The Saint of London
The Life and Miracles of
St. Erkenwald

medieval & renaissance texts & studies

VOLUME 58

The Saint of London
The Life and Miracles of St. Erkenwald

Text and Translation

Edited and translated by

E. GORDON WHATLEY

medieval & renaissance texts & studies
Binghamton, New York
1989

Library of Congress Cataloging-in-Publication Data

The Saint of London : the life and miracles of St. Erkenwald :
    text and translation / edited and translated by E. Gordon
    Whatley.
        p.   cm. — (Medieval & Renaissance texts & studies : v. 58)
Bibliography: p.
Includes indexes.
        Contents: Introduction — Vita sancti Erkenwaldi — Miracula
sancti Erkenwaldi / Arcoid.
        ISBN 0-86698-042-3 (alk. paper)
        1. Erkenwald, Saint, ca. 630-ca. 693.   2. Christian
saints — England — Biography — Early works to 1800. I. Whatley,
E. Gordon, 1944-   . II. Arcoid, Canon of St. Paul's, fl.
1132-1142. Miracula sancti Erkenwaldi. 1989. III. Vita sancti
Erkenwaldi. 1989. IV. Series.
BR754.E75S25   1989
270.2′092′4 — dc19
[B]   88-24159
                                                                CIP

This book is made to last.
It is set in Goudy, smythe-sewn,
and printed on acid-free paper
to library specifications.

Printed in the United States of America

Contents

Foreword

The *Vita sancti Erkenwaldi* (*VSE*) and the *Miracula sancti Erkenwaldi* (*MSE*) are the principal Latin memorials to a seventh-century monk, Erkenwald, who became the patron saint of medieval London. Erkenwald is also the protagonist of a much admired narrative poem in Middle English alliterative verse, *St. Erkenwald*.[1] The saint whose cult inspired these works was the founder of the great Benedictine abbeys at Barking and Chertsey, a few miles respectively east and west of the old City of London. He was also bishop of London and the East Saxons from 675 to 693. The cult devoted to his memory and relics, while less glamorous than that of Edward the Confessor at royal Westminster, flourished continuously, with only brief interruptions, from the closing years of the seventh century until the English Reformation. In the twelfth century and the later Middle Ages his shrine behind the high altar of old St. Paul's was one of the glories of the cathedral, and the object of frequent important donations and of a steady stream of smaller votive offerings and popular devotion.

The available evidence, to be discussed in chapter two, indicates that *VSE* was composed around the turn of the eleventh century. It is extant in two manuscripts of the late twelfth or early thirteenth century, one of the early fourteenth, and a seventeenth-century printed edition based on a twelfth-century manuscript that is now lost. The author is unknown, but the work was most likely written at St. Paul's, rather than at Chertsey or Barking. It is an expansion of an earlier shorter life, no longer extant, which in turn was derived mainly from a brief account in Bede's *Ecclesiastical History*. *MSE*, which I will treat as a single unified work and therefore grammatically singular,[2] survives relatively complete in only one manuscript of the late twelfth century, although there are later epitomes and redactions, all of which are listed in the course of the introductory chapters that follow. The original *MSE* can be dated with reasonable certainty between 1140 and 1145. The author was a priest and canon of St. Paul's, nephew to the former bishop Gilbert the Universal (d. 1134).

Despite the enduring status of Erkenwald's cult in medieval London, and despite the celebrity of the verse *St. Erkenwald* among modern students of medieval English,[3] *VSE* and *MSE* have been largely ignored by scholars of literature, history, and hagiography alike, partly, no doubt, because of their lack of conventionally useful historical information, and partly also because the texts themselves have been accessible only in the drastically abbreviated redaction by John of Tynemouth,[4] and in the uncritical and relatively rare edition of *VSE* alone, printed by Dugdale in 1658. Both editions lack translation and commentary.

One purpose of the present edition is to enable scholars and students of English literature and related disciplines to explore more easily and accurately the relationship between the Middle English poem and the Latin hagiography concerning St. Erkenwald.[5] Another, broader aim is to draw attention to a substantial corpus of England's literary remains that is virtually unknown except to a handful of specialist historians and hagiologists. I refer to the scores of *vitae* and miracle collections that constitute the twelfth-century renaissance of Anglo-Latin hagiography.

That there was such a renaissance is no secret,[6] but the few texts that have been published in good modern editions are not at all typical or representative of the great majority of the works in question. Eadmer's life of St. Anselm, Walter Daniel's life of St. Ailred of Rievaulx, and the life of Christina of Markyate, all edited and translated by eminent historians, are valuable historically because their authors were the contemporaries and confidants of their saintly subjects.[7] But they were in a distinct minority. The literary energy and creativity of the Anglo-Norman hagiographers were expended mainly on works dealing with the pre-Conquest saints of England, many of whom had been dead for centuries, but whose cults were being given new life and visibility by the great surge in church building during the century following the Conquest. Augustine, Dunstan, and the martyred archbishop Elphege at Canterbury, Swithun and Birinus at Winchester, Aldhelm at Malmesbury, Cuthbert at Durham, Edward the Confessor at Westminster, Edmund the martyr at Bury, Etheldreda and other female saints at Ely, Ethelburga at Barking, and her brother Erkenwald at St. Paul's, London: these are just a few of the saints whose remains were translated to new shrines in imposing new churches during the Anglo-Norman era, all of whom were honored with works of narrative art to match the more visible craftsmanship of the artisans in stone and glass and precious metals.

VSE and *MSE* are genuine if modest representatives of this important and largely unexplored phase in the literary history of England. Ostensibly works of history, they are in fact, like most medieval hagiography, hybrids of history and fiction, and they are perhaps as susceptible to literary analysis as to historical examination (the opening phrase of *MSE* is, significantly, "Eloquentiae uirtus"). If read with care and appreciation for their hybrid status, works like the two published here can offer substantial insights into the evolving art of medieval religious narrative, as well as the ecclesiastical, political, and cultural concerns of the hagiographers and their contemporaries. Written saints' legends are no longer regarded as the unreflecting effusions of the popular imagination;[8] they are now recognized as having been written by and for members of the ecclesiastical elites, whether monastic or secular, embodying the values, ideals, and aesthetics of such elites in the symbolic language of the miraculous.[9] An important aspect of English intellectual and literary history will therefore have been neglected unless the Latin hagiography of twelfth-century England is made more accessible for study and critical appreciation. The present volume is a contribution to that goal.

Acknowledgements

For research grants at various stages of a larger project, of which this book is the partial fruit, I am grateful to the following institutions: Lake Forest College, Illinois (faculty summer research grant); the National Endowment for the Humanities (Independent Study Fellowship); the American Philosophical Society (Penrose Fund); the Research Foundation of the City University of New York (PSC-CUNY grants); Queens College, CUNY (Fellowship-in-Residence). The Newberry Library, Chicago, generously gave me Research Associate status, a study carrel, and the use of its superb collections and facilities during the early stages of work on the edition. To the expert and ever-helpful staff, and particularly to Richard Brown, Director of Education and Research, I am deeply grateful.

In addition, many libraries, large and small, public and private, in the USA and the UK, have allowed me access to their collections of manuscripts and printed books and supplied me with microfilms, etc. The names of most of them are cited in the notes: to their directors and helpful staffs I am much indebted. I am particularly grateful to Professor R. I. Page, librarian of Corpus Christi College, Cambridge, for several courtesies, and to the Master and Fellows of the same college for permission to publish the unique Corpus text of the *Miracula sancti Erkenwaldi*. I am similarly grateful to the librarian of Stonyhurst College, Father Turner, for his kindness and assistance.

In addition to the scholars whose personal help is acknowledged in the notes, I would like to thank Charles Dahlberg, Mary Richards, and David Rollason for reading and commenting on portions of an earlier draft. I am indebted to Geneviève Brunel, John Corbett, Brenda Dunn-Lardeau, Richard Hamer, and Vida Russell, for timely favors and advice. At Queens College, my colleagues in the English Department, along with William Clark in Art History, and Dean Jack Reilly, have provided support and encouragement at opportune moments, as have, further afield, Jane Roberts, and Patrick Geary. Earl Anderson and Tom Hill have contributed indirectly but nonetheless essentially.

In some of the drudgery of the research and manuscript preparation I was helped at different stages by three Queens College student assistants: Michelle Brandwein, Sally LaForte, and, during the past three years, Meghan Ray, who has shared in the work of proof-reading and preparing the bibliography and index, besides performing other research chores with unwavering efficiency. I am also grateful to the Queens College Interlibrary Loan department for keeping the books and articles coming, and to the patience and professionalism of the several members of the Queens College Word Processing department who shared in typing the main draft. To the editors and staff of Medieval & Renaissance Texts & Studies, especially Mario Di Cesare, my heartfelt thanks for guidance, encouragement, and patience.

My wife, Mary Margaret, who has known St. Erkenwald as long as she has known me, and whose birthday is on the feast of his *translatio*, has cheerfully tolerated, fed, and fostered in sundry ways our mysterious triad from the beginning, as well as giving birth to our daughter Johannah a few hours after the completion of Erkenwald's spring octave in 1982. To all three of them this book is a gift of love and gratitude.

NOTES TO FOREWORD

1. *VSE* and *MSE* are numbered BHL 2600 and 2601 respectively by the Bollandists. Neither work is printed in ASS, which prints instead the 14th c. redaction by John of Tynemouth (BHL 2602) in a 15th c. recension attributed erroneously to John Capgrave: ASS Apr., 3:790–96. The Middle English poem, entitled *De Erkenwaldo* in the unique MS copy, BL Harley 2250, ff.72v–75v, has been edited most recently by Ruth Morse, *St. Erkenwald* (Cambridge/Totowa, N.J., 1975), and Clifford Peterson, *Saint Erkenwald* (Philadelphia, 1977). See also below, n. 4.

2. I follow scholarly usage with regard to such works as Chaucer's *Canterbury Tales* and Plutarch's *Lives*, which are treated as grammatically singular, despite their plural form and episodic contents, when reference is made to the whole work. The same usage

applies to medieval Latin works entitled "Gesta," such as William of Poitiers' *Gesta Guillelmi*. Cf. T. A. Dorey, *Latin Biography* (London, 1967), 139.

3. In addition to the recent editions cited above, n. 1, and three earlier editions (see Peterson, 144), the poem has been the subject of numerous separate articles, especially within the last twenty years. See Whatley, "Heathens and Saints: *St. Erkenwald* in Its Legendary Context," *Speculum* 61 (1986): 330–63, espec. n. 10, for a list of recent scholarship, to which may be added Alan J. Frantzen, "*St. Erkenwald* and the Raising of Lazarus," *Mediaevalia* 7 (1981): 157–71, and William A. Quinn, "The Psychology of *St. Erkenwald*," *Medium Aevum* 53 (1985): 180–93.

4. *NLA*, 1:391–405.

5. For an attempt to define this relationship, see Whatley, "Heathens and Saints," 353–59, and "The Middle English *St. Erkenwald* in its Liturgical Context," *Mediaevalia* 8 (1982): 277–306. The article by Sandra Cairns, "Fact and Fiction in the Middle English *De Erkenwaldo*," *Neuphilologische Mitteilungen* 83 (1982): 430–38, discusses the poem in relation to the 14th c. redaction by John of Tynemouth.

6. The strongest statement is that of Sir Richard Southern, "The Place of England in the Twelfth-century Renaissance," *History* 45 (1960): 208, rptd., but considerably revised, in *Medieval Humanism and Other Studies* (NY, 1970), 158–80. Cf. also Theodore Wolpers, *Die englische Heiligenlegende des Mittelalters* (Tübingen, 1964), 164.

7. Southern, ed., *The Life of St. Anselm of Canterbury by Eadmer* (London, 1962); F. Maurice Powicke, ed., *The Life of Ailred of Rievaulx by Walter Daniel* (London, 1950); Charles H. Talbot, ed., *The Life of Christina of Markyate* (Oxford, 1959). All these have facing translations. William of Malmesbury's life of St. Wulfstan of Worcester (d. 1095), ed. R. R. Darlington, Camd. Soc., 3rd Ser. 40 (London, 1928), provides no translation and is consequently much less well known than it deserves.

8. An influential proponent of the older view was H. Delehaye, *Les légendes hagiographiques*, 4th ed. (Brussels, 1955, rptd., 1973), ch. 2, passim.

9. On the role of elites in promoting saints' cults in the early church, see Peter Brown, *The Cult of the Saints* (Chicago, 1981), espec. 12–30. Recent studies of saints' cults and hagiography, stressing in various ways the importance of hagiography as a vehicle of thought and policy, are Frantisek Graus, *Volk, Herrscher und Heiliger im Reich der Merowinger* (Prague, 1965); J.-C. Poulin, *L'idéal de sainteté dans l'Aquitaine carolingienne, d'après les sources hagiographiques* (Montreal, 1975); D. W. Rollason, *The Mildrith Legend. A Study in Early Medieval Hagiography in England* (Leicester, 1982); A. M. Orselli, *L'idea e il culto del santo patrono cittadino nella letteratura cristiana* (Bologna, 1965); A. Vauchez, *La sainteté en occident aux dernières siècles du moyen âge*, Bibliothèque des écoles françaises d'Athènes et de Rome, 241 (Rome, 1981). The popular element in saints' literature has not been neglected, however. See W. W. Heist, "Hagiography, chiefly celtic, and recent developments in folklore," in Evelyne Patlagean & Pierre Riché, eds., *Hagiographie, cultures, et sociétés IVe–Xiie siècles. Actes du Colloque organisé à Nanterre et à Paris, 2–5 mai 1979* (Paris, 1981), 121–41; Elissa R. Henken, "The Saint as Folk Hero: Biographical Patterning in Welsh Hagiography," in Patrick Ford, ed., *Celtic Folklore and Christianity. Studies in Memory of William W. Heist* (Los Angeles, 1983), 58–74; and the works cited in the bibliography of Sofia Boesch Gajano, ed. *Agiografia altomedioevale* (Bologna, 1976), 279–80.

Introduction

Bodley MS Lat. liturg. d. 42, f. 46ʳᵛ (*by permission of the Bodleian Library, Oxford*).
The historiated intial P, showing St. Erkenwald as bishop instructing monks, is the recto
of a cutting from a lost leaf of the Chertsey Breviary. The verso preserves portions of
the text of the seventh and eighth lections at mattins on St. Erkenwald's feast day,
April 30. See below, pp. 4–5, 8 n. 31, 69 n. 48.

CHAPTER ONE

The Manuscripts and the Texts

1. The Manuscripts

There are three extant manuscript copies of the *Vita sancti Erkenwaldi* (*VSE*) and a seventeenth-century printed edition based mainly on a manuscript since lost. At least two other manuscript copies are known to have existed as late as the sixteenth century, but they also have disappeared.[1] In addition, portions of *VSE* have been preserved as lections in two medieval service books. Of the *Miracula sancti Erkenwaldi* (*MSE*), several medieval copies are known to have circulated,[2] but only one of them has survived, remaining unprinted until now. The other late medieval copies, together with the earliest printed edition, represent not the original *MSE* but a later reworking that thoroughly obscures the special character of the original, although the reworking remains of value as a witness to the textual tradition. Some additional light is thrown on *MSE* by several extracts, of varying length, preserved in some lections in one of the above-mentioned service books, and in some notes made by a sixteenth-century antiquary.

Of the manuscripts and early printed editions described below, A, D/Dm and L contain only *VSE*; S contains lections from *VSE* only; C contains both *VSE* and *MSE*, while Ch contains lections drawn from both *VSE* and the *MSE*. J and T contain useful portions of *MSE* only. The order of the descriptions corresponds to these categories.

A. London, British Library Cotton Claudius A.v. Vellum, 244 x 162 mm., s.xii ex.–xiv in.

The MS consists of three formerly separate books: a fourteenth-century Peterborough chronicle; William of Malmesbury's *Gesta pontificum*, of which bk. V is his *vita S. Aldhelmi*; and a group of saints' lives. The latter comprises the anonymous life of Erkenwald, VSE (BHL 2600), Robert of Shrewsbury's life and miracles of Winifred, an anonymous life of Neot (BHL 6052), and William of Malmesbury's life of Wulfstan of Worcester.[3] The portion containing these four lives, written around the turn of the twelfth century, belonged to the Cistercian Abbey of the Virgin Mary, Holme Cultram (Cumbria).[4] A's text of VSE, ff. 135–38, is divided into four chapters, indicated by large colored initials, but without numbers or headings, at VSE 1 (Post passionem); VSE 43 (Quadam uero die); VSE 56 (Beatus uero pater); VSE 79 (Interea cum uniuersa).

Judging from the choice of saints in this and other known Holme Cultram manuscripts, the monks there were interested not only in the heroes of the Cistercian and Cluniac traditions, but also in early English hagiology in general.[5] Such an interest would be sufficient to account for the apparently anomalous presence of a London saint's *vita* so far from the normal confines of his cult.[6] Certainly the manuscript was read: there are marginal notations, one of which, f. 135r, repeats the title of the work; others (135v) call attention to the monasteries Erkenwald founded at Chertsey and Barking; and on f. 137v there is a faintly pencilled chapter heading, opposite VSE 63, in a round cursive, probably thirteenth-century, that recurs throughout the manuscript.

D. Sir William Dugdale, A History of St. Paul's Cathedral (London, 1658); 2nd ed., E. Maynard (London, 1716); 3rd ed., Sir Henry Ellis (London, 1818).

Dm. ———, Monasticon Anglicanum, vol. 3 (London, 1673).

Dugdale's printed text of VSE, on pp. 181–84 of his first edition (2nd ed., appendix 5–8; 3rd ed., 289–91; Monasticon 3:299–301), is the sole witness to the copy (designated *b* below) in a manuscript which he identifies as MS B or "Liber B," from the Chapter Library of old St. Paul's Cathedral. Only two leaves are extant (Oxford, Bodley, Rawlinson A. 372). "Liber B" comprised, among other things, Ralph Diceto's Domesday Register, a collection of charters, deeds, and inquisition records compiled by the energetic Dean of St. Paul's on first assuming office in 1180–1181. The surviving leaves of the codex contain a table of contents that refers only to one portion of the manuscript, dealing with church property, and does not refer to VSE, which according to Dugdale began on f. 20, or to the charters among which it appears in Dugdale's edition. We cannot be sure, therefore, exactly how VSE was presented or incorporated in "Liber B" and it has not been mentioned by modern historians familiar with Diceto's Domesday.[7] VSE was most probably included in the St. Paul's book because it provided historical and narrative background to the early charters that dealt with the Cathedral's foundation, early properties, and privileges. If Dugdale's folio references to "Liber B" are reliable *VSE* was sandwiched between King Ethelbert's charter, granting Bishop Mellitus the manor of Tillingham, and King Athelstan's various charters confirming privileges Erkenwald himself had originally obtained from Rome and King Sebba of the East Saxons, as well as sundry property grants from subsequent kings.[8] In a later charter from the same codex King Edward the Confessor invokes the name and sainthood of Erkenwald in formulas reminiscent of Athelstan's various charters to grant additional properties and confirm the earlier grants and privileges (D, 189). *VSE* itself does not describe any such grants and exemptions, but it tells how Ethelbert built St. Paul's for Mellitus, touches on Erkenwald's early relationship with Mellitus, and relates that Erkenwald was made bishop "with the consent of King Sebba," and was "appointed so from the city of Romulus" (*VSE* 28, 77). Finally, by recording the story of his holy life and death and the ensuing wonders, *VSE* constitutes a kind of supernatural guarantee and spiritual authority for the mundane legal documents, in that it confirms the sanctity of Erkenwald's body in its shrine and his powerful posthumous presence in the cathedral.[9]

L. London, BL Lansdowne 436. Vellum, 335 x 216 mm., s.xiv in.

L is a legendary, from the Benedictine nunnery of the Virgin Mary and St. Elfleda, Romsey (Hants.).[10] It is a unique collection, devoted to the lives of English saints too numerous to list here,[11] many of whose *vitae* are epit-omes of older texts, but some of which, including *VSE*, on ff. 36–39, are quite close to their originals. *VSE* 1–5 are omitted, but otherwise the text is complete, and there are small explanatory additions.[12] L's text of *VSE* is in six chapters, numbered two through six in arabic numerals in text and margin. After the opening chapter, the divisions occur at *VSE* 27, 43, 56, 86, and 111.

S. Blackburn, Stonyhurst College, 52. Vellum, 148 x 103 mm., s.xv in., with later additions.

A portable Sarum breviary, of uncertain provenance, though the later owners appear to have been in the southeast, in view of additions relating to Erkenwald and Etheldreda. On a blank leaf, f. 468v, there are three lec-tions for Erkenwald's deposition, in a hasty cursive of the second half of the fifteenth century,[13] corresponding to *VSE* 27–41, 57–60, the last few lines of lection three departing considerably from the equivalent portion of text in the other MSS.

C. Cambridge, Corpus Christi College 161. Vellum, 302 x 208 mm., s.xii ex.

In the opinion of M. R. James this manuscript, entitled "Legenda Sanctorum" and containing lives and miracles of sixteen saints, nine of them pre-Conquest English (plus David of Wales), "took its present shape at Canterbury" but the greater portion was probably compiled in the London area. N. R. Ker declined to endorse James's view and the provenance remains uncertain, though most probably "southern."[14] The selection of English saints seems to indicate little more than that the compiler was interested in abbots and bishops of the Anglo-Saxon church, particularly those with feasts in the summer season, April through July.[15] *VSE* occupies ff. 31-33, *MSE* ff. 33-45v. *VSE* is divided into seven chapters, two through seven being numbered in the text with Roman numerals, but there are also individual headings at the beginning as a table of contents, f. 31r, which are printed in the text of this edition. *MSE*, which begins with a large decorated initial, has twenty chapters, unnumbered, but with brief headings in red. The exemplar of C seems to have had twenty-one chapters.[16] *VSE* and the first six folios of *MSE* are written by one scribe, the remainder by a second. The first was less tidy than the second, crossing out and rewriting a good deal as he went along, although the second did the same on occasion. Each was editing his exemplar even as he copied it (there are some bona fide corrections of both their work, in a small neat hand contemporary with the text hands). Some more sizeable cuts, however, were made in the immediate exemplar of C, for it lacks the following passages in *VSE*: 41-42, 84-86, 92-93, 104-110, 111-14, 117-18, 135-39. Similar abridgement of the *MSE* by the C scribes or their exemplar is more difficult to pinpoint, owing to the lack of other copies comparable in importance to C, but as will be shown below, C's text of *MSE* is certainly not a full-length version of the original.

Ch. Oxford, Bodley Library Lat. Liturg. e.39 (& d.42). Vellum, 200 x 132 mm., s.xiv in.[17]

Ch is a monastic breviary, sanctorale portion only (calendar and temporale are Lat. Liturg. e.6 & e.37 respectively), from the Benedictine Abbey of St. Peter, Chertsey (Surrey). The breviary is beautifully decorated in both margins and text, and formerly contained many fine historiated initials and some full-page illustrations.[18] But the book was vandalized at some point, apparently by a book dealer, and many of the folios containing particularly choice illuminations were removed. Some of the missing folios and some individual historiated initials, including a picture of Erkenwald addressing his monks inside a letter P, have turned up and are preserved in a guard book, Lat. Liturg. d.42 (the portrait of Erkenwald is f. 46). However, two whole gatherings at the end of the sanctorale, after f. 152, are lost, and many individual leaves also. The offices for Erkenwald are on ff. 38v–47r. One leaf at least is missing between 38v and 39r, which would have contained the night office and day hours for April 30, Erkenwald's deposition. So we lack the eight matins lections recounting the saint's life and death, except for a few words, *VSE* 35–36, 41–42, on the reverse of the historiated initial P mentioned above. Surviving in full, however, are the offices for the Sunday in the octave, with eight lections from *VSE*, beginning "Audientes uero canonici," and comprising *VSE* 63–68, 68–73, 73–78, 79–84, 86–91, 93–97, 111–16, 128–33, 139–43, 148–49, 152–54 (the last four sets comprising the eighth lection). These describe the struggle for Erkenwald's corpse and the funeral procession.

Ch also contains some valuable portions of MSE: ff. 42r–42v, three lections, from Mir. VI, for the second nocturn of May 2; ff. 47r–48r, eight lections, from Mir. I, for the first and second nocturns of the octave day, May 7.[19]

J. John Leland, *De rebus Britannicis collectanea*, 2nd ed. (London, 1770), 1:20–21.

Brief extracts, mainly from Mir. IV, from an untraced manuscript of indeterminate date and provenance. It apparently contained both *VSE* and MSE.

T. London, BL Cotton Tiberius E.i. Vellum, 286 x 173 mm., s.xiv med.

Given by Thomas de la Mare, abbot of St. Albans from 1349–1396, to the Benedictine Priory of St. Amphibalus (a cell of St. Albans), Redbourn (Herts.), T is the unique copy of the original version of the *Sanctilogium Angliae*, a massive legendary of English saints' lives, compiled around the middle of the fourteenth century by John of Tynemouth.[20] T was damaged in the Cotton fire, but it is legible on the whole. John's chapter on Erkenwald, a redaction of *VSE* and MSE, is on ff. 116v–21v. Later copies of T, representing a mid-fifteenth century revision, are Bodley Tanner 15, designated E by Horstmann (Erkenwald is on ff. 232–43), and York Minster XVI.G.23 (Erkenwald, ff. 144–45), Horstmann's MS Y. BL Cotton Otho D.ix, also of this type, is illegible due to the Cotton fire. The printed edition by Wynkyn de Worde, *Nova Legenda Angliae* (1516), represents an even later recension.[21] T and these related texts preserve much the same version of the life and miracles of St. Erkenwald, classified by the Bollandists as BHL 2602.[22] John of Tynemouth completely rewrote *VSE*, so T is of no value for the text of *VSE*. He drastically abridged, interpolated, and in places rewrote MSE, rearranging the order of the miracle episodes, which appear in T as follows: XVIII,

IV, XIV, XVII, VI, X, XII, III, II, V, IX, VIII, XI, I, XV, XVI, XIX. He did, however, retain considerable portions of MSE text, enough to make collation worthwhile in numerous instances, but he omitted the author's proem, large stretches of narrative, especially in the longer chapters, most of the homiletic effusions, comments, asides, introductions and conclusions, as well as all the autobiographical touches.

One further, very marginal witness to the manuscript tradition of *VSE* and *MSE* is BL Additional MS 35298, a late fifteenth century copy of the *Gilte Legende* (GiL), a Middle English prose rendering of Jean de Vignay's *Légende dorée* supplemented from other sources with numerous lives of English saints. The chapter on Erkenwald, ff. 53–57, is based partly on the *Sanctilogium*, but mainly on *VSE* and *MSE*, of which it is a free translation and abridgement. The order of miracles corresponds with that in C, not in T. Unfortunately, the translation is not close enough, except in rare instances, to be of real value in the study of the textual transmission of the original *VSE* or *MSE*.[23]

2.   THE TEXT OF THE *Vita sancti Erkenwaldi*

Collation of the manuscripts and printed texts of *VSE* reveals that while none depends on any of the others, the four main copies can be classified with some certainty into two distinct groups: AD and CL. In sixty-nine instances A and D share readings not found in C, not counting the passages C omits altogether, while AD agree on readings not in CL in thirty-one instances. A and C, on the other hand, agree on readings not in D in only fourteen instances, while C and D never agree on readings not found in A.

C and L appear to have a common ancestor, designated *r* in the stemma below. Although *r* did not abridge the text of *VSE*, it clearly made a number of changes to improve the grammar and bring its diction more in line with classical usage.[24] One would not expect a text composed in late eleventh- or early twelfth-century England to exhibit classical touches that were then altered in favor of cruder Latin by a later reviser. One must assume therefore that *r*'s improvements to the text of *VSE* were the work of a better educated if rather fussy scribe later in the twelfth century, possibly on one of the occasions when Erkenwald's relics were translated to their new shrines,[25] and that the less polished language of AD is more representative of the original text of *VSE*.

As mentioned earlier, individually both C and L present features that further distance them from the presumed *VSE* archetype, designated *p* in the stemma. C lacks a number of the more colorful passages, most notably in the debate between the Barking nuns and the Londoners. The cuts may have been the work of the C scribe or his immediate exemplar (not *r*). The motivation for the cuts is uncertain, since C does not seem to be designed specifically for liturgical use.[26] Possibly the abbreviations were intended to improve the text by removing awkward or offensive material. The former seems to be the case with C's omission of the intriguing but intrusive lines, *VSE* 41–42, without which the narrative proceeds much more smoothly.[27] The scribe of L, or his exemplar, while more faithful to *r* than C, nonetheless cut the opening eight lines and expanded the remainder of the text slightly here and there (see, e.g., the textual notes on *VSE* 9, 13, 24, and 57). L is also quite carelessly copied, compared to C or A, although it preserves some important variants missing from C.

C and L, then, both individually and as regards their common ancestor *r*, each represents a revised text of *VSE*. The AD group, on the other hand, seems to represent a relatively unrevised tradition and one closer to the presumed original, *p*. There is no evidence of abridgement of the sort one finds in C (and Ch) and the Latin is, as we have noted, slightly less correct, having escaped the attentions of the *r* reviser whose work is reflected in Ch as well as CL.

Collation of A with the various editions of D shows that A is the superior text. Dugdale states that his printed text was based on two manuscripts: the now lost *b* manuscript, the St. Paul's "Liber B," and our A manuscript. Collation of A and D, however, suggests that Dugdale relied much more on *b* than A, that A does not derive from *b* or vice versa, but that they have a common ancestor, designated *q* in the stemma, which seems to have been not far removed from *p*, the original *VSE*.[28] Over against the many instances, cited above, where AD agree against CL, there are twenty-five instances where D's readings differ from those of A, some of which are Dugdale's or his printer's errors (corrected in some cases in Dm or the list of *corrigenda* at the end of D), e.g., *VSE* 100, 172. But some D variants cannot be explained as his errors. Either they are deliberate emendations on his part, which seems unlikely, or they represent actual variants in *b*. For example, at *VSE* 9, where D has the weak "tramitem tute docendo," A has "tramitem uite docendo." Not only does A's reading make better sense, but it is supported by CL. Similarly in *VSE* 6–7 A shares with C the "harder" but more interesting reading "Dauiticis tympanis" against D's "Dauitici hympnis." Readings which A has in common with C and CL must be accorded strong authority as almost certain reflections of *p*.[29]

One would have expected a manuscript copied probably in the 1180s in the scriptorium of St. Paul's cathedral, yards away from Erkenwald's shrine, to offer a text of Erkenwald's *vita* superior to one copied a generation later in a remote Cumbrian monastery, three hundred miles from London. Doubtless this was Dugdale's supposition also. But it does not seem to have been correct. Leaving aside Dugdale's printer's errors and his own, we are still left with a significant number of D readings that are decidedly inferior to those of A. The manuscript Dugdale largely ignored outlived its rival *b* (which no doubt perished in the London holocaust of 1660) and survived the Cotton fire to be the best, indeed the only extant manuscript witness to the full, original text of *VSE*, and the obvious choice as the base text of this edition.

The relationship of the liturgical extracts, S and Ch, with the two main groups is more difficult to determine, owing to their highly abridged condition as lections, and it is not essential to our understanding of the extant texts of *VSE*. However, the subject is not without its own intrinsic interest, and deserves some further consideration here.

The Ch lections are the result of a more drastic editing than the text in C, and for that reason it was decided not to include Ch readings in the textual notes to this edition of *VSE*. But the Ch lections contain enough of the text of *VSE* to show that Ch has more in common with CL than with AD. Altogether Ch agrees with CL in ten instances of variants, and with AD against CL in only two instances.[30] This suggests that at some point between the twelfth and early fourteenth centuries, the monks of Chertsey had access to a text of *VSE* that derived at least in part from *r*. There is some slight evidence also, however, to suggest that the lost portions of the Chertsey offices may also have reflected an older, possibly pre-Conquest textual tradition, of which more will be said below.[31]

S is even more difficult than Ch to place in relation to the other manuscripts. As we noticed earlier, the three S lections correspond to *VSE* 27–42, and 57–60. That is, lections one, two, and the first sentence of lection three follow *VSE* 27–42 quite closely, but with no clear affiliation with either AD or CL,[32] while the remaining four lines of the lection correspond only in content and a few words to *VSE* 57–60, otherwise differing considerably, more so than can be explained by the need to abbreviate. In fact this portion of S is longer than the equivalent passage in ADCL. The language is simpler and has an archaic, quasi-heroic flavor lacking in the other versions. As in the case of the missing portions of Ch, we may have to do here with the survival of an older textual tradition than *VSE* proper. S may be a late and probably somewhat abridged witness to a lost version of Erkenwald's *vita*, a version preserved in liturgical lections, perhaps in some provincial oasis of devotion, long after it had been superceded as the official life by

VSE as we know it from ADCL. Both the author of *p* and the *r* reviser could easily have had access to this older *vita*, as apparently did Goscelin the hagiographer when he wrote the *Vita S. Ethelburgae* around 1087.[33] This would explain the even mix of AD and CL readings in S along with the unique readings and archaic flavor of the third lection.

The foregoing discussion can be best summed up in the form of the stemma below, which indicates the suggested relationships of the manuscripts and printed texts and the priority that should be accorded to manuscript A. Broken lines represent relations that are possible rather than demonstrable.

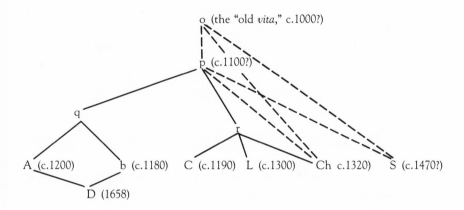

3. THE TEXT OF THE *Miracula sancti Erkenwaldi*

The textual situation of *MSE* is much simpler than that of *VSE*. As we have seen, there is but one manuscript copy that, with all its deficiencies, can claim to represent the original: C. The other witnesses are either, like Ch, extracts abridged from *MSE*, or, like T and its derivatives, later redactions that considerably distort the text of the original. C, which has not been printed or collated before, must therefore serve as the base text for this edition of *MSE*.

Despite the inferiority and unreliability of the other witnesses, however, they provide valuable information about the textual tradition of *MSE*. Collation of C with ChJT reveals in the first place that C itself is a somewhat abridged version of the original. It is apparent from the collation that Ch and T and the lost manuscript J (examined by Leland), while independent of one another, derive ultimately from exemplars somewhat closer to the presumed original than either C or its immediate exemplar. Some examples from Mir. I, IV, and VI will suffice to demonstrate this.

That C represents an edited text lacking some phrases from the original *MSE* is evident when we compare the C and J versions of Mir. IV 48–51, where the C scribe has left traces of his editorial efforts in the excised word *sede[m]*: J preserves the fuller and probably original text.

C	J
Et ut grauiora dampna	Et ut grauiora damna
pareant, episcopalem ~~sedem~~	pariant, episcopalem sedem
doctoris gentium pauli	doctoris gentium pauli uidilicet
basilicam	supramemoratam basilicam ausibus
in favillam redigendo	truculentis in favillam redigendo
satis mirabiliter exsufflauit.	satis miserabiliter exsufflauit.

C's exemplar, as is evident, had the word "sedem" retained by J's text. The C scribe saw a way of abbreviating the passage by eliminating what may have seemed to him the redundant "sedem" and simplifying the rest of the sentence.[34] But in doing so he has deprived "exsufflauit" of its direct object, so that "basilicam" now serves as the object of both "redigendo," as in J, and "exsufflauit." J preserves the better reading.[35] Similarly, C's "mirabiliter" seems less appropriate than J's "miserabiliter" in view of the plangent "Heu, heu" that immediately follows in both texts. I have therefore adopted J readings in this passage, even though they are not corroborated by a third witness, T's version of Mir. IV being a colorless précis.

Such is not the case in Mir. I and VI, where we have useful variant readings from both T and Ch, enabling us to reconstruct the archetype that is obscured in C by the abbreviations of either the scribe or his exemplar.

C	ChT
Interim magistro de animad-	Interim magistro anima-
uersione facienda offirmato	uersione facienda affirmato (T offirmato)
placuit puerum reddentem audire	placuit puerum (om., T) reddentem audire
ut	quatinus ex iusta ratione
quotiens eum deficientem in lectione	quociens eum deficientem in lectione
deprehenderet, tociens ei uerbera	deprehenderet tociens ei uerbera
ingeminaret	ingeminaret
(Mir. IV 42–44)	

There is no question of an error of omission here. C's "ut quotiens" is a deliberate substitute for the more complex "quatinus ex iusta ratione quociens" of the other texts, preserving grammatical coherence while simplifying the narrative flow. It is possible that Ch and T have independently preserved an interpolation, but this is unlikely, given the other verifiable instances of deliberate abridgement by the C scribe and his exemplar, both in *MSE* and *VSE*.[36] The phrase "ex iusta ratione" preserved in ChT suits the overly intellectual character of the master and strikes one as genuine, given the remarks made elsewhere in *MSE* about the opposition of simple faith and rational intellect (Mir. IV 2–4).[37]

Unfortunately, only two of *MSE*'s nineteen chapters were used for lections at Chertsey during Erkenwald's festival octave, April 30–May 7. The offices for the feast of his Translation, November 14, which would undoubtedly have contained lections from other portions of *MSE*, have not survived.[38] It is thus impossible to corroborate or reject the numerous other instances in the text where T offers potentially useful variants like those illustrated above. I have therefore chosen not to adopt any T readings that are not corroborated by Ch or J. As we have observed, T itself is a highly abbreviated redaction and on its own cannot be considered a reliable alternative to C. In Mir. I and VI, however, I have occasionally adopted readings from Ch that disagree with C and are not echoed in T, and where there is no visible evidence of excision by the C scribe. I have done so because in many instances in these two miracle episodes Ch agrees with C against T more frequently than CT against Ch. Furthermore Ch exhibits none of T's demonstrable tendencies to rephrase or tamper with the exemplar other than by simple abridgement. It is a liturgical text from a monastery where Erkenwald's memory was venerated as highly as at St. Paul's, it seems, and the monks would surely possess early and authoritative copies of the relevant texts associated with their founder. Finally, it is unlikely that a liturgist editing lections for the breviary would have *added* phrases and sentences to the text. Lections are much more likely to be abridged than expanded, and in those instances where we can compare, this is true of the Chertsey lections also. Therefore where Ch preserves phrases lacking in C, it seems legitimate to attribute these to the archetype of *MSE*.

Constructing anything like an acceptable stemma from these four texts is not practical. All one can say for certain is that C preserves the fullest and best extant text of the mid-twelfth century *MSE* of St. Erkenwald; that it is of the same type as the others now lost but known to have existed; that it is slightly abridged as compared to the archetype, though nowhere near as much as the fourteenth-century redaction of John of Tynemouth; and that some words and phrases omitted by one or more of the successive editors of the work can be restored with the help of the other extant copies. The two scribes who copied the *MSE* text in C were definitely responsible for some of the work of abridgement, possibly all of it. What is interesting is that there is no direct evidence that either of the scribes abridged anything but the strictly narrative portions of the miracles. There are no deliberate excisions in the homiletic passages. The scribes seem to have respected the suggestion of the author in his proem (Mir. Pr. 43–49), that the miracles should be read as much for their spiritual and moral instruction as for their literal truth.

CHAPTER TWO

Authorship and Date of
Vita sancti Erkenwaldi

VSE has never been, to my knowledge, the subject of a detailed study, but several scholars have used and referred to it incidentally and in the process have given the impression that the author and date of the work are firmly established, when in fact the opposite is the case. It has been asserted for example that *VSE* was written by the acknowledged author of *MSE*, who has been identified as Arcoid, nephew of Bishop Gilbert "the Universal" and canon of St. Paul's Cathedral. Arcoid died around 1145 and wrote *MSE* during the three or four years preceding his death.[1] As I will argue below, there is no real basis for attributing *VSE* to Arcoid and several reasons for assigning it to an earlier generation in the cathedral's history.

It has also been suggested, more plausibly perhaps, that the prolific Flemish hagiographer, Goscelin of St. Bertin and later St. Augustine's, Canterbury, who flourished between the 1060s and ca. 1110, wrote *VSE*. But here again the evidence is unfavorable and leads one to assert only that the work was composed after 1087, when Goscelin wrote his life of St. Ethelburga, and before 1124, when William of Malmesbury published the *Gesta pontificum* in which he appears to have drawn on *VSE* for his account of Erkenwald's episcopacy. Until more evidence comes to light, the identity of the author of *VSE* must remain unknown, but one may assume he was a member of the cathedral chapter of St. Paul's and, if not of Norman or French birth himself, was certainly sympathetic to and familiar with continental hagiographic tradition.

Since *VSE* has been attributed to the author of *MSE* in a few important and widely accessible modern works, it is necessary to trace briefly the source of this attribution and then to offer reasons for rejecting it, before examining the evidence for alternative attributions and an earlier date.

Sir Thomas Duffus Hardy in his *Descriptive Catalogue* of English historical manuscripts seems to have been the first modern scholar to suggest a single author was responsible for *VSE* and *MSE*. He remarks of *VSE* that although earlier scholars had ascribed it to Goscelin "it was more probably written by the nephew of Bishop Gilbert."[2] Hardy's information about the Bishop's nephew was culled from Henry Wharton's history of the bishops of London. As Hardy admits in a note, Wharton does not say that the "nepos" wrote *VSE*, but merely that "a certain canon of St. Paul's, nephew of Bishop Gilbert the Universal, who wrote the splendid history, *Of the Miracles of St. Erkenwald*, records that he was present at the translation on February 16, 1140." Wharton nowhere suggests that the canon wrote the other work.[3] Yet apparently following Hardy, a number of scholars, including Marion Gibbs, Christopher Brooke, Rose Graham and Bernard Scholz have repeated the notion that *VSE* and *MSE* were the work of this one man, Arcoid.[4]

It is true that *VSE* appears together with *MSE* in the Corpus manuscript and in John of Tynemouth's massive compilation of English saints' lives, the *Sanctilogium Angliae*, where they have been drastically rewritten and abbreviated. In this latter setting they do indeed appear to form one work. But the earlier manuscript texts create a different impression. In the Cotton manuscript, which we argued earlier represents the oldest extant form of the work, *VSE* has all the appearances of a self-contained and decidedly anonymous creation. There is no prologue or dedication, and no indication that the exemplar from which it was copied was a "Vita" and "Miracula" combined. This impression is supported by the fourteenth-century copy in the Landsdowne manuscript, in which *VSE* appears in full, except for the opening lines, and is similar to though not derived from the copy in the late twelfth-century Corpus manuscript.[5] Even in the Corpus manuscript, however, where *VSE* is followed immediately by *MSE*, the picture is the same. For *MSE* is preceded by an elaborate prologue, "Eloquentie uirtus," which marks an abrupt division between the miracle collection and the life. In his prologue, Arcoid says nothing about a "Vita" and nowhere does he even hint that he might have composed one before compiling the miracle collection. On the other hand he frequently draws attention to himself as author of *MSE*. Not only does he identify himself through his relationship to the former Bishop, but he also tells how he became involved in recording the miracles and on several occasions speaks as an eye witness and participant in the events themselves. It is unlikely that one who shows himself to be such a self-conscious writer in *MSE* could have suppressed his personal style and voice so completely as to have produced the restrained, impersonal *VSE*.[6]

There are a few faint echoes of *VSE* in Arcoid's prologue, and in three of the miracle episodes:[7] sufficient to establish that he knew the other work. But he evidently saw no reason to draw attention to it. It is possible that a writer as consciously literate as he might have been somewhat embarrassed by its simple style and occasional awkwardness of structure. He may even have been responsible for the *r* revision that is the common ancestor of the Corpus and Lansdowne copies, in an attempt to remove some of *VSE's* infelicities of grammar and style.[8]

In William of Malmesbury's *Gesta pontificum*, finished around 1124, there is a different, perhaps more compelling kind of evidence against the notion that *VSE* was composed by Arcoid in the 1140s. William gives the impression that he had seen, if not carefully studied *VSE*. For in his account of Erkenwald's saintly career, he describes a miracle which appears to be a deliberate and skillful conflation of two miracles in *VSE*: the wheel episode and the miraculous river crossing. He tells how one day, while touring the diocese in his horse-litter the old bishop and his followers came to a flooded turbulent stream. While they hestitated for fear that the cart would be overturned if they tried to cross, the waters suddenly subsided and held back "in a stationary mass" above them, allowing the party to proceed unharmed to the safety of the other bank. As soon as they had crossed, the river fell back into its channel. William then goes on to tell the story of the cart's healing properties, citing Bede as his source.[9]

Although he does not use the actual words of the river episode in *VSE* William does borrow a verse or two from Joshua,[10] to which *VSE* explicitly refers, and the nature of the miracle is obviously similar to that in the saint's life. At the same time, the followers' fear that the cart will overturn in the water strikes one as a skillful adaptation of the wheel miracle in *VSE*. It appears that he has conflated the two *VSE* miracles into one.

That the monk of Malmesbury, in his quest for stylistic individuality and originality of content, was capable of this creative kind of approach to his sources is evident in several other instances where his knowledge of the relevant sources is more certain.[11] Given the fact that he does not include anything in this passage that is not in *VSE* in one form or another, one can assert with some confidence that William knew the work and that its *terminus ante quem* can therefore be placed some years prior to the completion of the *Gesta pontificum*. *VSE*, in other words, was known in England at least twenty years before Arcoid wrote *MSE* and several years before he was even in England.[12]

William of Malmesbury provides us with one final piece of evidence for the existence of *VSE* before the 1120s, when he makes it clear that Erkenwald's cult had been flourishing in his own day for some time, to the great benefit of the canons of St. Paul's, and that both "recent report and ancient memory" had attested to the saint's miraculous powers. There are therefore no grounds for asserting, as do Gibbs and Brooke, that Arcoid wrote the life and miracles in the 1140s in order to revive the fortunes of a forgotten Anglo-Saxon saint. William's testimony encourages us to believe that, on the contrary, the beginnings of Erkenwald's Anglo-Norman cult and the likeliest composition date for VSE are to be sought in the early 1100s or even earlier.[13]

Another candidate for the authorship of VSE is Goscelin, a Flemish monk from St. Bertin who migrated to England just before the Norman Conquest and was active as a quasi-professional hagiographer between about 1070 and the turn of the century.[14] Goscelin is known to have written a large number of lives of Anglo-Saxon saints and it is not surprising that several vitae of uncertain attribution should be associated with his name. Most of these attributions seem to go back to John Bale, the Elizabethan antiquary, who found a manuscript in Leland's library containing several of Goscelin's known works along with three other vitae, one of which was recognizably VSE. Bale notes in his Index that Goscelin "is said to have written them." Moreover, among the "Collectanea" of a certain Thomas Langley, Bale lists four other works firmly attributed to Goscelin, of which the first is a Miracula Erkenwaldi beginning "Veterum vestigiis herentes."[15] The other three pieces listed are lives of the Barking saints Ethelburga, Hildelith, and Wulfhild, which we know were composed by Goscelin in the late 1080s, and two of which he dedicated to Bishop Maurice of London.[16] It is possible, then, that while he was at Barking, working on the lives of the abbesses, Goscelin also wrote a set of Erkenwald's miracles. Helmut Gneuss recently suggested that the Fleming may also have composed a set of short lections, De sancto Erchenwaldo, surviving along with excerpts from the Barking lives in one of the badly burned Cotton manuscripts, Otho A.xii.[17] It is reasonable to suppose that the lections, of which only a few words have survived, were excerpted from the miracula noted by Langley.

There are faint echoes of the wording of these fragments in Arcoid's elaborate "proemium" to MSE, and a quite close parallel in Mir. XVIII, so it is just possible he knew one or both.[18] If so, he denies it elsewhere in his proem, lamenting the failure of earlier generations to write down accounts of Erkenwald's miracles. It is probable that the lost Goscelin materials dealt only with miracles of Erkenwald associated with Barking, not with St. Paul's. Arcoid would therefore have less interest in them.[19]

Despite this evidence of Goscelin's possible authorship of some accounts of Erkenwald's miracles, there is no equivalent evidence to connect him with the composition of VSE and much that militates against such a connection.

Modern scholars who have attempted to establish the full corpus of Goscelin's works have invariably denied him the authorship of *VSE*, though without offering reasons for doing so.[20] Yet it is not hard to see why. Goscelin was one of the more deliberately ornate and grandiloquent writers of his day, and it is next to impossible to imagine that he is responsible for the prosaic and simple Latin of our text.

The author of *VSE* shows, like many of his predecessors in the art, a fondness for biblical echoes, and it is in these that his few flights of rhetoric and color occur.[21] Rarely does he indulge in Goscelin's habit of studied repetition and variation and nowhere does he exhibit anything like the Fleming's predilection for sustained periods of elevated diction and figurative language.[22] He usually states each event or idea once, in good order and clear sequence, with few obvious attempts at internal rhyme or cursus. He shows none of Goscelin's special fondness for word-play or for rare, esoteric and invariably polysyllabic vocabulary.[23] Although capable of a variety of rhetorical devices, he uses them in strictest moderation.

The incompatibility of the two styles may best be illustrated by comparison of the two following passages. The first is from *VSE*, and concerns Erkenwald's precocious piety as a youth, his influence on his sister and his conversion to the monastic life. The second passage, from Goscelin's life of St. Werburga, describes the virgin's early life and the growth of her religious vocation under her mother's care.

> Igitur ad doctrinam melliti episcopi puerulus quidam erkenwaldus nomine concurrebat; etate paruus sed mente maturus. Inter multa itaque alia legitur in hystoria anglorum *uita* eius uel *conuersatio fuisse tam sanctissima, ut in interiore homine diuicias glorie* perscrutatus, caduca uel secularia cuncta postponeret. Habebat autem germanam adleburgam nomine, quam ita disciplinis celestibus inflammauerat; ut ipsa uirgo uita et moribus et conuersatione sanctissima per omnia deo placere satageret. Predictus uir domini erkenwaldus, etate temporum et probitate morum roboratus pocius elegit solitaria antra quam popularibus interesse curis. Nam *duo preclara monasteria unum sibi alterum sorori sue construxerat*, etc.[24]

Notice how rapidly the narrative proceeds in this passage. It pauses only to gloss the quotation from Bede—"conuersatio ... sanctissima"—with an allusion to the Epistle to the Ephesians and to the familiar notion of *contemptus mundi*, before passing on to mention Erkenwald's sister and his influence on her. Then the "contemptus" theme is used again, in different words, to mark Erkenwald's adoption of the monastic life and his building of the two monasteries. The hagiographer's employment of simple balance and elementary rhyme in phrases like "etate paruus et mente maturus" and "etate temporum et probitate morum roboratus," exhibits only the humblest of stylistic aspirations, while the repetition of "conuersatio sanctissima" is inelegant and lazy in a way that a stylist such as Goscelin could not countenance. The *VSE* author's readiness to quote verbatim from his sources and from scripture, without any creative paraphrasing or oblique imitations, is likewise a trait one would not normally find in Goscelin, who is too firmly wedded to the principle of *amplificatio* to be content with word for word renditions when he can multiply by three! In the Goscelin passage below, one can see how little narrative ground he actually covers. He says little more here than that Werburga turned away from the world and from offers of earthly love, and chose Christ for her bridegroom, being encouraged in this by her mother. He is mainly interested in placing Werburga in the tradition of the Virgin and the virgin saints by weaving around her several strands of biblical imagery familiar from the liturgy and biblical exegesis.

A tenere ergo aevi flore, cum formae pulchritudo insigniter responderet generositati suae, coepit speciosa facie cum speciosissima mente ad illum, qui speciosus est forma prae filiis hominum (cf. Ps. 44.3), contendere: cujus ut inaestimabilem dulcedinem praegustare potuit, protinus in ejus amorem anhelo pectore exarsit, et, ut cervus ad fontes aquarum, virginalis anima ejus in ipso sitivit (cf. Ps. 41.2, 3): adeo dulcis et suavis Spiritus Domini a Patre dilectionis procedens illam attraxit, caelestes concupiscientias in ejus corde accendit, terrenas extinxit (cf. Ps. 44.11–12). Illa amore perpetuae virginitatis ad sponsum aeternae integritatis convolavit, procos et amatores regificos angelica pudicitia repulit, imo Christus electam sibi inhabitans omnibus appetitoribus eripuit. Sanctissima parens non cessabat assiduis monitis irrigare hortum Domini, et plantare in ea immarcescibilia germina paradisi (cf. Cant. 4.12), et accendere lampadem ejus oleo et flamma caritatis inextinguibili (cf. Matt. 25.1–13).[25]

[And thus from the first flowering of her girlhood, when her outward beauty gave striking evidence of her noble blood, the maiden with the lovely face but with a mind that was lovelier by far began to yearn for Him who is "fairer than the children of men": as soon as she caught a foretaste of that unimaginable sweetness, her panting breast was constantly aflame with love for Him, and as "the hart thirsteth for the water brooks," her virginal soul did likewise for Him. And so the sweet and pleasant Spirit of the Lord proceeding from the Father of delight drew her towards Him and kindled heavenly love-longings in her heart, and extinguished those of earth. In love with perpetual

virginity the maiden took flight towards the bridegroom of eternal purity; chaste as an angel, she rejected kingly suitors and lovers; Christ
took up His abode in His chosen one and freed her from all other ap-
petites. Her most holy parent did not cease meanwhile to water the
garden of the Lord with frequent instructions and therewith to plant
in her the seeds of the never-fading blooms of paradise and to keep
her lamp kindled with the oil and inextinguishable flame of charity.]

Goscelin may not be the author of the *Vita Erkenwaldi*, but his writings
are relevant to our inquiry in other ways. The *Vita Ethelburgae*, to which
we have already referred and which he wrote some time during 1086–1087,
devotes a good deal of attention to Erkenwald himself. Its opening chapters
provide us with sufficient evidence, in fact, to establish a *terminus post quem*
for the extant, full version of VSE in 1087, and to posit the prior existence
of a shorter *vita*, in length probably three short lections' worth, that was
little more than a creative paraphrase of the passage about Erkenwald in
Bede's *Ecclesiastical History*. The evidence of Goscelin's *Vita Ethelburgae*, in
other words, enables us to understand how and when VSE was composed,
if not by whom.

Goscelin begins his account of Ethelburga with a rather full description
of her brother's saintly life and career.[26] The purpose of this lengthy
preamble to the life of the abbess is four-fold. First, it explains, as does Bede,
how Ethelburga's sanctity was first aroused by that of her brother; second,
it casts some glory upon the sister by eulogizing the brother; third, it helps
Goscelin expand the rather sparse materials on Ethelburga's early life that
he found in Bede; and fourth, it serves as a compliment to Bishop Maurice
of London, to whom the work is dedicated and upon whose good will
depended the satisfactory completion of the extensive structural and liturgical
changes Abbess Alviva, Goscelin's patroness, had undertaken at Barking.[27]
Given Goscelin's habitual readiness to supplement his often meager early
sources with more recent legendary material, no matter how outrageous or unsuited,[28] it is rather surprising that he makes no mention of
the two most distinctive episodes in VSE: the miracle of the cartwheel and
the miraculous crossing of the flooded river after the quarrel over Erkenwald's
body. Goscelin leaves us with the same impression as Bede: that Erkenwald's
cult is still centered on the miraculous cart with its power to heal the sick,
and not on the saint's own body which is the main object of attention in
VSE.[29]

It is highly unlikely that Goscelin would have seriously misrepresented
the cult of the patron saint of the new powerful bishop to whom the *Vita
Ethelburgae* was dedicated. One can only conclude that whatever materials

Goscelin was able to consult concerning Erkenwald, besides Bede, they did not contain the episodes in the second part of *VSE* as extant today.

At first glance, indeed, Goscelin's account of Erkenwald seems merely to duplicate, in his characteristically verbose and repetitive style, what he could find in Bede. One could conclude from this that there was no life of Erkenwald at this time and that the readings for the saint's day were taken verbatim from the *Ecclesiastical History*. I hope to show, however, that while Goscelin certainly had Bede in front of him as he worked, and used him exclusively for chapters iv–x of his *Vita Ethelburgae*, he based the first three chapters on something very like the opening passages of *VSE* supplemented with additional material from elsewhere in Bede.

In the first place, Goscelin's narrative structure follows that of *VSE*, not that of Bede, although Bede's would have been more suitable. In the *Ecclesiastical History* we are told first how Theodore appointed Erkenwald bishop of London and how his holiness of life was confirmed by the miracles attributed to the horse-drawn litter. Bede next goes on to tell how Erkenwald had founded Chertsey and Barking before becoming bishop, installing his sister Ethelburga in the latter. With this introduction Bede begins his account, which occupies several pages, of Ethelburga's regime at Barking and the numerous miracles that occurred there.[30] It would have been natural for Goscelin to follow the same narrative order, since his main subject, like Bede's, is Ethelburga and not her brother. Instead Goscelin tells first how Augustine came to convert the English, and made Mellitus bishop of London, how Erkenwald became his pupil there and when he came to manhood renounced the world and used his patrimony to found two monasteries for himself and his equally devout sister. Goscelin then goes on in chapter three to tell how there came a second wave of Roman missionaries, led by the learned Theodore and Hadrian, how Theodore selected Erkenwald to be prelate in London, and how Erkenwald in spite of age and infirmity continued to preach the gospel by traveling the countryside in the wooden litter which later worked so many miracles of healing. Finally Goscelin reverts, rather abruptly, to Ethelburga in chapter four. His narrative order is thus precisely that of *VSE* in its opening paragraphs, except that he includes the material on Theodore and Hadrian lacking in *VSE*.

This naturally prompts one to consider *VSE* as one of the unnamed additional sources he alludes to in his dedication to Bishop Maurice,[31] and further evidence seems to confirm this. For Goscelin shares with *VSE* two narrative details not found in Bede: that Erkenwald was Mellitus' pupil; and that he rejected the glory and wealth of secular life and chose instead the solitary life of the monastery.[32] The only narrative detail in *VSE* that is not in Bede or in Goscelin is the statement that after Cedda's death Erkenwald was elected bishop with the consent of King Sebba and the people of London. Goscelin chooses instead to follow Bede here, saying simply that Theodore "ordained" Erkenwald bishop.[33] This permits him to maintain the symmetry he has created by balancing the two figures of Augustine and Mellitus, in Erkenwald's boyhood, against those of Hadrian and Theodore in his old age. Mentioning the latter also allows him to flesh out his narrative further with an effusive paean to the Latin and Greek learning they brought with them and in which, he claims, Ethelburga shared. It seems likely also that Goscelin, misunderstanding Bede, was indulging himself in the fantasy that archbishops in the late seventh century could appoint bishops without royal interference.[34]

In his search for exotic vocabulary and rare synonyms Goscelin, as we have already observed, tends to avoid repeating the exact wording of his more prosaic sources. We would not therefore expect to find the *Vita Ethelburga* depending too closely on the actual words of *VSE*. But Goscelin's knowledge of the latter work is discernible in a few verbal borrowings, as well as in the parallels of structure and substance we have noticed so far. A detailed demonstration of these verbal echoes would be tedious here and only the most telling correspondences will be touched on to complete this stage of the analysis.

One of Goscelin's main concerns in his account of Erkenwald is to increase Ethelburga's standing in relation to her brother. Whereas *VSE* depicts her as the passive fruit of Erkenwald's inspiration and example, Goscelin depicts her as his equal in holiness and fellow-mover in good works. This change is effected in part by simply attributing qualities to both of them that are confined to Erkenwald in *VSE*. The following passage from the *Vita Ethelburgae* is a good example of this device:

> Ut uero etiam beatum Erkenwaldum eadem *lectio* iungat sorori, quam sibi eadem *germani*tas eadem *probitas* eadem *mens* et diuina iunxit *caritas*. . . .

What we have here is little more than a clever synthesis in one sentence of a series of separate phrases from *VSE* characterizing Erkenwald's virtues:

> Erkenwaldus . . . mente maturus. . . . Habebat germanam. . . . probitate morum roboratus. . . . Erat enim . . . lectioni deditus; caritatis radice plantatus.[35]

Similarly Goscelin describes the conversion to the monastic calling in terms that combine echoes from *VSE*'s descriptions of Erkenwald's early religious vocation and of his conduct when appointed bishop. Thus *VSE*'s "in interiore homine diuicias glorie perscrutatus, caduca uel secularia cuncta postponeret," which refers to Erkenwald's youth, and a phrase referring to his episcopal period, "popularibus igitur pompis abrenuntiatis," turn up in Goscelin's work in a sentence describing Erkenwald's and Ethelburga's founding of the two monasteries: "*Renunciatis* ergo *seculi pompis gloriae* celestis amore terrenam dignitatem et ampla patrimonia in diuinam et ecclesiasticam hereditatem transtulere."[36]

Even more important than the direct verbal borrowing in this last sentence is Goscelin's statement that Erkenwald and Ethelburga put their inherited family wealth at the disposal of the church, giving up their secular nobility and prestige in return for eternal life. This is the only narrative detail which is unique to Goscelin's account of Erkenwald, for neither Bede nor VSE actually says how he could afford to found not just one but two religious establishments. Bede says simply that Erkenwald founded two monasteries. VSE by way of a preface to the dual foundation says that he gave up the world, preferring "the riches of glory" (in other words, the familiar treasure in heaven of Luc. 12.33),[37] rejecting *caduca uel secularia*, "transitory or worldly things." Here at least the issue of wealth is raised. But Goscelin is much more specific, making it quite clear that there was an "ample patrimony" available to Erkenwald which he and his sister appropriated to ecclesiastical use and for their "divine inheritance." Goscelin appears to have taken the word *caduca*, which in VSE is a neuter plural adjective meaning "transitory (things)," as the plural form of a specialized noun *caducum* which meant, among other things, "inheritance" or "inherited wealth." This late, learned, specialized form of *caducus* originated in classical Latin, where it meant a deceased person's wealth or goods passing to someone who is *not* the heir. It has this meaning in the Theodosian law codes and in the *Digest*. But by the twelfth century it had taken on the simple meaning of "inheritance," or, as Blaise defines it, "héritage qui revient a l'hériter legitime."[38] Goscelin evidently chose to understand the expression "caduca . . . postponeret" in VSE to mean that Erkenwald decided to reject the idea of using his inheritance for himself, surrendering it instead to the use of the communities he would found.[39]

Goscelin's sole contribution to the story of Erkenwald is explicable, then, as a highly specialized reading of a word used quite conventionally in VSE. We can only conclude from this that the numerous links between the first chapter of VSE and the opening chapters of Goscelin's *Vita Ethelburgae* result from Goscelin's having known and used a version of VSE which included the opening chapter but little else, since he appears to know nothing of its later chapters.

Neither Arcoid nor Goscelin composed VSE. Given the available evidence it can be dated between 1087 and ca. 1124; it also seems to be a composite work, an expansion of an earlier, shorter *vita* or set of lections. This "old *vita*," possibly preserved in the form of the Stonyhurst lections, was based closely on Bede and did not include either the wheel miracle or the longer narrative that follows the saint's death. These two episodes were added, in my view, by the author of the work extant as *VSE*. There is no evidence to indicate who the author may have been. Intellectual life at St. Paul's, as elsewhere in England, was improving during the period in question, as we know from charters issued by Bishop Richard in the early years of the twelfth century, defining the duties and providing for the material welfare of the Cathedral's "magister scholarum." The men appointed to this task, which also entailed supervising all the schools and scholars in the city, not just those of St. Paul's, must have been learned and literate beyond the common level and possibly capable of putting together the several parts of *VSE*.[40]

Certainly a new life of the saint was appropriate at this time, and necessary. If we can trust *MSE's* account of the great fire of London, 1087 (see Mir. IV), people of the time believed that Erkenwald's bodily relics and shrine had miraculously survived the fire, which destroyed the Anglo-Saxon cathedral. Erkenwald's standing in the eyes of the Normans must have risen dramatically thereafter, since the fire had virtually constituted a test of the authenticity of the relics.[41] But even if the *MSE* story, composed 1140–1145, is fictitious, it is certain that after the fire Bishop Maurice and the predominantly Norman chapter were very much in need of local London support for the construction and decoration of the vast new cathedral they now planned to build, which William of Malmesbury, for one, criticized for its ambitious scale.[42] Even if they had ignored or slighted Erkenwald before, sheer need might well have prompted them, after 1087, to promote official observance of the London saint's feast day and to commission a new *vita*, one that suited Norman tastes, however, and expressed and justified their idea of church and priesthood. An appropriate time for publishing *VSE* would have been the occasion when Erkenwald's pre-Conquest shrine was moved from wherever it had been kept since the fire to the great new crypt which was completed by the time Maurice died in 1107 (Mir. V 3–4). A similar combination of unearthly and mundane factors seems to have occasioned the composition of *MSE*, to which we may now turn.

CHAPTER THREE

Date and Authorship of
Miracula sancti Erkenwaldi

Internal and external evidence, to be discussed later in this chapter, indicate that the *Miracula sancti Erkenwaldi* was written between 1140 and 1145, and probably in 1141, by Arcoid, a canon of St. Paul's cathedral in London, and nephew to the former bishop, Gilbert the Universal (1128–1134). The work is thus the product of one of the more colorful and stormy periods in the history of St. Paul's.

It is alleged by some modern historians that Arcoid was one of the leading protagonists of a conflict over elections and ideology in the London chapter in the 1130s and '40s, and that his writings are in part an expression of it. But this view is not supported by the contents of *MSE* or by the external evidence. Authors of miracle collections and saints' lives were, it is true, quite capable of mingling sacred and secular history when they chose: the miraculous "works of God" could be and frequently were used as propaganda to promote political viewpoints as well as religious devotion, and to defend ecclesiastical privileges and possessions.[1] And *MSE* is by no means free of propaganda, but it bears no discernible relation to the election squabble of the London chapter. Arcoid's purpose is first of all to provide suitable reading matter for the lections on the saint's new feast day, that of the "translatio." At the same time he aims to publicize the miraculous powers of Erkenwald's relics, so as to encourage devotion to the shrine and raise money for its beautification. Another related goal of *MSE* is to promote and defend the veneration of relics and saints in general, and to foster a traditionally credulous acceptance of miracles in the face of contemporary scepticism and incredulity. Finally, *MSE* is an argument for the providence of God, designed to buttress and justify the long-standing Christian belief that even the worst kind of suffering can be shown to have a beneficent end and

purpose: "And truly there is no evil in the city that is not of the Lord's doing, for he creates misfortune so that in himself we might find relief and
peace" (Mir. XI 13–14).

To provide modern readers of *MSE* with the local historical background,
so that they may decide for themselves as to its relevance to Arcoid's work,
the first section of this chapter is devoted to an unavoidably detailed sketch
of the Anglo-Norman history of St. Paul's during the period covered by Arcoid's narrative. In the process, however, I will present my own arguments
against what appears to be the received interpretation of events in the
cathedral chapter in the 1130s. The second section of the chapter discusses
the evidence for the date of composition of *MSE*, and of the author and
his professional milieu. The specific circumstances that prompted the composition of the work are discussed in detail in chapter four, since they are
an important part of the history of St. Erkenwald's cult and shrine. The
final section of this chapter deals, instead, with *MSE*'s intellectual context.

1. ANGLO-NORMAN ST. PAUL'S, 1087–CA. 1150

A coherent view of the course of Anglo-Norman history at St. Paul's, London, has been presented by C. N. L. Brooke in a succession of studies building
on the work of Marion Gibbs.[2] In the valuable and wide-ranging introduction to her edition of the cathedral's charters in the so-called "Liber A," Gibbs
at one point offers an interpretation of the struggle among the canons to
elect a successor to Bishop Gilbert during the long vacancy between 1134
and 1141. Her tentative suggestions have been developed by Brooke into
an attractive scenario revolving around a conflict between opposing factions
of reform and reaction. According to Gibbs and Brooke, the two bishops
who preceded Gilbert, namely Maurice and Richard I (of Belmeis), fostered
a worldly, prosperous cathedral chapter in which clerical marriage and concubinage, hereditary prebends, absenteeism and other typically secular abuses
of the clerical life, were all too common. By 1127, when Richard died, St.
Paul's had become a target for Hildebrandine reformers. Under the next
bishop, Gilbert, a reform party with ascetic, monastic tendencies emerged
and a lengthy struggle ensued between the reformers on the one hand and
the reactionary old guard, led by Richard of Belmeis' legacy of nephews and
sons, on the other. This struggle culminated in the temporary success of
the ascetic reform faction, with the ten-year episcopacy of a monk, Robert
de Sigillo (1141–1150), during whose time the cult of the Anglo-Saxon monk-
bishop, Saint Erkenwald, was revived as a sort of symbolic focus for the
monastic ideals of the reformers, one of whose leaders, Arcoid, wrote the
saint's life and miracles.[3]

Anyone working on the history of St. Paul's and Anglo-Norman London quickly becomes aware of the fundamental importance of the scholarship of Gibbs and Brooke. Their studies are and should remain the standard introduction to medieval St. Paul's. It is with considerable diffidence and reluctance, therefore, that I have found myself forced to disagree with their published views on this particular issue. The several objections raised below, as well as those made earlier with regard to the dating and authorship of *VSE*,[4] are not intended to imply any general criticism of the work of Gibbs and Brooke as a whole, but merely to correct one aspect of it.

As Marion Gibbs established through her work with the St. Paul's charters, the Anglo-Norman era at the cathedral begins in earnest with the episcopacy of Bishop Maurice (1086–1107), former archdeacon of Le Mans, clerk to William the Conqueror and chancellor in the king's later years. Maurice seems to have been responsible for beginning, if not completing, the reorganization of the chapter according to the Norman model, instituting the system of prebendal stalls for thirty senior canons, a dean and several archdeacons, and possibly incorporating the existing pre-Conquest rule, with its semi-monastic flavor, into more modern statutes designed to suit the requirements and lifestyle of a more cosmopolitan body of secular clerics.[5] Apparently some of Maurice's reforms cut across the traditional autonomy of the cathedral canons, particularly with regard to the right to select new canons to occupy vacant prebends. Maurice repented of his abrogation of such chapter rights in a death-bed charter, but, as Gibbs points out, the bishop's right to "present" his own nominees to vacant stalls had been established and became a regular feature of episcopal authority in London in the twelfth century.[6]

Maurice's other main achievement as bishop was to supervise the planning and initial construction of the new Norman church, to replace the Anglo-Saxon minster destroyed by fire in the summer of 1087.[7] William of Malmesbury is our earliest witness for the vast scale on which Maurice planned the new building, criticizing him for the extravagance of its conception and the immense burden it became for his successors who were left to complete it. William also accuses Maurice of philandering, but grudgingly admits he was efficient as an administrator.[8] Other writers, however, suggest that Maurice was more than the womanizing clerical tycoon of Malmesbury's portrait. Ordericus Vitalis, a younger contemporary with ample contacts in the English church, calls Maurice "uir bonus et religiosus,"[9] and there are further indications, besides the death-bed repentance singled out by Gibbs, that his religiosity went deeper than a taste for expensive vestments and grandiose buildings. Denis Bethell[10] has pointed out that the Ramsey life of St. Osyth attributes to Maurice a more than obligatory devotion to the shrine of the virgin martyr of Chich (near the episcopal estates in Essex), describing how he elevated her relics, enriched the shrine and organized its keepers into a college of priests. He also received the dedication of Goscelin's lives of SS. Wulfilda[11] and Ethelburga,[12] and, if we can trust John Bale, the lost miracles of St. Erkenwald, also apparently by Goscelin.[13] Finally, there is charter evidence that he was a benefactor of the nuns at the Abbey of St. Amand, Rouen.[14]

This does not prove that Maurice was a saint, but it does suggest he was a more complex ecclesiast than William of Malmesbury was willing to allow. The same ambiguity surrounds his successor, Richard I of Belmeis, who was a royal clerk like Maurice, and one of the most powerful and long-serving of Henry I's provincial administrators. He was Henry's viceroy in Shropshire both before and after his consecration as bishop of London.[15] In addition to serving the royal interest in Shropshire, sometimes with ruthless efficiency and invariably to his own benefit, he continued at St. Paul's where Maurice had left off, both in the reorganization of the chapter and the construction of the new church.

From the charter evidence, for example, Gibbs concludes that although there certainly was a school in Maurice's time (and probably before), Richard of Belmeis seems to have taken particular care to clarify the schoolmaster's rights and responsibilities and to provide him with a suitable income.[16] He also contrived to provide for his own numerous family: no less than two sons and four nephews obtained canonical prebends during his episcopacy and of these, three held office as dean or archdeacon. The Belmeis dynasty thus founded continued to thrive at St. Paul's for the rest of the century and beyond, retaining and obtaining prebends through inheritance or family influence, and furnishing later deans, archdeacons, and even another bishop, Richard II (1152–1162), nephew of the first Richard.[17]

While the prebendal estates were yielding comfortable livings for his younger male dependents, Richard ploughed his own episcopal income back into the work on the new church. William of Malmesbury is specific about this, as is the author of *MSE*. But whereas the historian monk says Richard saw the building progress hardly at all despite his great efforts and expenditures,[18] the hagiographer canon credits the red bishop with "marvellously" advancing the work on the cathedral walls and with securing the urban demesne around the church by means of numerous purchases of lay property and the construction of a great wall round the whole churchyard.[19]

Contradiction also marks the evidence for Richard's generous endowment of a new Augustinian priory at St. Osyth's, Chich, in 1118/19. Whereas Malmesbury, in the passage just cited, implies that Richard turned from St. Paul's to St. Osyth's out of frustration and exhaustion, the St. Osyth hagiography and relevant charters reveal that he founded the new priory as a result of a near fatal stroke that at first left him blind and mute as well as paralyzed. He apparently believed that his attempt to appropriate some of the collegiate property of St. Osyth, for enclosure in his own hunting park at Clacton, provoked the saint's anger and the seizure was the result, but his repentance prompted her to initiate his partial recovery. He was unable to walk for the rest of his life, another nine years, but his sight, speech and mental powers returned. Besides his careful provision of ample funds and distinguished personnel for the priory, he also introduced the cult of St. Osyth at St. Paul's and presented the church with a reliquary containing one of the virgin martyr's arms.[20]

Like his predecessor Maurice, Richard issued charters shortly before his death deploring and retracting several predatory acquisitions of property in both Shropshire and the London area, eagerly branding himself as a great sinner fully repentant of his misdeeds.[21] Malmesbury's portrait emphasizes the sinner and seems to have colored Brooke's view of Richard and his "tribe" as the embodiment of "old corruption" in the St. Paul's chapter. But his memory was revered not only at Chich, where the canons of St. Osyth eulogized their founder in a verse panegyric,[22] but also at St. Paul's, where Arcoid, the author of *MSE*, praises Richard for his morality as well as for his energy and his many gifts to the cathedral.[23] Yet according to Gibbs' and Brooke's scenario, Arcoid should have had only distaste and pity for the arch-Belmeis. Generations later, Master Henry of Northampton, canon of the cathedral and a distinguished royal clerk, thought highly enough of Bishop Richard to have his portrait embroidered on one end of his maniple; St. Erkenwald adorned the other end.[24]

Little is known about the character of the St. Paul's canons before Maurice's time, but by the 1120s they constituted a group of worldly, privileged, often talented men, most of whom had powerful connections with the court, as had Ralph Flambard or Angar of Bayeux, or among the City's leading families, like Thomas Becket and the Canon Ralph who was also an alderman, or within the episcopacy itself, like the Belmeis clan and Arcoid himself. Others were simply the sons of earlier canons, from whom they had inherited the prebendal estates and the seats in the choir.[25] How much time and energy each of the thirty "majores" or senior canons devoted to the liturgical and choral round that was ostensibly at the heart of the Cathedral's existence, we do not know exactly. Already by Maurice's time there were twelve so called "minor" canons and thirty "vicars," one for each of the senior canons.[26] According to the thirteenth-century statutes which are regarded as a reliable guide to post-Conquest customs there was a rota system whereby only two canons at a time, named by the "cantor" or precentor in advance,

were required to lead the singing at the day and night services over a specified
two week period. And even they could be represented by their vicars on
all but major feasts, "si voluerint."[27] The minor canons and vicars could undoubtedly handle most of the pastoral work in the local community. Small
wonder that Osbern of Canterbury, the hagiographer of St. Dunstan writing
in the late eleventh century, characterized the secular canons' life as consisting of "women's embraces, spacious homes, and troops of friends."[28]

Osbern was indulging in monkish exaggeration, of course, but the St. Paul's
canons undoubtedly enjoyed a comfortable and flexible existence. Their
relative freedom from the demands of the "opus dei" allowed them to devote
themselves to the various executive branches of chapter business or the
management of their prebendal estates and other properties if they had them,
or to other private interests or public careers. Even in the early years of the
century, at least seven of the thirty canons were completely nonresident,[29]
a figure that increased steadily as St. Paul's prebends became a standard source
of income for royal clerks or a stepping stone to higher office in the
church.[30] Public opinion and various forms of official pressure gradually
reduced the number of wives and concubines living in the canons' houses
in or near the churchyard or out on the manors in Essex, and there were
therefore fewer sons waiting to inherit the choir stalls. Hereditary prebends
were a thing of the past not long after the mid-century. But nepotism,
celibacy's answer to primogeniture, and particularly episcopal nepotism, went
from strength to strength.[31]

Richard of Belmeis, who was both father and uncle to a portion of his
chapter, passed away in 1127 and was succeeded a year later by Gilbert the
Universal, a well known theologian and teacher, former head of the cathedral
school in Auxerre.[32] Gilbert's appointment need not be taken as an indication of "spiritual panic"[33] on King Henry's part, or as a belated attempt to
inject a more intellectual or more religious spirit into his episcopal ranks.
As Beryl Smalley has argued, Gilbert recommended himself to Henry because
of his skills as a canon lawyer and by his readiness to switch to the king's
side during some litigation at the papal court in the winter of 1125–1126.
The case involved the perennial dispute between York and Canterbury, and
Gilbert's support for the king and Canterbury was apparently crucial in securing York's discomfiture.[34]

It is true that Bernard of Clairvaux wrote to Gilbert at some point during
his episcopacy, congratulating him on living the life of a poor man even
while a bishop,[35] and this has been taken as an indication of a new ascetic
spirit at St. Paul's during Gilbert's regime.[36] But all of the other evidence
suggests that what Bernard interpreted as a kind of apostolic poverty was
more likely to have been the old man's avarice and miserliness. Gilbert appears

to have done very little during his declining years in London except amass a fortune and acquire a reputation for meanness.[37] Even the author of *MSE*, his own nephew, after referring to Gilbert's "frugality," declines, on the grounds of insufficient learning, to offer an account of his uncle's "great gifts" to the church.[38] The fact is that Gilbert died intestate, part of his treasure was seized by the king, and it is plain that he had spent as little as he could in his six year term.[39] *MSE* makes no mention of any progress in the construction of St. Paul's during that time, whereas the considerable contributions of Maurice and Richard in this sphere are described and praised.

What we do know is that in June, 1133, Gilbert outraged the monks of Westminster by seizing the offertory money collected at the Mass he celebrated there on the feast of SS. Peter and Paul, and there is other evidence to suggest that he attempted to seize a church belonging to the Augustinian priory of Holy Trinity, Aldgate.[40] It is possible that his last act as bishop, shortly before he died in August, 1134, was an effort to make amends to Westminster, for he had been reprimanded by the Pope for his treatment of the monks and ordered to refrain from any interference at the Abbey in the future. He is known to have assented to the founding of Kilburn Priory in North London for three female recluses, and to have relinquished all episcopal jurisdiction over the new priory, which was highly unusual. The person responsible for the founding and funding of Kilburn was Osbert of Clare, prior of Westminster Abbey.[41]

There is no evidence, apart from his nephew's composition of *MSE*, that Gilbert made much difference to the intellectual life of the cathedral. As instances of "a new infiltration of learned men into the chapter" in Gilbert's time, Brooke offers only two names: Arcoid himself, and Master Alberic, author of a treatise on mythology.[42] Alberic's first definite appearance as a canon, however, is dated 1148/9, long after the period in question. It is true that he is known to have witnessed two charters that are datable anywhere from 1138–1154, due to the lack of more specific dating criteria.[43] But this means that at the very earliest Alberic makes his first mark at St. Paul's fully four years after Gilbert's death. It is unlikely that any of Gilbert's nominees or protégés would secure a prebend after the old man's death. Whereas Arcoid witnesses his first extant charter in 1132 and is indubitably Gilbert's nominee,[44] there is no evidence at all to link Alberic the mythographer with Gilbert the Universal.

It should also be pointed out that Richard of Belmeis in no way discouraged intellectual activity at St. Paul's. We have already noted his provisions for the cathedral school and his foundation of St. Osyth's, which became quickly famous for the learning and piety of its canons. There is even a scrap of evidence for some literary sophistication at St. Paul's itself during his time:

namely a set of rather elaborate verses penned in 1122 by a certain cleric
of St. Paul's, identified as Ralph, son of Fulcred of Caen, on a mortuary
roll in honor of Bishop Vitalis of Avranches.[45]

Bishop Gilbert's death in August, 1134,[46] ushered in a vacancy of seven
years in the London episcopacy, which coincided with the first part of the
troubled reign of King Stephen. The ostensible reason for the long vacancy
was the failure of the St. Paul's chapter to agree on a successor to Gilbert.
For the first time since the Conquest they were permitted to exercise their
right to elect a bishop themselves rather than simply confirm a royal
nominee.[47] London was the first episcopal vacancy of Stephen's reign. In
having the canons hold their election at his first Easter council at Westminster (late March, 1136) he may have been attempting to impress the other
bishops and abbots with his respect for the freedom of the Church,[48]
because he was hoping to receive oaths of fealty from them later in the council. In the event, what the assembled notables witnessed was an early
demonstration of the divisive effects of the new king's approach to gov-
ernment.

A later dean of St. Paul's, Ralph de Diceto, is the main source of our
knowledge of this affair,[49] for MSE completely ignores the election and its
sordid sequel. Ralph tells how Dean William of Belmeis, nephew of Bishop
Richard I, was summoned to Westminster along with the rest of the canons,
to settle the choice of Gilbert's successor in the see. To the great displeasure
of the king and council, the chapter could not come to an agreement and
"many of the canons deserted the Dean and against his wishes voted in favor
of Abbot Anselm." This Anselm was a nephew of St. Anselm of Bec and
Canterbury, a former papal legate, former abbot of St. Saba in Rome, and
currently abbot of St. Edmund's, Bury.[50] He had been among the most prominent of the regular clergy during the reign of his friend, Henry I, but undoubtedly by this time he had ceded first place to the Cluniac Henry of
Blois, abbot of Glastonbury, bishop of Winchester, and brother of King
Stephen. Ralph de Diceto does not say why Anselm got the majority vote
among the canons. He does say that Dean William' closest adherents, those
"who were accustomed to dine with him everyday," appealed against the
vote and apparently had the backing of the lay and ecclesiastical barons
and the king himself, all of whom disapproved of Anselm's candidacy. The
king was so angry with the Anselm faction, says Ralph, that he soon afterwards appropriated the benefices of several of them.[51]

Undeterred, Anselm's supporters took the case to Rome the following year,
laden with "the treasures of the church of London," and accompanied by
Anselm himself, "his saddle bags bulging," but whether with his own or St.
Paul's coin, Ralph does not say. In Rome they obtained their suit, with the

help of "the gleam of the rusty purse." On their return, Anselm was enthroned in triumph and promptly began to act in a tyrannical and acquisitive manner, taking possession of all the church's temporalities (which were supposed to be held partly by the canons in common, partly by individual prebendaries, partly by the bishop) and extorting feudal dues, and oaths of obedience and fealty from the chapter's tenants. But his joyride was brief. Two of Dean William's personal staff, his nephews Ralph of Langford and Richard of Belmeis, both canons, went to Rome also, and got the case reopened, with a result that Pope Innocent II and his chancellor Ammericus called upon the other English bishops to submit their opinions on the matter. The only one Ralph de Diceto records is that of Archbishop Thurstan of York, a former canon of St. Paul's, who replied that considering the quality of Anselm's life and his public reputation, it would be safer to remove him from his abbacy than to promote him to the bishopric of London.[52]

The papal decision was to declare the election of Anselm uncanonical and void, since it had been opposed by the Dean, who should have had "first voice." Anselm was expelled and regained his abbacy at St. Edmund's only after a struggle, while Bishop Henry of Winchester was appointed bishop-in-charge of the diocese. The London *cathedra* was finally filled in June, 1141, when Robert de Sigillo, former chief clerk in Henry I's chancery and briefly a monk at Reading Abbey, was appointed bishop by Empress Maud during her short-lived ascendancy over Stephen. Robert managed to retain his new post even after the empress was driven from London, although he appears to have been in exile for a short time. Later in the decade he was one of three English bishops who defied the pope in favor of King Stephen, and was among those who effected a reconciliation between Stephen and Archbishop Theobald. He died in 1150, amidst rumors that he had been poisoned, and was succeeded, after a struggle, by Richard of Belmeis.[53]

The split in the chapter in 1136–1138 has been explained by Gibbs and Brooke[54] as, in part, the consequence of an ideological conflict between, on the one hand, the worldly Belmeis clan and their adherents, and on the other a "theological party" that had formed around Bishop Gilbert the Universal and survived his passing. The starting point of the conflict, Gibbs argues, was in the late 1120s, soon after Gilbert arrived, when one of the issues confronting the English hierarchy was whether or not to institute nationally the Feast of the Immaculate Conception. According to a letter written by Osbert of Clare to Abbot Anselm of Bury in 1128, Gilbert the Universal supported this campaign for the feast, along with Anselm himself and Abbot Hugh of Reading. Osbert, who seems to have succeeded Eadmer of Canterbury[55] as the driving force and chief spokesman of the campaign, tells Anselm how he had recently attempted to celebrate the feast in the face of complaints from unspecified opponents, "mei emuli," who had taken their complaints to, among others, Roger of Salisbury. He urges Anselm to join with Gilbert and Hugh to defend the feast against such detraction.[56] Edmund Bishop, the liturgiologist, speculated that Osbert's "emuli" in this matter might be Dean William and other members of the Belmeis family at St. Paul's, but Bishop based his speculation not on any contemporary evidence but solely on the fact that eight years later Dean William opposed Anselm of Bury's election as bishop of London.[57]

Building on this rather flimsy base, Marion Gibbs further speculated that Anselm's faction in the chapter in 1136 constituted an "anti-secular tendency," other symptoms of which, besides the promotion of the Marian feast, were the later revival of Erkenwald's cult and the foundation of Holy Trinity Convent, Caddington, during the episcopate of the erstwhile monk, Robert de Sigillo. Christopher Brooke has gone even further than Gibbs, redefining her "anti-secular tendency" as an "ascetic movement" fiercely resisted by the Belmeis clan in their role as representatives of the "old corruption."[58]

There is not much good evidence for any of this. In the first place, Bishop's suggestion that Osbert's "emuli" were of the Belmeis family is rendered even shakier by the editor of Osbert's letters, who points out that at the time in question, 1128, Osbert was supposed to be in exile from Westminster Abbey and that there is nothing to indicate therefore that the mysterious "emuli" were in London at all.[59] More suspicious, in my view, is his use of the phrase "mei emuli," which implies that these people were conducting some sort of vendetta against Osbert personally, presumably in connection with his troubles as prior of Westminster, and were opposing the feast as a way of discomfiting him. Since we lack any evidence that Osbert had enemies at St. Paul's, it seems likely that the "emuli" were monks of Westminster Abbey. A third weakness in Bishop's proposal is of course its dependence on an event that occurred so many years later, when the feast of the Conception was no longer controversial (a church council of 1129 approved it).[60] The fact is Dean William's opposition to Abbot Anselm was seconded by every bishop and baron attending the Westminster council of 1136[61] and Archbishop Thurstan's searing rebuff to his candidacy ought to convince one that Dean William had other reasons besides the Immaculate Conception for not wanting Anselm inside St. Paul's.

The assumption that the St. Paul's chapter divided sharply into worldly Belmeis reactionaries and ascetic newcomers is also misleading and too simple. The abortive election of Abbot Anselm was secured by the very Belmeis clan who we have been told were his implacable enemies. Diceto is quite clear on this point. It was Dean William's "consanguinei," his own relatives, who withstood him most of all in the election itself and who later carted Anselm off to Rome with the cathedral treasure to pay their expenses.[62] Just why half the Belmeis canons and a majority of the others should have supported Anselm in defiance of their dean, we shall probably never know. But it is most unlikely that it had anything to do with either the Immaculate Conception or asceticism. Certainly there is nothing in Anselm's record to suggest that he was qualified to be the leader of an ascetical movement. He was, as far as one can tell, an opportunist and a careerist. Always happier out of the cloister than in it he was in constant attendance on his friend King Henry both before and after he secured the abbacy of St. Edmund's.[63] His association with St. Saba's and St. Edmund's should not obscure what was evidently a long-term ambition: to be a bishop.[64] Furthermore he was the father of at least one son. The testimony of Thurstan, himself a great supporter of the regular life, and Anselm's own behavior during his brief tenure of the see, make it highly unlikely that the wandering abbot of St. Edmund's was to be the spearhead of an ascetic revival at St. Paul's, London.[65]

Ironically it can be argued that the ostensibly worldly, secularist leaders of the Belmeis family were more interested in promoting the regular life than Bishop Gilbert, Abbot Anselm, or Robert de Sigillo. We have already noticed Richard I's foundation of St. Osyth's priory and his fostering her cult at St. Paul's itself. To this should be added his apparently crucial role in the foundation of St. Bartholomew's Priory in London by Rahere, former minstrel of Henry I, in 1123.[66] Richard's involvement in such foundations is more impressive than Gilbert's mere assent to the foundation of Kilburn. Similarly, the charters of 1145 recording the foundation of Holy Trinity Priory, Caddington, of which Christina of Markyate was first prioress, indicate that the land for the priory was donated by the St. Paul's chapter, led by the Belmeis brothers, Dean Ralph and Archdeacon Richard, acting independently of the ex-monk, Robert de Sigillo, whose name appears nowhere in the extant documents.[67] One should also be cautious about positing Robert himself as an ascetic reformer. One of the few things that is known about his activities as bishop is that he provided one of his sons to a St. Paul's prebend.[68]

In *MSE* itself there is no mention of either Anselm or the Immaculate Conception, despite the assertion of Brooke that Arcoid the author was a friend of Anselm's and shared with him in the promotion of the feast.[69] Perhaps significantly, Arcoid's narrative completely ignores the period 1136 to 1138 when Anselm's candidacy was an issue. The miracles of St. Erkenwald begin to proliferate in 1138–1139, after Anselm had gone for good. Moreover, Arcoid shows no special sympathy for or interest in the regular or ascetical life, and there is some evidence that he valued the freedom and flexibility afforded by the life of a secular chapter.[70] What is uppermost in *MSE* is an enthuasiasm for the *liturgical* life of the secular cathedral and for the colorful splendor of a big city church with its crowds of worshippers and pilgrims

at its shrines. There are remarks about the dangers of becoming too absorb-
ed in worldly pleasures and prosperity, but they are no more than the commonplaces of medieval Christianity. The religious life as it is understood
in MSE consists in the ordinary practice of Christian virtues, with a special
emphasis on faith in the merits and miracles of the saints, and of St. Erkenwald in particular; devotion to the liturgy; and the willing observance of
feast-days. Of asceticism in the strict sense, as reflected, for example, in the
contemporary lives of English hermits such as Christina of Markyate herself
or Godric of Finchale, there is no trace, nor of the *vita apostolica* espoused
by the new orders of regular canons.

If there had been a conflict at St. Paul's between ideological factions such
as Gibbs and Brooke posit for the 1130s and 1140s, it is likely that the *Miracula sancti Erkenwaldi* would have registered its existence in some way. Instead it reflects the more general concerns of a secular cathedral in a thriv-
ing commercial metropolis in the mid-twelfth century. There is no effort
to exalt one form of religious life over another, but there is a continuous
effort to assert and defend the time-honored values of the ecclesiastical tradition against its habitual enemies, intellectual scepticism and lay indifference.

2. "ARCOIDUS PRESBYTER":

THE DATE AND AUTHORSHIP OF MSE

Unlike VSE, MSE can be dated with some precision. Its subject matter
covers the period from the late-eleventh century up to 1140–1141, but the
main historical focus is on the years when St. Paul's was without a bishop,
1134–1141, and more specifically the years 1138–1141, when Henry of Blois,
bishop of Winchester and brother of King Stephen, was in charge of the
diocese following the expulsion of the temporary bishop, Anselm of Bury.
Among the last events described, and the only event in MSE to be given
a precise date, is the hasty translation of Erkenwald's coffin from the crypt
to a stone "housing" in the upper church, most probably in the nearly completed choir, on February 16, 1140. This is related in Mir. XIV. Of the remaining five miracle stories, three concern events that supposedly occurred
before the translation (Mir. XVI–XVIII) and a fourth (Mir. XIX) cannot be
dated at all, except after ca. 1073; the remaining miracle (XV) seems to refer
to Erkenwald's feast day, April 30, in either 1140 or 1141.

If the author had waited longer than the latter date to write up his account of the 1140 translation and the miracles that led up to it, he would
have had to mention the nomination and consecration of the new bishop

of London, Robert de Sigillo, in June, 1141, or at least to address him in a prologue or dedication. But there is not a hint of his existence. In the "proemium" the author addresses only his "fratres karissimi," presumably his fellow canons of the cathedral chapter of St. Paul's. In a preamble to Mir. V he briefly describes the episcopates and building achievements of the three twelfth-century bishops who had preceded the long vacancy, and therefore not to acknowledge Robert's accession to the *cathedra* would have been not only odd but also a breach of decorum.[71]

Individual portions of *MSE* may have been composed before 1140–1141, such as the strictly narrative passages of Mir. VII,[72] but in the absence of strong evidence to the contrary, we can assume that the work was composed as a whole rather than piecemeal and probably during the latter half of 1140 or early in 1141. This agrees with what is known of the author.

In an important passage early in Mir. V the author of *MSE* reveals himself in a self-effacing but not entirely modest fashion as the nephew of the well-known theologian Gilbert the Universal, who was bishop of London from January, 1128, to August 1134.[73] After briefly touching on Gilbert's wisdom, natural authority, frugality, and Old Testament scholarship, the writer excuses himself from offering any fuller account of the bishop, on the grounds that the task of describing Gilbert's generosity to the church and his personal probity would require, he says, "a man of gifted intellect, not his nephew, it being beyond his (i.e., the nephew's) power to recount the deeds that all of Latin Christendom praises." (Mir. V 16–19).

Beryl Smalley, in the article cited several times above, identified this "nepos" as a certain Canon Arcoidus[74] who is listed in the surviving records as a holder of the cathedral prebend of Brondsbury (earlier Bromesbury) in North London from ca. 1132 or before to ca. 1142, and who witnessed a respectable number of St. Paul's charters during this period, some of which are cited by Diana Greenaway in her edition of Le Neve's *Fasti*. Greenaway, Marion Gibbs, and Christopher Brooke, have followed Smalley in identifying this Arcoid as Erkenwald's hagiographer.[75] However, just as Smalley refrained from attributing both the Miracles *and* the life of Erkenwald to this nephew of Gilbert, she was also cautious in her identification of him. She said that Arcoid "may be" the writer.

Gilbert apparently had more than one nephew. Another "nepos episcopi Gilberti," named Henry, occurs in the St. Paul's prebendal catalogue like Arcoid, but as prebendary of Islington. Henry is otherwise a mystery, for he witnessed no extant charters. He would have assumed the prebend, Greenaway argues, before his uncle died in August, 1134. His successor in the Islington stall, Jocelin of Bohun (later bishop of Salisbury), was archdeacon of Winchester under Henry of Blois and was doubtless appointed to the St. Paul's prebend while the latter had charge of the London diocese from 1138–1141, before Robert de Sigillo became bishop.[76]

This means that Henry, "nepos Gilberti" and either brother or cousin of Arcoid, relinquished his stall and presumably his earthly life only shortly before Arcoid himself, who does not appear in any charters later than 1142 and was certainly dead, says Greenaway, by 1145.[77] Since MSE, as we have argued, was most probably written by 1141, Canon Henry could conceivably have been the author just as well as Arcoid.

Yet Arcoid seems the more likely candidate, at least on the evidence available. For one thing, his dates are more definite. Whereas Henry's demise could have occured as early as 1138, Arcoid died no earlier than 1140 and possibly as late as 1142–1145; he was certainly alive therefore at the time of the translation of the relics, February 16, 1140, which is the *terminus post quem* of MSE, whereas Henry could have been dead before. Equally important, Arcoid was the more influential and respected of the two nephews, and demonstrably more involved in the residential life and business of the chapter. And this matches the impression MSE's author conveys of himself, as we shall see in more detail below. Given Henry's total lack of visibility in the surviving documents, except the prebendal catalogue, it is very possible that he was one of the full-time absentees, of whom there were about ten others at this time, by Brooke's estimate.[78] Unless new evidence emerges therefore, it seems reasonable to leave this other "nepos" of Gilbert to his former oblivion and to credit Arcoid with the authorship of Erkenwald's miracles.

Although twice named "priest," Arcoid is never entitled "canon" in the charters, prebendal lists, or MSE. But with a prebendal stall he was *ipso facto* a canon, and he implies as much in Mir. XIV (58–59) when he refers to Canon Theoldus of St. Martin's-le-Grand as "consocius noster." As we observed earlier, the canons of St. Paul's formed a privileged circle of secular clerics, provided with ample if not enormous incomes and with the freedom to add to their wealth by other business or employment if they chose. Not a few, as we have seen, were non-resident, pursuing careers in the civil service and the church that would lead to positions of even greater wealth and eminence. Arcoid, however, does not appear to have been of this ilk. He may have served on his uncle's personal staff up to 1134, but there is no evidence that he was a pluralist (though no particular stigma was attached to this in his day) or that he was married or engaged in business dealings of any kind outside the chapter. It is probable that he was not a young man when he came to London with his uncle in 1128 or later. Gilbert himself is described as already "of great age" when he became bishop,[79] and his nephew might easily therefore be middle- aged in 1130. Ten years later he writes of himself and other members of the chapter as of "advanced age, nay, approaching our end" (Mir. I 63–64). Arcoid, in other words, was probably past careerism when he came to London and was no doubt pleased to give himself wholeheartedly, though an alien immigrant, to the life of the English cathedral close.

He had his own house in London, apparently near the cathedral (Mir. XI 45), besides whatever properties were included in the manor out at Brondsbury. He was sufficiently well-to-do to play host to one of the royal clerks, Adam, with whom he may have discussed medicine as well as miracles (Mir. XI 4–5, 46–47). In the charters he witnesses, he appears invariably with, among others, Robert de Auco, an elderly married canon whose house in St. Paul's churchyard was next to the schoolhouse. The head of the school, Master Henry, who had received his education and upbringing as a ward of the previous magister, Hugo,[80] likewise appears in most of Arcoid's charters. Similarly Robert of Caen, and canons Geoffrey and Robert, sons of a former canon, Wilfred, were Arcoid's frequent co-signers of charters between 1132 and ca. 1140. In two of the latest dateable such documents, involving agreements between the chapter and various of its lay tenants, Arcoid actually heads the list of canons, which seems to indicate a degree of seniority on his part. One charter he witnesses even in the absence of either the dean or any of the archdeacons.[81]

Apart from their approximate life-spans and the names of their prebends and of their fathers in some cases, we know very little about any of these men, except Arcoid through MSE, and Master Henry, whose duties as schoolmaster can be surmised on the basis of the thirteenth-century statutes and who is himself the subject of more than one charter.[82] But we do know that over a period of twelve years or more Arcoid was closely associated, in cathedral affairs if not socially, with a group of canons who represented the hereditary continuity of the chapter, who took an ostensibly active part in the day to day business of the great ecclesiastical corporation, and who doubtless fulfilled their religious duties as conscientiously as they could. Whatever else they meant to him, for Arcoid they must have been a link with the early days of the Anglo-Norman cathedral under Bishops Maurice and Richard I of Belmeis.[83] Probably it was through these men, or others like them, that the traditions regarding the great fire and the other miracles from before Arcoid's time were passed on to him to be dressed in suitable hagiographical and homiletic guise.

Despite their obvious fascination for the historian, and their importance for the study of topography, onomastics, economics, and chronology, charters leave a lot unsaid about the people whose names they record, and merely encourage one to speculate about the unknowable. Without MSE one would have never dreamt that the busy immigrant canon, whose uncle the bishop had obtained for him the comfortable prebend of Brondsbury in the early 1130s, was also a writer of no mean ability and, to judge from what he wrote, a deeply religious man in love with the old-fashioned values of the established church. In the *MSE* he has left us a highly selective account of the Anglo-Norman world of St. Paul's and of his own involvement in, and interpretations of, the events he considered worthy to be memorialized for the benefit of posterity, "posteris . . . nostris temporibus."

The historian in search of new information about the great events and personalities of the mid-twelfth century will be disappointed by what Arcoid chose to memorialize. Of the role of London and St. Paul's in the so-called anarchy of Stephen's reign, or of the squabble over the episcopal election in the cathedral chapter, there is scarcely a trace,[84] and the oblique manner in which he does touch on such things indicates very well that Arcoid as a hagiographer is little interested in secular, "non-miraculous" history. The miracles of the saint happen in the temporal world, it is true, but they are not human events or even, strictly speaking, temporal events; rather they are "signs," signs from the higher world, revealing to mortal men the reality and essence of God's eternal order and providence. They are intended to draw men back to God, to bring hope and consolation amidst the suffering and disorder caused by human evil, and to give assurance that everything that happens in the world, good or bad, does so according to God's will. These divine signs are extraordinary in the fullest sense of the word, and quite distinct from the natural course of human history. For Arcoid, the "divina opera" he records constitute a precious "historia" quite separate from and markedly superior to the sordid business of the chronicler.[85]

He even dispenses with the chronicler's traditional concern for the linear passage of time. As we shall see in the next chapter, Miracles IV through XV do seem to be in chronological order, and from them a narrative history of Erkenwald's shrine can be pieced together. But most of the references to time and dates are vague, and what we learn about the shrine and the liturgical cult is incidental to the recounting of the miracles themselves. The first three miracles, moreover, which comprise almost a third of the whole work, lack any sense of historical time whatsoever. It is impossible to determine even which century they belong to. Miracles XVI–XIX, on the other hand, move backwards in time, one by one, from the year 1140–1141, into the eleventh century. All we can say of Mir. XIX is that it must have occurred, if at all, after ca. 1070 when the diocese of Lincoln was established. Clearly we are dealing with a "hystoria" (Mir. II 54) that cannot be comprehended merely through a traditional historical reading. As I hope to show in a separate study, the more esoteric tools of literary analysis are necessary to begin to understand *MSE*'s elusive structure.[86]

3. "Erubesce, ergo, Vigilanti!"

Arcoid and the critique of saints' cults

As will become clear in the next chapter, pragmatic considerations such as the St. Paul's cathedral building program, funding for a new shrine, and the attendant need for publicity and promotion, influenced the timing of the 1140 translation of Erkenwald's relics and the subsequent composition of *MSE*. But of considerable importance to Arcoid the author, to judge from the attention he gives them in the text, were the theology of the saint's cult and the attendant problems of authenticity and credibility. More than is usual for a twelfth-century hagiographer, Arcoid interrupts and comments on his miracle narrative in ways that reveal not only his aims as a hagiographer but also his sensitivity to criticism, from among his contemporaries, of his craft and of the relics, miracles, and cult that are his stock-in-trade. In order to understand and appreciate Arcoid's own thoughts on this subject, we must look first at the relevant historical background and the contemporary context of his ideas.

Arcoid was writing at a time when attitudes towards the veneration of saints and their relics were shifting, at least among certain types of people. Not that there was any real decline in the general popularity of the saints' cults. On the contrary, they continued to play an important and increasing role in medieval religious life and they remained a great stimulus to devotion, art, literature, and economics.[87] The number of new saints "created" in the twelfth century was to exceed that of the eleventh century by a considerable margin.[88] But like so many aspects of Christian life during the late eleventh century and throughout the twelfth century, sanctity became the subject of more scrutiny, debate, clarification, and control than in the past, and it ceased to be a merely local concern.[89] Up to the end of the eleventh century, bishops, archbishops, and sometimes national church councils had determined whether or not someone should be venerated as a saint, and the translation or elevation of relics by one or more bishops in itself constituted a virtual canonization, although the term was not used.[90] In England, moreover, particularly before the coming of the Normans, secular monarchs and lay magnates often played a crucial role in fostering and even initiating saints' cults, some of which had little or no ostensible religious basis.[91] But in the course of the twelfth century, the creation of a new saint came to be associated more and more with the deliberate act of canonization by the pope. The idea that canonization was the pope's exclusive prerogative would not be made explicit in so many words until 1171, nor would it be incorporated into canon law until after 1230, but the sentiment was widespread long before,[92] as is evident from Osbert of Clare's decision to go to Rome in 1139 and seek the canonization of King Edward. The Confessor's relics had been translated in 1102, apparently, though not certainly, by Bishop Gundulf of Rochester, but the first miracles did not occur until the 1130s. Osbert must have felt that the cult was insufficiently validated by the episcopal translation, and so he became the first to seek the canonization of an English saint.[93]

The papacy's gradual assumption of control over the making of saints was only one aspect of the growth of the Roman curia's prestige, power, and effectiveness in the twelfth century. It is a commonplace of modern scholarship that the popes had no need to seek actively to extend their power at this time. Rather it was pressed upon them by the quickening tide of eager litigants who came to the papal court from all over Christian Europe to claim old and new privileges and benefits for themselves, and for their abbeys or chapters, as well as to have disputes settled by the supreme authority in all things ecclesiastical.[94] The same was true of canonization. Sought initially by eager promoters of a new saint to confer a "supplementary lustre" on a cult already sanctioned by local authorities,[95] the approval of the papal court gradually came to be a juridical necessity in an age when people felt more and more impelled to obtain the highest token of legitimacy for their respective causes. The final stage in this process occurred when the popes themselves began to claim canonization as their exclusive right.

I have not seen it suggested by scholars who have studied the history of canonization, but it seems to me likely that one factor helping to provoke the shift away from episcopal control of saints' cults and towards exclusive papal canonization was that clerics of the late eleventh and early twelfth century were more sophisticated than their forebears in their thinking about the cults, the relics, and the literary memorials of the saints. Although a thorough study of this topic has yet to be attempted, there is a good deal of testimony that many more clerics were looking at the stories of the saints' lives and miracles with a sharper, more critical eye than in the past, and demanding better evidence of the authenticity of relics and the reliability and veracity of hagiographical writings.[96] Under such circumstances, it is not surprising that the promoters of new and old cults were willing to incur the frustrations and expenses of the canonization procedure, for papal confirmation of a saint's authenticity would be a powerful form of protection against critics and sceptics.[97]

In the early middle ages and down into the eleventh century, one encounters the occasional hagiographer who was, at least ostensibly, concerned to get at the truth of his subject and resist the temptation to lie on the saints' behalf,[98] but for the most part the authors and redactors of the Merovingian and later *vitae* and *passiones* paid only lip service to the notion of historical accuracy, preferring, as is now generally recognized, to fashion idealized portraits of their subjects based on biblical and hagiographical models.[99] It did become customary, after the Carolingian reforms, for bishops and even diocesan and provincial synods and councils to examine the written accounts of the life and miracles of a putative saint, or to hear oral testimony on which the *vita* or *miracula* would be based, before allowing the new cult to proceed.[100] These hearings were the forerunners of the more elaborate, more searching *processus* of the formal canonization inquiries that became the norm in the thirteenth century. The ecclesiasts who conducted the inquiries in the earlier centuries, however, and the sporadic papal commissions of the twelfth century, appear to have been easily satisfied and largely uncritical in their approach to the evidence presented. They were mainly interested to see that the *vita* of a new saint should be sober and edifying.[101]

Certainly the hagiographers themselves, to judge from their prefaces and prologues, were more concerned to ward off adverse criticism of their style of writing than to anticipate questions and complaints as to their historical accuracy and credibility. More often than not, one finds that they take for granted the truth of their subject matter, "veritas rei gestae," and, invoking an early Christian hagiographical topos, they offer this "veritas" in place of, and as a justification for, their lack of eloquence and erudition. Qualities such as the latter, they claim, are more likely to obscure the truth than help reveal it.[102] But the truth that they assert on behalf of their plain style (sermo humilis) is not simply fidelity to mere fact, as in our modern legal definition. Rather it is the notion of fidelity to the Christian life: the hagiographer offers a pattern of human action that is "true" in that it has been gleaned from the testimony of good men or from previous written accounts, conforms to the precepts of Christ and the Church, and is worthy of belief and imitation.[103] The high style or "sermo grandis," on the other hand, is to be avoided because it is perceived to be inextricably linked to the secular skills of logic and hair-splitting dialectic, which were anathema to the patristic proponents of the ideal of "sancta simplicitas." The ultimate authority for this way of thinking was St. Paul: "Sapientia huius mundi stultitia est apud Deum" (1 Cor. 3.19)[104]. In other words, inherent in the rhetorical tradition of medieval hagiography there is a basic antipathy towards the rational intellect that concerns itself with mundane historical truth. In order to accept or to describe the "veritas" of Christ and his Church one needs the unlearned simplicity, the "stultitia" and "rusticitas," of the fishermen whom Christ chose as his apostles.[105]

As is well known, in the course of the eleventh century logic and dialectic began to regain some of the prestige they had enjoyed in pre-Christian education and culture, and came to occupy a position of increasing importance not only in the proliferating secular schools but also in the developing disciplines of civil law, canon law, political theory, and theology itself. It was inevitable that, like these other branches of clerical knowledge and practice, hagiography and hagiology would be affected by the renaissance of secular learning. An early illustration of this impact is the Norman scrutiny of the cults of native English saints.[106] The Norman prelates and abbots who assumed the leadership of the English church were critical of the Anglo-Saxon saints, many of whom lacked written memorials, at least in Latin. It is probably true that a good deal of this antipathy was motivated by Norman chauvinism, rather than by a genuine concern for authenticity. But in Lanfranc's discussion with Anselm, over the validity of the cult of St. Elphege, we have a specific instance of a more rigorous type of hagiological thought.[107] Here there was no problem of historical authenticity: Lanfranc did not doubt that Elphege existed, or that he was "a good man," or that he had been cruelly murdered by heathen Danes. What the former lawyer and teacher of logic queried, in Anselm's presence, was whether someone who preferred to die rather than pay a heavy ransom price should be venerated as a martyr, since the glory of a martyr's crown was supposed to be reserved to those who gave their lives in witnessing to their faith in Christ.[108]

It is unlikely that such a question had been posed in England before. As we observed above, the Anglo-Saxons seem to have been particularly generous and indiscriminate in conferring martyrdom on their fellow countrymen. In Elphege's case, it would be sufficient for most of them, as it was for the author of the entry in the Anglo-Saxon Chronicle, that a respected primate of the English church had been slaughtered by infidel Danes.[109] The basic structure of the event conformed to the pattern of martyrdom; the details were unimportant. That miracles should occur at the dead man's tomb shortly after his death could only be expected (no doubt expectation helped facilitate their occurrence) and merely confirmed what was already believed. The war might be lost, but the people had another martyred saint to console them.[110] Theological precision of the sort Lanfranc wished to introduce had a low priority in such matters.

The outcome of the discussion between Lanfranc and Anselm was innocuous enough. Anselm was able to persuade the archbishop that it was sound theology to venerate Elphege as a martyr. What is of interest here is that Anselm won Lanfranc over not by resorting to the traditional tools of the hagiographer, but by means of the syllogisms and analogies of the dialectical method of reasoning. Using as an analogy the martyrdom of John the Baptist, who died witnessing to the truth rather than to his faith in Christ, Anselm argued that Elphege had died for the sake of justice. Since Christ himself is justice, Elphege had died for Christ and was thus a true martyr.[111]

Neither Eadmer, Anselm's biographer, nor Osbern, who wrote a *Vita S. Elphegi* some time after Lanfranc endorsed the cult, fully appreciated what Anselm had done. Each of them turned to hagiographical models in order to improve Elphege's image and quite simply created incidents that made the saint more conventionally acceptable as a martyr.[112] In effect, the two Englishmen implied that Anselm's rationally argued defense of their saint was inappropriate to the sphere of hagiology. The real conflict that emerges here, therefore, is not between Anselm and Lanfranc: their debate was easily resolved, because their manner of thinking was much alike. The conflict is between the new intellectual rigor of the Italian emigrés and the more traditional hagiographical notion of "truth" displayed by the Englishmen, Eadmer and Osbern. In the late eleventh and early twelfth century and later, it appears that Lanfranc's questioning approach to saint's cults and legends was shared by increasing numbers of clerics, and there is evidence of a more general desire to think about old and new saints in a more disciplined and methodical fashion than was previously thought necessary.

The first theological treatise in about seven hundred years devoted solely to saints' relics was composed early in the twelfth century by Thierry of Echternach. The treatise, entitled *Flores epitaphium sanctorum*,[113] draws heavily on biblical precedents and the writings of the Fathers, and is wholly positive and effusive in its celebration of the virtues of the "pignora sanctorum." But it is nonetheless an exercise in apologetics, intended to justify and defend certain aspects of the veneration of relics (e.g., the expensive practice of enshrining them in gold and silver) against the criticisms of unnamed detractors.[114] Thierry is not a landmark theologian but his treatise is important as an early attempt to provide a rationale in scripture, patristic thought, and historical tradition, for certain staple features of popular religion, which some among his contemporaries were no longer willing to take for granted. In a similar vein is a short work by Eadmer of Canterbury, written probably in the late 1120s and preserved among other *opuscula* in a manuscript believed to be by his own hand, CCC 371. The *Sententia de memoria sanctorum quos veneraris*,[115] a homily divided into three lections and intended for liturgical use, is much simpler and narrower in scope than Thierry's *Flores*, but it shares with the latter the same defensive tone, the same awareness of a climate of doubt and criticism. Eadmer focuses on the idea of intercession, attempting to convince his "fratres" that the saints do indeed intercede with God on behalf of their devotees. "The suppliants prostrate their bodies before the saints' relics, they grovel on the ground on bended knees, they bend their faces to the floor – and we are to believe that the saints stand before God rigidly indifferent to these prayers, that they refuse to listen, that they care nothing for them? Who could say such a thing? The devotion of these suppliants will not be useless, it will not be in vain, it will not go unrewarded."[116]

Quite different in style, tone and intent from these essentially uncritical, eulogistic tracts is Guibert de Nogent's critique of saint's cults and relic-veneration, *De pignoribus sanctorum*, finished towards the end of his life in the early 1120s.[117] The work is regarded by many historians as being far in advance of its time, in that it exposes and mocks, with a coolly rational scepticism and methodical logic, the typical absurdities, falsifications, and excesses of medieval hagiology. At the same time, it argues forcibly against the elevation, enshrinement, and veneration of corporeal relics, in other words, against the most visible, lucrative aspect of the cults of the saints which Thierry of Echternach defends at elaborate length. Guibert felt that the prevalent Christian obsession with such bodily objects impeded the fulfillment of the "interior man," the spiritual goal that was attainable only through prayer and contemplation. Thus Guibert criticized the cults of relics on both rational, moral grounds, for their frequent offences against truth and authenticity, and also on theological grounds, as a violation of every man's natural fate, including Christ's. "Dust you are, and to dust you will return. . . . How can it be fitting for anyone to be enshrined in gold and silver, when the Son of God was buried and cut off within a vile and dingy cave of rock."[118]

Studies of Guibert have emphasized his precocious modernity, uniqueness, and lack of obvious dependence on any tradition, and they find him to have had no discernible impact on twelfth-century thought or practice. Only a thorough study of eleventh- and twelfth-century hagiography and hagiology can establish a proper context for the *De pignoribus*, but my own impression is that Guibert was far from alone in his attitudes.[119] He was simply one of the more eloquent and respectable members of a sizable minority of clerics and laymen, in the late eleventh and early twelfth century, who found the cults of relics theologically unjustified and much hagiography offensive to reason and truth.

Sources of information about heretical movements in the early twelfth century are fragmentary and often willfully distorted or vague, but it seems certain that among the many facets of organized religion that were rejected by charismatics such as Henry of Lausanne and Peter of Bruys (c.a. 1110–1145) was the cult of the saints, particularly as a source of income for the clergy and as a means of intercession for the salvation of the faithful. Neither sect believed, for example, that churches "built of stone or wood" were necessary for proper Christian worship and prayer: in other words, they rejected the whole idea that God could be approached only in specific and hallowed physical locations and that his power and grace were accessible to people only via the consecrated material "media" controlled by the priesthood; they insisted that, on the contrary, God's grace was available to the humble penitent individual anywhere.[120] Since the cults of most of the saints were nothing if not deeply rooted in the church's traditional belief in the holiness of place and object, one is not surprised to learn, from Geoffrey of Auxerre's life of St. Bernard of Clairvaux, that Henry of Lausanne's followers in Languedoc, in 1145 and earlier, were boycotting not only infant baptism and prayers and offerings for the dead, but also pilgrimages to saints' shrines, invocation of the saints, and holidays on saints' feasts and other holy days. Eberwin, abbot of Steinfeld, wrote to St. Bernard in 1143 or '44 complaining of similar attitudes among a group of self-styled imitators of the apostles in Cologne.[121] Finally, there is the somewhat earlier evidence of the letter which Hildebert of Lavardin wrote when he was Bishop of Le Mans (1095–1125), attempting to refute an unknown correspondent's argument that veneration of the saints was invalid because the saints in the afterlife have no knowledge of what happens here on earth and are therefore incapable of interceding with God on behalf of the living.[122]

Less extreme evidence of the changing hagiological climate in the time of Guibert de Nogent is afforded by many of the hagiographers themselves. Osbern of Canterbury, in his preface to the *Miracula S. Dunstani*, written in the late 1080s, obviously feels it is necessary to persuade his readers, particularly those of later generations, that he is telling the truth. In a lengthy piece of logical argument he attempts to demonstrate why it is reasonable and right for his readers to lend credence to his account of Dunstan's miracles. One objection he anticipates is the reader's refusal to accept as authentic anything that cannot be matched from his own experience: "If the kind of thing we are bound to relate here should be unheard of in their day, they ought not immediately to reject it as false on that account, as if God in his providence is incapable of doing in one era, for men's correction and reproof, what he has not seen fit to do in another."[123] As in this quotation, Osbern's language is for the most part measured and polite. But at one point the irritation and anger he evidently feels breaks through the calmly logical prose: "Should we deny that the blessed John the Evangelist drank the poison and lived, or that he brought back to life those who died of the poison, simply because some slanderous busybody did not see it happen (quod ista nescio quis impostor et calumniator non viderit)?"[124] The basis of his defence of his miracles stories is an appeal to the power of faith. He asks his readers to believe him, in order that they in turn may be believed when they come to write such things themselves, and he concludes, rather cleverly one must admit, by asserting that if his readers believe first of all in the events that they have not seen, they, like Osbern, will be permitted eventually to see such miraculous events take place before their eyes.[125]

The arguments of Osbern's preface presuppose the existence of critically-minded clerics and laymen devoted to the crudely empirical philosophy of "seeing is believing." He expects his miracle tales to be greeted with disbelief on the grounds that they are outside of normal human experience. Even allowing for a certain amount of literary posturing on Osbern's part, the preface certainly seems to reflect a sharpening of the critical faculty among his contemporaries. A similar impression is conveyed by Henry of Huntingdon in the prologue to the book of miracles he compiled in the 1140s, shortly after Arcoid. Henry's attitude is quite different from Osbern's, however. Having announced his intention to round off his secular history with an account of famous English miracles, he feels obliged to dissociate himself from the gullible folk and from similarly credulous clerics who accept fictitious tales as true miracles.

> The gullible folk and some who bear the name and habit of religion seem to be the worst offenders, immediately believing and accepting miracles that are either wholly fictitious or impossible to confirm with any real certainty. The people indulge in this kind of thing out of their stupid taste for novelty, but the religious have grown accustomed to this kind of deception and falsehood for their own personal enrichment and to enlarge the shrines of their saints beyond what is reasonable. Furthermore, if they happen to find some piece of miracle literature they make no effort to ascertain the author but instead they quite fearlessly presume to recite and preach such stuff in God's presence and at his holy altar. If miracles of this sort are related to me, on the other hand, I do not openly reject them, unless they are blatantly frivolous, but neither do I leap to their defense, unless I can see that they are corroborated by convincing evidence and by witnesses of impeccable character.[126]

As a result of Henry's pious scruples, his "libellus" of miracles is one of the more disappointing and unoriginal in the twelfth century, being composed almost completely of verbatim extracts from Bede, whose credentials as a "verax auctor" were, of course, beyond question. Henry adds only a few post-Bedan stories that he is familiar with and cares to vouch for.[127] Whereas Osbern of Canterbury insinuates that those who are cautious in accepting miracles lack faith, the archdeacon of Huntingdon applies the epithet "infidus," faithless, to anyone who fabricates miracle stories or who publishes miracles that lack reliable sources. While he does not seem to share Guibert's aversion for cults of corporeal relics *per se*, he echoes precisely the Frenchman's attitude towards hagiography: "Antequam ergo eum deprecer, necesse est ut de ueritate sanctitatis ejus altercer." (Before I will pray to a saint, I feel obliged to dispute the fact of his sanctity.[128])

Benedicta Ward, in her recent study of medieval miracle collections, cites a related development noticeable in twelfth-century discussions of biblical miracles. She argues that the authors of the new "sententiae" and "quaestiones,"such as Peter Lombard and Robert of Melun, deal with biblical miracles in a manner subtly but significantly different from that of the more traditional biblical commentators who are content to synthesize the exegetical wisdom of the earlier fathers and their imitators. Whereas Anselm of Laon in the *Glossa ordinaria* treats a miracle such as the creation of Adam or the raising of Lazarus as a divine *signum*, rich in typological and allegorical meaning, "that tends to establish the reign of charity," Lombard goes further and questions how the miracle was achieved. He does not express any doubt that it occurred, but he has the scholastic's interest in exploring and explaining it as an actual event.[129]

A similar tendency is to be seen in the growing controversy over the Eucharist. Ward quotes Hugh of St. Victor's outburst against the "dialecticus" and "sophista" who were apparently seeking to examine the mystery of transubstantiation with the tools of logic. The dialecticians were interested in explaining how the change took place and what it involved, a curiosity that Hugh obviously found repugnant and hostile to the whole notion of "mysterium." Here again there is no question of actual scepticism regarding the sacred event, but merely a desire to know its "quomodo" as well as the more traditional "quare."[130]

Ward also remarks, following M. D. Chénu, that the Chartrean Platonist philosophers, including William of Conches and Thierry of Chartres, likewise affected people's thinking about miracles, by focusing on the operation of natural causes in the natural world.[131] In what Ward calls the Augustinian or sacramental view of the universe, everything that exists or happens in the world is the miraculous result of God's continuous and direct action and is therefore divinely meaningful. But the new philosophers worked to distinguish the truly miraculous events from the natural phenomena that occurred according to nature's God-given but autonomous laws. Only something that could be shown to have no explanation in nature deserved the name of "miraculum." Chénu sums up the motivation of these thinkers as "a search for the causes of things."[132] This search inevitably resulted, as Ward points out, in their restricting the variety and number of acknowledged miracles, and equally inevitably it aroused the resentment of those who had a vested interest, as well as a genuine faith, in the notion of a sacramental and miraculous order of creation. Such traditionalists were the object of an attack by the Platonist William of Conches, himself a contemporary of Arcoid of St. Paul's.

Ignorant themselves of the forces of nature and wanting to have company in their ignorance, they don't want people to look into [inquirere] anything; they want us to believe like peasants and not to ask the reason behind things. . . . But we say the reason behind everything should be sought out. . . . If they learn that anyone is inquiring, they shout out that he is a heretic, placing more reliance on their monkish garb than on their wisdom.[133]

In Ward's view, medieval miracle collections on the whole do not betray or acknowledge the impact of these new modes of thought, and she cites only a late twelfth-century example from William of Canterbury's book of the miracles of St. Thomas Becket.[134] But as we have seen in the case of Osbern of Canterbury the controversy affected hagiography before the end of the eleventh century, and may be said to have influenced even the literary form of miracle writing, as exemplified in Henry of Huntingdon's careful separation of his book of miracles from the "temporalia" of English history. No doubt further research in the printed and unprinted hagiography of the period would turn up more examples. It is unlikely, however, that one will encounter a hagiographer more sensitive than Arcoid of St. Paul's to these various but related currents of thought. To his response to the new intellectualism we can now turn out attention.

Unlike Osbert of Clare, who was disappointed in his bid to secure the canonization of Edward the Confessor, Arcoid was fortunate in being the promoter of a long-established cult and of a saint whose holiness was vouched for, if only briefly, by no less an authority than Bede himself. There was therefore no question of going to Rome or of seeking papal consent to the projected translation of Erkenwald's relics to their new shrine. Yet Arcoid exhibits a striking awareness of the critical tendencies we have outlined above. At one point he even hints, in the person of a pious canon in Mir. II, that Erkenwald's cult actually has been sanctioned by the Pope.[135] In his views on miracles and relics, he is solidly in the tradition of Thierry of Echternach and of Eadmer and Osbern of Canterbury, but he is more vehement than they are in expressing his awareness and resentment of the spirit of scepticism. His miracle stories both individually and collectively dramatize the controversy outlined above in a manner and to a degree that I have not encountered in other comparable miracle collections of the period. Not only is there in MSE an unusually high percentage of punitive miracles (Mir. II, VI, X, XIII, XVI), in which the offense is disrespect for or mockery of the saint's cult and feast day, but Arcoid also draws attention on several occasions throughout the collection, not just in the prologue, to the cynics and sceptics for whom miracle stories and relics are so much nonsense.

As we have seen in the case of Osbern of Canterbury and Henry of Huntingdon, a hagiographer usually touches on topics such as veracity, incredulity, and scepticism, if anywhere, in the prologue or dedicatory epistle. Arcoid's proem, however, gives little indication that these things are to be among his major concerns until in its last few lines. Among the rhetorical topoi he employs in the body of the proem is that of neglect, "negligentia," by which initially he means the failure of the "faithful folk" to record in writing the wonders they have witnessed at Erkenwald's shrine in former days.[136] But at the close he extends the topos to caution his fellow canons and priests against listening in careless fashion, "negligenter," to *MSE* being read aloud. He does not explain what he means by "negligenter" here, except by quoting from Matt. 7.6, "ne margarite ante porcos misse ... uideantur," lest pearls should seem to have been strewn in front of swine. In view of the traditional exegesis of this verse, it seems in this context to be a warning to his audience not to be incredulous or scornful of the miracle stories,[137] but rather to seek for their inner meaning, the spiritual mystery veiled beneath the surface narrative: "de gestis exemplum ... spirituale salutis nostre summamus" (Mir. Pr. 43–46.)

That Arcoid intends the literati among his listeners and readers to pay attention to the "spirit" of the miracles, rather than to the "letter," is evident from his tortuous attempt, at the end of Miracle I, to expound its allegorical significance, and also from his frequent homiletic asides and conclusions throughout the collection. Arcoid is not suggesting that his miracles are not literally and historically true. Particularly in his handling of Mir. IV-XV he makes a habit of indicating that he was a witness of the miracle in question or that he knew the person involved. But he seems anxious to discourage at least his more learned listeners from concentrating solely on the miracles' historical, factual aspects. They should be read, he suggests, with the kind of faith and spiritual consent with which people are accustomed to read the holy scriptures. "Whatever is written is for our instruction," he writes at the end of the proem, quoting St. Paul, Rom. 15.4, "so that with patience and the comfort offered to us by the scriptures, we may have hope" (Mir. Pr. 46–49) Later, in the preamble to Mir. IV, he is more explicit about how the miracles should *not* be read, describing the preservation of Erkenwald's coffin through the fire of 1087 as "an event that is virtually impossible to narrate, that was wondrous to behold, and must be judged more on faith than on appearance, and evaluated more with the help of theology than according to rational standards" (Mir. IV 2–4). Osbern of Canterbury had said essentially the same thing years before, though less succinctly, when he denounced those who refused to believe anything that was outside their everyday experience.

Similar sentiments are voiced even within one of the miracle narratives, by the anonymous canon of St. Paul's who rebukes the blasphemous layman for working on Erkenwald's feast day. More than a simple rebuke, the priest's long speech is both an assertion of the importance of observing feast days in general and a defense of the validity of Erkenwald's cult in particular. In support of Erkenwald's sanctity the canon refers to the "many miraculous works" the saint did during his lifetime, and to the miracles that occurred soon after his death and later. "Nor is it any man's place to press for an accounting (enumerare) of these miracles, or for an explanation of them; rather it is our duty to write out the history of them, nothing more. For who can count the number of times God, through the prayers and merits of St. Erkenwald, has granted sight to the blind ..."[138] (Mir. II 51–56).

Even in these few contexts we can see clearly the interplay of the various schools of thought we referred to earlier. Arcoid is evidently conscious of and opposed to those, like William of Conches, who are prone to ask questions, seek rational explanations, and try to understand the "quomodo" as well as the traditional "quare" of miraculous events. He openly instructs his readers to interpret the miracles as the church fathers did the scriptures, mystically, and implies that to approach them in any other spirit is tantamount to heresy or lack of faith. Unlike Henry of Huntingdon who espoused the new rational epistemology, at least in some respects, and sought to implement it in his treatment of miracles, Arcoid shows only impatience with the "higher criticism."

In Mir. I, for example, he comes to a point in his narrative where a potential critic would be likely to pounce on him for disregarding logic and probability. Describing how a fugitive schoolboy, fearful of his teacher's anger takes refuge at Erkenwald's tomb, Arcoid admits that what the boy said and felt as he prayed to the saint is unknown (there being no witnesses), "and we must not affirm as fact something we cannot demonstrate from a reliable source (auctore veraci). We must believe, however, that the contrite, humbled heart of the boy was pleasing to God...." Arcoid here is as close to the stance of Guibert de Nogent or Henry of Huntingdon as he ever comes, but it is difficult to avoid the impression that he is paying lip service to a more rigorous critical standard, with which he is not very comfortable. The phrase, "We must believe, however (credendum tamen est)," indicates better where he stands. It is simple, unquestioning faith that is imperative for understanding the miracle, not this quibbling over reliable sources.

The whole story of Miracle I could be taken as an exemplum of what Arcoid considers the truly Christian frame of mind for hearing and receiving his miracle stories: not the strict, disciplined, judgmental habit of the teacher, ready to pounce on every small inaccuracy in the boy's recital of his "lectio"; but rather the feckless insouciance of the child who humbly trusts in the virtues of the saint rather than his own intellect, and is therefore vindicated while the master is put to shame. The story, as Arcoid tells it, is strongly anti-intellectual and quite appropriate for the first chapter in his *MSE*. It is as if he is inviting his readers to put away their rational scruples and to read his miracles in a childlike manner that will be "pleasing to God" and to St. Erkenwald.

Arcoid's most vivid personal complaints against the sceptics and other opponents of saints' cults occur in Mir. IV and XI. In the latter, which I touch on first as the shorter of the passages in question, Arcoid has just told of the miraculous recovery, from a liver disease, of a certain Adam, a clerk skilled in medicine who had despaired of a medical remedy for his illness and had turned to Erkenwald. After remarking on the public rejoicing over the miraculous cure, Arcoid suddenly adds that it is pointless "to be sceptical and critical over this great new miracle," and he launches into a brief but virulent attack on "those who are driven mad by the miracles of the saints rather than being inspired by them to grow in increase of faith." He characterizes his potential detractors as "those who would rather mutter and carp and rot in the slimy dregs of their filth" than be raised to virtuous living under the influence of the miracles, and he warns them to keep quiet lest they bring harm on themselves by disparaging St. Erkenwald (Mir. XI 39–44). I do not know why Arcoid should have chosen this particular miracle in which to deliver such a broadside, but it is not inappropriate in the context. He associates himself especially closely with this miracle, since "Adam notarius," the beneficiary of Erkenwald's healing powers, was evidently his friend and guest, and scepticism in this case seems to have struck him as a personal affront, despite his rhetorical disclaimer, "It matters very little to me if I am condemned" for publicizing the cure (Mir. XI 39–40). Moreover the episode is intended in part to illustrate the superiority of "celestial medicine" (Mir. XI 7) over human medical knowledge, and therefore an attack on those who rely on human intelligence to query supernatural phenomena likewise suits the context.

The most sustained and virulent passage of this type, however, forms the conclusion of the long and in many ways central episode, Miracle IV, in which Arcoid offers a quasi-legal proof of the authenticity and power of Erkenwald's relics. After describing how Bishops Maurice and Walkelin found the feretrum of Erkenwald and its flimsy linen drape totally unharmed by the great fire, and after giving the year in which the miracle occurred, he suddenly launches into an apostrophe addressed to the fourth-century Gallic priest Vigilantius (Mir. IV 136 ff.). "So blush with shame (erubesce), Vigilantius, worst of heretics," he begins, and proceeds to pour out a stream of uncomplimentary epithets climaxing in "great mountain and monster of Gaul." Vigilantius is well known as the author of some outspoken tracts in which his targets were clerical celibacy, several aspects of the liturgy, the cult of the Virgin Mary, and cults of relics in general, for which he was attacked by St. Jerome in a caustic pamphlet that is the only surviving evidence of the whole affair.[139] Arcoid imagines Erkenwald as a second Jerome, brandishing against the "heretic" the very flames that he has withstood during the destruction of London and St. Paul's. Ignoring the issues of celibacy and the Blessed Virgin, Arcoid reduces the scope of Vigilantius's criticisms to one theme: the veneration of bodily remains. He credits Vigilantius with having described the relics of the saints as mere "dry bones ... ashes ... vile cadaver[s]," and with having complained about the futility of spending money to illuminate the relic shrines. By emerging unscathed from the inferno, says Arcoid, Erkenwald has provided a devastating new rebuttal of Vigilantius's complaints and arguments. The London saint has shown that the cult of his relics is far from being a pointless waste of money and candle wax for the sake of a dusty corpse; rather, it is nothing less than "the redemption of souls" and a means by which God is glorified, faith is strengthened, and sinners brought to repentance by the realization of divine power in their midst.

Arcoid here has turned his attention away from rationalist criticism of *miracula* and *legenda* to the very topic that occupies so much of the attention of Guibert de Nogent in his *De pignoribus*: the earthy, material aspect of the cults of the saints. For Vigilantius such cults were a sheer waste of precious resources, all to glorify the "vile flesh" that Christians were supposed to despise in favor of the spirit that transcends the carnal existence. Guibert felt the same way about corporeal relics: for him they constituted a travesty of religion and an obstacle to the inner life of the spiritual man. We may assume that the advocates of the more heretical kinds of "vita apostolica," including Henry of Lausanne and Peter of Bruys, argued in a similar vein during their several campaigns to promote a true church of the spirit in opposition to what they saw as the materialism of the ecclesiastical establishment, of which the lucrative saints' shrines were such a prominent feature. Bishop Hildebert of Le Mans, in the letter to the unnamed cleric who had declared the saints' cults invalid and pointless, recognized that the arguments he was attempting to refute were variations on an ancient theme and he twice compares his opponent to Jerome's Vigilantius.[140]

It is not improbable that Arcoid was familiar with the careers and opinions of the continental heretics, and he may be consciously echoing Hildebert's letter in alluding to Vigilantius in such a context. In my view the passage that ends Mir. IV of MSE is less an attack on the long-dead pamphleteer of Roman Aquitaine than on the many and various revivers and developers of his ideas who were active in Arcoid's own time,[141] including not only Hildebert's opponent but also Guibert himself. It may be coincidental, but at the beginning of Mir. IV Arcoid describes Erkenwald's shrine in language that seems to recall and rebuff Guibert's objections to the elevation of saint's relics above ground. Guibert had insisted that the saints should be buried, below ground, even as Christ himself had submitted to burial in the "saxo vilissimo." Since our bodies are made of earth, "terra," that is where they belong in the end.[142] Not so, says Arcoid. Erkenwald's sarcophagus was elevated higher than the height of a man above ground level because "someone who shines forth so gloriously in the heavens should surely not be buried in such a foul garment as the earth (tam vili scemate sepeliri in terra)" (Mir. IV 20–21).

Two widely divergent views of Christianity are involved here. Arcoid speaks for the medieval majority, deeply committed to a sacramental theology whereby divine grace is transmitted to sinful man from the day of his birth, through a multitude of material channels, such as water, oil, wine, bread, precious metals, the fingers of priests, and the hewn and painted stones and carved wood of the churches. It is surely no accident that the story of Erkenwald's cult, as told by Arcoid, is linked at each of several stages with either the building of the Anglo-Norman church or the refashioning and decoration of his shrine. For Arcoid, much more than for Guibert, *ecclesia* is a physical place rather than an inner condition. It is where God's presence can be felt and enjoyed through His "friends," the numinous bodies and resplendent shrines of the saints, and through the ministrations of His "servants," the consecrated priests. Heavenly life is foreshadowed, in Arcoid's eyes, on a great feast day of the saint, when the people of London put away their everyday working habits, don their holiday finery, and make their way to the "domus dei" to hear the mass and office sung in honor of Erkenwald "who reigns with God" (Mir. II 13–20, 48).

For Guibert de Nogent, the principal value of the saints lies in the moral pattern of their holy lives as recorded in the "legenda" (provided these are authentic!), inciting the people who hear and read them to follow the saintly examples and live virtuously. But for Arcoid one senses that it is not what Erkenwald was when he was alive that is important; rather it is what he is now that he is dead. For now he is a living member of God's kingdom in heaven, and lord and bishop of London at the same time. He is the "friend of God" and "the great priest whose wish the Lord will not deny" (Mir. Pr. 30, 34–35), able to intercede with the Almighty on behalf of his helpless devotees on earth, to whom he is a living attentive presence, animating the bones inside the shrine, and active in the world for the good of his people.

The materialism and carnality of Erkenwald's relics, which is such a repugnant notion to Guibert and his ilk, is precisely what Arcoid delights in contemplating, for the same reason that Augustine of Hippo in his old age modified his earlier objections to relics' cults and became the promoter of the cult of St. Stephen's relics in his own diocese.[143] The very liveliness of Erkenwald's dead body offers a continuous demonstration of the promised glorious resurrection of the flesh, and of the total redemption of man from the mortal consequences of the Fall. ". . . non est ista perditio, sed animarum redemptio. . . . humanorum corporum resurrectio indicitur . . ." (Mir. IV 144-45, 149-50). The miraculous activity around the shrine, including the cures of the incurably sick, the impossible phenomena affecting solid stone, wood, and linen, the strange noises, the beautiful visions of the resplendent bishop in his pontificals, the sudden violent deaths of his detractors — all this, as Arcoid points out more than once, is "contra cursum nature," against the course of nature (Mir. IV 111). The very life that is in the saint's ashes, and the life-giving power that emanates from and through them, denies the effects of the Fall and of Original Sin on created nature. Erkenwald's shrine is a glimpse of the eternity of redeemed spirit and flesh.[144]

It is thus highly appropriate that the "sarcophagus" should be visible, approachable, tangible, and also gloriously encased in silver and jewels, immune to moth and rust. With its gabled roof surmounted by silver angels, and with its sculpted and jeweled silver "walls," the shrine was the image on earth of the saint's home in the new Jerusalem and of the eternal material existence and spiritual life that Erkenwald's devotees hoped, with his patronage and help, to share with him in turn.

CHAPTER FOUR

The Cult of St. Erkenwald
in the Middle Ages

I. THE ANGLO-SAXON PERIOD, 693–1087

The historical facts about Erkenwald of London can be quickly summarized from a paragraph in Bede's *Historia ecclesiastica*, 4. 6, the main authority for the saint's life and early cult.[1] Erkenwald's date of birth and family origins are unknown, but he was evidently rich enough to found not one but two monasteries. The first, of which he himself was abbot, was St. Peter's, Chertsey, in Surrey, and the other, in which he installed his sister, St. Ethelburga, was St. Mary's, Barking, a few miles east of London, in Essex. Erkenwald provided each house with monastic rules that in Bede's opinion were excellent, which means they were almost certainly modeled on the rule of St. Benedict. In 675, when no longer young, Erkenwald was chosen by Archbishop Theodore to succeed Wine, a simoniac, as bishop of the East Saxons, a role that Erkenwald seems to have filled not only with piety but also with considerable practical success, establishing Christianity on a firm footing in a diocese notorious for earlier backsliding. We know from other sources that he was the trusted advisor of Ine, king of Wessex, whose laws he may have helped draft, and he was apparently instrumental in ending the estrangement of Archbishop Theodore and St. Wilfred.[2]

Bede does not record when or where Erkenwald died (charter evidence makes 693 a likely date), but he mentions the old man's "most holy life and conduct" (*uita et conuersatio . . . sanctissima*), both before and after his episcopacy, and as evidence for his sanctity refers to the miracles of healing reputedly still being performed in Bede's own time, ca. 730, through the medium of a wooden litter or cart on which the aging saint would travel when he was ill. Bede, whose source of information for all this was probably the London priest Nothelm, tells us specifically that the litter had been kept by the saint's followers (discipulis) and that people would pluck splinters from it to bring healing and relief to those too ill to come to the cult center themselves. Erkenwald's miraculous wooden litter is one of three such relics described in the *Historia ecclesiastica* with obvious parallels to the wood of the cross.[3]

We may infer from Bede's account of the litter that Erkenwald's cult was no spontaneous popular effusion around his grave but something initiated and fostered by clerics who had reason to believe that the physical objects with which their bishop had been in close contact would prove to be thaumaturgic. Erkenwald thus passed from history into the yearly cycle of liturgical cult.[4] Until the Anglo-Norman era, however, when *VSE* and *MSE* were composed, there is very little information about the cult, or indeed about other aspects of the history of St. Paul's church in London. One Anglo-Norman hagiographer, Hermann of Bury, writing his history of the eleventh-century miracles of St. Edmund ca. 1100, implies that in London in the early eleventh century there was no active cult of Erkenwald or any other saint, but he consoles the saintless Londoners with the prospect of St. Edmund's arrival. "You have mourned long enough in your barrenness," he tells them in a rather labored apostrophe. "Now, barren as you are, you can be happy, you who have begotten no saints nor possess any . . . , for out of East Anglia there comes someone who will be your intercessor." Hermann goes on to relate how a priest and devotee of St. Edmund, to protect his patron's body from Danish invaders, brought it to London, and how eighteen people were cured of various bodily diseases as he trundled the holy load from Aldgate to St. Paul's; he tells also how later, when it was safe for the saint's body to be taken back to Bury, the bishop of London, Aelfhun, tried to appropriate it permanently for St. Paul's.[5]

Hermann's story is obviously intended, perhaps not very seriously, as a monkish insult to the secular canons of London and their episcopal saint, who, although a monk himself, was no martyr. In depicting London as a city without saints, Hermann is indulging in the hagiographer's licence to reconstruct the past according to the present needs of his patron saint. For his allegation is just as untrue of the period he is writing about, the early eleventh century, as of the late eleventh century when he lived and wrote. The early eleventh-century gazetteer of English saints and shrines, *Secgan be Godes sanctum*, states unambiguously that "resteð sante Eorcenwald se bisceop on Lundenbyrig,"[6] and the frequent occurrence of the saint's April 30 feast day in calendars from churches all over later Anglo-Saxon England indicates that the cult was liturgical as well as thaumaturgical, and that Erkenwald was virtually a national saint before the Norman Conquest.[7]

2. THE ANGLO-NORMAN CULT AND SHRINE: 1087 THROUGH THE THIRTEENTH CENTURY

It is possible that as late as 1087, the year in which the great fire of London destroyed the Anglo-Saxon minster of St. Paul's, the wooden litter described in Bede was still an "active" cult object, for Goscelin of Canterbury speaks of its healing powers in the present tense at this time.[8] But it is also evident that the saint's corporeal relics were a prominent feature of the cult already, occupying a tall shrine of stone and wood directly behind the main alter of the minster. Whether the wooden litter survived the fire or not, we do not know, but *VSE*, written, as we have argued, around the turn of the century, refers to the litter in the past tense, indicating that it was no longer part of the cult.[9] According to *MSE* Erkenwald's bodily relics, on the other hand, miraculously survived the fire, and the cult devoted to them survived the Norman take-over and reorganization of the cathedral chapter in the decades that followed. The most visible effect and symbol of the new regime was the vast new Norman church begun by Bishop Maurice after 1087, but Erkenwald was also renewed and recast at this time.[10] His acceptance by the predominantly Norman chapter of canons by the early 1100s is borne out by William of Malmesbury in his survey of episcopal saints and sinners, *Gesta pontificum*, completed in 1124. He describes Erkenwald as "Lundoniae maxime sanctus," pre-eminently the saint of London, whose miracles are the subject of not only "ancient memory" but also "recent fame." The latter phrase refers to either recent miracles at the shrine or, possibly, the recent publication of the new *Vita sancti Erkenwaldi* which William seems to have known and used in his account of Erkenwald.[11]

Besides implying that by ca. 1100 the wooden litter was no longer Erkenwald's principal relic, *VSE* offers little information about the contemporary cult of the saint. Its interest is primarily ideological, a topic we will pursue in more detail in chapter five. In Arcoid's *MSE*, on the other hand, we have an important source of knowledge regarding the cult during the late eleventh century and the first forty years of the twelfth, and an interesting example of the relationship between cult and hagiography.

Arcoid's ostensible purpose in writing *MSE*, is, as he states himself, to publish a record of Erkenwald's miracles "to the glory of God and to the honor of His friend, Erkenwald, and for the benefit of those who come after us . . . that all who hear them, whenever they are laboring in anguish of mind or body, might take refuge in the favor of the blessed and most pious shepherd Erkenwald, and need not fear that a just petition will fail of fulfilment" (Mir. Pr. 29–34). The miracles are to be a reminder to future generations that the shrine of the London saint can provide healing and comfort for the afflicted.

Accordingly of the twenty-three miracles described in the nineteen chapters, fourteen are miracles of healing and include examples of blindness, various kinds of paralysis and fever, deafness, intestinal pain, and a liver complaint. These were common enough afflictions and would presumably help recommend the shrine to the ailing. Although written in Latin for an obviously clerical audience, copies were no doubt made available to the clergy at other major churches in the city and at the other places where Erkenwald was traditionally venerated (for example, St. Albans, Winchester, Westminster, and Bury, as well as Chertsey and Barking), in the hope that the stories would in turn be passed on in vernacular homilies or by other more informal means to the laity.[12] We know, for example, that at Chertsey in the early fourteenth century the monks used two of the miracles (Mir. I & VI) for the lections at Matins during Erkenwald's octave, April 30–May 7, and they undoubtedly used others as lections for the feast of his translation on November 14,[13] but whether this practice was already established by the mid-twelfth century when Arcoid wrote, we have no way of knowing. Certainly, to judge from the passage quoted above, Arcoid appears to have been confident that his work would reach a wider audience beyond the walls of the cathedral and chapter-house where it doubtless received its first hearing.

His interest in reaching this larger public was, in my view, not wholly altruistic or devotional. Several of the miracles, and the order in which they occur, allow us to see a more specific cultic reason for publicizing the shrine miracles in the early 1140s. His aim was to raise money, not for any profane or selfish reason, but rather for "the glory of God and the honor of His friend, Erkenwald," in the form of a new silver "ferculum" or reliquary for the saint's remains. Before discussing this new development further, it is necessary to summarize MSE's unique information regarding the earlier history of Erkenwald's shrine.

In Mir. IV we learn that the saint's body enjoyed a place of honor in the pre-Conquest church of St. Paul's. It was behind the main altar inside a wooden "theca" or chest which was covered with a small "pallium" or cloth of linen. The wooden reliquary rested on a stone plinth, which Arcoid calls a "mausoleum," and the whole structure was "higher than a man" (Mir. IV 17–20, 107).[14] It seems likely that the body itself was in a sealed lead coffin inside the wooden "theca" (Mir. XIV 20–21, 29). The latter was probably shaped, like many early and later medieval reliquaries, in the form of a gabled house or church with a steeply pitched roof, positioned at right angles to the altar and thus forming a letter T with the leg towards the east behind the main altar. The west end of the shrine, therefore, would form a kind of reredos on which very likely there were carved or painted images of the saint and his legend or other suitable subjects, visible from the west.[15]

In June of 1087, less than a year after Bishop Maurice was consecrated, much of London, including the Saxon church of St. Paul, was destroyed by a great fire.[16] According to Arcoid's account of it, which is the longest and most elaborately written episode in MSE, only Erkenwald's shrine and its humble, linen pall, survived the disaster. Although certain features of this miracle seem to derive from hagiographical tradition, and the whole account is a literary tour de force, the core of the story is probably true. Arcoid is careful to state that Bishop Maurice and Bishop Walkelin of Winchester inspected the ruin as soon as the fire had died down, and saw the untouched shrine for themselves.[17] As was suggested earlier, it is possible that this in itself contributed to Erkenwald's standing in the eyes of the Normans, since it constituted, albeit by "accident," a successful test of the saint's relics such as Lanfranc had recommended some years earlier to a Norman abbot sceptical of Anglo-Saxon sanctity.[18] It seems to me very likely that, given Arcoid's noticeably defensive posture throughout MSE and his frequent references to sceptics, he intended this episode which culminates with a diatribe against the ancient skeptic, Vigilantius, to serve as the outstanding proof of the authenticity and power of Erkenwald's remains.[19] It opens, moreover, what is the properly historical or chronological portion of MSE, Mir. IV–XV, and thus forms a spectacular division between the Anglo-Saxon past and the new Anglo-Norman era to which Arcoid himself belonged.

By the end of Maurice's episcopacy in 1107, Erkenwald's shrine, at least the wooden "theca" portion with its lead coffin, was installed in the vast new crypt to await completion of the new church (Mir. V 3–4). Thirty years later, despite the wealth and energy of Richard of Belmeis, the cathedral was still far from complete. At least two more serious fires, not mentioned by Arcoid, had swept through London in 1132 and 1135 or 1136,[20] at least one of them doing considerable damage to the church and no doubt retarding the progress of the builders. The result was that Erkenwald's temporary shrine down in the crypt had begun to seem more like a permanent home. Although at first it was evidently "on the right side of the altar of St. Faith" (Mir. XVI 15–16) to whom part of the crypt was dedicated as a church,[21] the shrine must have been given a chapel of its own, with an altar (Mir. XIV 4, XVII 7). The crypt ceiling above the altar was decorated (Mir. XVII 6, 11–12) and the immediate area formed what Arcoid terms an "oratorium" (Mir. XVII 11) that was enclosed by some kind of partition or railing with gates that when locked were large enough to prohibit access to altar and shrine (Mir. XIV 4, 25; XVII 11). This was the situation when Arcoid arrived at St. Paul's, either in 1128 with his uncle Gilbert or shortly afterwards, and also in 1137–1138, "in the fourth year" after the bishop's death.

On an unspecified occasion during this year, the events comprising Mir.
V occurred. A woman from Tuscany named Benedicta, afflicted from birth
with a withered and palsied hand, who had visited most of the major healing shrines in Europe, was completely healed of her infirmity through Erkenwald's intecession. She evidently made a deep impression on Arcoid, for
not only does he honor her with the epithet "uenerabilis mulier," but he
also makes of her the most individualized character in the whole *MSE*.
Although the episode is in many respects a model of hagiographical con-
vention, the portrait of Benedicta, brief as it is, has naturalistic features that
I have not encountered elsewhere in miracle collections.[22]

The air of authenticity that Arcoid imparts to this episode may be simply
an effect of his own personal respect and fondness for the woman herself,
but it may also be a deliberate device to lend credence to the events that
followed. For Benedicta's is the first of the miracles that supposedly took
place in Arcoid's own time at St. Paul's and inaugurates a new level of activity at the shrine in the crypt. The next miracle (VI) is about a miser who
forbade his wife to donate money towards the cost of a new silver reliquary
for St. Erkenwald, and, although it is not so stated, one may infer from this
positioning of episodes that the healing of Benedicta's hand led to the decision to provide the saint with a more splendid home. That at least is the
impression given by *MSE*.

Such a decision would not be made lightly, however, since it involved
a considerable investment of time and money at a far from propitious moment in the history of the chapter.[23] Another factor that may have influenced the decision to undertake the new "ferculum" was very likely the
long awaited but imminent completion of the Romanesque choir.[24] The
shrine of the saint, if placed behind the main altar as it had been before
the great fire, would be the centerpiece of the new building and a major
devotional attraction. But the simple wooden "theca" of the much more
modest pre-Conquest basilica was doubtless too austere and old-fashioned
for the tastes and pretensions of the Anglo-Norman chapter. Well in advance, therefore, they commissioned a new silver shrine and began to col-
lect funds. Mir. VI includes the interesting information that London's
wealthier citizens were not quick to respond to the call for contributions,
"donating little or nothing," but that the poorer people organized collections
throughout the city (Mir. VI 3). In Mir. X we learn that a little over a year
later, that is in 1139, the work was under way, a new wooden "feretrum"
had been made to support the silver exterior, and the silversmiths were engaged in the slow and expensive task of fashioning the artifact itself.[25]

There is independent corroboration of the silvering of the feretrum, and
of lay contributions to it, in a St. Paul's charter which can be dated to the

late 1130s or early 1140s, and according to which a certain Galio came to an agreement with the canons of St. Paul's over the leasing of some of their communal land at Sandon in Essex. Under this "consentio," Galio was to hold the land from them for his lifetime, and restore it to the chapter on his deathbed along with a substantial quantity of livestock, "for the redemption of his soul." By way of concluding the agreement, Galio gave the canons forty shillings (solidos) and "half a mark of silver to St. Erkenwald for the work on his reliquary."[26] The charter is an interesting, if unfortunately solitary, example of the commercial and legal ramifications of the saint's cult, and it also illustrates the importance of the London shrine even in rural Essex.[27]

Besides attracting donations for the silver ferculum, Erkenwald's holy bones, according to Arcoid, were performing miracles in abundance during the two years or so following the healing of Benedicta's hand (Mir. VII 1–15, XIV 2). As news of the heightened activity around the shrine spread, it so aroused the envy of "certain English monasteries" that they tried to steal the precious body from its sanctuary in the crypt (XIV). The attempted "furtum sacrum" failed but, to prevent any second efforts, the canons quickly had a stone "habitaculum" made for the lead coffin, "in a safer place," and the coffin was translated there three days after the break-in. That this "safer place" was in the upper church, and in or near the choir, transpires from the next miracle episode, Mir. XV, the account of Baldwin the foreigner, who is healed of a persistent fever after falling asleep "at the entrance to the choir" while listening to the canons singing the mass of St. Erkenwald. He has been taken there by his friends to be near the saint's tomb (Mir. XV 13–15).[28]

The date of the rather hasty and disorderly translation was February 16, 1140 (Mir. XIV 48–50). That there was a translation of Erkenwald's relics in 1140 was not widely known in the later Middle Ages, because it was soon superseded by a second translation, that of November 14, 1148. The second date is echoed in all subsequent calendars, and 1148 is the year cited by Matthew Paris and Ralph of Coggeshall.[29] This is not surprising, for even though there is no surviving account of the 1148 translation, it is likely that as a liturgical ceremony it would be more impressive and official than this of 1140. For one thing, in 1148 St. Paul's had a bishop, Robert de Sigillo, who doubtless presided at the translation in that year, whereas in 1140 the episcopacy was vacant and the ceremony was performed by the canons, Arcoid among them, without even the assistance of the bishop-in-charge, Henry of Winchester. A more important and memorable feature of the 1148 translation, however, must surely have been the new silver shrine. Thomas Boase has suggested that Erkenwald was translated in 1148 to mark the completion of the choir.[30] This is possible, but the evidence of *MSE*, as we have seen, indicates that the choir was already functional in 1140 or, at the latest, the following year. It seems to me more likely, therefore, that the ceremony of 1148 was the translation of the lead inner coffin from its temporary stone housing, located just inside or just outside the choir entrance, to the new silver feretrum begun ten years earlier and now finally complete. According to the description preserved in an inventory of 1245, it was of wood inside and silver plates on the outside, which were decorated with pictorial images and studded with gems. Perched on the top, presumably astride the apex of the gabled roof at each end of the shrine, were two silver angels weighing three pounds apiece.[31] In size the reliquary was at least the length of a man, since in Mir. X a silversmith lies down inside it, and it is unlikely that in height it would be any shorter than its predecessor, described as "above the height of a man" when resting on its stone plinth. In 1245 the shrine is said to have been on the main altar itself, alongside a less sumptuous reliquary containing some relics of St. Mellitus. There is no reason to believe that the shrine was anywhere else but on or abutting the main altar throughout the preceding century.[32]

We have suggested that *MSE* was probably written, in part at least, to publicize the ferculum project and the miracles that had led to its inception, in the hope of eliciting devotional and financial support for the continuation and completion of the opus. But Arcoid himself did not live to see the finished article nor the glorious re-enshrinement of his patron. He was content to end the chronological portion of his story with accounts of the interim translation of the relics from the crypt to the upper church, and of the subsequent miracles (XIV and XV). It must be admitted that as a result *MSE* is in the end unsatisfying and somewhat anti-climactic from the point of view of historical narrative. Having aroused his reader's expectations, Arcoid does not fulfil them. A finely written description of the translation or elevation of the relics to the finished silver feretrum in the romanesque choir would have been the most fitting and logical conclusion to the story begun in Mir. IV. Instead we have the rather unlikely tale of the attempted theft of the relics and the unpremeditated, unceremonious translation to the plain stone shrine.

I have no doubt that there was an 1140 translation. Arcoid is careful not only to give a precise date (the only one in the whole *MSE*) and to stress his own presence and participation in the rite, but also to include among the witnesses the name of a known contemporary, Canon Theoldus of St. Martin-le-Grand, whose existence is verified in a charter dated 1137 from St. Bartholomew's Priory and other documents from around the same time.[33] The 1140 translation is also confirmed in the *Annales Paulini*.[34] I am sceptical, however, about Arcoid's explanation as to why the body was translated at this time. It seems highly unlikely that a group of English monasteries would conspire in the middle of the twelfth century to steal the relics of St. Erkenwald of London. The heroic days of the "furta sacra" were long past, at least in Europe, and neither ecclesiastical nor lay authorities would have tolerated such an outrageous caper. Erkenwald had been at St. Paul's for 500 years: that he might be suddenly spirited away and divided up between the monks of Westminster or Bury or St. Albans is unthinkable, even during the reign of Stephen. It is also difficult to see how, if the "thieves" were neither seen nor arrested, Arcoid can identify them as monastics. The story is a patent fiction, although it is to Arcoid's credit that he has avoided the sensational elements usually found in examples of this hagiographical topos.[35]

Bernard Scholz argued some years ago that the quickening of interest in Erkenwald in the late 1130s may have been the St. Paul's response to the expected canonization of Edward the Confessor, whose relics lay at Westminster.[36] The monks' energetic prior, Osbert of Clare, finished a new *vita*[37] of Edward in 1138, obtained letters of support from Bishop Henry of Winchester, King Stephen, and the canons of St. Paul's, and took his new dossier of the Confessor to Rome late in 1139 or early 1140. He came home about a year later virtually empty-handed. Pope Innocent II politely recognized Osbert's zeal and devotion to his patron, but declined to add his blessing to the cause until Osbert could provide evidence that Edward's sanctity was fervently upheld, and his canonization desired, by the English church and people at large.[38]

It was Marc Bloch's view that Osbert's mission was a political ploy engineered by Stephen and Henry his brother to legitimize their rule, and that it failed for political reasons.[39] But Scholz showed that, on the contrary, the affair was an act of individual enthusiasm, a one man show, on Osbert's part. The letters of Stephen and Henry are more in support of Osbert than of St. Edward, while the brief St. Paul's letter is blatantly lukewarm, as Scholz pointed out.[40] But the failure of the mission would be difficult to predict before it occurred. Osbert had been successful in two earlier pet projects: the promotion of the Feast of the Immaculate Conception, and the foundation of Kilburn Priory.[41] So it is possible that there was some anxiety at St. Paul's over the prospect of a halo rising in the west. Erkenwald's silver shrine, begun in 1138, and the 1140 translation could well have been symptoms of such anxiety.

This would explain the choice of the "furta" topos, and the charge that "certain English monasteries" hatched the conspiracy, as Arcoid's device to discredit Westminster's claim for Edward's sanctity. The attempted theft not only enhances Erkenwald's prestige by implying that he is worth stealing; it also insinuates that he is more precious and desirable than the relics presently in the possession of the monasteries themselves.

We have no way of proving these links between Osbert's and Arcoid's efforts to promote their respective patrons. Although there is no doubt that Arcoid, through chapter business at least, would know of Osbert's suit to Rome, and may well have seen the *Vita Edwardi*, no contemporary historian or chronicler remarks on any cultic rivalry between St. Paul's, London, and St. Peter's, Westminster, nor does Arcoid's "quibusdam monasteriis" necessarily include the Abbey up-river. Scholz's idea is attractive, but it must remain a matter for conjecture.

More than likely, the example of Osbert at Westminster acted as an additional stimulus to rather than as the sole initiating factor in the 1140 translation and the subsequent composition of *MSE*. My own hypothesis is that, since the choir was to all intents and purposes ready, and the new shrine was not, Arcoid and his confrères, goaded perhaps by events at Westminster, decided to move Erkenwald's relics in order to make them more accessible to the lay public, and in turn to stimulate devotion, miracles, and support for the silver feretrum project. Arcoid's personal literary task was to publicize the recent miracles, the translation, and the new shrine, among the literate clerical community and through them to bring in visitors from further afield and from the urban and rural laity. The chapter was undoubtedly hard up, given the loss of episcopal revenues and the various other depredations during the long vacancy, and it was probably necessary that the shrine be a self-supporting project.

3. THE LATE MIDDLE AGES

The silver shrine that is the object of so much attention in *MSE*, and that was reported as resting on the main altar of the cathedral in 1245, was most probably dismantled like the great Norman choir above it by the end of the thirteenth century. The choir was replaced between 1258 and 1314 by a more extensive Gothic structure, the so-called "New Work" in the Perpendicular style, which is depicted in the engravings by Hollar in Dugdale's *History*.[42] Erkenwald's relics were then furnished with an even more imposing shrine, likewise in the Gothic style, which took twelve years (1314–1326) to construct, and which was located not on or abutting the main altar, but just behind it in a separate, new chapel of St. Mary. The St. Paul's chronicler tells how the body of the saint was moved by night, on the feast of the Purification (Feb. 1, 1326), to avoid the crowds and mass hysteria that would have resulted if the relics had been exposed during the daytime.[43] The superstructure of the new shrine was of elaborately carved stone and alabaster, but the inner shrine, which would presumably be visible through the openwork of the superstructure, was made of precious metals. In 1319 a canon of St. Paul's left all his gold rings and jewels to the work on the new shrine, and there are records of further expenses for gold, silver, and gems, by the dean and chapter in 1324, in preparation for the translation in 1326. Again in 1339 we learn that three goldsmiths were put to work on the shrine for a whole year. Among the more generous and notable pilgrims who paid their respects before it in the early 1340s was the royal prisoner, King John of France, who donated twelve nobles.[44]

In the late fourteenth century Erkenwald's feasts, along with other major saints' feasts, apparently suffered some neglect in London, and Bishop Braybroke in 1386 had to issue diocesan letters to reinstitute the full liturgical observance of the saint's octaves of April 30 and November 14.[45] Further promotion of the cult by both clergy and laity took place in the decade following, in the form of expensive gifts, elaborate processions, more work on the shrine by the goldsmiths, and the construction of an imposing and costly ironwork fence around it. By a bequest of 1407, Dean Thomas provided a row of houses the rents from which were intended to finance the permanent upkeep of the shrine, the burning of lights on the two feast days, and the support of a chaplain for a fraternity of St. Erkenwald at the cathedral.[46]

These material evidences of the cult's importance in the later Middle Ages are matched by various kinds of liturgical and literary testimony, which can be briefly summarized.

While Erkenwald's cult was celebrated after the Norman Conquest at fewer centers outside London than was the case in Anglo-Saxon times, the surviving calendars indicate that by the thirteenth century his April feast was kept at St. Albans and Westminster Abbey with twelve lessons, and he was honored with at least a commemorative prayer by the monks of Chester, Abbotsbury in Dorset, St. Guthlac's abbey in Croyland, Ely cathedral, Hyde Abbey in Winchester, and elsewhere.[47] The major monastic centers of the cult were of course Chertsey and Barking, the saint's own foundations. A beautifully written and illuminated set of offices for his April octave, somewhat mutilated, survives in the early fourteenth-century Chertsey Breviary in Bodley, which includes a historiated initial P marking the incipit of *VSE* and showing Erkenwald as bishop instructing his monks.[48] From Barking, in the abbey's late fourteenth-century customary, we have an abbreviated set of rubrics for the mass and office of both the April and November octaves.[49] Also from the fourteenth century, in a single manuscript copy of an influential legendary – John of Tynemouth's *Sanctilogium Anglie* – there is the radically revised edition of Erkenwald's life and miracles, based on *VSE* and *MSE* but with many alterations, which underwent further revisions in the fifteenth century.[50] John of Tynemouth's redaction in turn supplied the lections for the November offices at Barking (those in April were taken from *VSE*), as well as those for April 30 in other London diocese churches later in the fifteenth century. John's version is also the source of the lections for Erkenwald's feasts in the late printed editions of the Sarum Breviary.[51] The adoption of the revised life and miracles for the lections in the fifteenth century indicates, besides the standardization of the English liturgy, not only a continued interest in the saint but also a desire to keep the liturgical cult up to date.

Modernizing the *legenda* may indicate sustained devotion to the cult in clerical circles, but what of the laity in the later Middle Ages? Here also there is evidence of continuing devotion to London's local saint. Laymen provided two of the more costly offerings to the shrine in the 1390s,[52] and at Lincoln's Inn in 1431 St. Erkenwald's November feast day was proclaimed as one of the four major feasts to be celebrated annually by the members of the Inn.[53] This association between Erkenwald and the London lawyers appears also in the custom, recorded in the early sixteenth century but probably of earlier vintage, whereby newly appointed sergeants of law on the occasion of their induction would walk in procession through the City to St. Paul's, make an offering at Erkenwald's shrine, and then each be assigned a pillar in the nave as a regular place for meeting with prospective clients.[54] One of London's most famous lawyers, Sir Thomas More, himself shows his familiarity with St. Erkenwald by citing one of the miracles in two different contexts in the course of his polemical tract, *A Dialogue Concerning Heresies*, published in 1527.[55]

Two important instances of the cult's appeal to lay audiences involve hagiography in the vernacular. The first, written in the late fourteenth or early fifteenth century, is the alliterative poem to which we referred earlier, the Middle English *St. Erkenwald* which is extant in a late fifteenth-century N. Midlands recension of the *South English Legendary*.[56] The poem adds another miracle to the saint's "dossier" by recasting the legend of Pope Gregory and the Emperor Trajan in a London setting and with numerous motifs and themes borrowed from *VSE*, *MSE*, and the liturgy of Erkenwald. It also further reflects the importance of the legal profession in Erkenwald's cult, as noticed above, for the other chief character in the story besides the bishop himself is the speaking corpse of a London judge.

For reasons unknown, but possibly because of its provincial dialect and authorship, the poem had no influence on the late fifteenth-century author of the other important vernacular treatment of Erkenwald, a Middle English prose redaction of his life and miracles, which is extant only in a single recension of the *Gilte Legende*. Unlike most of the other chapters of the *Gilte Legende*, which are translated quite closely from the *Légende dorée* of Jean de Vignay, the Erkenwald chapter is an apparently independent effort to combine the more original features of John of Tynemouth's *De Erkenwaldo* with the earlier *VSE* and *MSE*, marking one more stage in the evolution of the saint's hagiography. This version in turn was adapted and considerably shortened by Caxton for his *Golden Legend*.[57]

Finally there is a good deal of evidence that Erkenwald, while undistinguished iconographically from dozens of other bishop confessors in the church calendar, was not neglected by medieval English artists. Probably the earliest visual image extant is the interesting historiated initial from the Chertsey Breviary (ca. 1300), mentioned previously, depicting Erkenwald instructing his monks.[58] More usually he is represented alone, simply as a bishop in pontificals. His mitred head appears twice in the stained glass (1280–1350) of Wells Cathedral, in the retrochoir (south side, south window tracery lights) and in the south window of St. Catherine's chapel in company with St. Aldhelm and other early English saints.[59] A crude and much restored portrait of him is to be seen alongside that of Edmund, king and martyr, in two panels of a splendid wooden rood screen, of fourteenth-century date, in the parish church of Guilden Morden, some miles south west of Cambridge.[60] A more imposing portrait survives in another corner of East Anglia, in the late fifteenth-century stained glass of St. Peter Mancroft, Norwich, where Erkenwald, young, beardless, in a pearl-studded mitre, occupies a prominent position at the top center of the tracery lights in the great east window, next to St. William of York (the archbishop, d. 1154). Unfortunately the window is mainly a collage assembled in the seventeenth century of pieces that originally belonged in other windows of the church. While Erkenwald's portrait clearly derives from the same window as that of St. William, there is no way of knowing what other saints accompanied them.[61]

Although a systematic search might yield more, I know of only two miniatures of Erkenwald in fifteenth-century books of hours. One of these, MS 105 in the Morgan Library in New York City, was beautifully executed at Rouen, 1420–1425, for Sir William Porter, a Lincolnshire knight. The saint is portrayed as a richly dressed bishop (the face is smudged) in a rural landscape, bearing a crozier and reading a book.[62] There is a portrait by an English artist in another Morgan *horae*, MS 46, of the same period but of undetermined ownership. Facing the miniature, however, is an anthem for the saint's feast day which strongly suggests a London provenance and which provides a suitable conclusion for this survey of the history of Erkenwald's cult:

O decus insigne nostrum pastor atque benigne
lux lundonie pater Erkenwalde beate.
Qui super astra deum gaudes spectare per euum
aspice letantes tua gaudia nos celebrantes
et tecum uite fac participes sine fine.

(O thou illustrious glory of our city, our shepherd and blessed father Erkenwald, light of London, thou who beyond the stars rejoicest to gaze on God eternally, look down on us, as we in gladness keep thy joyful feast day, and grant us to share with thee in the life that never ends.)[63]

CHAPTER FIVE

The *Vita sancti Erkenwaldi*
and the *Miracula sancti Erkenwaldi*:
Hagiography and History in the Anglo-Norman Era

In the decade or so following the Norman Conquest of England, nearly all the important positions in the English church came to be filled by foreign ecclesiasts from Normandy and other parts of the Continent. This copious influx of personnel brought with it substantial changes in the structure, customs and basic character of the English church, which was considered decadent and provincial by many of the Normans when they arrived, including the new archbishop of Canterbury, Lanfranc.[1] Among the various aspects of native English Christianity with which the Normans found fault was Anglo-Saxon hagiology.[2] Lanfranc and the other immigrant bishops and abbots were confronted with a multitude of saints with seemingly uncouth Anglo-Saxon and Celtic names, about whom little was known in some cases except the location of their cults and the dates of their feasts. Latin *vitae* were rare and vernacular lives do not seem to have been as common as one might have expected in a country that had produced the first effective vernacular literature in Europe. Many of the local saints were apparently commemorated mainly through oral tradition.[3] Accustomed to their own saints and to higher standards of hagiology and hagiography, the Normans were at first contemptuous of the native cults and in a number of cases attempted to suppress them.[4] Lanfranc himself initially downgraded the feast of such a well-known English saint as Dunstan, and it took no less than the subtlety of Anselm of Bec to persuade the archbishop that St. Elphege, who was murdered by pagan Danes in 1012, was worthy of his status as Canterbury's only martyr saint.[5]

The Normans' objections to the native saints were doubtless motivated as much by chauvinistic prejudice as by learned scepticism or scruples about authenticity. As the years passed and the mutual suspicion and friction between conqueror and conquered waned, the Anglo-Normans, as they deserve to be called by the end of the century, began not only to tolerate the native cults but also to enhance and promote them, in part by refurbishing existing shrines or translating the relics to new shrines in the new Norman churches and cathedrals,[6] and in part by encouraging the composition of new written *vitae*, such as *VSE* itself, for liturgical readings and other public and private forms of celebration and commemoration. Much of this "rehabilitation of the Anglo-Saxon saints,"[7] represented by dozens of individual *vitae* and sets of *miracula* from the period of 1070 to 1150, was the work of a small group of hagiographers. Two of the earliest writers were Goscelin and Folcard, both originally from the abbey of St. Bertin in Flanders. Somewhat younger were Osbern and Eadmer of Canterbury, Englishmen who were among the first conspicuous products of the Normans' efforts to raise the level of latinity among the English clergy. Other contributors included William of Malmesbury, Dominic of Evesham, and Osbert of Clare.[8] Others, some of whose names we know, wrote only one or two works, while many, including the writer of *VSE*, are still anonymous.[9]

It has been said that the unprecedented resurgence of Latin hagiography in Anglo-Norman England was in large part a native English reaction to the "Normanization" of the English church and resulted from an urge to recover and preserve the Anglo-Saxon heritage of England before all trace of it was obliterated by the Normans' energy and zeal for modernization. Denis Bethel has suggested that for the Anglo-Normans the relics of the Anglo-Saxon saints came to be "symbolic of the old kingdom and the old language, liturgy, literature and devotion,"[10] and Sir Richard Southern has argued with his customary eloquence that the revival of hagiography signaled the burgeoning of a historical spirit that, as reflected in the works of William of Malmesbury and Simeon of Durham, was the "greatest intellectual achievement of twelfth-century England."[11] This may well be true in the case of William and Simeon, particularly with regard to their histories of contemporary events, but one should not overemphasize either the nationalism or historicism of the majority of the Anglo-Norman hagiographers. To do so would be to ignore some important considerations and to risk projecting upon the early twelfth century the values and perspectives of our own time. It is surely significant that the works of Latin hagiography from this period that are best known to modern scholars and students are the lives of Anselm of Bec and Christina of Markyate, both published in splendid editions and translations by Southern and C. H. Talbot.[12] Neither of these lives is remotely representative of the bulk of the hagiography of Anglo-Norman England. Each was written soon after the death of its subject and is of real historical value because the legend-making process had had little time to distort the facts. By contrast, most of the typical hagiographical output of the period deals with the distant past which is largely reconstructed with the help of legend and outright fiction. The lives of Anselm and Christina are also unusual, and historically valuable, in their approach to the depiction of saintly character, for they reveal their subjects with an individuality and naturalism, and with a simplicity of style, that are quite foreign to medieval hagiography in general and to other Anglo-Norman lives. In other words, of this hagiographical revival that Professor Southern and others have valued so highly, the characteristic, representative works remain inaccessible and unread while its anomalies have achieved the status of set books in the history schools because they come closest to what is recognized today as authentic history.

As is obvious from any medieval artist's depiction of a classical Greco-Roman subject, the medieval sense of history was quite different from the modern. Antiquarianism was virtually unknown. The past was not valued for its own sake and there was no premium on recovering its exact likeness. Even for the most literate intellectual of the twelfth-century renaissance, what mattered was its practical relation to the present and future,[13] and in the term "practical" I include the notion of mystical typology as well as legal precedent. For example when a cleric of this period read the Old Testament account of Joshua leading the Israelites across the Jordan with the ark of the covenant (Ios. 3 & 4), nothing in his education or culture led him to analyze or appreciate it as history in any literal sense. He did not wonder how the waters were immobilized above the crossing point or what they looked like as they hung suspended, or whether the river bottom was muddy and difficult to traverse. Nor was he troubled by the rather confused references in the text to the twelve stones. What he got from the story was that it confirmed his own special status as a priest and showed how his role in the sacrament of Christian baptism made him a vital intermediary between man and God. In other words, he read the story for its allegorical and typological significance and in his own immediate interests.[14]

The same attitude is illustrated in the forging of charters by such ostensibly pious, God-fearing clerics as Eadmer of Canterbury, the biographer of St. Anselm and author of the *Historia novorum*. M. T. Clanchy recently explained this phenomenon as follows: "Forgery was necessary because contemporaries had no historical sense. A good oral tradition or an authentic charter of an early Anglo-Saxon king might be rejected by a court of law because it seemed strange (i.e., was not couched in contemporary formulas), whereas a forged charter was acceptable because it suited contemporary notions of what an ancient charter should be like."[15] If we can understand why people like Eadmer and Osbert of Clare habitually forged charters, we should be careful not to credit the audience of their saints' lives with anything like a modern comprehension of or interest in the historical past.[16]

In addition to this lack of developed sense of history, one must also take into consideration the basically ahistorical character of the saints' cults themselves. Although attitudes towards saints and their relics were changing and growing more sophisticated and sceptical in some quarters, for the medieval majority, both laymen and clerics, a saint was not really a matter for history at all. Rather he was the living spirit of a holy place, the powerful "patronus" of those who worshipped in his church, tended his shrine, and had their homes within his domain. The holy man or woman who had lived for a short space centuries before was dead: but the saint that he or she had become at the moment of death was believed to be very much alive. In his prologue to the MSE, for example, Arcoid remarks that not only did Erkenwald perform "admirable works" during his lifetime, "but not even death has been able to hold him back, even as a dead man, from giving the most certain proofs of the liveliness of his soul, to the glory of God and for the salvation of the believers, and from showing forth acts of surpassing power to the faithful people" (Mir. Pr. 14–17). From inside his shrine, the saint protected his devotees and the temporal wealth they had acquired in his name, while at the same time acting as their spiritual advocate and patron in the court of heaven.

It is unlikely that anyone as alive and emphatically "present" as a powerful saint would be regarded as a nostalgic symbol of a vanished culture, and the evidence of the Anglo-Norman vitae and miracula suggests the opposite. Native Englishmen like Osbern and Eadmer, although they did not agree with everything their foreign mentors did or said, were not at all nostalgic about old pre-Norman England. Osbern attributes the destruction of the Saxon cathedral of Canterbury in 1067 to the fact that the spirit of St. Dunstan had deliberately deserted the church some time before, because the Anglo-Saxon monks had permitted earl Harold's unbaptized son to be buried inside and had ignored the saint's warnings to "shove the body outside."[17] Similarly in the MSE of Erkenwald, when describing the miraculous preservation of the saint's shrine in the great fire, Arcoid expresses no regret that Erkenwald permitted the destruction of the pre-Conquest church while saving himself. Instead the hagiographer rejoices at his patron's victory over the flames and at the fact that the Anglo-Saxon bishop is now able to become the episcopal saint of the vast new Norman cathedral. Erkenwald, like Dunstan, is represented as being content to see the old culture destroyed and to assume the patronage of the new regime.

Rather than indulging an urge to discover the past for its own sake or to project themselves back to their Anglo-Saxon origins, the authors of the new vitae and miracula were seeking to bring the past into the present, to accommodate the written memorials of the Anglo-Saxon saints to the new conditions and tastes that had emerged out of the Anglo-Norman synthesis. The most prolific of the new hagiographers, Goscelin of Canterbury, who spent the last part of his long career at St. Augustine's, addresses the issue of past and present in the preface to his "magnum opus," the life and miracles of St. Augustine, the missionary and first archbishop of Canterbury. More by rhetoric than reasoned argument, Goscelin offers a defence of the idea of up-dating the past, of rewriting old texts in modern style, and of attributing old miracles to later saints:

> I hope that no devotee of antiquity will take offense at this new work of mine because I have fashioned something new out of old materials or because I write in an up-to-date style about recent events. For whoever takes offense at what is new might well appear to be impugning God himself, who is forever creating things afresh. The God of Abraham is the God of Augustine. He who worked wonders in ancient times effects the same miracles today through the relics of saints of the modern age, and in the persons of the saints of our own day. To him the prophet cries out, "Show us new signs and new miracles," and he creates new heavens and sitting on his throne he makes all things new. If the fathers of old had not accepted what was considered new in their day, nothing that we venerate as old today would exist. But the Jews and all the other incredulous enemies of new and sacred truths prefer to remain in the darkness of the past with all its errors, rather than be illumined by the light of new grace.[18]

Underlying Goscelin's efforts to "make all things new" in his life of Augustine and many of his other works, is a literary confrontation with Bede, whose *Historia ecclesiastica* was the principal "auctoritas" for the lives and miracles of the early Anglo-Saxon saints. Even where Bede devotes several chapters to a particular saint, as he does to Augustine of Canterbury, it is not nearly enough for Goscelin and his fellow monks.[19] Not only is Bede's account quite short with hardly any miracles, but it clearly lacks the heroic tone, richness of rhetorical color and range of incident and emotion that the Anglo-Norman literati felt appropriate for the "historia major" of the apostle of the English. So Bede's concise, understated biography is transformed by Goscelin into a sprawling romance of quite different character and intent, replete with new incidents and a new Anglo-Norman image of the saint. Bede's rather diffident, hesitant Italian missionary is transformed by Goscelin's rhetoric into the mighty conqueror of Britain, which he claims for Christ and Pope Gregory as the spoils of spiritual warfare.[20] The militaristic metaphor could not fail to appeal to the Norman hierarchy at

St. Augustine's where a rebellion of Anglo-Saxon monks had been put down by force of arms, with typical Norman vigor and efficiency, a year or so before Goscelin arrived there. Another example of Goscelin's approach is his inclusion, in the first part of the *Vita*, of a long, detailed account of Augustine's supposed adventures and miracles in Angers on the western Loire. There is no trace of this tale in Bede. Goscelin got it, as he tells us, from a certain "Guiffridus" (presumably Geoffrey), bishop of Angers, who visited Canterbury some time in the 1090s. The tale links Augustine with the larger Anglo-Norman world and at the same time introduces into his mythology a strongly anti-feminist element that was apparently congenial to the monks of Canterbury.[21]

The anonymous author of *VSE* likewise had to come to terms with Bede. At some point during the Anglo-Saxon period, Bede's one-paragraph account of Erkenwald (*Hist. eccles.* 4.6) had been reworked into a brief *vita* of the saint sufficient for three lections at the night office. This pre-Conquest life was used by Goscelin in 1087 for the opening of his life of St. Ethelburga, Erkenwald's sister. The author of *VSE* in turn incorporated this still essentially Bedan portrait of the saint into a new, more extensive narrative framework, largely borrowed from continental saints' lives that would be familiar and acceptable to the Norman canons of St. Paul's. At the same time, by virtue of the type of hagiographical episodes he chose to imitate, the *VSE* hagiographer made the saint's legend more in harmony with the contemporary character of the cult and more nearly representative of the Anglo-Norman regime whose patron he had become.

The main contribution of the anonymous hagiographer to Erkenwald's legend is the story of how the canons and layfolk of London triumphantly claimed the body of the saint, shortly after he died, from the monks and nuns of Chertsey and Barking (*VSE* 63–172). The story is not historical. There is no reason or evidence for supposing that any such struggle occurred at the time of Erkenwald's death or at any subsequent time. The whole episode, which constitutes well over half of the extant *VSE*, is a literary fiction, the culmination of several centuries in the development of a hagiographical topos.[22] Its "truth" lies in its fidelity to the history and ideology of the author's own time, not to that of the Anglo-Saxon past. It is a piece of myth-making, inventing a past to make sense of the present.

In practical terms, it provides lections for the saint's feast that shift the focus of devotion from the wooden horse-litter emphasized by Bede to the corporeal relics that had become the center of the saint's cult even before the Norman reorganization and rebuilding. Equally important the new episode effects a change in the image of the episcopacy itself. As William Bright pointed out, Bede's attention to the healing virtues of the wooden litter highlights the apostolic, pastoral character of the bishop in early Anglo-Saxon society.[23] The cart in Bede's scheme of things is Erkenwald's cross, the symbol of his redemptive pastoral ministry and of his vital personal importance to the salvation of his people. It was the cart that enabled him to move about his diocese, preaching, baptizing, confirming, and dedicating parish churches, even after he was infirm and unable to walk or ride; so it is the cart, like Oswald's cross and Aidan's wooden pillar, that embodies his sanctity to Ango-Saxon posterity. VSE, on the other hand, reflects the Christianity of a later age, to which Bede's imagery is no longer appropriate. The numinous corpse of Erkenwald, surrounded by its attendant canons and priests, miraculously fording the River Hile like the ark of the covenant crossing the Jordan, is a much more apt embodiment and symbol of the more remote, legalistic episcopates of Anglo-Norman England, and of the sacramental rather than pastoral character of the Christian church as a whole at this time. As we pointed out earlier, the crossing of the Jordan was universally recognized by Christian clerics as a "figura" or type of salvation through baptism, and specifically baptism by priests. The priestly role is emphasized in VSE when the canons of St. Paul's pause for a time, after crossing the river, to let the laypeople go on ahead, in an apparent allusion to Ios. 3.4, where the people are told to keep their distance from the ark, which only the priests are allowed to accompany.[24]

One might add that the triumph of the urban secular canons and layfolk over the rural monastics in VSE may well have been viewed at St. Paul's as an endorsement of the strongly secular character of the Anglo-Norman chapter under Bishops Maurice and Richard I of Belmeis, from 1086–1127, the period during which VSE was composed. As C. N. L. Brooke has shown, under Maurice and Richard the quasi-monastic traditions of the Anglo-Saxon St. Paul's were largely abrogated, although the post-Conquest statutes of the cathedral still preserve some portions of the pre-Conquest rule, just as VSE itself incorporates the Bedan account of Erkenwald's life. But there is little in either to suggest any sort of nostalgia for the earlier age.[25]

The author of VSE included the Bedan portrait of Erkenwald but he did not expand on it or dwell on it. The life that Erkenwald lived as abbot and monk-bishop was much less important to the Anglo-Normans than the dead body they had inherited from the Anglo-Saxon past. A monk-bishop was not the most ideal patron for the secular chapter organized by Maurice in the late eleventh century and we should not be surprised that the hagiographer was content to leave the saint's life story so undeveloped. The one major addition to the old sources in the first part of VSE is the innocuous story of the cart's missing wheel (VSE 43–51), which increases the length of the work, provides a much needed miracle during the saint's lifetime, but does nothing to expand or elaborate the portrait of the holy man himself. What Erkenwald was when he was alive remains vague, abstract, and by far the less striking and memorable portion of the new mythos of his cult. The primary and final emphasis falls on the body of the dead saint as a source of miraculous power, ecclesiastical symbolism, and religious meaning. The composition of the work is a vivid example of the way the Anglo-Norman hagiographers used the past (or what they could discover of it) for their own present purposes, supplementing what they knew or chose to preserve with what they could borrow or imitate from other pasts that were more congenial to their tastes and more appropriate to their current needs.

VSE, then, is the myth on which Erkenwald's cult rests. It explains the origins of the present veneration of the saint at St. Paul's in such a way as to justify the dominant ideology of his Anglo-Norman "patrocinium." The MSE that was written a generation or two later has somewhat different though parallel concerns, and the same ambiguous relation to history. It deals with the cult itself and with the saint's miraculous activity or "divina opera" during the Anglo-Norman era, looking back over a period of fifty years or so (1087–1140) but concentrating on events just prior to the composition of the work itself. We observed earlier that in some cases the medieval hagiographer who writes about a contemporary or near-contemporary is apt to be more reliable as a historian than one who reshuffles legends in order to reconstruct the distant past. It is true that in the MSE there is a good deal of what appears to be valid and valuable historical information, particularly about Erkenwald's cult at St. Paul's and some aspects of church and city life in the first part of the twelfth century. It would be misleading, however, to treat the MSE as a work of history. In its selection of incidents and its development of themes, in the narrative techniques of individual episodes, and in its overall structure, the Miracula reveals itself as just as much a hybrid of history and fiction as VSE. It represents the genre of hagiography in a relatively pure, unmixed form, for unlike many earlier such collections it is not concerned to safeguard ecclesiastical property, or the judicial privileges and exemptions of the church against secular encroachments.[26] As a result the amount of economic, social, legal and topographical data in the successive episodes is limited. Moreover the major political, social, and ecclesiastical issues of the age, including the breakdown of public order under King Stephen, and the long troubled vacancy in the London episcopacy, are all but invisible here, except, as we shall see in the case of Mir. VII, in a form that no conventional historian could use. St. Paul's property was under attack during the period covered by the MSE, by no less than the king himself and Geoffrey de Mandeville, but Arcoid never refers to any such material depredations.[27]

The *Miracula* does have something to protect, but it is a state of mind and a quality of faith, not a piece of real estate. The conflict of ecclesiastic and layman that unfolds in many of the episodes involves the very assumptions and bases of organized religion in the High Middle Ages. As we observed earlier, the practical purpose of the work is to celebrate and publicize the wonder-working shrine of St. Erkenwald, but implicit in the whole collection, and openly stated in several episodes, is essentially the same theme as the anonymous vernacular poet would explore, more than two centuries later, in the Middle English *St. Erkenwald*: namely the vital necessity of traditional, sacramental modes of Christianity, of which the saints' cults were perhaps the most vivid and visible expression. Arcoid shows us several laymen and one cleric being humbled and punished in a variety of ways, two of them fatally, for doubting or slighting the sacramental system of the church as represented in the liturgical cult and the relics of St. Erkenwald. In the most extensive of these episodes, Mir. II, the wider implications of this lack of respect for the saint's cult are made clear in a blasphemous layman's scathing attack on the uselessness of the "opus dei" and the lives of the cathedral canons devoted to it.

Equally important throughout the *MSE* is a collateral effort on Arcoid's part to explain and vindicate the workings of divine providence. Not only does he at one point, in his Proem, actually refer to the miracles as "heavenly sacraments"; he also embodies this idea in the very structure and narrative technique of the individual episodes, treating them as divine "signa" that reveal and communicate the grace and nature of God to sinful men and women, and that turn them from sin and suffering towards the promise of eternal life.[28] Rather than fill out the narrative with the sort of circumstantial detail that appeals to social historians, Arcoid prefers to amplify his account of the miracles themselves with homiletic asides, apostrophes, and explanatory commentary, helping us to see Erkenwald's miraculous activity as exemplifying the pattern of God's providence and imminent justice, or, in Arcoid's own rather cloudy phrase, as an "exemplum . . . spirituale salutis nostre." To this end he also makes copious use of biblical language and quotations both for narrating and explicating, and he frequently makes open or implied allusions to miracles in the Bible and in lives of other saints, that are parallel to those of Erkenwald. He is even careful to specify on occasion that Erkenwald's "novitates" (as he sometimes calls the miracles) surpass certain comparable Old Testament "mirabilia," just as the New Law of grace fulfilled and surpassed its types and foreshadowings in the Old Testament. Underlying the *MSE*, in other words, is the notion of sacred history or salvation history familiar to students of medieval historiography.[29]

The clearest, most conventional example of "Heilsgeschichte" in the *MSE* is Mir. IV. Arcoid here takes a well-known important event in temporal history – the destruction by fire of most of the buildings of London, including the Saxon cathedral – and proceeds to explain both its cause and effects in terms of divine intervention and control over human affairs. First of all, the fire is God's punishment of the evil deeds of the Londoners (Mir. IV 24-26, 46-48), and the destructive ferocity of the flames is described in biblical language that recalls similar occasions in the history of Jerusalem (Mir. IV 33-39, 57). In addition to being the instrument of God's anger and justice, however, the fire is also the means of glorifying Erkenwald, God's saint. The holy bones and their shrine, even the flimsy cloth covering the shrine, are completely untouched by the fire that destroys everything else around them, just as the three Hebrew youths endured the fiery furnace of Nebuchadnezzar unharmed (Mir. IV 105-32). Thus while evil men are punished, Erkenwald's relics are glorified and authenticated by their ordeal, sceptics are shamed and rebuffed, and God's providence is vindicated.

Nowhere else in the MSE does Arcoid attempt to treat notable secular history in these sacred terms. Most of the miracle episodes involve little-known people, and miracles of a narrowly ecclesiastical frame of reference. Although he does allude vaguely, in Mir. VII, to the turmoil of Stephen's reign, he chooses to deal with it symbolically and remotely in the person of the young Frenchman, William, who is suddenly stricken with a cataleptic seizure at a dinner on St. Erkenwald's feast day. William's resulting blindness, paralysis, and "stupor" are presented by Arcoid as an image of the collective stupor and spiritual blindness of society at that time, which he specifically identifies as the reign of Stephen (Mir. VII 99), the only reference to the king in the whole MSE.

In order to propagate the kinds of truth that he considered important, Arcoid was able to invoke the hagiographer's license to attribute to Erkenwald miracles recorded elsewhere of other saints. This is apparently what he did in Mir. I. This episode almost certainly has little or no basis in historical fact. Although one of the protagonists is named – the schoolmaster of St. Paul's, Elwin – there is no trace of him in the copious Anglo-Norman records of the cathedral. Arcoid offers no direct indication as to when the miracle took place, but it was apparently before 1087, and belongs to the obscure period when, as Arcoid himself admits in his Proem, no one wrote down the miracles that occurred and as a result they were lost forever. In Mir. I, therefore, as in Mir. II and III, which together form a kind of literary prologue to the more historically verifiable events of the rest of the MSE, Arcoid is following in the footsteps of the anonymous author of VSE, inventing and creating a suitable past to meet the needs of the present.

The episode as whole is an artful synthesis of two distinct hagiographical topoi.[30] In one of these a saint miraculously enables a devotee or disciple to perform some ostensibly impossible task that involves reading or memorizing a written text. In the other topos, schoolboys expecting a flogging from their master (usually for no specific offense), pray to a saint to save them, and the saint either miraculously enables them to avoid the flogging, or chastizes and humbles the master for having flogged the boys after they had put themselves under the saint's protection. In Arcoid's Mir. I a truant schoolboy, fearing the consequences of not having done his homework, takes refuge at St. Erkenwald's shrine, but the master drags him away, orders him to recite his lesson, and promises him a lash for every mistake he makes. The boy startles the master (and himself) by reciting faultlessly by heart not only the pertinent lesson but also the one that was to be assigned for the following day! The master is so ashamed of his disrespect for the saint that he resigns his teaching post, gives away his property, and goes into exile abroad.

The combination of the two topoi results in a clever short story that easily surpasses any of its analogues in craft and charm. It also provides Arcoid with an ideal introduction to his collection in that it preaches the necessity of cultivating a child-like and unquestioning faith in the intercessory power of St. Erkenwald. Given Arcoid's recurrent warnings to his readers throughout the MSE that they should believe in the relics and miracle stories and not question their truth and authenticity, the story is clearly designed to inculcate a receptive attitude to the miracles that follow it. It is a warning to Arcoid's distinguished "fratres karissimi" in the cathedral chapter not to fall into that species of pride and intellectual self-sufficiency that places a higher priority on self-discipline and personal accomplishment than on a humble, trusting dependence on the mediation of the saints.

Modern educational historians may be intrigued that Mir. I's information about pedagogical techniques at St. Paul's grammar school anticipates by some twenty years John of Salisbury's famous account of the similar teaching methods of Master Bernard of Chartres.[31] But Arcoid of St. Paul's, although his uncle Gilbert had been head of the cathedral school at Auxerre, was not interested in educational history as such. The story to him is an exemplum, to be read, as he shows in its final paragraphs, for its spiritual meaning and truth rather than for its literal information. Elwin's pedagogical system is simply one of Arcoid's ways of adapting older stories, concerning other saints and institutions, to the context of St. Paul's and Erkenwald in 1141. The story is quite unreliable as educational history, although it is valuable evidence of the wider influence of St. Anselm's opinion, as reported by Eadmer,[32] that the foibles of children should be treated with kindness and understanding, not with the rod, which was the prevailing medieval orthodoxy. Its main interest for us today, however, is as a specimen of literary and hagiographical composition in Anglo-Norman London, and as an illustration of the tension between the traditional religious attitudes that had fostered the cults of the saints, and the newer habits of intellectual rigor and logical inquiry that were increasingly prevalent in the secular schools of the time.

The artful and purposeful blend of historical fact and legendary fiction that VSE and the MSE have in common is characteristic of the literary genre—hagiography—to which they both belong. But while Arcoid and his anonymous predecessor at St. Paul's share the typical hagiographical conception of history and truth, each implements it in his own distinctive fashion. VSE and the MSE were written at different times for different liturgical occasions, and they each belong to a distinct hagiographical sub-genre. VSE, as the vita associated with the saint's "depositio," describes what is known of his life, career, death and burial, in a unified linear narrative. It is a portrait of one saint and his holy end. The MSE, on the other hand, written for the feast of the saint's "translatio," is an assortment of discrete miracle episodes, ostensibly self-contained and unconnected, focusing on separate individuals who are related to one another only in that each has had, once in his or her life, a dramatic and transforming encounter with the power residing in the saint's relics.

In addition to this generic distinction between them, the two works differ also in literary character. VSE is anonymous in narrative method as well as in authorship. The author, whose style is simple, concise, and unpretentious (though not by any means artless), remains hidden and impersonal. A prologue or dedicatory epistle revealing his identity and circumstances may have been lost in transmission, of course, but there is no evidence for this. In the work itself he never refers to himself or volunteers to comment on the events in any obvious way.[33] He does not reach out to his audience to admonish or prompt them, or to moralize for their benefit. The "historia" is left to speak for itself. The author of the MSE, by contrast, is frequently audible above his narrative, and at times even visible in it. Not only does he comment on all the miracles, sometimes at length, sermonizing, exhorting, interpreting, remonstrating, apostrophizing, even cursing, he is also personally involved in some of the episodes as an eye witness and occasionally as a participant in the action.[34] As a stylist he is more self-conscious and more ambitious than the VSE hagiographer; as a Latinist—at least to my eye—he is more accomplished. Altogether the MSE is a more accessible work than VSE, and more complex.

The two works, it is true, have more in common than is usual with hagiographical duos of this type. In such cases one is often struck by the abrupt discrepancy between, on the one hand, the humble, amiable, self-denying character of the saint in the *vita*, and on the other hand the rather flashily aggressive, acquisitive, and occasionally violent behavior of the same saint in his or her posthumous *miracula*. The French hagiologist Sigal has explained this recurring *volte face* as the natural consequence of the saint's becoming, after death, the patron of a monastery or cathedral church. Inevitably the saint as "dominus" of an ecclesiastical fief assumes those fiercer, more worldly qualities that were the conventional attributes of earthly lordship and rule in a warlike and honor-conscious society.[35] In the case of Erkenwald, an analogous but by no means identical contrast in the saint's character before and after his death is already visible in *VSE* itself, as we suggested earlier. The transformation of the saint from holy man to holy thing, from pastoral "sanctus" to sacramental "corpus," embodying the spiritual and material power of the London church, is already achieved in the long *contentio* episode added to the earlier Bedan portrait sometime in the late eleventh century or early twelfth. The *MSE*, written several decades later, may be said to develop and elaborate the complex of meanings implicit in *VSE* in the densely symbolic crossing of the river. The second part of *VSE* shares with the whole *MSE* a strongly sacramental view of the Christian church and of St. Erkenwald's posthumous role within it.

The *MSE*, however, goes beyond *VSE* not only in its being a much more explicit, self-reflexive work, but also in its defensive posture and tone. Arcoid has to demonstrate, explain, argue and defend the sacramental, ecclesiastical system that in *VSE* is taken for granted and left to reveal itself in symbolic narrative. The reasons for this are presumably in part merely a matter of personal style and the limits of the respective genres. But the different historical contexts of the two works are surely an important factor also.

In *VSE*, for example, the focus is on reconciliation and renewal: in the guise of the legendary conflict between the monastics and the secular canons and layfolk, which is resolved through prayer and miracle, *VSE* reflects the integration of previously hostile national and ecclesiastical traditions that was achieved in England during the late eleventh century, as English and Normans settled their differences to create the new Anglo-Norman order. There is no quarrel over the church's sacramental character as symbolized by Erkenwald's precious corpse and the miracles accompanying its progress towards London. The quarrel is about who will possess it, just as in England up to the 1090s the principal conflict in society and church was over possession and power, as the Normans steadily extended their control of the Anglo-Saxon inheritance.

But in the late eleventh and early twelfth century, as is well known, a more settled political situation, a quickening intellectual climate, and the rapidly rising prestige and influence of the papacy and papal ideology, conspired to focus attention and debate on the nature of the church, the character of the priesthood, and the church's relation to secular society and lordship. Arcoid's MSE mirrors some aspects of the intellectual conflict within and around the church itself, particularly as this concerned the validity of the saints' cults but also the more fundamental issue of the church's traditional, sacramental character, as the sole and necessary mediator between man and God. Heretical attacks on, among other things, the sacraments, priestly authority, and saints' cults, were engaging the attention of some of Europe's most prominent churchmen during the second quarter of the twelfth century. There is also evidence that in more orthodox clerical circles learned scepticism regarding some aspects of traditional hagiology and hagiography was increasingly in vogue during the same period. Arcoid's MSE is by no means a polemical tract on the order of Peter the Venerable's *Contra Petrobrusianos*, but it is certainly a response to various critiques of the modes of faith and worship that he and a majority of clerics treasured and wished to preserve.[36]

That Arcoid's preoccupations were of lasting relevance to St. Paul's is indicated by the late fourteenth-century Middle English poem in which St. Erkenwald is one of the two chief protagonists.[37] For in the poem we find a similar confrontation between ecclesiastical and secular values, represented in the contrasting figures of bishop and magistrate, and a similar concern for preserving the sacramental essence of the visible church. The poem goes beyond the MSE, of course, as the MSE goes beyond VSE in its exploration of this sacramental theme. The lay figure in the poem is a much more formidable and sophisticated embodiment of secular values than any of the benighted laymen who cross Erkenwald's path in the MSE: and this is only to be expected, given the tremendous progress in secular education and professionalism in the intervening centuries. But the striking similarities between all three works, including moreover the fact that the narrative climax of both the poem and VSE is the rite of baptism (literal in the former, allegorical in the latter), bears witness to the late medieval continuity of conservative ecclesiastical values at St. Paul's and in the literary persona of its local patron, St. Erkenwald, "lux londonie."

Texts & Translations

Vita Sancti Erkenwaldi

Post passionem ac resurrectionem dominicam cum catholica fides per orbem terrarum diffusa esset, atque per suos athletas dominus sparsim semina uite erogasset, sicut dauiticis canitur in tympanis,[1] *in omnem terram exiuit sonus eorum, et in fines orbis terre uerba eorum.*[2] Tandem ad usque celi cacumen erecta britannie occidentalis aduolarunt partibus, per beatum augustinum a Gregorio papa missum. Qui primus tramitem uite docendo in dorobernensis ecclesie sede *quasi solis* radius *fulgere* cepit.[3] *Mellitum* igitur sancti certaminis commilitonem partibus *orientalium saxonum a cantia* destinauit; *quorum metropolis ciuitas lundonia super* 10 *flumen tamense posita est.*[4] In qua athelbertus rex in honorem doctoris gentium pauli ecclesiam construxit, ubi mellitus predictus pontificali fungeretur officio.[5] Igitur ad doctrinam melliti episcopi puerulus quidam erkenwaldus nomine concurrebat, etate paruus sed mente maturus.[6] Inter multa itaque alia legitur in hystoria anglorum *uita* eius uel *conuersatio fuisse* tam *sanctissima,*[7] ut *in interiore homine diuicias glorie*[8] perscrutatus, caduca uel secularia cuncta postponeret.

Habebat autem germanam adleburgam nomine, quam ita disciplinis celestibus inflammauerat, ut ipsa uirgo uita et moribus et conuersatione sanctissima per omnia deo placere satageret. Predictus etenim uir domi- 20 ni erkenwaldus, etate temporum et probitate morum roboratus, pocius

The Life of St. Erkenwald

After the passion and resurrection of the Lord, the universal Christian faith had been poured forth throughout the world, and the Lord by means of his strenuous ministers had scattered and sown the seeds of life far and wide, in accordance with that verse we sing from David's psalter: "Their sound has gone out into the whole world, and their words to the ends of the earth." At last the apostles' words ascended to the very roof of the heavens and in the person of blessed Augustine, sent by Pope Gregory, winged their way to Britain in the west. Like a radiant beam of sunlight was this Augustine, and the first to teach the true way of life in the see of the church of Canterbury. From Kent he in turn dispatched Mellitus, his comrade in the sacred struggle, to the country of the East Saxons, whose capital city, London, was situated on the river Thames. There King Ethelbert built a church in honor of Paul, the preacher to the Gentiles, and there the aforesaid Mellitus performed the office of bishop. And thus it came to pass that a certain small boy named Erkenwald, young in years but mature in mind, would hasten to hear the teaching of Bishop Mellitus. In the *History of the English*, among many other things concerning him, we read that in life and conduct he was so very holy that he sought and found riches and glory in the inner man, and put behind him all transitory and worldly things.

He had a sister, Ethelburga, in whom he kindled such enthusiasm for celestial discipline that the maiden herself proved most holy in her life, both in character and conduct, and strove to please God in all things. Moreover the aforesaid man of God, Erkenwald, reaching adult age and further strengthened by the steadfast purity of his life, preferred to seek out the solitude

elegit solitaria antra quam popularibus interesse curis. Nam *duo preclara*
monasteria unum sibi alterum sorori sue construxerat, quod utrumque regularibus
disciplinis optime instituerat. Sibi quidem in regione suthe |f. 135v| *rie iuxta*
fluuium tamensem in loco qui uocatur ceroteseya, sorori autem in orientalium
saxonum prouintia in loco qui uocatur berchingum, ubi et constituta *est mater*
animarum.[9]

    Contigit autem ut episcopus lundonice sedis, cedde uocabulo, migrauit
ad dominum. Consensu uero regis, sebbe uocabulo, et uniuerse plebis
uir domini erkenwaldus in cathedra pontificali sublimatus est.[10]

30 Popularibus igitur pompis abrenuntiatis, quicquid sermone docebat operum exhibitione implere curabat. Erat enim sapientia perfectus, sermone
modestus, peruigil in orationibus, corpore castus, lectioni deditus, *cari-*
tatis radice plantatus.[11]

    Post multa siquidem imminentis uite certamina sanctus uir artubus
corporis cepit *infirmari.* Precepit uero *feretrum caballarium* preparari quo
portaretur per uicos et ciuitates uerbum domini predicando. Vnde *fer-*
tur per multa tempora hoc *seruatum* esse *a discipulis* atque plurimi, qua-
licumque dolore grauati essent, mox eo tacto atque deosculato ab
infirmitate liberabantur. Verum etiam *hastule* ab eo *abscise* et *ad* egrotos
40 *allate citam* eis salutem parabant.[12]

    Aduenit ergo tempus quo talentum preciosum celesti sacrario con-
deretur,[13] et pii patris manipuli ad horreum dominicale reportarentur.[14]

    Quadam uero die, uerbi dei pabula commisso sibi gregi ministratu-
rus, dum duarum rotarum ferretur uehiculo infirmitate prepediente uel
senio, contigit ut altera rotarum semite difficultate axem relinqueret et
ibidem socia relicta remaneret. Cumque diu rota reliqua sola officii sui
cursum continuaret, ignorabant enim qui aderant; subito currus ex altera parte uacuus sustentamine cernitur, cuius tamen cursus usu nouo
immo insolito mirabili|f. 136r|ter perficitur.[15] O deus mirabilis per om-
50 nia laudabilis super omnia, cui bruta sunt obnoxia insensata obedien-
tia. Sed quoniam uir sanctus huius uite laudem fugiebat dum eterne
beatitudinis fructum appetebat, remunerator celestis serui sui compen-
sans merita, de ualle lacrimarum et huius uite miseria uocat eum ad reg-

of caves rather than mingle with the throngs in the courts of men. For he built two renowned monasteries, one for himself and the other for his sister, each of which he provided with an excellent rule of monastic living. He built the one monastery for himself in the region of Surrey near the Thames, in a place called Chertsey, and the other for his sister in the province of the East Saxons at Barking. There she was appointed mother of souls.

It came to pass after this that the bishop of the see of London, who was called Cedd, departed to the Lord. And so with the consent of the king, who was named Sebbe, and of the whole people, the man of God, Erkenwald, was elevated to the episcopal throne. As bishop he utterly avoided all public and worldly display, taking care to show forth in his works whatever he preached as doctrine. For he was perfect in wisdom, humble in speech, tireless in prayers and vigils, chaste in body, devoted to study, and the plant of charity was rooted deep within him.

After he had endured many of the contests of this present life, he began to grow infirm in his bodily members. So he ordered the construction of a horse-drawn litter to carry him from one village and town to the next, preaching the word of God. It is said of the litter that it was preserved for a long time by his followers, and that very many people, no matter what illness afflicted them, the moment they touched or kissed it, were delivered from their infirmity. Indeed even splinters broken off from it and taken to the sick would bring them speedy recovery.

In due course the time came for the precious ransom to be placed in its heavenly treasury and for the sheaves of the good father to be carried back to the storehouse of the Lord.

One day when he was on his way to administer the nourishment of God's word to the flock under his care, travelling in the two-wheeled litter because sickness or old-age made walking impossible, it happened that one of the wheels was jarred loose from the axle by the bumpy track. The companion wheel, however, stayed in place. For some time none of those present noticed that the remaining wheel was performing alone its appointed task of supporting the litter. Then suddenly they realized that one side of the vehicle had nothing to hold it up. Yet in this new, not to say unprecedented fashion, the journey was miraculously completed. O God how wonderful you are in all things, and above all things worthy of praise. To you even brute beasts are submissive, and inanimate things are obedient.

But since the holy man always fled the glory to be won in this life and desired instead the fruit of eternal blessedness, the celestial Recompenser rewarded his servant for his merits and summoned him from out of this vale of tears, from the misery of this life, to the kingdom of heaven. And

na celestia. Quod ubi uir sancte conuersationis agnouit, uocationem suam secretis suis familiaribus imminere predixit.

Beatus uero pater erchenwaldus cum dei dispositione berchingum ueniret, infirmitate graui corripitur qua uitam temporalem finiuit. Qui dissolutionem sui corporis imminere prenoscens, conuocat filios suos ac salubri admonitione omnes instruxit, suaque benedictione deo commen-
60 dauit, sicque inter manus illorum spiritum exalauit. In cuius transitu tam mira suauissimi odoris flagrantia, cellulam ubi ipse iacebat impleuit, ac si ipsa domus tota perfunderetur balsamo.[16]

Audientes[17] uero canonici lundonie et monachi certeseye sanctum dei uirum scilicet de hoc mundo transisse, illuc confestim uenerunt ut secum corpus inde tollerent. Quod uidentes sanctimoniales, illos scilicet sancti uiri corpus inde uelle transferre, constanter restiterunt, affirmantes dignissime illic sanctum corpus humandum, quia fundator ac pater loci ipsius extiterat, et de hac causa corpus eius habere uolebant. E contrario monachi certeseye responderunt dicentes, "Nobis extitit abbas, noster[18]
70 erit iam defunctus; et ideo huc uenimus, ut eius corpus nobiscum hinc tollamus. Scimus enim eum uestram ecclesiam fundauisse, sed tamen prius nostri cenobii fundator extitit; insuper et nos ibi constituit, ac deinde abbas noster deo uolente factus est." Tum uero clerus ac populus urbis lundonie indignantes de tali certa|f. 136|mine, ex abrupto ad utrosque responderunt dicentes, "Frustra contenditis; quia nec uos illum habebitis nec iustum est ut eum habeatis. Uerum si mos antiquitus seruatur institutus, in urbe qua presul ordinatus est immo de urbe romulea destinatus deo iubente sepulchrum habebit."[19]

Interea dum hec dicerentur, plebs certatim accurrit lundonie, ac deo
80 annuente sui pontificis corpus inde secum sustulere. Condolentes uero monachi uerum etiam et sanctimoniales de beati uiri corpore sibi sublato, plorando beati uiri corpus prosecuntur eiulantes. Exeuntibus illis de cenobio facta est tempestas maxima uidelicet de pluuia et uento ad declarandum uiri meritum, ita ut uix aliquis sufferre posset. Nec mirum fuit, si cerei ardentes qui circa beati uiri corpus erant appositi in tali tempestate fuissent extincti. Sequentes igitur sanctissimum corpus in huiusmodi tempestate ad fluuium usque uenerunt nomine hyla,[20] ubi sine dubio transire putabant. Sed cum illuc uenissent inuenerunt ipsum fluuium de se ipso tam magnum atque profundum, qui de siluaticis riuulis
90 ita creuisse ac superhabundasse,[21] ut si quis hunc transire uoluisset,

when that man of holy life realized this, he warned his closest followers that his summoning was at hand.

And so when the blessed father Erkenwald came by the design of God to Barking, he was seized by a serious illness which ended his earthly life. Knowing beforehand that the death of his body was close at hand, he called together his sons and gave them all instructions and wholesome guidance, commending them to God with his blessing; and thus in their arms he breathed forth his spirit. And as he passed from among them, a most marvellous fragrance and sweetest odor filled the cell where he lay, as if the whole house were drenched in perfume.

When the canons of London and the monks of Chertsey heard that the holy man of God had in truth departed from this world, they came hurriedly to Barking, so that they might remove the body. When the nuns realized that the visitors did truly intend to take the holy man's body away, they steadfastly objected, insisting that the most fitting thing must be to bury the holy corpse in the place where he had been both founder and father; for this reason they themselves wished to keep the body.

The Chertsey monks replied, on the contrary, "He has been our abbot in life, and he will be ours now that he is dead; and we have come here for the purpose of taking him away from here with us. We know he founded your church, but he founded our monastery earlier; and besides he gave us our rule and with God's will became our abbot thereafter."

But then the clerics and people of the city of London, growing impatient with this argument, suddenly broke in and answered both sides as follows: "You are quarreling in vain, because you are not going to have him and it would not be right if you did. Instead, if the custom established in ancient times is to be observed, he will have his tomb, God grant it, in the city where he was ordained prelate and appointed to that office by Rome."

While this was going on, the lay folk of London ran forward eagerly and, with divine consent, carried off with them the body of their bishop. And the monks and nuns, grieving that the dead man's corpse had been taken from them, followed after, weeping and wailing for the body of the blessed man. Just as they were leaving the convent there arose a great storm of wind and rain, as if to manifest the man's worth; and it was so violent that people could scarcely stand upright. Nor was it any wonder in such a tempest that the lighted candles which had been arranged around the blessed man's corpse were all blown out.

So in this storm they all followed behind the most holy body until they came to the River Hile. Here they were expecting to cross without any difficulty. But when they arrived they found that the river, which was wide and deep in any case, had risen and swollen so much with the waters of

nullo modo absque nauis adminiculo transire potuisset. Semita nusquam
ibi inueniebatur aliqua. Nauis etiam nulla uel pons ibi aderat, per quem
aliquis ultra ire posset.[22] Cumque monachi simul et sanctimoniales hoc
uidissent, exclamauerunt dicentes, "Eya, Eya, nunc apparet iniuria quam
nobis intulistis de sanctissimi uiri corpore." Dicunt etiam et sanctimoniales, "Vere per hanc nimiam aque inundationem demonstrat hic
dominus quo in loco ipse disposuerit ut requiescat uir iste tumulandus.
Quare uobis summopere curandum est, ut ab isto uestro proposito citis-
sime redeatis et corpus ad locum sibi |f. 137r| a deo destinatum refera-
100 tis, ne propter inportunitatem et concupiscentiam uestram deum
offendentes et incomparabile dampnum incurratis. Nam iccirco ad nos
illum adhuc in carne uiuentem atque *multis* nos *exhortationibus
spiritualiter*[23] corroborantem misit dominus deus, ut nos saltem post eius
transitum celeberimum atque sanctissimum eius corpus haberemus. Sed
uos quidem deum nil metuentes cum summa uiolentia loca nostra ueluti peruasores crudeliter introistis, et ut lupi famelici caulas gregum ir-
rumpentes querendo rapiendo, laniando quascunque inuenire possent,
inuentasque deuorando consumunt: et sic seuiendo et minitando nos
inuasistis, in super et basilicam nostram de tali ac tanto uiro exspolias-
110 tis. Quamobrem iudicet dominus deus omnipotens inter nos et uos."
    Audientes uero hoc ciues lundonie, responderunt e contra tali affamine,
"Diu quidem quod satis patienter opprobria et conuitia uestra sustinui-
mus, nichil uobis e contra obicientes. Sed unum pro certo habeatis, et
ne diutius credere differatis: quia nec uos ut supra diximus eum habebitis; nec nos unquam a proposito nostro alicuius metu flecti uidebitis,
neque dampnum aliquod inde nobis euenire gaudebitis. Adhuc autem
uolumus et uos scire nos non quasi lupos, sed sicut uiros fortes et stre-
nuos per medias acies bellatorum non segniter irrumpere, et uerum etiam
urbes munitissimas armis et gentibus debellare, subruere atque subuer-
120 tere, antequam dei seruum et patronum nostrum amittamus. Quia certe
per eum nos et omnis populus lundoniensis, cum omnibus suis prouin-
tialibus, insuper et ecclesia metropolitana[24] quam ipse iuste et sancte lon-
go rexit tempore, deo miserante ipsoque patrocinante, ab inimicorum
nostrorum insidiis presentibus scilicet et futuris credimus et confidimus
potenter nos eripi atque saluari |f. 137v|. Ideoque et nos ipsi uolumus
ut de tali patrono corroboretur et honoretur tam gloriosa ciuitas talisque
conuentus."
    Interea cum uniuersa multitudo tumultuaretur pro thesauro sacro sancti
corporis obtinendo, quidam uir[25] religiosus et eruditus in disciplinatu ip-

woodland tributaries that it was impossible for any one who wished to cross over to do so except by boat. There was not a fordable place to be found anywhere, nor was there either boat or bridge in sight, by which any one might be able to get to the other side.

When the monks and the nuns together realized this, they jeered at the Londoners and cried aloud, "Now is made manifest the wrong you have done us in taking the body of that holiest of men." And the nuns said also, "Truly, by sending this great flood the Lord is revealing the place which he himself has selected for Erkenwald's rest and burial. Therefore you had best decide to retreat in haste from your intention, and return the body to the place destined for it by God, lest by your insolence and greed you offend him and suffer some terrible harm. For the Lord God sent that man to us in the flesh, while he was still alive, to fortify us spiritually and to hearten us with the thought that we should at least have his most celebrated and holy body after his departing hence. But as for you, who fear God not at all, you have cruelly invaded our grounds with outrageous violence like bandits, just as famished wolves burst in upon the fold of a flock of sheep, pursuing, seizing, and mangling whatever sheep they can find, and then devouring and consuming them: even so, raging and full of threats, you rushed in among us, and then you robbed our church of this good and great man. Wherefore let almighty God be the judge between us and you."

When the townsfolk of London heard this, they countered with this reply: "We have borne with your insults and revilings patiently enough for a long time; nor have we hurled any back at you. But you may be certain of one thing, and you cannot ignore it any longer: as we said before, you will not have him, and you will never see us deflected from our purpose for fear of anyone, nor will you ever rejoice at any misfortune befalling us for having done so.

"Furthermore, we would have you know that we are not like wolves but rather we are like strong and vigorous men who will burst at full tilt through the midst of battle-lines of warriors, and even batter, undermine and overturn cities heavily fortified with men and weapons before we will give up the servant of God, our protector. For truly we, and all the people of London and of the province, and especially the church metropolitan which he governed with justice and holiness for a long time, we all strongly believe and trust that through him, with God's mercy and his protection, we will be rescued and delivered from the snares of our enemies now and in the future. Therefore, we ourselves intend that such a glorious city and congregation should be strengthened and honored by such a patron."

Just at this moment, while the whole crowd of people was in uproar and confusion over possession of the sacred treasure of the saint's body, a cer-

130 sius pontificis sancto spiritu plenus in eminentem locum ascendit, et hu-
iuscemodi sermonem facto silentio exorsus est. "Uoluntas uestra laudabilis
est ac omnipotenti deo acceptabilis; uidelicet, quod gubernatorem animarum uestrarum penes uos habere nitimini. Ceterum nimis a regula ueritatis exorbitatis, qui hoc sanctum opus[26] simultate ac odio aggredimi-
ni. Scriptum est enim quoniam caritas *legis est plenitudo;*[27] et *qui in uno*
offendit, id est in caritate, omnium reus est.[28] Si uos ergo estis discordes ac rixantes, quomodo deus *holocaustomata* precum *uestrarum*
suscipiet[29] cum ipsum offenderitis? Quippe, sicut sacra pagina testatur,
deus caritas est.[30] Quapropter *unitatem caritatis* unanimes seruate,[31] et
140 flexis genibus, creatorem uniuersitatis inplorate quatinus reuelare dig-
netur ubi reliquias sui preciosi confessoris nostrique patroni collocari
uelit." Huic exhortatorie predicationi omnes assensum uoluntarie ad-
hibuerunt. Clerus letaniam et psalmodiam gemebundus preciniuit; turba uero utriusque sexus pusilli ac maiores se in terram prostrauerunt;
et gemitibus ac lacrimis dei misericordiam implorauerunt, ut indicio
alicuius signi tantam litem et seditionem diuinitus dirimeret. Ut psalmista
perhibet, *prope est dominus omnibus inuocantibus eum in ueritate et deprecatio-*
nem eorum exaudiet.[32] Nam dum proni orationibus unanimiter insuda-
rent, unda fluminis se diuisit et uestigiis illorum siccum iter prebuit,[33]
150 uti quondam fluenta iordanis siccata sunt, cum filii israel terram promis-
sionis ingrederentur,[34] uel cum helias in carne in re|f. 138r|quiem in-
tronizandus siccis pedibus transmeauit.[35] Quod cum uidissent iubilantes
et deum glorificantes, eleuato feretro cum magna reuerentia et concor-
dia transieunt, et usque ad flumen quod nuncupatur stratford iter
fecerunt.[36]

Hic statuerunt paulisper pausare quoniam locus amenus erat, uiridi-
tate florigera uestitus, donec plebs aliquantisper precederet. En iterato
deus gloriosus in sanctis suis miraculum ostendit nequaquam pretereundum. Etenim dum nimbosa tempestas sopita esset et pluuiose nubes
160 rarescerent ac decrescerent ac solis radii rutilantes calorem generarent,
cerei circa libitinam celitus illuminati sunt.[37] Quesitum est ilico quis-
quamne ministerium ignis adhibuisset. Cum uero cognouissent diuina
potentia actum esse, multo magis tripudiantes et exultantes domini
maiestatem collaudauerunt et glorificauerunt, et consurgentes ad ciuita-

tain devout and learned man, who was in the retinue of the bishop, being filled with the Holy Spirit climbed up onto a higher piece of ground and when there was silence he began to address them as follows:

"What you desire is praiseworthy and acceptable to almighty God: namely, your striving to have among you the guide of your souls. But you stray too far from the path of truth when you approach this holy task with rivalry and hostility. For it is written, that the fullness of the law is love, and he who offends in one thing, that is, in love, is guilty in every way. For if you are contentious and quarrelsome, how might God, whom you will thus offend, accept the sacrificial offerings of your prayers? Truly, as holy writ bears witness, God is love. Therefore with one mind preserve the bond of love and beseech the creator of the universe, on bended knees, that he might deign to reveal where he wishes the remains of his precious confessor, our leader, to be laid to rest."

To the preacher's words and exhortation all gave their willing consent. The clergy solemnly intoned the Litany and Psalms, and as for the crowd of people, young and old of both sexes prostrated themselves on the ground and with groans and tears beseeched God's mercy, that he might put an end to this great strife and upheaval by means of divine revelation, by giving them a sign of some sort.

As the Psalmist declares, "in truth the Lord is near to all who call upon him, and he will hearken to their prayers." For while they lay prone on the ground, toiling with one mind at their prayers, the waters of the river divided and offered a dry pathway for their feet, just as once the waters of the Jordan were dried up when the children of Israel passed over into the land of promise; or when Elijah, just before he was taken up to his rest and a heavenly throne, while yet in the flesh, crossed over dryshod.

When they saw what had happened, they rejoiced and glorified God. Raising the litter with great reverence and in complete concord, they walked across and made their way to the river now known as Stratford.

Here they decided to pause for a while, for it was a pleasant place, garbed with greenery and flowers, to let the people go on ahead of them. And lo, a second time God who is glorious in his saints revealed a miracle which must not be passed over. For when the violence of the storm had subsided, and the rain clouds were growing thin and few, and the sun's shining rays warmed the air, the candles around the funeral couch were kindled by the power of heaven. At once inquiry was made as to whether anyone had tendered the flame. And when indeed they realized it was done by divine power, they were even more beside themselves with joy and exultation, praising and glorifying the majesty of the Lord; and so they rose up and bent their way towards the city of London.

tem lundoniensem tetenderunt. Cum autem didicissent qui erant in ciuitate aduentum sancti presulis, exierunt obuiam ei cum hymnis et canti-
cis inenarrabiliter colletantes, quod locus suus exequiis tam uenerandi
pastoris sublimatus sit. Quotquot autem gestatorium sancti uiri tetige-
runt, a quacumque infirmitate uexabantur liberati sunt, et cotidie ad tum-
170 bam eius sanitas egrotis recto corde petentibus exhibetur, prestante domino nostro ihesu christo; qui cum patre et spiritu sancto uiuit et regnat
deus per omnia secula seculorum amen.

Explicit uita sancti erkenwaldi episcopi et confessoris.

When the people who had remained in the city learned of the approach of the holy prelate, they went out to meet him singing hymns and canticles, unspeakably happy that their own city should have been honored with the burial rites of the sheperd who was so much revered. Moreover, however many people touched the funeral carriage of the holy man, they were delivered from whatever infirmity was afflicting them; and daily even now at his tomb health is restored to the sick, provided they ask him in purity of heart and our Lord Jesus Christ consents, who with the Father and the Holy Spirit lives and reigns, one God, ages without end, Amen.

Here ends the life of St. Erkenwald, bishop and confessor.

Appendix

THE STONYHURST LECTIONS

|Stonyhurst College Library, MS 52, f. 468v.|

lectio prima. Postquam beata sebba londoniensis episcopus migrauit ad dominum consensu regis sebba nomine et uniuerse plebis uir dei erken-waldus cathedra pontificali est sublimatus popularibus igitur pompis abrenunciatis quicquid sermone docebat operum exhibecione inplere curabat erat enim sapientia perfectus sermone modestus peruigil in ora-cionibus corpore castus lectioni deditus caritate radice plenus.

lectio secunda. Post igitur multa presentis uite certamina beatus uir er-kenwaldus artibus corporis cepit infirmari precepit feratrum caballorum preparari quo portaretur per uicos et ciuitates uerbum dei predicando
10 unde fertur per multa tempora hoc seruatum esse a discipulis atque plu-rimi qualicunque essent a dolore grauati mox de tacto ac de osculo eius ab infirmitate liberabantur. Verum etiam hastule ab eo abscise et ad egrotos allate cito eis salutem prestabant. Tu autem.

lectio tertia. Pereuenit itaque tempus quo talentum preciosum in domi-ni celestis sacrario conderetur et pii patris manipuli ad orreum dominicale reportarentur. Sciens itaque sui corporis dissolucionem ad presens fore conuocauit filios ecclesie eosque multis exhortacionibus spiritualiter at-que in dei famulatum fortiter ut starent exhortans sic inter manus caro-rum emisit spiritum. Tu autem domine.

Appendix

Lesson one. After the blessed [Cedd], bishop of London, departed to the Lord, with the consent of the king, who was named Sebba, and of the whole people, the man of God, Erkenwald, was elevated to the episcopal throne. He utterly avoided all public and worldly display, taking care to show forth in his works whatever he preached as doctrine. For he was perfect in wisdom, humble in speech, tireless in prayers and vigils, chaste in body, devoted to study, and the plant of charity was rooted deep within him.

Lesson two. After he had endured many of the contests of this present life, he began to grow infirm in his bodily members. So he ordered the construction of a horse-drawn litter to carry him from one village and town to the next, preaching the word of God. It is said of the litter that it was preserved for a long time by his followers, and that very many people, no matter what illness afflicted them, the moment they touched or kissed it, were delivered from their infirmity. Indeed even splinters broken off from it and taken to the sick would bring them speedy recovery. Thou [O Lord have mercy on us.]

Lesson three. In due course the time came for the precious ransom to be placed in its heavenly treasury and for the sheaves of the good father to be carried back to the storehouse of the Lord. And so, knowing that the death of his body was at hand, he called together the sons of the church, and urged and exhorted them to stand bravely steadfast in the spirit and in obedience to God, and thus in the arms of his dear ones he sent forth his spirit. Thou O Lord [have mercy on us.]

Miracula

Eloquentie uirtus quam sit in negotiis efficax non solum secularibus uerum etiam sacris, quibus fideles edocentur atque ortantur deum ue-rum agnoscere ipsumque pro uiribus mentis et corporis appetere, tam litterarum apicibus quam doctorum eruditionibus[1] multipliciter explana-tum est. Qua creatorem omnium atque rectorem, qui non *solum* in se uerum etiam *in sanctis* est |f. 33v| *mirabilis, predic*are atque *laud*are[2] oportet ut quanto gloriosior intelligatur eo uehementius ab uniuersis fideli-bus honoretur atque ametur.

Nobis itaque ad diuina sanctissimi presulis erkenwaldi opera mentis
10 aciem conuertentibus supraquam dici potest admirabile illud occurrit, quod non solum humane uite temptatio atque oppugnatio, que modo ab hominibus modo a demonibus modo etiam a carnalibus desideriis grauius consurgit,[3] hunc uirum uiuentem admirabilium perpetratione operum retrahere nequaquam preualuit; sed ne mors quidem defunc-tum retinere potuit quin ad dei laudem fideliumque salutem argumenta uiuentis anime certissima daret, precelseque uirtutis acta fidelibus populis demonstraret.

Quorum profecto miraculorum enarrationes nullius iam hominis memoria comprehendit. Fidelis etenim populus diuinorum operum in-
20 nouationem recognoscens ad gratiarum quidem actionem festinauit, sanc-tumque dei erkenwaldum quanto laudabiliorem frequentatione signorum perspexit, tanto tenatiori amore complecti curauit. Sed que audita et

The Miracles of St. Erkenwald

Eloquence is a powerful instrument for transacting the business of the world; but it is also effective in the sphere of religion, for instructing and exhorting the faithful to acknowledge the true God and to ask him for strength of mind and body. And this is clearly demonstrated in various ways, as much on the written page as in the spoken art of preachers. And so we should proclaim and praise with eloquence the creator and ruler of all things, who is wonderful not only in himself but also in his saints, so that the more glorious he is understood to be, the more passionately will he be honored and loved by all the faithful.

But when we direct our attention to the godly works of the most holy prelate Erkenwald, we find something that is wonderful beyond words: for not only did human life's temptations and assaults, arising from men, demons and, even worse, carnal desires, in no way at all prevent this man from the performance of admirable works while he was alive; but not even death could hold him back, even as a dead man, from giving the most certain proofs of the liveliness of his soul, to the glory of God and for the salvation of the faithful, and from showing forth acts of surpassing power to the faithful people.

Today not a single person can give a full account of these miracles. For the faithful folk, when they recognized that divine works were being renewed among them, hastened to give thanks and endeavored to embrace the holy man of God with a more steadfast love, the more praiseworthy they saw him to be because of the frequency of his miracles. But they fondly commit-

uisa dulciter memorie mandauerat, litteris ligare ne aufugerent, proh dolor, neglexit.[4] Irruens itaque mors et ipsos uirtutum diuinarum testes absorbuit et sanctitatis inditia quibus diuinus floruit pontifex ex magna parte deleuit.

Nos itaque, licet omnia uirtutum insignia quibus sanctissimus effulsit erkenwaldus nequaquam attingere ualeamus, cum sint hec plura quam humana possint comprehendi memoria, pauca de pluribus[5] ad gloriam
30   dei et honorem amici eius erkenwaldi successorum nostrorum prouec-tui modo producam in medium: quatinus omnes hec audientes, si quando anxietate mentis aut corporis laborauerint, ad beati piissimique pastoris erkenwaldi suffragia confugiant, neque iuste peticioni effectum defore optatum umquam diffidant. Hic enim est *sacerdos magnus*[6] cuius uolun-tati nichil prorsus abnegat deus. Nam psalmigrafo teste, *uoluntatem timen-tium se faciet; et deprecationem eorum exaudiet.*[7]

Sanctorum igitur patrum exemplum sequentes, posteris acta nostris temporibus propinamus, eandem successoribus solicitudinem exhibentes quam ipsi nobis paternis affectibus ministrarunt. Inuidia namque liuet
40   qui recitanda silet, ea maxime que celestia spirant sacramenta,[8] que deum mirabilem in sanctis predicant, que dei gratiam ultro se offeren-tem surdis hominum auribus intonauit.

Nos igitur fratres karissimi *magnalia dei*, et preconia sancti erkenwal |f. 34r|di negligenter *audire*[9] nequaquam debemus, ne *margarite ante porcos* misse atque ipsorum *pedibus conculc*ate[10] uideantur; sed de gestis exemplum etiam spirituale salutis nostre sumamus. Hoc etenim aposto-lus, in quo locutus est christus, sensit dum romanis ita scripsit: *Quecumque scripta sunt ad nostram doctrinam scripta sunt: ut per pacientiam et consolatio-nem scripturarum spem habeamus.*[11]

EXPLICIT PROEMIUM.

INCIPIVNT MIRACULA SANCTI ERKENWALDI, LVNDONIENSIS EPISCOPI

I   *Quomodo puer qui ad sancti erkenwaldi tumbam confugit lectionem eate-nus ignotam minaci magistro reddidit*

Fuit itaque in doctoris gentium[1] familia lundonie didasculus quidam, nomine elwinus,[2] moribus bonis insignis et artibus, qui inter cetera pie-

ted to memory the things they heard and saw, neglecting, alas, to bind them with letters to prevent their escape. And so death rushed in and swallowed up the very witnesses of his divine virtues, and erased in large part the traces of sanctity which had flourished in the godly bishop.

And so, although we cannot touch on all the evidences of the virtues with which the most holy Erkenwald shone, since they are more than can be comprehended in human memory, I will publish a few from the many, to the glory of God and to the honor of his friend, Erkenwald, and for the benefit of those who come after us: enough, that is, that all who hear them, whenever they are laboring in anguish of mind or body, might take refuge in the favor of the blessed and most pious shepherd Erkenwald, and need not ever fear that a just petition will fail of fulfillment.

For he is the great priest whose wish the Lord will not deny. For the psalmist bears witness that God will do the will of the fearful and he will hear their prayers.

Following, therefore, the example of the holy fathers, we are setting forth his acts for the generations after ours, showing the same solicitude for our successors as the fathers affectionately bestowed upon us. He must be green with envy indeed who keeps silent about things that should be uttered aloud, especially these acts which breathe abroad the heavenly sacraments, which preach the Lord wondrous in his saints, which thunder forth the grace of God offering itself to the deaf ears of men.

We therefore, dearest brothers, ought not negligently to hear the marvels of God and the praises of St. Erkenwald, lest pearls should seem to have been cast before swine and ground beneath their feet. Rather let us take from these acts a spiritual pattern of our salvation. For this the apostle meant, in whom Christ spoke, when he wrote thus to the Romans: "Whatever things are written are written for our instruction so that we might have hope through patience and the consolation of the scriptures."

End of Proem

HERE BEGIN THE MIRACLES OF SAINT ERKENWALD, BISHOP OF LONDON

Miracle 1 *How a boy, who took refuge from his angry schoolmaster at St. Erkenwald's tomb, recited the lesson he had not known until then.*

In the cathedral community of St. Paul's in London there was a certain schoolmaster, Elwin by name, a man noted for his morality and learning.

tatis opera puerorum disciplinis uigilantissimam impendere curam soli-
tus fuit; id nimirum studens ut cum post obitum in se bona exercere
opera non ualeret, in discipulis quos promouisset docere multosque ad
dei seruitium promouere non desisteret.[3]

Hic cum die quadam puero lectionem postero die reddendam iuxta
morem scolasticorum ostendisset,[4] penamque uerberum ipsi grauium si
reddere non posset etiam atque etiam intentasset,[5] ea que fecerat at dix-
10 erat puero sufficere posse credens, ad alia se conuertit negotia que necessitas monstrabat non esse differenda.[6]

Puer autem, etatis tenere lubrico[7] et coetaneorum ludo seductus, tam
didascalice comminationis quam proprie lectionis est oblitus. Sequenti
autem die cum reddendi tempus instaret, formidoque pre oculis ex ig-
norantia lectionis occursaret puerili memorie, quid faceret nichil tutum
inuenit, qui nec leccionem reddere neque ire magistri reperire valebat
remedium. Post multas ergo cordis anxietates incidit in animum pueri
ut fuga penam uel alicuius precibus deuitaret ac euaderet uel saltem in
aliud tempus, dum indignacio magistri deferueret, cruciatum differet.[8]
20 Circumspiciens igitur si quis adesset qui eum fugientem magistro pro-
dere uellet, cum tutum oppinaretur diffugium, concito surrexit, aufugit,
et ad ecclesiam in qua sancti erkenwaldi requiescit corpus peruenit, ibique
prostratus iuxta sanctum erkenwaldum iacebat.

Quibus uerbis oraret qualibusque affectibus liberationem impetraret,
non est humane cogitationi proditum; neque pro certo est affirmandum
quod auctore ueraci nequiuimus demonstrare tunc fuisse gestum. Credendum tamen est cor contritum et humiliatum deo fuisse placitum in puero,
quem preclaro constat liberatum extitisse miraculo.

Pretaxatus quippe magister more solito scolas[9] ingrediens puerumque
30 non inueniens, ut eum fugisse persensit, modo suas oppiniones secutus
deuenit ad locum quo puer iacebat suppliciter orans ad sanctum. Ira
igitur instigante puerum apprehendit, illumque ad scolas puniendum ue-
lociter ducere |f. 34v| proposuit. Puer autem doctorem sequi timens sanc-
toque monumento adherere cupiens, pallam piissimo pontifici super-
positam[10] utraque manu quantis potuit uiribus arripuit, tenuit, et ne
abduci posset pertinacissime laborauit.

Among other works of piety, he was wont to devote the utmost care and vigilance to the education of boys, being truly desirous that after his death, when he was no longer able to do good works himself, he would not cease, in the person of the disciples he had educated, to go on teaching and training many others for the service of God.

One day he had expounded to one of his pupils, in the usual grammar-school fashion, a passage that the boy was to recite the following day, and he threatened him repeatedly with a severe flogging if he should not be able to recite it. Believing the boy to be capable of fulfilling the task he had assigned him, the master then turned to other pressing business that he could no longer put off.

The boy, on the other hand, who was at that tender, undisciplined age, was seduced by his peers into playing games, and forgot both his teacher's warning and his own lesson. On the following day, when the time for the recitation was at hand, fears of what lay in store for him, for not knowing the lesson, thronged into the boy's mind. But he could not think of any way of saving the situation since he was incapable either of reciting the lesson or of devising a means to avert the schoolmaster's ire. After much fretting and anguishing it occurred to the boy that he might avoid and escape punishment by fleeing or by praying to a special person, or at least that he might put off his expected torment long enough for the master's wrath to have cooled. Looking around therefore to see if anyone was about who might wish to betray his flight to the master, and considering it safe to make his escape, he quickly got up and fled away and came to the church in which rested the body of St. Erkenwald, and there he prostrated himself at St. Erkenwald's side.

It has not been revealed to human understanding what the boy said as he prayed, or what he felt as he begged for deliverance; and we must not say for certain that something we cannot demonstrate from a reliable source actually did take place. We must believe, however, that the contrite, humbled heart of the boy was pleasing to God, and it is generally thought that he was delivered by a splendid miracle.

Well, the master whom we mentioned earlier went into the school as usual, and when he did not find the boy there, realizing that he had run away, he acted on intuition and came straight to the place where the boy was lying in humble prayer to the saint. There the master flew into a rage and seized his student with the intention of marching him back to the school for speedy punishment. But the boy, fearing to follow the teacher and desiring rather to stay close to the holy monument, seized the cloth which covered the most holy bishop and, holding onto it with all the strength he could muster, strove with the utmost stubbornness to resist being taken away.

Sed quid puer contra uirum, quid timidus contra animosum ualeret?
Separatis igitur discipuli manibus a palla pontificis extrahitur puer ab
ecclesia. Statuitur in scolis sub preceptoris commoti censura;[11] de liber-
40   atione aut euasione iam nulla restat fidutia.

Interim magistro de animaduersione facienda offirmato placuit puerum reddentem audire, quatinus ex iusta ratione quociens eum deficien-
tem in lectione deprehenderet, tociens ei uerbera ingeminaret. O nunc
infelicem puerum, nisi citius habeat liberatorem clementissumum erkenwaldum. At miro modo, cum sancto multa liberationis genera suppeterent
hunc liberandi delegit modum, qui et pueri studio et magistri proposito
plurimum congruebat.

Precibus itaque et meritis preclari doctoris erkenwaldi affuit puero
sapientia, que *apperit os mutum et linguas infantium facit disertas*,[12] affuit,
50   inquam, ac diuinitus eum edocuit quod a nullo magistrorum[13] ante au-
diuit. Cum enim lectionem puer sine libro proferre cogeretur, non solum quod magister eius tradiderat absque obstaculo atque adminiculo
reddidit, uerum etiam illud quod preceptor eius traditurus fuerat, ob-
stupescente magistro, memoriter diuque recitauit.

Tunc uero didasculus, tandem ad cor reuersus,[14] iram remisit
ueniamque fuge puero concessit, atque se ipsum, quod sancto puerum
subduxit neque honorem tanto patrono dignum exhibuit, grauiter
condempnauit. Penitentis etenim uoto, rebus distractis pauperibusque dis-
persis, uoluntario se statim exilio tradidit neque in patria post modum
60   comparuit.

Si igitur tenere etatis puer iram sui doctoris sapienter preuidit, effugit,
meritisque sancti erkenwaldi declinauit, ut quid nos etatis prouecte, iam
iamque finiende,[15] uenturi iudicis sententiam incommutabilem non ex-
pauescimus, nec pietatis operibus sanctorumque intercessionibus uin-
dicis animum placare contendimus? Et si puer, salubri usus consilio, non
solum sancti meritis a pena est absolutus, uerum etiam scientia quam
magister non docuit ad laudem dei eruditus, cur nos proximis nostris
salutaria monita pro uiribus non inculcamus, neque sanctorum prophetarum atque apostolorum exhortationibus ad exorandam dei misericordi-
70   am, ipsisque ad dei noticiam in |f. 35r| inuestigandam omni uirtutis
studio[16] non conuolamus?

But what can a boy do against a man, or the fearful against the furious? Pulling the schoolboy's hands from the bishop's pall, the teacher dragged him out of the church and made him stand in the school to suffer his angry judgment. Of deliverance or escape he now had no hope.

Meanwhile it pleased the schoolmaster, who was resolved on administering punishment, to hear the boy recite to him; he intended that as often as he found him making an error in his lesson he would give him two stripes with the rod, a proportion he considered fitting in this case. O what an unhappy boy he will be now if Erkenwald does not speedily become his most compassionate deliverer! But in wondrous fashion, although many kinds of deliverance were at the saint's disposal, he chose to effect the rescue in a way that was appropriate both to the boy's course of study and to the master's assignment.

For by the prayers and merits of Erkenwald, himself a wonderful teacher, wisdom was suddenly with the boy, she who opens the mouths of the dumb and makes eloquent the tongues of children; she, I say, was with him and taught him by divine grace things he had heard from none of the masters before. For when the boy was forced to recite the lesson without looking at his book, not only did he repeat, without stumbling and without assistance, what the master had assigned, but also, to the latter's amazement, he recited at length and completely from memory what the teacher had been about to give him for the next assignment!

Then indeed the schoolmaster came to his senses and put away his anger and forgave the boy for having run away. As for himself, because he had plucked the boy away from the saint and not shown proper respect for his great patron, he severely condemned himself. He took a vow of penance, divided up his effects and distributed them to the poor, and went immediately of his own free will into exile, nor did he appear in his own country again after that.

If therefore a boy of a tender age foresaw, fled from, and then, by the merits of St. Erkenwald, turned aside the anger of his teacher, ought not we, of advanced age and virtually at our inevitable end, to shudder at the thought of the incommutable sentence of the judge when he comes, and ought we not to strive to placate the anger of the avenger by works of piety and by the intercessions of the saints? And if the boy, by resorting to wholesome counsel, was not only absolved by the saint's merits from punishment, but also was imbued, to the glory of God, with a knowledge which the master had not taught him, why do we not flock together to pray for the mercy of God, as exhorted by the holy prophets and apostles, and, as they exhorted us likewise, strive for the knowledge of God with all the zeal for virtue we can muster?

Si doctor predictus se ipsum exilio dignum iudicauit, eo quod puerum puniendi studio reuerentiam sancto dei dignam non exhibuit, qua pena dignos censere debemus qui, nec dei beneficiis inuitati nec penas seculi presentis uel futuri perterriti, *preuaricatione legis*[17] diuine delicta delictis, peccata peccatis in dies miseri cumulamus?[18]

At nunc, fratres karissimi, incommune deum nostrum omnes exorare studeamus, quatinus ipse, qui nichil odit eorum que fecit, sancti erkenwaldi obtectu, nos a commissis omnibus absolutos et sanctorum consi-
80   lio adherere et beatificam dei presentiam attingere concedat.

II   *De quodam ob temeratam sancti festiuitatem repentina morte multato*[1]

Illud quoque quis fidelium audiat et non expauescat, quod per excellentissimi pontificis erkenwaldi prerogatiuam[2] credendum est accidisse cuidam homini, non minus iustitia quam rerum inopia laboranti, qui sicut uite ita et fame fuit obscure usque quo in se iram dei eiusque amici erkenwaldi contumelia graui prouocauit, ac morte terribili omnibus beati presulis parrochianis innotuit.

Gloriosi enim pontificis solennitate appropinquante, iuxta morem ecclesie denuntiatum est[3] uniuersis in territorio degentibus ut, secularibus studiis intermissis, in die quem sanctissimi patris ad paradisum
10   transitus insigniuit ad ecclesiam christi conuenirent, suisque precibus ac tanti patroni erkenwaldi meritis tam corpori quam anime necessaria obtinere laborarent.

Cum ergo dies optatus, dies letie spiritualis, dies non minus angelis quam hominibus uenerandus adesset, conati sunt quisque pro uiribus ciues ciuibus, uestimentorum ornatu ac morum, ostendere quanta deuotione studebant beati pontificis honorificentie curam impendere. Uniuersi nimirum populi sexus, etas, et conditio tanta gestiuit exultatione ut quisquis alienus superueniret, studiumque religionis in clero ac populo animaduerteret, celestis ierusalem conuersationem, ubi spiritus beati sem-
20   piterno fruuntur gaudio, ad memoriam reuocaret, nisi maligni spiritus instinctu tabesceret.

If this same teacher judged himself worthy of exile because in his desire to punish the boy he did not show a worthy reverence for God's saint, of what punishment ought we to judge ourselves worthy, we who are neither seduced by God's goodness nor terrified by the thought of punishment in the present or the future life, and who in our misery heap delight upon delight and sin upon sin in transgression of divine law day after day?

But now, dearest brothers, let us all together earnestly pray to our God that he who hates nothing that he has made will, with St. Erkenwald's protection, absolve us of our sins and allow us to hold fast to the counsel of the saints and to attain to the blessed presence of the Lord.

Miracle 2   *Concerning a man punished with sudden death for scorning the feast day of the Saint*

Let each of the faithful hear but not be disturbed at what we must believe happened, through the power of the most excellent bishop Erkenwald, to a certain man who was ground under no less by justice than by poverty, and whose mode of life was as wretched as his fame was obscure until by his gravely insulting behavior he provoked the ire of God and of God's friend, Erkenwald, and by his terrible death became famous among the parishioners of the blessed prelate.

For once, when the feast day of the glorious bishop was approaching, according to the church's custom the proclamation went out that all the people living in the diocese should refrain from secular pursuits on the day which the most holy father had honored with his passing into paradise, and that they should come together in Christ's church and in that day they should labor for the necessities of body and soul by means of their own prayers and the merits of their great patron.

When therefore the wished-for day arrived, the day for paying the levy of the spirit, the day which angels no less than men revere, the townsfolk, each one according to his means, strove to show to one another, by their fine clothes and best behavior, with what great devotion they were taking pains to honor the blessed bishop. Indeed, people of both sexes and of all ages and conditions throughout the whole town were moved to such a great pitch of exaltation that a foreigner who came and witnessed the religious zeal in clergy and people alike would have been reminded of the way of life of the heavenly Jerusalem, where the blessed spirits enjoy everlasting delight, if the occasion had not been spoiled at the instigation of a wicked spirit.

Enim eius quippe deuotissime ciuitatis celebritate quidam ignobilis, cuius supra mentionem succinctam fecimus, deo ac magistris ecclesie in-obediens extitit, cetibusque fidelium segregatus, seruili operi[4] intentus. Non solum indicte festiuitatis religionem preuaricari presumpsit, uerum etiam, cum impietatis argueretur, quod nequaquam deo sanctoque ip-sius erkenwaldo condignam exiberet gloriam, uesanus, peccatis peccata coaceruans, in prestantissimi pontificis contemptum erupit.

Cum enim sacrorum ministrorum unus, quadamne necessitate coac-
30 tus, ab ecclesie fuisset egressus, ecce, impius ille de quo dictum est, graui fasce onustus, occurrit obuius et, iuxta mo|f. 35v|nasterii parietem ex-oneratus, cepit resistere uacuus, quid quisque loqueretur de irreligiosi-tate ipsius nequaquam sollicitus. Nam diuitias quas solas optauerat quoniam quidem laboribus suis assequi non ualebat, famam bonam om-nino neglexerat.[5]

At minister qui fuerat ecclesia egressus, ut uidit hominem publico scan-dalo propalatum, proprium negotium intermisit uerbisque admonitio-nis pie ad impium loqui cepit. "Quis," inquit, "es tu, homo miserande, qui dei misericordiam et sancti erkenwaldi plus aliis indiges, et adoran-
40 dum deum dilectumque ipsius erkenwaldum, aliis festinantibus, tu so-lus non accedis? Quotiens enim dei uicarius[6] festum omnipotentis dei et sanctorum ipsius denuntiat et contempnitur, indignissima deo iniur-ia exoritur, sicut ipsa ueritas testatur dicens, 'Qui uos audit me audit; et qui uos spernit me spernit. Qui autem me spernit, spernit eum qui me mis-it.'[7] Porro cunctis in diocesi sancti erkenwaldi indicta est hodie celebri-tas per ministros dei sacerdotes[8] pro necessitatibus nequaquam ipsius sancti, sed populi. Iam enim sanctus cum deo regnat; nichil nostri nisi salutem exoptat. Huic autem tanta est fidutia committenda, ut nemini de beneficiis eius impetrandis ambigendum sit, nisi ei qui iniusta
50 petiuerit.

"Huic profecto assertioni fidem faciunt mirabilia opera que ipsius ui-tam commitata sunt, et nichilominus signa diuinitus monstrata que obi-tum ipsius mox et post modum subsecuta sunt;[9] quorum numerum aut explanationem euoluere nequaquam hominis exhortantis sed hystori-am scribentis est.[10] Quis enim enumerare queat quotiens deus per preces et merita sancti erkenwaldi cecis uisum, surdis auditum, mutis loquendi usum, claudis gressum, et, ut breui plura comprehendam,

For amid the celebration that this most devout city was carrying on the wretched man, whom we have briefly mentioned above, disobeyed God and the masters of the church and kept himself apart from the crowds of the faithful, being intent on his lowly work. Not only did he presume to violate the order of the festival as it had been proclaimed, but also, when he was accused of impiety for refusing to acknowledge the honor and glory of God and St. Erkenwald, he burst forth like a madman into open contempt for the most excellent bishop Erkenwald, heaping sin upon sin.

One of the holy ministers had left the church on some necessary business, when, lo, that wicked man of whom we speak encountered him as he was hurrying along bearing a heavy bundle of timbers. Then, throwing down his burden against the wall of the minster, the vain man began to oppose him, quite heedless of what anyone said about his irreligious behavior. For having been unable, by his own efforts, to amass the riches he desired more than anything else, he had utterly ceased to care about his good name.

Now the minister who had left the church, upon seeing the scandalous spectacle the man was making of himself, interrupted his own business and began to speak to the impious one with words of pious admonition, saying, "Who are you, wretched man? You need the mercy of God and St. Erkenwald more than the others, and yet you alone, while all the others are celebrating the festival, do not draw near to adore God and his beloved Erkenwald. For as often as the pope proclaims the festival of God and his saints and it is scorned, then God is most disgracefully insulted. Just as truth itself bears witness, saying, 'Whoever hears you, hears me also, and he who spurns you, spurns me. And he who spurns me, spurns him that sent me.' Moreover, the priests serving God in the diocese of St. Erkenwald have decreed that his feast day be observed by all who live here, not because the saint himself is in any need of it, but rather for the good of his people. For the saint already reigns with God; he asks for nothing from us except our salvation. And yet such power is granted him that no one who asks him for favors need doubt of his granting them, except someone who asks for unlawful things.

"We make this assertion with confidence on account of the many miraculous works which accompanied his life, and likewise on account of wonders revealed by divine grace which followed close upon and somewhat after his passing. Nor is it any man's place to encourage either an investigation into the number of the miracles or an attempt at explaining them away; rather it is our duty to write out the history of them, nothing more. For who can count how many times God, through the prayers and merits of St. Erkenwald, has granted sight to the blind, hearing to the deaf, to the dumb the power of speech, to the crippled the power to walk, and, to sum up all in

uniuersis hominum morbis medelam pie petitus reddidit? Quod corporis morituri commodis tam beniuolus tam prestabilis fuerit, quis anime
60   utilitatem semper uicture eum cuique negasse putauerit?
    "Resipisce igitur, miser, resipisce! Penitentiam age! ad misericordis dei
clementiam, ad ecclesiam curre! Patronum in causa tua dei amicum erkenwaldum aduoca. Nam licet peccando sanctum iniuriaueris, toto corde conuersus eum tibi mox propitium feceris. Uerum tamen quicum que
post transgressionem nequaquam fuerit conuersus, profecto non erit diu
inpunitus."
    Hec autem et his similia pius ad impium, canonicus[11] ad prophanum,
est exhortando locutus. Sed uesanus ille furibundo silentio conuitiorum
ac contumeliarum uenenum preparans, tandem in doctorem suum indi-
70   gna coaceruauit, et in contemptum sancti erkenwaldi plura eructans,
ad canonicum sic est ex|f. 36r|orsus.[12] "Magna otia clericis qui, suis
negotiis omissis, aliena curent. Vobis, certe, uobis uacat cotidie feriari,
quibus contigit otio dissolui, et alieno cibo nutriri. Secure potestis die
noctuque cantare, quos nulla necessitas cogit laborare. Vestra vita magis inter ludicra quam inter negotia est computanda. Si quis esset qui
gratis me uellet cotidie pascere atque uestire, peream nisi ei contenderem
seu uellet alta seu uellet humili uoce cantare.
    "Quotiens ex nostris laboribus precium cibi ac potus abundantius ad-
quirere ualemus, tunc saltationibus, tunc uociferationibus diem festum
80   in conuiuio agimus. Si nostris gaudiis interesse uelletis, uestras solenni-
tates et uociferationes parui faceretis. Nos quidem utiles uicissim exerce-
mus labores, uicissim uero iocundis uocibus et leticie usibus opera damus.
Vos autem clerici semper inutiles et clamosi uitam nostram contempni-
tis; opera nostra, quia uestris sunt dissimilia, superbe condempnatis. Quin
etiam in patrocinium uestre pigritie erkenwaldum nescio quem producitis,[13] et uite mee sustentamentum per eius auctoritatem mihi adimere
temptatis. Uult me erkenwaldus pascere, si eius gratia questum meum
incipiam omittere? Ridiculus essem, si ego, deserto officio, uictum a uestro patrono expectarem. Ite, igitur, et uestras ferias uestrasque cantile-
90   nas cum erkenwaldo uestro sine inuidia uobis habetote, et opus uirorum
fortium, ignaui, nobis relinquite. Qui mihi persuadere poterit ut, neglecta
operatione, occupatus uestra existam religione, ipse mihi persuadere hoc
simul ualebit ut uiuere queam absque ciborum perceptione."
    Dum uero impius ille in hunc modum plura eructare feditatis uerba

one word, healing to all sick men when they have asked him in holy wise? And since he has been so grandly benevolent towards the needs of this mortal body, who could think that he would deny to anyone what is good for the immortal soul?

"Come to your senses, therefore, wretched man! Recover yourself, repent, run to the clemency of merciful God, run to the church. Enlist Erkenwald, our patron, the friend of God, as advocate in your case. For although you have insulted the saint with your sin, if you turn to him with your whole heart, you will soon make him kindly towards you. But if anyone after transgressing does not repent at all, he will not long remain unpunished."

With such words then, and more in similar vein, did the holy man, the canon, exhort the impious and heathen layman. But the madman in silent rage was all the time preparing his poisonous brew of revilings and insults, and finally he gathered up all his reproaches against his teacher and belched forth a heap of abuse in despite of St. Erkenwald. This is what he said to the canon: "You clerics have so much time on your hands that you neglect your own business and meddle with what doesn't concern you. You people, honestly, you're free to keep every day as a holiday, and you get to grow soft with idleness and to eat other folks' food. You can sing without care both day and night, for no necessity compels you to work. Your life should be thought of as more a game or stage play than a real occupation. If someone would feed me every day for free, and clothe me, damn me if I wouldn't strain myself for him, no matter if he wanted me to sing high or low.

"Whenever we manage to make enough money from our work for food and a bit more to drink, then we spend our feast day having a good time, dancing and shouting. If you were to take an interest in our type of enjoyment, you would come to think very poorly of your own solemnities and clamorings. For one thing, the jobs we work at are useful, and for another, we do them with cheerful voices, and for the sake of happiness. But you clerics, with your everlasting useless dirges, you despise the life we lead, and because our type of work is not like yours, you proudly condemn it. And then you bring in some Erkenwald or other to defend your idleness, and by his authority you try to deprive me of what sustains my life. Will Erkenwald feed me if I begin to lose my income on his account? I would be a laughing stock if I gave up my job and expected to be fed by your patron. So go on then, and keep your festivals and your old songs and your Erkenwald to yourselves, and leave off envying us, drones that you are, and let us get on with the work that strong men have to do. Whoever could persuade me to busy myself with your religion and to neglect my work, could also persuade me that I can live without eating."

While this impious man was trying to utter more words of vileness in this

temptaret, increpatus a dei ministro, iussus est tacere, ne iusticia dei sine dilatione inciperet peccatorem secundum merita multare. Sed ipse, quasi esset fugatus, sic profecto sub omni celeritate, onere subleuato quod contra sepulcrum sancti erkenwaldi extra monasterium deposuerat, sic, inquam, est auersus, sic in uiam amens est progressus. Dumque festinaret hoc
100 seculis est proditum[14] atque probatum quod homo ille perditus ad caput mortui semisepultum offendens, in proprium caput est prolapsus et suimet ruina conquassatus et extinctus.

Ut autem ea que facta fuerant populi auribus fama diffudit, mox ab omnibus, a plateis, a uicis, mox etiam sacris locis, innumerabilis hominum cetus est egressus et circa mortui cadauer stans stupefactus. Post interuallum, recepta mente, ordinem rerum que contigerant diligentius est perscrutatus. Cognouit itaque populus hominem infelicem, per inobedientiam et uerborum petulantiam, summi iudicis sententia mortem incurrisse subitaneam, dum in sanctos dei contumeliam grauem di-
110 uulgaret.

His igitur acceptis, quidam qui affuerunt, humanam infirmitatem et ignorantiam attendentes, querimoniam lugubrem ediderunt; quidam uero, iusticie dei fauentes et sancti erkenwaldi reuerentie astantium alios inclinare uolentes, merito ac condigne omni peccatori penam obtigisse grauissimam confirmauerunt, et summam reuerentiam deo sanctoque ipsius erkenwaldo exhibendam in perpetuum statuerunt. Iste autem miserrimus, sed nulli iure miserandus, qui uniuersorum domino extitit inimicus. Non est contentus ut sancti dei festum pollueret, sed peccatis peccata, minoribus maiora, impius addidit, qui adusque peccator in
120 profundum malorum ueniens contempsit. Pium monitorem, de conuersione et emendatione sapienter agentem, uesanus irrisit. Ministros altissimi dei proprios clericos spreuit, et bachantibus in conuiuiis post posuit. Postremo linguam magniloquam, linguam mortiferam, aduersus sanctum erkenwaldum extulit, sed deus uindictam non diu distulit.

Nos itaque, fratres karissimi, fidelium monitis animati, peccatorumque penis a peccatis absteriti, amicum dei erkenwaldum humiliter deprecemur, ut sua intercessione nobis transgressionum ueniam obtineat, quo nostro domino reconciliati cum eo regnare ualeamus, cuius regnum perdurat ultra omne quod extat.

manner, he was loudly rebuked and told to be silent by the minister of God, lest divine justice should punish the sinner without delay as he deserved. But he, suddenly, like one hunted, in great haste picked up his bundle, which he had put down by the tomb of St. Erkenwald outside the minster, and thus, I say, he turned and went off on his way, quite beside himself. And, as has been well known and affirmed for generations, as he was hurrying along, this desperate man stumbled over the half-buried skull of a dead man, and pitching forward he fell on his own head, and struck it with such force that he was killed.

News of what had happened reached the ears of the people, and soon from everywhere, from every street and neighborhood, and even from the religious houses, an innumerable crowd of people had gathered together and stood stupified around the body of the dead man. After a while, when their shock had subsided, they began to inquire more thoroughly into the sequence of events that had taken place. And thus the people realized that that unhappy man had met his sudden end by the sentence of the highest judge, because of his disobedience and the impudence of his words as he published abroad his outrageous abuse of God's saints.

After everything had been explained, several who were there were very sad and were inclined to question what had happened and to complain about it, pointing out that men are by nature weak and ignorant. Others, on the other hand, who delighted in God's justice in the matter and wished to incline other bystanders to reverence St. Erkenwald, affirmed that the weightiest penalty that befell any sinner was both deserved and fitting, and they concluded that the utmost reverence be shown henceforth and at all times to God and to Erkenwald, his saint. For that man, wretched as was his fate, should on no account be pitied or mourned, for he was the enemy of the lord of all. Not content with polluting the festival of God's saint, in his impiety he added greater to lesser sins and pursued his wicked contempt to the very depth of evil. In his madness he laughed at him who, acting according to wisdom, warned him to turn and make amends. He scorned the clergy dedicated to the service of the most high God and despised them in favor of his drunken feasting. Finally he raised his boastful voice, his fatal voice, against St. Erkenwald, and God did not delay his vengeance for very long.

Therefore, dearest brothers, having been inspired by the counsels of the faithful, and made fearful of sinning by witnessing the punishment of sinners, let us humbly pray to Erkenwald, the friend of God, that he by his intercession obtain forgiveness for us for our transgressions, and that, having been reconciled by him with our lord, we might be worthy to reign with him whose realm will endure beyond everything that now is.

III   *De uincto soluto*

Quodam igitur tempore, cum in sancti erkenwaldi solennitate[1] eramentorum sonitu, quo christianorum cetus uocari solet, uniuersa ciuitas quasi tonitru inciperet concitari, captiuus quidam quantum potuit compeditus illuc festinauit, templumque dei quo festiuitas sancti colebatur ingressus, in hunc modum est exorsus.

"Deus, quem nemo petit in uanum nisi uanus, uanitatem meam tua ueritate euacua. Deus illuminator mentium me tua pietate illumina, ut norim quod expediat orare, ut possim tibi placita postulare atque impetrare. Multa sunt, domine, que uidentur mihi necessaria, sed nichil
10 uolo petere, nichil etiam optare, nisi que tibi sint beneplacita.

"Benedicta sit, domine, tua iusticia que me coniecit in corporis uincula, quia per hec sum recordatus quam fortiter ligata sit anima mea. Si adhuc liber essem corpore, libertatem fortassis neglexissem anime mee. O beatifica uincula quam nunc mihi estis iocunda, per uos enim mihi uia salutis est ostensa. O deus, quis enumeret miserationum tuarum modos et multitudinem, qui cum uideris irasci benignissime misereris, qui uerberans et plagas inferens perpetuam sanitatem procuras?

"Ecce me, domine, presto sum tolerare quicquid mihi disponis irrogare. Nunc tandem sentio summe bonum esse quicquid procedit a tua boni-
20 tate. O utinam domine obtinere a tua misericordia ualeam ut temporaliter puniar, et eternaliter absolutus inueniar. Sed tamen si ui|f. 37r|des domine ad utilitatem ecclesie tue, ad honorem etiam sancti erkenwaldi, qui tam deuotus predicator extitit omnipotentie tue,[2] absolutionem meam et liberationem meam pertinere, corporis mei uincula rumpe, et anime mee absolutionis fidutiam impende. Sperabunt uehementius de tua misericordia ceteri, cum me reum, me uinculis strictum, tam celeriter, tam mirabiliter uiderint absolui, diuinitusque liberari.

"Quis etiam a tuis cessabit laudibus, cum te uniuersorum deum ac dominum curam prospexerit impendere miseris et abiectissimis hominibus?
30 His adde, gloriosissime domine, quod si absolutus fuero nequaquam mee importunitati, sed honori ac dignitati beati pontificis erkenwaldi ascribetur. Concede igitur, si concessurus es, liberationem meam sancto tuo erkenwaldo et hoc quo signo qualiter carus est tibi ostende populo tuo."

Miracle 3 *Concerning the prisoner who was set free*

Once, at the celebration of St. Erkenwald's feast day, the whole city as in a thunderstorm was rumbling and shaking with the sound of the bronze bells, with which it is the custom to summon the congregation of the faithful. On this occasion a certain prisoner hastened thither as best he could in his fetters, and making his way into the temple of God where the festival was being held, he began to speak as follows:

"O God, whom no one petitions in vain unless he be vain and false himself, cleanse away my falsehood with your truth. O God, the light of men's minds, enlighten me with your goodness that I might know what I should best pray for, and that I might ask and plead for things pleasing to you. There are many things, O Lord, which are needful for me, but I do not wish to ask or beg for anything except what is pleasing to you.

"Blessed be your justice, O Lord, which cast me into the chains of the body, because by these chains I am reminded how strongly my soul is bound. If I were still free in body, perhaps I would be paying no heed to the freedom of my soul. O blessed chains, what a joy you are to me now! For through you the road to salvation has been shown to me. O God, who may explain the ways of your mercies, or enumerate them? For when you seem to be angry you are actually most kind and most merciful, since by the strokes of your rod and the plagues you inflict upon men, you procure perpetual health for them.

"Behold me Lord, who am ready to bear whatever you decide to impose upon me. For now at last I feel that whatever proceeds from your goodness is the greatest good. O would that I might, of your mercy, be granted temporal punishment here and find myself hereafter absolved eternally. But if you consider, Lord, that to absolve me and set me free will benefit your church and bring honor to St. Erkenwald also, who preached your omnipotence with such devotion, then burst the chains of my body and assure me of the deliverance of my soul. The rest of the people here will the more ardently hope for your mercy when they have seen me, a guilty man bound with chains, so speedily and marvellously forgiven, and divinely delivered.

"Who will then cease from praising you when he has seen the God and the Lord of all things bestowing his care on wretched and abandoned men? And, moreover, O most glorious God, if I am set free, it will by no means be ascribed to my importunings, but rather to the honor and dignity of the blessed bishop Erkenwald. If you will therefore grant it, grant my deliverance to your St. Erkenwald, and show your people by this token how dear he is to you."

Dum hec et his similia effudisset captiuus coram domino, astante sacrorum ministrorum choro, audiente atque intuente uniuerso populo, intrantibus eius custodibus et hominem arripere destinantibus, fragore maximo rupta sunt uincula captiuique orantis, cum admiratione cunctorum qui astabant, dissoluta sunt crura.

40   Ut uero rumor uiri peruenit ad episcopum,[3] uerba de miraculo fecit ad populum, et quem sanctus erkenwaldus dignatus est absoluere, prohibuit cunctis predictum hominem custodia ulterius iniuriare. Quanta uero tunc secuta est populi exultatio, quantaque in deum et eius dilectum erkenwaldum prodita est laudatio, nullius eloquium edere, nullius ingenium ualet excogitare.

    Rogitemus autem, fratres dilectissimi, quatenus possibile est, quam magna multitudo dulcedinis dei quam abscondit timentibus se, qui nichil facit homini in hoc tempore, quod est tempus misericordie, nisi quid homini proficit, siue bonum siue malum uideatur. Dum flagellis[4] expur-
50 gatur homo aut probatur, dum beneficiis ad regnum perhenne inuitatur. Sic enim medicine peritus nunc suaui nunc insuaui egros curat remedio, ita in mirum omnipotentis dei sapientia, modo prospera, modo aduersa, perpetue sanitatis prospectu hominibus ineffabiliter dispensat. Vices etiam prosperitatis et aduersitatis tam mirifice commutat, ut misericordia eius et iusticia in ipsa commutatione laudentur, et sancti eius, ad auxilium inuocati ut tristibus amotis leta succedant, pro impetratione uotorum glorificentur.

    Quod in hoc miraculo patuit, quando sanctus erkenwaldus captiuum absoluit. Ligauerat enim deus peccatorem ut ligamina interiora cog-
60 nosceret, et inuocato dei amico erkenwaldo absoluit orantem conuersum, ut misericordiam dei post iusticiam |f. 37v| comprobaret. Vtilis fuit igitur homini ligatio qua dei cognouit iusticiam; utilis[5] etiam solutio per quam dei expertus est misericordiam.

While the prisoner was pouring forth these and similar prayers in the presence of God, with the choir of the holy ministers close at hand and the whole congregation listening intently, in came his prison-guards and made as if to seize the man. But just at that moment, with a mighty crack his chains burst asunder and, to the wonder of everyone standing there, the prisoner's legs were freed of his fetters even as he prayed.

As soon as the news about the man reached the bishop he issued an order concerning the miracle, to the effect that since St. Erkenwald had seen fit to set the said man free he forbade anyone to wrong him with further imprisonment. As for the great rejoicing which then ensued among the people, and the great praise both of God and his beloved Erkenwald which went abroad, there is no one with either the tongue to describe it or the mind to imagine it.

But let us consider as far as we can, beloved brothers, how great a store of God's sweetness there is, which he conceals from those who fear him. He does nothing to man in this lifetime, which is a time of mercy, that is not for man's good, whether it appears to be good or evil. As long as man is being purged and tried with the lash of affliction, he is at the same time being drawn by kindness to the eternal kingdom. For just as the skillful doctor cures the sick, now with a gentle remedy, now with a harsh one, in the same way the wisdom of the Almighty God wondrously and ineffably dispenses prosperity and adversity to men by turns, by way of providing for their perpetual well-being. Moreover, he rings the changes on prosperity and adversity in this marvelous way so that people will praise his mercy and justice as they feel the force of each in turn, and so that they will call upon his saints for help in replacing their sorrows with happiness, and will glorify them in their prayers.

All of which is exemplified in this miracle, whereby St. Erkenwald freed the prisoner. For God bound the sinner so that he would recognize the chains binding him within; and when he called upon Erkenwald, the friend of God, he set the convert free as he prayed, and thus displayed mercy after justice. The man's imprisonment therefore, was profitable to him, for through it he came to know God's justice; equally profitable was his deliverance, for in that he experienced God's mercy.

IV   *Qualiter inter uasta urbis et ecclesie incendia sepulcri eius palla perdurauit illesa*

Temporibus pie recordationis mauricii[1] lundoniensis episcopi, in lundoniensi urbe res contigit relatione inenarrabilis, uisu mirabilis, fide magis estimanda quam spetie,[2] diuinitatis uirtute quam humanarum rerum censenda ratione.

Fvit in supradicta ciuitate, in honore doctoris gentium pauli,[3] basilica antiquo lapideo tabulatu fabricata,[4] que non solum cathedra episcopali sublimata, uerum etiam thesauris inestimabilibus fuerat adornata. Thesauris, inquam, celestibus illius celestis ierusalem lapidibus preciosissimis et auro mundissimo precipue fuerat coronata. Felix lundonia, talibus
10 munita presidiis, que beati pontificis erkenwaldi sanctique sebbe regum mitissimi, aliorumque sanctorum[5] quam plurimorum sacrato glebas seruat sub aggere. Isti namque sunt inestimabiles diuitie, gaze perpetue, incomparabiles sapientie et scientie thesauri absconditi de quibus dicitur, *Porte ierusalem ex saphiro et smaragdo edificabuntur, et ex lapide mundo et candido omnes platee eius sternentur et per omnes uicos eius alleluia cantabitur.*[6]

In supramemorata itaque ecclesia beatissimi erkenwaldi corpus post altare dominicum sub theca lignea quiescebat, que altius quam statura sit hominis, super structuram lapideam in altum porrecta, ueteri pallio-
20 lo tegebatur.[7] Nempe qui tanta in celestibus emicat gloria non debuit tam uili scemate sepeliri in terra.[8]

Enim uero paulo ante natiuitatem beati iohannis baptiste[9] circa mediam noctem in occidentali ciuitatis parte, uidelicet in ipsius porte uestigio, meritis mortalium exigentibus, ignis tam ualidus accenditur, ut urbem ante se positam usque ad exitum orientis[10] inuolueret, et furorem offensi dei altius gementibus uideatur aperire. Interea turbati ciues et stupefacti domorum interruptione uoraces conantur reprimere flammas, sed illis incassum laborantibus, summi furor tonantis[11] post laboranti-um miserorum terga salientes patitur incendiorum insultare uoragines.
30 Et iam turrium seu ecclesiarum cacumina atrox flamma mirantibus cunctis conscenderat, atque matrici sue media deuoranda deserens, ad anteriora tumultuosis anfractibus progredi haud segnius conabatur.

Miracle 4   *How amid the great burning of the city and church the pall on his tomb survived unharmed*

In the days of Bishop Maurice of London, of blessed memory, there oc-curred in the city of London an event which is virtually impossible to nar-rate, which was wondrous to behold, and which must be judged more on faith than on appearances, and evaluated more with the help of theology than according to rational human standards.

In the aforesaid city, in the honor of St. Paul the teacher of the Gentiles, there was a basilica which had been built with a roof of ancient stone. This church was not only exalted by virtue of its being the episcopal cathedral, but it was also adorned with priceless treasures. With celestial treasures, I say, it was crowned, and in particular with the most precious stones and with the purest gold of that celestial Jerusalem. Happy London, to be for-tified by such protectors, for beneath that sacred pile you keep the mortal remains of blessed bishop Erkenwald and holy Sebbe, mildest of kings, and of many other saints besides. For they are inestimable riches, inexhaustible hoards, incomparable treasures of wisdom and knowledge stored away, of which it is said, "For the gates of Jerusalem will be built with sapphire and emerald, and all her roads will be paved with pure and shining stone and her streets will ring with alleluias."

In this church of St. Paul, the body of the most blessed Erkenwald lay behind the altar of the Lord in a wooden coffin which, resting on a stone plinth, stood higher than the height of a man and was covered with an an-cient altar cloth. For someone who shines forth so gloriously in the heavens should surely not be buried in such a foul garment as the earth.

But it came to pass that, shortly before the feast of the Nativity of John the Baptist, in the middle of the night a fire broke out in the western part of the city, that is, at the foot of the gate: a fire brought on by the ill deserv-ings of mortal men, a fire so great that it overwhelmed the city in its path all the way to the east gate, and seemed to unleash God's fury on those who had offended him even as they groaned and lamented before it. At times the townsfolk, shaken and amazed at this onslaught on their homes, attempt to beat back the ravenous flames, but they labor in vain, for the fury of the great thunderer suffers the whirling, devouring fires to mock them and leap over the backs of the wretched people even as they toil. And now the fierce flame had scaled the tops of the great houses and churches to everyone's amazement, and leaving the intervening buildings to be devoured in its womb, it strove energetically, with violent twistings and turnings, to advance upon the foremost.

Quasi ortus uoluptatis ciuitas *coram ea et post eam solitudo deserti, nec est quo effugiat eam. Quasi aspectus equorum aspectus* incendiorum et *quasi equites sic* currebant. *Sicut sonitus quadrigarum super capita montium exiliebant, sicut* |f. 38r| *sonitus flamme deuorantis stipulam, uelut populus fortis preparatus ad prelium. A facie eius cruciabatur populus; omnis uultus redigebatur in ollam.*[12] *Unusquisque fratrem suum,* timore perterritus, *coarcabat,* urbem exibant cum sarcinulis.[13] Mulieres quippe sicut nocturno incen-
40   dio consternate surrexerant nudis pedibus, sparsis crinibus, manibus complosis, lacrimarum imbre perfusis uultibus, circumcursabant, atque lamenta uel saxea corda penetrantia cum eiulatibus crebris multiplicabant. Adhuc diuersi diuersa deflent incommoda et quicquid acciderat aut singulorum aut paucorum hominum reputabatur esse periculum.

A tanti autem *facie* discriminis lundonia contremuit, *moti sunt* populi eius, *obtenebrati sunt* principes ipsius, quia erkenwaldus *splendorem suum retraxerat,*[14] et dominus deus potestatem in tanto discrimine *sathane tradiderat.*[15] Nulli parcit qui super omnia laxatis habenis dimittitur. Et ut grauiora dampna pareant, episcopalem sedem doctoris gentium pau-
50   li, uidelicet supra memoratam basilicam, ausibus truculentis in fauillam redigendo satis miserabiliter exsufflauit. Heu, heu, uolatu citissimo ignis alta corripit, tectorum culmina uiolenter inuoluit, ac repente tota lignorum strues accenditur, ac omnino combusta deperit. Nondum arcus lapideos, quos uulgo dicimus uoltas, nostri manus artificis ita plene, sicut nunc, attigerat, sed trabibus parietibus superiectis uniuersam ecclesiam uenusta testudine superficies integra palliabat.[16]

Templum ad solum diruitur; dissipata est, et scissa et dilacerata[17] domus dei, ruunt fastigia, moles tanta subuertitur, trabes fulminee pauimenta subuertunt, altaria diruunt, utensilia incendio tradunt. Stat erkenwal-
60   dus in medio,[18] inter fulgurantes lignorum acies relinquitur, frementis flamme circumquaque sustinet impetus, semiustorum roborum ab alto cadentium sistitur ictibus.

Quid inter hec facies erkenwalde? Quis commouebitur super te? Ac si commotus fuerit, quomodo per tot et tanta discrimina, ut tibi ferat auxilium, ad te poterit peruenire? Ea propter exurge, obsecro, *letare et exulta*[19] in cubili tuo! Ostende uirtutem mortuis mortuus, quam uiuus

The city in front of it was like a garden of delight, but a desolate wilderness behind it, nor was there anywhere to escape it. The forms of the flames were as the shapes of horses, and like horsemen they rode. With the sound of four-horsed chariots rumbling along the mountaintops, or of the crackling of flames devouring the stubble, they hurtled along, like a strong nation prepared for war. And before the face of the fire the people were in anguish, and every cheek grew pale as ashes. Each man shook with fear, embraced his brother, and fled the city with his belongings. The women also, as if the nocturnal fire had made them demented, rose up, their feet bare, their hair flying and disshevelled, beating their hands together, their faces wet with showers of tears, and ran here and there with fierce laments and with loud and repeated moans that pierced even the hardest hearts. Different people bewailed different misfortunes, and whatever had happened was believed to be the fault of either isolated individuals or of a few men.

Yes, London trembled in the face of such a calamity—its people were troubled and its princes plunged in gloom because Erkenwald had withdrawn his radiance and the Lord God had handed over his power in such a crisis to Satan. Given a free rein to range at will over all, he spares no one. And the losses appear more and more serious, for he has vented himself on the episcopal see, the church of Paul, apostle of the Gentiles, which we described earlier, reducing it all too pitifully to ashes with his ferocious assaults. Alas, alas, in its lightning flight, the fire attacks the heights and whirls itself violently all the way to the very rooftops, and in no time the timber edifice is burning and totally consumed. For at that time the hand of our architect had not yet mastered the art of building stone arches, which in the vernacular we call vaults, as he has now done; rather, the roof, which was all of one piece, covered the whole church over with an elegant ceiling by means of wooden beams strung across between the tops of the two walls.

The temple is razed to the ground; the house of God is broken in pieces; the roofs collapse; this great edifice is overturned, blazing beams destroy the pavement, and the altars topple, hurling the vessels into the flames. In the midst of it all Erkenwald remains; he is left amid the fiery onslaughts of the timbers; he endures the attacks of raging flame from every side; he is hemmed in by the blows of half-burned logs which fall from above.

And while all this is taking place, O Erkenwald, what do you intend to do? Who will bestir themselves on your behalf? And if anyone were moved to help you, how could he get to you to bring you help through so many and such great dangers? Therefore rise up, I beg you. Rejoice and be happy on your couch. Although you have died, reveal your strength to the dead, which you revealed to the living when you were alive! It is a greater thing

ostendisti uiuis! Maius est puluerulenta ossa uirtute intima incendia deuitare, quam menbra spiritu plena mortuos suscitare.[20]

Mellitus magister tuus cantuariam secessit;[21] chedda, predecessor
70   tuus,[22] hominum meritis occultantibus, nondum apparuit; gloriosus rex
sebba, dilectissimus tuus, sua reuelatione nos indignos iudicauit.[23]
Omnes sanctissimi college tui, lundoniam abdicando, tibi deferendo, occulto terre gremio sua preciosissima corpora uisitationi suppreme custodiunt.[24] Tu solus es qui sub nostro aere paruisti; tu solus es qui patris
officium maternaque uiscera sensisti; tu solus, inquam, nostris successibus et cotidianis periculis tua presentia subuenisti |f. 38v|. Peccatores
quidem sumus et indigni ut uiuamus, sed poterit pater suorum obliuisci
filiorum? Et si ille oblitus fuerit, tu numquam, obsecro, obliuiscaris.

Presentia tua demones fugat, uitia calcat, deum inducit, uirtutes nutrit,
80   animam mundat et reficit.[25] Feretrum quo uiuus ad seminandum dei
uerbum deferebaris, et cetera quibus humandus lege naturali accubuisti,
tactu suo corporibus humanis, mirabile dictu, integram restituunt sanitatem.[26] Quid faceret corporis tactus, cum tot et tanta faciat lapis superpositus?[27] Quid sanitatis afferret puluis sanctissimus, cum languida
corpora sanet ligni uermiculus?[28] O beate erkenwalde, te presente uidet
cecus, ambulat claudus, contrectat aridus, sanitatem recipit egrotus.[29]

Absentia tua tribuit contrarium, et cum sine peccato non possit duci
miserabilis uita mortalium, tui combustione corporis execrabile parabis
detrimentum et ineuitabile dampnum. Certe non decet tuam dignita
90   tem ut ossa tua concrementur, in puluerem redigatur. Salua tua reuerentia
loquor, turpe est ut reliquie tue, edacibus flammis fauille facte, ui uentorum sparsim per aera deuoluantur et tandem uestigiis hominum conculcanda trudantur. Absit hoc a te, absit pater sanctissime: immo
attendant karissimi ciues tui et admirentur miraculum pontificis sui.

Uideant nouitatem, immo supereminens nouitas nouitatum[30] subito
resplendeat eis, et resipiscant a peccatis quibus tenentur, et te solum
post deum presulem et patronum cognoscant et uenerentur.

Audite igitur populi omnes et attendat terra et plenitudo eius.[31] *Audite*
igitur *hoc senes,*[32] ad quos magis spectat, et a magnitudine miraculi *re-*

for dusty bones by their own power to ward off the flames than for limbs full of life to raise the dead.

Mellitus, your master, has gone away to Canterbury. Your predecessor, Cedd, perhaps because men do not seem to deserve it, has not yet shown himself. Glorious king Sebbe, your beloved, has made it plain that we are not worthy to see him. All your most holy colleagues have foresworn London, deferring to you, and in the secret bosom of the earth they keep their most precious bodies in readiness for the supreme visitation. You are the only one who has appeared beneath our sky; you alone have felt a father's sense of duty and a mother's heart; you alone, I say, have with your presence supported our successes and helped us in our daily perils. We are indeed sinners and unworthy that we should live. But will the father be able to forget his children? And even if he should, I beg that at least you will never forget them.

Your presence puts demons to flight and treads vices underfoot, while it brings God to the soul, and fosters virtues therein, cleansing and refreshing it. The litter on which you were carried about during your lifetime, to sow the word of God, and the other things on which you lay down to be buried according to nature's law—with their very touch, amazing as it seems, they restore perfect health to human bodies. What would the touch of your body do, when the stone laid over it will do so many wonders? What health might that most holy dust provide, when a purple dye from a tree will bring healing to diseased bodies? O blessed Erkenwald, in your presence the blind man sees, the lame walks, the paralytic regains the feeling in his limbs, the sick man receives his health again.

Your absence brings just the opposite. And since the miserable life of mortal men can never be lived without sin, you are preparing for them, with the burning of your body, an accursed loss and inevitable destruction. Truly it is a dishonor to you that your bones should be consumed and reduced to powder. Saving your reverence I speak, but it would be a vile thing if your remains were to be turned to ashes by the greedy flames and flung and scattered in the air by the force of the winds, and then at last to be trodden and ground down by the feet of men. Let not such a thing happen, most holy father! Let it not be! Rather let your dearest citizens look to see and marvel at a miracle from their bishop.

Let them see something new. Let a rare thing, an unparalleled wonder, suddenly shine down upon them, and let them recover from the sinfulness in which they are held and let them know and venerate you as their bishop and protector, saving God only.

Therefore hear ye, all ye peoples, and may the earth in her fullness bear witness. Hear this, therefore, ye old men, whom it much concerns, and by

100 *dite ad cor uestrum;*[33] respicite super hoc, *si factum sit in diebus uestris,*
aut in diebus patrum uestrorum. Super hoc filiis uestris narrate et filii uestri
filiis suis; et filii eorum generationi alteri.[34] Omnia que fuerant in domo
domini alimenta facta sunt incendii, nil latere potuit quin fieret cibus
ignis. Residuum erkenwaldi ueretur flamma contingere; palla superposita ethneas[35] uoragines uidetur artare.[36] Ante et retro, dextrorsum et
sinistrorum super etiam torridum uoluitur incendium, ut taceam de membris pontificis et de lapideo mausoleo et de strue lignorum superposita,
lintheamina serico contexta *odorem ignis non*[37] sentiunt.

     Magnitudo miraculi crescit uilitate panni. Virtus erkenwaldi crescit
110 immanitate incendii. Obstupesco dum refero, naturam namque confundo,
usus assuetos destruo. Contra namque cursum nature, arida pallia atroci-
bus flammis resistere et, ut ita |f. 39r| dicam, stupam leuem fulmina ab
alto supra se cadentia procul a se repellere.

     Tercia autem die, cum uix basilice patuisset ingressus, intrant ciues
optato adueniunt et duo pontifices, supra memoratus urbis episcopus
lundoniensis mauricius et wintoniensis walkelinus,[38] necnon et sacerdotes quam plurimi sacrorumque ordinum et inferiorum ministri. Quod
factum diuina prouidentia non dubitamus, ut simul uiderent quod simul
predicarent, unde posteris fides certior haberetur.[39]

120   Uerum quia dicit scriptura, 'ubi amor ibi oculus,'[40] illuc spargunt lumina quo corpus sancti reliquerant. Mirabile uisu, cernunt erkenwaldum ignes uicisse, naturam superasse, omnia in circuitu in cineres
deuenisse, et nec filum pallii suprapositi uirorem suum in tanto discrimine perdidisse.[41] Preterea trabes maxima ardens super idem pallium
inuenitur, pannique superficies integra conseruatur. Plumbeus liquor et
uiui carbones obliti fuerant sue conditionis, uim uirtutis sue perdiderat
ignis. Fit gaudium inter ciues, letatur clerus et populus, et quibus altius
datum est sapere magis contemplantur factum istud, et usque ad ulti-
mum electum qui legerit que scribimus mirari poterit mysterium istud.
130 Dicat quisque quod senserit. Humana ratione coactus assero, plus afferre
nouitatis erkenwaldi cineres igneos superasse impetus quam uiua puerorum corpora incendia deuitasse.[42]

the greatness of the miracle recover your senses. Look closely and see if its like has been done in your days or in the days of your fathers. Relate it to your sons and have them tell it to theirs, and their sons to the next generation. For everything which had been in the house of the Lord became food for the flames; nothing could hide or escape being fodder for the fire. But the flame is afraid to touch the remains of Erkenwald. The cloth which covers them seems to fend off the blazing volcanic jaws. Before and behind, to the right and to the left also, the fire rolls and destroys, and yet not only were the bishop's limbs, and the coffin of stone, and the wooden super-structure completely untouched, but the very fibers of woven silk and linen in the flimsy pall did not catch even a trace of the fire's smell.

The magnitude of the miracle increases when one considers the small size of the thin cloth; Erkenwald's power seems all the greater when one considers the immensity of the fire. I am dumbfounded even as I tell the story, for I am refuting nature and confounding time-honored truths. For against the course of nature, the dry cloth was impervious to the greedy flames, and it was as if that piece of oakum beat back the blazing bolts which fell upon it from on high.

On the third day, when it was still barely possible to enter the basilica, the townsfolk went in, and two bishops came along with them as they desired, the aforementioned Maurice, bishop of London, and Walkelin, bishop of Winchester, as well as very many priests and ministers of lower rank. We have no doubts that by divine providence they saw what they simultaneously proclaimed, as a result of which those who came after have a firmer faith.

For truly, because it is written that "The eye follows the heart," they turn their eyes to where they had left the body of the saint. They see, and it is a wondrous sight, that Erkenwald has overcome the flames, and has triumphed over nature; while all around him has become ashes, not a thread of the pall which covered his tomb has lost its freshness of hue, even in the midst of such a disaster. Moreover a huge beam is found burning on that same pall and the surface of the cloth is quite unmarked. Liquid lead and live coals had forgotten their nature, and the fire had lost the force of its power. There is joy among the townsfolk, the clerics and the people rejoice while those who have the gift of deeper wisdom are more prone to meditate on the event. And everyone who reads what I have written, even the most elite member of my audience, will be capable of wonder at that mystery. Let everyone say what he feels. Compelled by human reason, I maintain that for Erkenwald's ashes to have overcome the fiery onslaught is a greater miracle than for the living bodies of children to have lived through the flames.

Patrata sunt ista in urbe lundoniensi in cathedra episcopali sub mauritio eiusdem ciuitatis episcopo, mense junio, eiusdem mensis die
septima.[43]

Erubesce ergo uigilanti heretice,[44] pessime, crudelis, sine misericordia,
sine affectu, sine pietate et quod est peius sine fide, uniuerse mons et
monstrum gallie. Contra te semel scripsit ieronimus, et cum *sola gallia*
careat *monstris* et montibus, te monstrum gallie nuncupauit,[45]
140   hereticumque comprobauit per omnia. Iterum contra te dimicat erkenwaldus, flammas quas superat in te uibrat, igneis iaculis te transforat
que deuitat. "Ad quid," ait uigilantius, "lumen ante arida ossa succenditur? Vt quid tanta perditio pro cineribus humanis? Uile cadauer tanto lumine non debuit decorari."[46] Vilis heretice, non est ista perditio
sed animarum redemptio. Non uile cadauer a sapientibus estimabitur,
quod tantis ignium resistere potuit conatibus, immo qui pallium supra
se positum igni uomis seruauit anfractibus. Pereas ergo uigilanti, tu et
complices tui.[47] Nos uero gaudeamus in tanta nouitate miraculi, in quo
deus mirabilis in sanctis predicatur,[48] humanorum corporum resurrec
150   tio indicitur, sanctitas erkenwaldi supra modum extollitur, peccatores
ad penitentiam reuocantur, iustorum perseuerentia roboratur.

V   *De constructione augustiore lundoniensis ecclesie et muliere manca que*
post multa per orbem precipuorum sepulcra sanctorum lustrata a sancto
erkenwaldo salutem optinuit

In huius nouitate miraculi supradictus |f. 39v| episcopus aliam ecclesiam
a fundamentis incepit, opus, uidelicet, ut multis uidetur inconsummabile, uerum si consummari posset, honor et decus lundonie.[1] Peractis
denique criptis, sanctissimi corpus erkenwaldi ibidem collocari precepit.
Mauricio autem uiam uniuerse carnis ingresso,[2] dominus Ricardus, uir
uenerandus, curam suscepit regiminis, uir, inquam, prudens et strenuus,
nobilitate et moralitate conspicuus. Iste quidem incepte muros ecclesie
mirabiliter auxit, necnon et plateas circa eandem ecclesiam permaximas,

These events took place in the city of London in the episcopal cathedral, during the time of Maurice, bishop of London, in the month of June, on the seventh day of the month.

So blush with shame, Vigilantius, worst of heretics, cruel man, lacking mercy, feeling, and goodness, and what is worse, lacking faith: great mountain and monster of Gaul. Jerome once wrote against you and, since only Gaul lacks both mountains and monsters, he named you the monster of Gaul and proclaimed you a heretic through and through. This time it is Erkenwald who contends with you and brandishes against you the flames he has overcome, pierces you with the fiery darts he himself avoids. "What's the point of burning a lamp before dry bones?" says Vigilantius. "Or why such a great expense for human ashes? One should not honor a vile cadaver with such a show of light." Vile heretic! There's no loss involved here, but rather the redemption of souls. The corpse which could withstand such a furious onslaught of the flames is not considered vile by the wise, the corpse, I say, of someone who kept safe the cloth covering him while flames were twisting and roaring about him. Perish, therefore, Vigilantius, you and your accomplices. For we rejoice in such a strange new miracle, in which wondrous God is made known in his saints, and the resurrection of the body is symbolized, the sanctity of Erkenwald extolled beyond measure, sinners brought back to repentance, and the righteous strengthened in their perseverance.

Miracle 5   *Concerning the building of a more splendid church in London, and concerning the crippled woman, who after journeying to many tombs of famous saints throughout the world, obtained her health from St. Erkenwald*

While this miracle was still new, the aforementioned bishop [Maurice] began to build another church from the very foundations, a task which to many people seemed impossible to complete, but if it could be completed, it would be the honor and glory of London. When the crypt was finished, he ordered the body of the most holy Erkenwald placed in it.

When Maurice had gone the way of all flesh, the lord Richard, a man worthy of veneration, assumed the burden of the episcopacy, a man, I say, both wise and energetic, distinguished for his nobility of character and for his morality. He marvellously advanced the work on the walls of the new church; also he acquired, at his own expense, the broad streets around the

que ante domibus laicorum obsesse fuerant, proprio sumptu adquisiuit,
10 et in circuitu muro fortissimo pene cinxit, aliisque quam plurimis beneficiis
lundoniensem ecclesiam ampliauit.[3]

Post hunc cathedram Gislebertus, qui uniuersalis dictus est, ab au-
tisiodoro, ciuitate gallie, uocatus, feliciter ascendit.[4] Hic nempe litteris
et sapientia, necnon auctoritate et frugalitate media cumulatus ante episcopatum uetus instrumentum ad liquidum exposuerat.[5]

Que uero uel quanta, episcopii onere suscepto, ecclesie sue contulerit,
cuiusue integritatis extiterit, non est huius operis enarrare, cum corda-
tum uirum, non eius nepotem, tale negotium expetat, ut supra uires illius sit actus describere que uniuersa latinitas laudat.[6]

20 Post mortem illius quarto anno,[7] quedam uenerabilis mulier, benedicta nomine, ad sancti feretrum diebus singulis ueniam postulabat, ut quod
natura subtraxerat optinere erkenwaldi precibus flagitabat. Siquidem duo
pessima simul ei a natiuitate contigerant: manus uidelicet ariditas atque
contractio.[8]

Hec italicam[9] se asserebat, et pro sanitate recipienda fere extremas
hominum nationes, ubi religio christiana peruenerat, pede lasso lustrauer-
at. Certe, uidi eam herilem feminam, et quamuis iuuenis uideretur, mas-
culina uestigia, facies ardore combusta, habitus et loquela argumentum
erant discriminis et angustiarum que fuerat passa.

30 O quam ineffabilis secretorum dei profunditas![10] Quam uniuersus
mundus cum suis reliquiis abdicarat diuina prouidentia reseruat erkenwaldo, ut mirabiliorem in sanctis suis deum britannia recognoscat. O
beate erkenwalde, apostolorum principes, petrus et paulus, tibi defer-
unt, alumnam suam tibi mittunt, ut gloriosior appareas et lundonia te
melius ueneretur et colat. Habundat roma in martyrum, confessorum,
uirginumque corporibus, ut qui hodie uiuunt in urbe ad comparatio-
nem sanctorum paucissimi uideantur. E contrario, pater gloriose, solus
caput tenes britannie, solus inter homines cubas in domino in lundoniensi
ciuitate. Que uirtutis nouitas, si tot sanctorum legiones muliercule ma-
40 num restituant?

Tibi ergo soli mittitur, ut in urbe tua nouum appareat. Innumerabiles

church which had previously been occupied by the houses of the laity, and which he virtually surrounded with a very solid and strong outer wall, and in general he enhanced and enlarged the church with very many additional gifts.

After him Gilbert, who was named the Universal, was summoned from St. Auxerre in France to ascend the episcopal throne. This was a happy event, for he indeed was filled with both learning and wisdom, and was possessed also of natural authority and the spirit of frugal moderation. Before becoming bishop he had written a most lucid commentary on the Old Testament.

But it is not within the scope of this work to describe the gifts, the great gifts, he bestowed upon his church after undertaking the burden of the see, or to describe the purity of his life, since such a task requires a man of gifted intellect, not his nephew, it being beyond *his* power to recount the deeds which all Christendom praises.

In the fourth year after his death, a certain venerable woman named Benedicta was wont to come every day to the saint's tomb to pray for mercy, and at the same time she would earnestly beg to obtain, by the prayers of Erkenwald, what nature had witheld from her. For since birth she had had two grievous afflictions, namely, that one hand was shrivelled up and at the same time stiffened in a permanent cramp.

She said that she was Italian, and that to regain her health she had made a wearisome jouney through virtually the most remote and isolated countries to which the Christian religion had penetrated. In truth, I saw this noble woman, and although she was apparently still young, her hardened masculine features, with her face burnt by the heat of the sun, her bearing and her speech, all were eloquent proof of the trials and tribulations she had endured.

O the unspeakable depth of God's secret workings! Her, whom the world with all its relics had rejected, divine providence reserved for Erkenwald so that Britain might recognize the wonderful working of God in his saints. O blessed Erkenwald, the princes of the apostles, Peter and Paul, defer to you and send their foster child to you that you might be revealed in greater glory and London might the better honor and revere you. Rome abounds in the bodies of martyrs, confessors and virgins, so much so that the actual living inhabitants of the city today seem very few in number compared to the saints. By contrast, glorious father, you possess the capital city of Britain all alone, you among men lie at rest in the Lord, in the city of London. What sort of miracle would it be for so many legions of saints to heal the hand of one poor woman?

To you alone therefore is she sent, so that in your city the miracle might be seen. Saints innumerable and of incomparable holiness of life refrained

et incomparabilis uite sancti cessant a miraculo, ut gloriosior appareas in hoc sancto.

Diebus continuis missa romanorum, flexis genibus, lacrimabili gemitu, corde contrito et humiliato uultu, a tua misericordia postulat quod sanctorum uniuersitas denega|f. 40r|rat. Quid plura? Quadam die, ut religionis est non sub hominum obtutibus sed in ecclesie angulis occultata aures summi pulsaret artificis, absconditorum cognitor deus,[11] meritis erkenwaldi exigentibus, manu miserationis manum alleuat deprecantis. Enim
50   uero prolixius illa propensiori cura ad sancti tumulum flagitante, nerui qui, ex nimia strictione, sui extorres animalis uiuacitatis extiterant, digitis ad ordinem reuocatis, ad cursum naturalem subito redeunt, et usui competens succus uiuificus manum restituit sanitati. Manus ariditas humectatur, et neruosa soliditas denodatur. Naturalis uigor miraculo depellit uitium, et putrefacta manus usuale sentit officium.[12] Erkenwaldi precibus admiratur digitorum discretionem, quod pregnantis nature dimiserat in gremio. Reddit erkenwaldus oblite iura nature, dum humane membrum restituit creature.

Sanata itaque mulier, ad memoriam tanti miraculi recolendam, ma-
60   num ceream[13] super sancti tumulum sincera deuotione apposuit, et post paucos dies, nobis ualedicens, erkenwaldi misericordiam circa se singulis referens, apud monasterium cui marcilliacum est nomen, in prouincia uidelicet lugdunensi, supra ligerim fluuium, inter sanctas feminas multo tempore deo seruire studuit.[14] Sed postea ad nos reuersa, quod pro temporali lucro non uenisset, immo ut curatori suo gratias referret satis ostendit.

VI   *De homine qui coniugem ab honore sancti compescuit punito et secundum ipsius sancti monitum reparato*[1]

Igitur cum dispensatori omnium deo parare argenteum erkenwaldo ferculum[2] placuisset, diuitibus urbis nostre parum aut nichil conferentibus, pauperum larga manus collectas per ciuitatem constituit.[3] Ubi

from performing this miracle in order that your glory might be manifested in this holy event.

Day after day on bended knees at the Roman Mass, with groans that would make one weep, with contrite heart and looks of humility she begs of your mercy for what the whole company of saints had denied. What more is there to tell? One day when she was assailing the ears of the supreme artificer, not under the eyes of men but—a sign of true religion—discreetly alone in a corner of the church, God who knows all things hidden, being importuned by the merits of Erkenwald, with his merciful hand brought comfort to the hand of the woman as she prayed. For as she poured out her entreaties more and more copiously and in deepening sorrow at the saint's tomb, the nerves which had been bereft of their essential life and vitality, on account of being so tightly cramped and constricted, suddenly returned to their natural state, and her fingers were recalled to their ordinary positions: life-giving fluid, returning to its normal use, restored the hand to health. The hand that had been shrivelled and dry became fleshy and moist, the tightly knotted nerves relaxed and untangled themselves. By means of the miracle, nature's power dispelled the palsy and the hand that had been corrupt and useless became sensible of its normal function. Thanks to Erkenwald's prayers she can marvel at the separateness of her fingers, a feeling lost to her even in the womb of teeming nature. Erkenwald restored the laws which nature had forgotten, when he healed the limb of this human creature.

The woman herself, to encourage people to remember and reflect on so great a miracle, with sincere devotion placed a hand made of wax on the tomb of the saint and a few days later she bade us goodbye, giving thanks to everyone for Erkenwald's kindness to her. Her desire was to serve God for a long time among the holy women in the monastery called Marcillac, in the province of Lyons on the river Loire. But afterwards she returned to us and showed plainly enough that she had not come for worldly gain, but so that she might give thanks to her healer.

Miracle 6   *Concerning the man who prevented his wife from honoring the saint, his punishment, and the restoring of his health in accordance with the saint's instructions*

On the occasion when it pleased God, dispenser of all things, that a silver shrine be made for Erkenwald, although the wealthy citizens contributed little or nothing, the generous hand of the poor set up collecting stations

cum quedam mulier, ut aliquid offerret mente deuota pergere preoptas-
set, a uiro suo acrius increpata, quod proposuerat implere non potuit.
Sequenti nocte infelix ille graui renum passione corripitur et tam acriter
dira humorum collectione[4] per non paucos dies uexatur, ut medicorum
iudicio in desperationem uerteretur. Verum quia dicit paulus, *Salua-*
bitur uir infidelis per mulierem fidelem,[5] ecce intempeste noctis silen-
10   tio mulieri in somnis sanctus noster apparuit et certa reuelatione perdocuit
quatinus sine aliqua procrastinatione uirum suum propensius animaret,
ut ad ipsius mausoleum se ferri preciperet. Itaque mane facto, uxoris
monitu humeris famulorum uir ille sustentatus, ad beati pauli basilicam
humilis ac deuotus abducitur, ubi, auxiliante sepedicto pontifice, languoris sui sanitate percepta, sui compos efficitur, et qui alienis adiutus
uenerat, pedibus propriis ad propria reuertitur.

Nimirum summam discretionem contra se stultus armauerat, cum ux-
orem a collectis retraxerat. Vnde, crudelibus uexatus iniuriis, in illorum
constituitur exemplum qui contradicunt operibus pietatis.

VII   *Qualiter honorem exhibitum sibi esse placitum mira beneficiorum largitate*
probauit

Ea tempestate erkenwaldus noster primitiue tempora |f. 40v| ecclesie
in omnium oculis renouauit,[1] et certe prodigiorum copia infideles nos
iudicauit, iuxta illud, *signa sunt pro infidelibus non pro fidelibus.*[2]
Nimirum preter anime pabulum quod nobis in tot miraculis exibuit, opus
quod inceperamus fore sibi beneplacitum ostendere curauit.[3]

Iacebat ante tumulum beati pontificis turba innumerabilis, pauci ani-
mas, multi corpora curari cupiunt, sed ne incassum diu postulantium
gemitus laborarent et corpora, pristinam subito sanitatem recipiunt. Hu-
manitas dolet supplicium, contra uirtus erkenwaldi superat uitium. Pel-
10   litur contrarium contrario, dum medela sancti datur imperio. Aucta fides
operum augmenta requirebat, sed hominum nefanda crudelitas inhor-

throughout the city. A certain woman, of devout heart, wanted to go to one of them to offer something, but her husband rebuked her bitterly and she was unable to do what she had proposed.

On the following night the miserable man was seized by an intense pain in his stomach and for several days he was afflicted so sharply by a terrible swelling of the humors that, in the judgement of his doctors, his situation was hopeless. But Paul says, "the unfaithful husband will be saved by the faithful wife"; and lo, in the silence of the dead of night our saint appeared to the woman in a dream and instructed her clearly to press and urge her husband, without delay, to have himself carried to the saint's sepulcher. And so when morning came, at his wife's urging, leaning on the arms of his men-servants, the man was conducted, devout now and humble, to the church of the blessed Paul. There, with the help of the famed bishop, he was healed of his affliction and was made whole and sound, and though he had relied on others to bring him there, he returned home on his own two feet.

The stupid man had gone too far and had aroused the supreme justice against himself when he had kept his wife from going to the collection. As a result, afflicted by cruel pains, he was set up as an example of those who stand in the way of the works of holiness.

Miracle 7   *How he demonstrated, with the wonderful largesse of his merciful acts, that he was pleased with the honor being shown him*

It was at this same time that our Erkenwald revived the age of the early church before the eyes of all men, and indeed, by the profusion of wonders he performed, he passed judgement on us as unbelievers. For it is said: "Miracles are for unbelievers, not for the faithful." Besides proferring us spiritual nourishment with this abundance of miracles, he took care to show us that the work we had begun would be well pleasing to him.

Usually there was before the tomb of the blessed bishop an enormous crowd of people, a few of whom desired him to heal their souls, while most wanted their bodies healed. But lest the suppliants should groan and suffer for a long time in vain, they were permitted to recover at once their pristine health. Humanity bewailed its suffering, but Erkenwald's power overcame its im-perfection. The hostile force was driven back by its opposite, as long as the power of healing was the saint's to command. As people's faith increased, so did their demand for miracles, but the unspeakable cruelty of men con-

rescebat. Vniuersitatis conditor uniuersorum sanabat iniurias sed nostra peruersitas onus depositum non pensabat. Crescebat sanitatum
presidia, sed decrescebant uirtutum culmina. Criminum diuersitas aug-
mentabatur et morborum uarietas superabatur.[4]

De multis unum referam, quasi de pluribus singulare, de innumerabili-
bus speciale, quod *qui audierit*, pre stupore nimio *tinnient aures eius*.[5] Ut
uel sic impenitens cor nostrum durius arguatur, et dei circa nos misericordia sollicius recolatur.[6]

De iuuene subite mortis presentia retracto

20   In fine igitur anni supramemorati, quasi ad anniuersarium miraculi
in tusca muliere ostensi,[7] quadam dominica clerus et populus ante
dominum erkenwaldum ut consuetudinis erat stationem fecit.[8] Erat ibi
iuuenis, nomine Willelmus, qui de gallia exercende negotiationis causa
fines nostros intrauerat. Qui, completa processione, ad hospicium dum
inter conuiuantes socius discumberet, subito tam atroci infirmitate concutitur, ut cathalepticum[9] hominem iudicares, et magis mortem quam
periculum minitares.

In tam lacrimabili euentu, turbatur dominus domus, uir bonus hameli-
nus, et uenerabilis albereda [10] uxor eius; turbabantur et socii, quibus
30   unum genus et una patria altius gemere prouocabat. Vnde statim de
mensa ad lectum satis eum miserabiliter prestolantes, nichil preter mortem pensare presumunt. Videres hominem in tanta mestitudine laboran-
tem minime respirare, toruis luminibus,[11] mortem minitari, continuis
malphationibus[12] spiritum exalare, nec dubium quin sepius mentem
perdiderit, cum in tanto positus discrimine et lumen amiserit et membrorum omnium caruerit sensualitate. Ex ipsa desperatione signum domini nostri ihesu christi ante infirmum apponitur, sacerdos, ut fidelium
mos est. magis ad exequias quam ad infirmi uisitacionem, inducitur, et,
omnibus rite paratis, iam tedio fessi qui aderant, magis eius mortem quam
40   tam pessime cruciari propensius inhiabant.

O genus infelix hominum, tot nefandis casibus immo tot miserabili-
bus mortibus inuolutum. Tam uili |f. 41r| ordine propagaris, tam uili-
bus secundarum apertionibus lucem istam ingrederis, et si forte

tinued to raise its horrid head. The creator of the universe healed the ills of all men, but in our perversity we did not consider the responsibility this kindness imposed upon us. Healing remedies grew in number, but the heights of virtue sank lower. For the diversity of criminal acts increased, even as the variety of diseases was being overcome.

I will relate one out of the many, something singular from the plurality, one miracle in particular from the countless numbers of them (and whoever hears it, his ears will ring in stupified amazement) the more sternly to rebuke our impenitent hearts, to make us reflect with more feeling on God's mercy toward us.

Concerning the young man who was rescued from sudden death

Almost a year later, on the anniversary of the miracle that manifested itself in the woman from Tuscany, one Sunday the clergy and the people were attending a processional mass according to custom before the lord Erkenwald. A young man was there by the name of William, who had come to our shores from France to transact some business. After the procession was over, when he was seated at table back at his lodgings being sociable with a group of fellow revellers, he was suddenly stricken with such an awful illness that you would have taken him for a cataleptic and predicted death forthwith, let alone danger.

The lord of the house, a good man, Hamelin, was much disturbed by this lamentable occurrence, as was his honored wife, Albereda. Likewise upset were the fellows of the stricken man who, being of the same race and country as he, were moved to even louder lamentations. At once they carried him from the table to bed, and there stood attendance on God's mercy, not presuming to expect anything but the young man's decease. You could see him struggling in his great misery, scarcely able to breathe, with wild staring eyes as death menaced him and as he continually gasped out his spirit in fits of swooning. Nor is there any doubt that he was frequently out of his mind, the matter having come to such a pass that he had lost his sight and lacked all feeling in his limbs. Out of sheer desperation, they placed the sign of our Lord Jesus Christ in front of the sufferer and a priest was summoned, as is the custom among believing Christians, more to perform the last rites than actually to visit the invalid. All those present were weary and exhausted; everything needed for the last rites was ready, and everyone longed more eagerly for him to die than for him to go on suffering in such terrible agony.

O unhappy race of men, involved as you are so often in unspeakable accidents and in so many wretched kinds of death. Conceived in such a vile fashion, you emerge into the light through the equally vile passages of the

cunabulorum uagitus euaseris, quasi pendulam naufragus fluctuanti tabule
uitam uentis expositis derelinquis. Heu, lamentabilis uita mortalium, *que
quasi flos egreditur et conteritur et fugit uelut umbra; et nunquam in eodem
statu permanet.*[13] Transit uelut *folium quod uento rapitur et siccate stipule*[14]
non incongrue comparatur. *Aggrauata est manus* omnipotentis *super gemi-
tum* nostrum. Sed *quis* nobis *tribuat ut cognoscam*us altissimum et *inuenia-*
50   *mus* illum, et ascendamus *usque ad eius solium* et *perueniat ad uictoriam*[15]
huius miserabilis exilii detrimentum? *Ue soli, quia si ceciderit, non habet
subleuantem.*[16] Soli sumus dum ab eo in quo sunt omnia exulamus, iuxta quod beatus iob plangit dicens, *Si ad orientem iero non apparet* deus
meus, *si ad occidentem non intelligam eum. Si ad sinistram quid agam?
Non apprehendam eum. Si me uertam ad dexteram; non uidebo* eum. *Ipse
uero scit uiam meam, et probabit me quasi aurum, quod per ignem transit.*[17]
   Ecce homo[18] iste, iocundus et letus, robustus et sanus, diues et felix!
In momento, in ictu oculi[19] marcescit, perit decor eius, in uile cadauer
soluitur.
60   Iam tertia subintrauerat dies nec adhuc ex circumstantibus ciuibus aliquis erkenwaldi potentiam implorarat. Silent siquidem erkenwaldi uicini,
ubi transmarinus non siluit. Obliuiscuntur ciues quod de gallorum gente
genitus recognouit. Profecto, ad nostram[20] uesaniam obtundendam, diuina dictante elementia, quidam ex infirmi sodalibus repente prosilit,
quod antea de uirtutibus mirandi antistitis a sacerdote audierat non sur-
dus auditor attollit, ut egrotus se totum reddat, totum uoueat, totum
se precibus sancti pontificis conferat nutu diuino laudando, consulit.
   Currit citus, cereisque oculis ceci oculos tangit, et festinus equo ante
sanctissimum corpus adueniens, super hastam que imminebat eosdem
70   oculos diligenter apposuit.[21] Res miranda! Vir boni consilii cera tangit
squalentes oculos, et illuminator noster preciosissimus erkenwaldus sentire
uidetur de tumulo. Ponit ille umbram luminum, sed hic sublata umbra
lumen reddit oculorum. Res stupenda! Nondum iuuenis doctoris gentium pauli basilicam exire poterat, et, ecce, priuationem luminis habitu
subsequente, letius egroti palpebra palpitabat, et qui antea maniacus uidebatur iam naturaliter in omnibus menbris usualem cursum recuperauerat.

lower organs, and if you are lucky enough to survive the mewling and bleating of the cradle, you eventually leave this uncertain life behind like a shipwrecked sailor clinging to a plank that pitches and plunges in the force of wind and waves. Alas, the lamentable life of mortal men, which fades and wears away like a flower and flees like a shadow, never remaining for a moment in the same state. It passes like a leaf seized by the wind and is not inaptly compared to a dry stalk of grass. The hand of the Almighty has grown heavy above our groaning. But who may grant us to understand and know the most high, or to ascend to his throne so that our present loss may turn to victory over this miserable exile? Alas for the man alone, for if he should fall, he has no one to raise him up. For we are all alone as long as we are exiled from him in whom are all things, just as the blessed Job laments, saying: "If I turn to the east, my God does not appear; if to the west, I will not grasp him. If to the left, what am I about? I will not lay hold on him. If I turn to the right, I will not see him. He indeed knows my way, however, and he will try me like gold which passes through the fire."

Behold that young man, genial and happy, robust and healthy, rich and successful. In a moment, in the twinkling of an eye, he begins to droop, his beauty perishes and he is changed into a vile cadaver.

Now the third day is upon them, and still none of the citizens present there had thought to call upon the power of Erkenwald. Erkenwald's neighbors are silent, where one from over the sea was not silent. The men of his city forget what one born of the stock of France remembers. For truly, one of the sick man's companions suddenly leapt up, impelled by divine power to shock us out of our insanity, and recalled what he had by no means inattentively heard from a priest, and he counselled the sick man to give himself up utterly and to promise and consign himself totally to the holy bishop's prayers, lauding all the while the will of God.

He ran quickly and touched the eyes of the blind man with a pair of wax eyes, and then hastened away on horseback to where the saint's body lay. Arriving there he placed these same eyes carefully on the railing suspended above the shrine. Then, a wonderful thing! The man of good counsel had touched with wax the darkened eyes of his friend; and now Erkenwald, our most precious bringer of light, seemed to understand from within his tomb. The one man laid down the mere shadow of a pair of eyes, but the other removed the shadow from those eyes and gave them light again. An amazing thing! For the young man could not have left the basilica of Saint Paul, doctor of the gentiles, to return to the hostel when, lo, the sick man's lost sight begins to return and his eyelids begin to flicker joyfully, and he who had earlier seemed but a maniac has now already recovered the natural and

O hominem de perdicione anime et corporis erkenwaldi precibus ab-
solutum.

Sciscitantibus qui aderant quomodo se haberet, tale dicitur dedisse
80 responsum: "Ego, per beatum erkenwaldum, qui mortuus fueram iam
uiuo, qui lumine priuatus extiteram iam uideo, et certe uenerabiles ip-
sius digitos sensi orbatis luminibus dignanter appositos |f. 41v|. *Et hoc
uobis signum.*[22] Crucem illam huc afferte." Qua allata, arrepta acu que
crucem et crucis baculum consuebat extraxit, et iterum, cunctis uidentibus, lumine preuio acu foramen impleuit.

O raphaelis noui stropha! Ille *oculos* tobie *piscis felle li*niuit, et lumen
amissum reddidit; iste spirituali digitorum appositione non solum oculis, immo membris uniuersis sanitatem restituit. Ille, phisica usus scientia, iusto homini in senectute in aliquo profuit; iste, preditus celesti
90 theoria, peccatori in iuuentute corpus et animam reparauit. Raphaelis
industria, tobie filius in terra non sua iecoris fumo a demonis letali imperio defenditur; hic piissimi erkenwaldi presidio, solo nutu, a tot demonibus quot premebatur criminis nexibus alienigena liberatur.[23]

Dantur ergo laudes deo altissimo, et tante nouitatis odore referta ciuitas;
una cum illis qui fuerant presentes currunt uelocius ad maiorem ecclesiam;
nunciatur clericis, pulsantur signa, letatur simul clerus et populus, 'Te
deumque laudamus' a sacerdote incepto. Mihi, qui aderam, scribendi
miraculum onus iniungitur.

Factum est autem istud mirabile signum, uacante cathedra lundoniensi
100 sub rege stephano, a partu uirginis anno millesimo centesimo tricesimo
nono, mundi machinam gubernante rege regum domino nostro ihesu
christo.[24]

VIII   *De puella ceca cita luce donata*[1]

Nec hoc pretereundum est quod diebus illis quedam matrona filiam
propriam, utriusque sideris lumine destitutam, ad asilum preciosissimi
corporis in multorum presentia secum lacrimabiliter adduxit, et statim,
oratione completa, subitam illuminationem puella cunctis mirantibus
euidenter obtinuit.

normal use of all his limbs. O young man, freed from destruction of body and soul by the prayers of Erkenwald.

When those present asked him how it had come about, he is said to have replied thus: "I who was dead am now alive through the blessed Erkenwald; I who was deprived of my sight can now see and truly I have felt his holy fingers gently touching my sightless eyes. And this will be a sign to you. Give me the cross." And they brought the cross to him and he gripped the pin which held the cross-piece to the stave and drew it out. And then, everyone watching him, with his own eyes guiding him he put the pin back in the hole.

Behold, Raphael's device made new. He daubed the eyes of Tobias with the fish's gall and restored the sight he had lost; but in this case by the ghostly touch of his fingers, the saint cured the eyesight and also healed all the limbs. In the former case, using the physician's science, Raphael did some good to a good old man; but here with celestial expertise, Erkenwald repaired both body and soul in a young sinner. With Raphael's active help, the son of Tobias in a foreign land was defended from the fatal power of a demon by the smoke from the liver; but here, under most holy Erkenwald's protection, simply by his willing it, a foreigner was freed from the bonds of sin by all the demons with whom he was afflicted.

Thanks were given to God on high and the city was filled with rumors of this great miracle. People ran with all speed to the great church, along with those who had witnessed the miracle; the clerics were informed, the bells rung, and both clergy and people rejoiced, while a priest began to sing Te Deum Laudamus. The task of recording the miracle was laid on myself, for I was there.

This marvellous event occurred during the time when the episcopal throne of London was vacant, in the reign of Stephen in the year 1139 since the Virgin bore a child, this cosmic order being governed by the King of kings, our Lord Jesus Christ.

Miracle 8   *Concerning the blind girl whose sight was speedily restored*

Nor should we pass over another event from the same period. A certain matron had a daughter who was bereft of sight in each eye, and she brought her weeping one day into the sanctuary of the most precious body, in the presence of many people; and there, as soon as she had finished her prayer, to the wonder of all, the girl without doubt suddenly received her sight.

IX   *De languido confestim sanato*

|Hiisdem temporibus quidem iuuenis languidus et atroci infirmitate
correptus, postquam admodum diu ante sepulchrum sepedicti presulis
iacuit, sanitate recuperata coram omnibus exclamauit: "Gratias tibi refero,
erkenwalde, qui infirmus huc veni et modo tua opitulante clementia sa-
nus et incolumis quo voluero possum exire."|

X |*Rubric missing*|

   Nec multo interposito tempore, uir quidam, eustachius nomine, cum
domus in qua supramemorata theca fabricaretur limina sepius attriuisset —
erat enim argentarius — quadem die, malo suo, in eadem argentarios nostros stolide uisitauit.[1] Et ut habebat consuetudinis fere ebrius, statim
iam dictam domunculam uanis atque superfluis tumultuationibus oc-
cupauit. Et quia similem similis diu non querit,[2] potius qui aderant gar-
rulitati eius aures prebuerunt, quam a temulentis gannitibus cohiberent.
   Porro ibi erat sepulchrum ligneum argento et auro tegendum, in quo
erkenwaldi membra condere fixeramus.[3] Credidit stultus se posse cum
10 celestibus quemadmodum ludebat cum coeuis mortalibus. Credidit, quia
blasphemando placuit lusoribus, quod similiter placeret sanctorum numi-
nibus. Enim uero, fatui, crescente insania, cepit miser supramemorato
ligneo locello non tantum quedam inhonesta proferre, uerum etiam ausu
temerario fabrica lignea sulleuata, ad modum sancti corporis quiescen-
tis interius latitare ac dicere,[4] "Ego sum erkenwaldus sanctissimus: mihi
munera deferte! A me auxilium po|f. 42r|stulate! Michi argenteum fer-
culum preparate!"
   Cum hec et his similia infelix rauco gutture perstrepuisset, graui infirmitate correptus, a circumstantibus foras eicitur, et ad lectum satis lacrima-
20 biliter deductus, infra paucos dies diuino percussus iudicio expirauit. Nimirum erkenwaldi miracula eiusdemque sanctitatem pertinaciter spreuerat,
unde secreti iudicii rimatorem ad percutiendum penitus animarat. Nec mirum si unus pro tanta animaduersione percutitur; cum prophetarum ira

Miracle 9 *Concerning a sick man speedily restored to health*

[During this same time, a young man who had been suffering from a terrible affliction, after he had lain by the tomb of the oft-named prelate, recovered his health and exclaimed before all present, "I thank you, Erkenwald, for with your aid and mercy I who came here sick can go hence whole and sound whither I will."]

Miracle 10 *[Rubric missing]*

Not long afterwards it happened that a man by the name of Eustace, being a silversmith, was in the frequent habit of slouching across the threshold of the house in which the reliquary, mentioned above, was being constructed. One day, unlucky for him, he paid one of his silly visits to our silversmiths in this same house, and being somewhat drunk as was his custom, he began at once to fill the little workshop with idle and unnecessary noise and buffoonery. It does not take long for a fool to find his fellow, and the others present lent a ready ear to his garrulity instead of ignoring his drunken yapping.

Now the wooden sepulcher that was to be covered with silver and gold, in which we planned to preserve Erkenwald's bodily members, was in the workshop on this occasion, so the stupid man thought he could act the fool with the spirits of heaven just as he was doing with his mortal peers. He thought that because his blasphemy amused his bantering friends, it would likewise delight the godlike souls of the saints. For to tell the truth he became even more out of his mind; not only did the wretch begin to make disgraceful remarks about the wooden shrine but also with wild presumption and daring he raised the wooden lid and hid himself inside as though he were the saint's body at rest; and thus he spoke:

"I am the most holy Erkenwald: bring me gifts; ask for my help; make me a sepulcher of silver!" When the unfortunate creature had bawled out these words, and others like them, in his raucous voice, he was suddenly seized by a severe pain. Whereupon, he was snatched out of the coffin by those around him and they bore him weeping profusely home to his bed. Within a few days, by the stroke of divine judgement, he died. Truly, he had stubbornly scorned the miracles and the sanctity of Erkenwald, and he had thereby provoked the agent of secret justice to strike him deep inside. Nor is it any wonder that one man was struck dead for such a great

quinquagenarios et quinquaginta suos celestibus incendiis, et duobus ursis quadraginta duos pueros tradat.[5]

XI   De medico a letali egritudine sanato

Per idem tempus egrotantium multitudo copiosa ante sancti tumbam sanitatis remedia poscebat, inter quos quidam uenerabilis clericus, cuiusdam magni nominis notarius,[1] spe sanitatis recipiende, omnibus qui eum nouerant mirantibus, se medium interiecit. Nam cum medicus esset et se minime per se uel per alios curare potuisset, odore miraculorum sancti pontificis refertus, tandem prouectione fidei roboratus, medicine celesti totum se destinauit.

Rerum enim euentus sepius a fluctiuaga mundi huius delectacione mortales solent retrahere, quos diuina clementia nullatenus potuit emen-
10   dare. Vnde euangelicus filius, quia fame peribat, ad patrem reuertitur,[2] et in Osee mulier fornicaria, post multas fornicationes ad se reuersa, loquitur, *reuertar ad uirum meum priorem, quia* melius *erat mihi tunc quam nunc*.[3] Et bene non est in ciuitate malum quod non faciat dominus; quia ad hoc creat malum, ut in ipso pacem habeamus.[4]

Verbi gratia.[5] Juuenis pretaxatus cum mundo ruente deliciis irretitus ruebat, cum subito morbo siccatus epatico, quem mala uoluntas suggesserat, hoc propria necessitas abdicabat. Et quia in mortem peccati deciderat diro flemone percutitur ut resurgat.

Erat autem, ut est illius infirmitatis, ita macie et omnium membro-
20   rum dissolutione fatigatus, ut potius expirare uideretur quam uiuere. Igitur, ut prediximus, miserabilis ille satis adam protoplastum imitans, cuius erat omonimus, inter alios debiles ipse debilior dei misericordiam prestolatur, uigiliis, ieiuniis, orationibus ante corpus sanctissimum deum lacrimabiliter deprecatur ut et suorum ueniam facinorum languorisque remedia consequi mereatur.

insult, when the wrath of prophets could deliver up captains and their troops of fifty to be destroyed by the fire from heaven, and two and forty boys to be devoured by two bears.

Miracle 11   *Concerning the doctor who was healed of a deadly sickness*

During the same period, a great number of sick people were wont to beg to be healed of their illnesses before the saint's tomb. Among these there was a certain noble cleric who was chancery clerk to a person of high standing and who, in the hope of recovering his health and to the surprise of all his acquaintances, thrust himself into the crowd of suppliants. For, being a physician who had been unable to cure himself by his own or others' efforts, and his head being filled with stories of the holy bishop's miracles, and encouraged in the end by an increase of faith, he decided to trust himself utterly to celestial medicine.

For mortal men who have not felt impelled to amend their lives in any way by the thought of God's power are very often pulled back from the dizzily unreliable pleasures of this world by the simple pressure of events. The son in the gospels who returns to his father does so because he is dying of hunger, and in the prophet Hosea, the adulterous woman, after many successive love affairs, comes to herself and says, "I will return to my first husband, because things were better with me then than they are now." And truly, there is no evil in the city which is not of the Lord's doing, for he creates misfortune so that in himself we might find relief and peace.

For example, the young man we spoke of was rushing along in this headlong world, tangled and snared by its pleasures until, suddenly exhausted by a liver disease brought on by his wicked desire for pleasure, his own vital need compelled him to renounce it all. And because he had fallen into the death-in-life of sin, he was stricken with a terrible inflammation, so that he might be lifted up again.

For, as is characteristic of that illness, he was so worn out by its emaciating effects and by the degeneration of his bodily organs that he seemed more likely to die than to live. And so, as we said earlier, this miserable man, imitating Adam the first man, whose name he shared, awaited, among others of the infirm, God's mercy upon such people, and before the most holy body tearfully besought God with his vigils, fasts, and prayers that he might be found worthy of obtaining forgiveness for his sins and recovery from his disease.

Quid plura? Properantibus nobis die tercia ad ecclesiam post uesperti-
nam sinaxim ut horam duodecimam diei compleremus,[6] subito obuium
habuimus supramemoratum languidum erkenwaldi precibus adiutum,
immo pristine sanitati restitutum, in huiusmodi preconia in omnium
30   presentia resolutum.

"Sciat hoc uniuersus clerus et populus, me ante paucas horas letali
infirmitate pregrauante ita mei impotem extitisse, ut non solum manu-
um officia perdidissem, uerum etiam omnium amminiculis caruissem.
Modo sancti uestri meritis interuenien|f. 42v|tibus, sanitate recuperata
ita ualidus existo, ut non solum manducare et bibere, uerum etiam,
incredibili dei uirtute, uiribus propriis equum ascendere et quo placuerit
ualeam equitare."

Si fuerit inexplicabile gaudium inter audientes, uanum est querere,
uanius autem tante nouitati obtrectando non credere. Michi autem pro
40   minimo est si ab illis iudicer qui sanctorum uirtutibus magis desipiunt,
quam in augmentum fidei crescant, magis murmurando in amurca sor-
dium putrescunt, quam tot uisis miraculis ad uirtutum foramina sur-
gant. Ceterum qui se sentit meritis inferiorem erkenwaldo, sileat, ne magis
sibi noceat detrahendo.[7]

Certe in domo mea per paucos dies dietauit, in quibus a laudibus erkenwaldi non cessauit; et inter cetera istud quod sequitur crebrius narrando frequentauit.

"Videbatur," inquit, "mihi dum in ecclesia pernoctarem audiri strepitus
circa hominis dei sepulturam. Quotienscunque usque ad candelabrum
50   ligneum, cui impressa fuerat, ignis consumpserat candelam, concitus ilico altius cereum inherebam, sed si paulo lumina clausissem, statim soni-
tum audiebam; unde timore perterritus, iterum cereum subleuabam."[8]

Nimirum eadem misericordia que ab egritudine peccatorem uoluit liber-
are, ad orationem dignata est incitare, ut quemadmodum corpore
sanabatur ita a spirituali sanie in anima curaretur.

What more is there to say? On the third day, as we were hastening to the church after vespers to complete the observance of the twelfth hour of the day, we suddenly met the aforesaid invalid who, with the help of Erkenwald's prayers, had been restored to his pristine state of health and set free to proclaim his delivery in the presence of all and in the following manner:

"Let all the clergy and people know this, that a few hours ago a deadly illness lay heavily upon me, rendering me utterly powerless, in that I had not only lost the use of my hands but I also lacked any means of supporting or helping myself. But the merits of your saint came to my aid and I have regained my health and am strong enough not only to eat and drink but also, by God's wonderful power, I can mount a horse without assistance and ride wherever I please!"

It is a pointless question, to ask if there was joy inexpressible among those who heard him, and it is equally pointless to be skeptical and critical over this great miracle. It matters little to me if I am judged unfavorably by those who are driven mad by the miracles of the saints rather than being inspired by them to grow in increase of faith; or by those who would rather mutter and carp and rot in the slimy dregs of their filth, than rise to the corridors of virtue after seeing so many wonderful miracles. But he who feels himself inferior to Erkenwald's merits should nonetheless keep quiet, lest he do more harm to himself by such detraction.

That man stayed on for a few days at my house, during which time he did not cease from praising Erkenwald, and among the various things he said, he would repeat most often the story that follows.

"When I was spending the night in the church," he said, "it seemed to me that I heard noises by the sepulcher of the man of God. As often as a flame burned a candle down to the wooden candlestick into which it had been thrust, I would quickly push the candle down deeper inside; but if I were to diminish the light a little, I would immediately hear a noise, at which in my terror I would raise the candle back up again."

Truly the same mercy which wished to deliver the sinner from his sickness deigned to urge him on in his prayers, so that just as he was being made well in body, he might also be cured of the spiritual corruption in his soul.

XII   *Quomodo festiuitatis eius preuaricator ipso suo opere punitur*

Illud quoque magnificentiam dei sanctique pontificis erkenuualdi gloriam aures audiendi habentibus[1] predicat, quia cum quidam christiane
religionis contemptor indictam festiuitatem sepenominati presulis opere
sacrilego uiolare presumpserit, penam condignam nec euitare nec etiam
differre preualuit.

Artifex etenim quidam, nomine uitalis, qui studium exercebat in pel-
libus expurgandis, quibus uulpinum fieret indumentum in urbe sancti
pontificis, aliis feriantibus, ipse opus exercere solitum conatus est. Fal-
cem enim arripuit, pellemque radere cepit. Contigit interea conciues il-
10   lac transire ad templum doctoris gentium ob honorem sancti erkenwaldi
festinantes.

Vt autem pellificem postpositis diuinis operibus humanis intendere
persenserunt, quidam eorum pereunti fratri condoluerunt; quidam uero
tanquam sacrilego insultauerunt. Nec defuerunt qui fraterno affectu ab
illicito ausu transgressorem temperarent. Hi quippe dixerunt, "Irato deo
uitalis hodie surrexisti, cum sis permissus tale perpetrare opus, quo parum lucraris, et anime detrimentum uehemens pateris. Episcopo ciuitatis, immo deo patrie celestis, inobediens existis, cum indictum negligas
festum,[2] cum conciuibus tuis uidentibus ingeras scandalum. Proice,
20   infelix, proice pellem de manu tua! Opus tuum immo te ipsum grauiter
condempna! Curre ad edem sa|f. 43r|cram et corde contrito implora
ueniam. Sanctum dei amicum erkenuualdum si petieris, intercessorem
ad dominum obtinebis, quem ad uindictam peccati tui prouocasti operibus prophanis."

His uero atque similibus aliis admonitionibus diutissime protractis, per-
mansit in opere cepto morte dignus uitalis. Parum illi fuit ut amicos
salubriter exortantes neglegeret, addidit etiam ut pro admonitione derisionem aliam et aliam proximis ingereret. Cum ergo contumeliis pretereun-
tibus ingerendis operam daret, ferramentum quo pellem scalpebat
30   inprouidus extraxit, oculumque proprium perforauit.

Miracle 12   *How a man who profaned Erkenwald's festival was punished by his own hand*

This incident likewise declares, to all who have ears to hear it, the greatness of God and the glory of the holy bishop Erkenwald, concerning as it does an occasion when a certain man, one who despised the Christian religion, dared to desecrate the festival of the oft-named prelate with a sacrilegious act, but had no power to avoid or even put off the punishment he deserved.

This man, whose name was Vitalis, was a craftsman who was in the business of cleaning the hides from which fox-skin cloaks were made in the city of the holy bishop. One day he made a point of carrying on his day-to-day business when others were celebrating the saint's day. He had taken up his knife and was starting to scrape a hide when, as it happened, some of his fellow citizens passed that way, as they hurried to the church of the doctor of the gentiles in order to do honor to St. Erkenwald.

When they realized that the pelterer was neglecting the works of God and concentrating on those of man, several of them pitied their brother, whom they considered lost, while others were inclined to abuse him for his sacrilege. And there were those who with brotherly affection would rather prevail upon the transgressor to give up his illicit presumption, and they said to him, "God must have been angry with you today when you arose, Vitalis, in order for you to have been permitted to work at this sort of thing. You will gain little money from it, and you will suffer with bitterness the loss of your soul. You have been disobedient to the bishop of the city and, further, to God in our heavenly home, since you are neglecting a festival which is to be observed by all, and with your fellow citizens looking on you are making a public spectacle of yourself. Wretched man, cast that hide from your hand, cast it away, I say. Condemn the work you are doing, and condemn yourself sincerely and deeply. Run to the holy temple and with a contrite heart beg forgiveness. If you ask Erkenwald, the holy friend of God, you will obtain him as your intercessor with the Lord, whom you have aroused to vengeance by your works of evil."

Although they urged these and similar warnings upon him for quite a long time, Vitalis, who was truly fit for death, carried on with his work. Nor was it enough for him to ignore the wholesome exhortations of his friends, but added to this, in return for their warnings, he hurled back one derisive comment after another at those closest to him. However, while he was busy lobbing abuse and scorn at those passing by, unbeknownst to him he slipped the blade out of the tool with which he was scraping the hide and it pierced his own eye.

Sic igitur luit homo iniquus instructionem piam quam frustra perfecerat illi populus amicus. Et qui noluit feriari ob sancti erkenuualdi honorem, opus abiecit ob oculi sui grauissimum dolorem.

Casu nempe miserandi hominis sunt uarii sermones exorta, insultacionem pro insultacione reddentibus his, ac misericordiam misero prestantibus illis. Omnis tamen in commune laudauerunt deum, ac sanctum erkenuualdum certatim predicauerunt; hunc quia sanctos suos non tantum in celis, uerum etiam in terris mirificat; illum autem quia diligentibus se securitatem, atque negligentibus seueritatem correctoriam,
40   procurat.

Nos autem fratres timeamus deum, qui nichil impietatis relinquit multum; diligamus quoque ipsum qui remunerabit quicquid bene fuerit gestum.

XIII   De ceca illuminata[1]

Nec hoc pretereundum existimo, quod in omnium oculis quedam uicina nostra, de eiusdem sancti erkenuualdi parrochia, lumine cecata, in omnium oculis lumen amissum obtinuit. Quod tanta admirationis euidentia statim claruit, ut in sequenti dominica ad spectaculum non uocati ciues concurrerent, et, uisa muliere, laudes non modicas una clerus et populus domino decantarent. Enim uero tam precelebre et tam euidens extitit, ut nullus qui inde dubitaret in tanta multitudine fuerit.

XIV   De insidiatoribus corporis eius frustratis; eiusque transpositione et sarcofago diuinitus adaucto concurrentibusque miraculis [1]

Imponebatur tunc temporis quibusdam anglorum monasteriis,[2] quod fama miraculorum attonita corpus sancti noctu furari uoluerint. Vnde intempeste noctis silentio non pauci homines ualuas criptarum in qui-

Thus the wicked man paid for the devout and well-intended instruction given him in vain by a friendly people. And he who had no wish to take a holiday for the sake of honoring St. Erkenwald cast off his work from him on account of the terrible pain in his eye.

Different opinions were voiced regarding the case of this wretched man, some people reviling him for his blasphemy, others offering him sympathy in his misery. But all together, however, praised God and enthusiastically proclaimed the holy Erkenwald. They praised God because he glorifies his saints on earth as well as in heaven, and they acclaimed Erkenwald because for those who love him he provides safety and for those who neglect him he provides bitter reproof.

Let us therefore fear God, brothers, for there are few impieties he ignores, and let us love him also, since he will reward whatever we do that is good.

Miracle 13   *Concerning the blind woman who received her sight*

I do not think I should pass over the incident of the woman, a neighbor of ours, from the same parish of St. Erkenwald, who as everyone knew was blind, but who in the presence of all obtained the sight she had lost. And there was such clear and immediate evidence of this wonderful event that on the following Sunday the citizens hastened to see the wonder without being summoned, and having seen the woman, clergy and people together chanted exuberant praises to the Lord. For this miracle was so well known and so plain that there was no one in that great multitude who doubted it had happened.

Miracle 14   *Concerning the foiling of an attempt by some thieves to steal his body, and concerning the translation, and the supernatural enlargement of the sarcophagus, with the concurrent miracles*

It was imputed to several English monasteries at that time that, astonished at the fame of Erkenwald's miracles, they wanted to steal the body of the saint by night. So it happened that in the dead of night, a goodly number of men broke down the doors of the crypt where the saint was buried and

bus idem sanctus condebatur confregerunt, et ianuas altaris[3] usque
uenientes, ausu temerario, prope frangere presumpserunt.

Quorum strepitu euigilans quidam, tunc pueritiam exuens, qui solus
cum duobus clericulis, locum custodum occupans,[4] in ecclesia pernoc-
tabat, clamoribus suis totam illam multitudinem ita dementauit, ut, diuino perculsi iudicio, ad uocem tanti hominis cursu concito per portam
10 qua uenerant repedarent.

His igitur tumultuationibus ecclesie superioris editui conclamantes, et
tintinnabuli pulsatione auxilium conuocantes, illos quidem comprehen-
dere nequiuerunt |f. 43v|, sed pro tanta animaduersione usque ad mane
ibidem excubias celebrarunt.

Facto autem mane, octo presbiteros tam uenerabili thesauro custodes
delegauimus, donec tercia die in tuciori loco interim parato sancti reliquias clauderemus.

Omnibus igitur rite paratis, cum crucibus et cereis sacerdotibus etiam
ad tam uenerabile obsequium prestolantibus, cum processione et letaniis
20 ad tumbam uenimus erkenuualdi pontificis, cuius loculo ligneo subleuato,
repperimus corpus sacratissimum isdem sigillorum munitionibus quibus
iam pridem fuerat premunitum.[5]

Certe per nos nulli in urbe fuerat nuntiatum, et diuina tamen prouidentia tantus factus est concursus populorum ut, toto nisu renitentibus qui
pro foribus aderant, ipsas fores serris postibusque excuterent, nec a suo
desiderio defraudari, una nobiscum tam ineffabile sacramentum per-
spicerent.[6]

Quid plura? Impetum multitudinis ultra sustinere non ualentes, ar-
repto plumbeo sepulchro in quo corpus sanctissimum quiescebat, ad
30 preparatum habitaculum cum lacrimis illud ferebamus, et ecce omnis
nostra preparatio irrita apparuit. Sarcina enim nostro edificio tam in
longitudine quam in latitudine permultum amplior innotuit. Res miranda!
Cui per ignorantiam artificis negatur sepultura, per celos extendentis
dexteram[7] amplior in lapide fit apertura. Vbi cum sanctus includitur,
saxea duricies emollitur. Obliuiscitur lapis sue conditionis et paret ob-
tutibus conditoris.

Certe ego, qui hec scribo, ad mensuram plumbei sarcofagi lapideum
edificium nostrum ita aptum et conueniens inueni, ac si regula et per-
pendiculo ad plumbi magnitudinem fuisset extructum; unde sepius

coming to the altar gates dared, with shameless audacity, to begin to break their way in.

But the noise they were making awoke a youth, just barely out of boyhood, who habitually spent the night alone in the church and who had the job, along with two boys from the cathedral school, of guarding the place. His shouting and yelling frightened the crowd of thieves out of their wits, so much so that, disheartened by this divine judgement, at the sound of the mighty little fellow's voice they ran off at top speed back through the door by which they had entered.

Although the custodians of the upper church added their own shouts to this uproar and called for help by ringing the bell, they were unable to catch the thieves. But they made great joy over the watchmen for their opportune vigilance, until the following morning.

When morning came, however, we appointed eight priests to be watchmen to guard the precious and holy treasure until, after three days, we could enclose the saint's relics in a safer place which was to be got ready for them in the meantime.

And so when all things were prepared for the rite, and the priests with crucifixes and candles were present in readiness for this holy ceremony, we came in procession, singing litanies, to the tomb of Bishop Erkenwald, and having raised the lid of the wooden shrine, we found the most sacred body still protected by the same seals with which it had long before been secured.

Certainly we had not announced any of this to any one in the city, but divine providence brought it about that a crowd of people assembled and those who were outside the doors, their way being blocked by the great press inside, tore the very doors off the hinges and posts, refusing to be cheated of their desire, which was to see with us the inexpressibly holy rite.

What more? Since we could not withstand the onrush of the multitude any longer, we picked up the lead coffin in which the most holy body was resting, and tearfully we bore it to the new home that had been prepared for it. And lo, all our preparation appeared to be in vain, for the coffin was clearly too large both in length and breadth, for the structure we had built to house it. But then a marvellous thing happened. For the sake of him who was being denied burial by the craftman's ignorance, the opening in the stone was made larger by the right hand of him who extends the heavens. When the saint was being placed inside it, the hardness of the slabs became soft, the stone forgot its natural condition and submitted to the gaze of its creator.

Truly I myself who write these things found our stone housing fitted the measurements of the lead coffin as well as if it had been constructed by rule and plumb-line to the exact size of the coffin. For I frequently checked it

40 propriis manibus attrectaui, deum testem inuoco, quod inter plumbum
    et lapidem in aliqua parte digitum figere nequiui.

    Affirmabant qui aderant eadem sorori sue, sanctissime edelburge, olim
    euenisse.[8] Nec dubium quod de sancto Sebba Rege uenerabilis Beda,
    anglorum gemma, in historia sua scripsit, sapientiores quoque, qui in
    presentia fuerunt, recoluisse.[9] Incredibili igitur gaudio animati cum tan-
    ta deuotione *te deum laudamus* cantauimus, ut et tam clerici quam populi
    pia lacrima uultus perfunderetur.

    Translatum est igitur sanctissimi corpus erkenuualdi anno ab incar-
    natione domini millesimo centesimo quadragesimo, mense februario, die
50 eiusdem mensis sextodecimo.[10]

    In cuius translatione, preter illud quod supra posuimus et alia multa
    que propter quorundam tedium omittimus, duo miracula claruerunt.
    Alterum in omnium oculis in quodam canonico nostro presente, forte
    tunc febricitante; alterum uero in puero quodam absente et iam per
    dimidium annum et eo amplius usque ad mortem egrotante. Presens prop-
    ter presentes, absens curatur propter absentes. Presenti subuenitur sancti
    presentia, absenti uero pulueris de ligno in quo sanctus iacuerat aspersura.

    Referebat enim eiusdem pueri dominus, theoldus |f. 44r|, consotius
    noster, ecclesie beati martini, que in lundoniensi ciuitate est sita, canoni-
60 cus,[11] quod collectum puluerem statim ut cum aqua infirmo tradidit,
    infirmitatem omnino euasit. Adiungebat etiam quod thuris, in eodem
    ligneo locello a se reperti, tenui fumigatione nares infirmantis impleuerit,
    et quasi thimiamate compellente morbum uniuersum depulerit.

XV *De curato febricitante ipso sancto eum uisitante*

    Libet compendiose commemorare qualiter duo grauiter febricitantes
    ad sepulchrum eiusdem patris nostri erkenuualdi sunt sanati, ut et
    presentes et futuri spem et fiduciam habeant pietatis et misericordie si
    ex toto corde inibi petierint.

myself with my own hands, and, God be my witness, I could not fit my finger between coffin and stone at any point.

Those present affirmed that the same thing had happened once to the most holy Ethelburga, his sister. Nor is there any doubt that the wiser men present also called to mind what the venerable Bede, jewel among Englishmen, wrote concerning the holy king, Sebbe. Filled with boundless joy, therefore, we sang the *Te Deum* with such fervor that the faces of clergy and people alike streamed with pious tears.

And thus was the body of the most holy Erkenwald translated, in the year eleven hundred and forty after the incarnation of the Lord, in the month of February, on the sixteenth day of the month.

Two miracles in particular shone forth in this translation, besides those we have told already and many others we will pass over so as not to be tedious. One of them, which happened in front of everyone, involved one of our canons, who by chance at that time was sick with a fever; the other befell a boy who was not present but who for half a year and more had been sickening even unto death. The one was healed for the benefit of those present at the translation, the other for the benefit of those not present. As for the former, it was the saint's close presence that relieved him, while the latter was healed by a sprinkling of the dust from the wooden shrine in which he had lain.

The master of this boy, Theoldus our colleague, canon of the church of the blessed Martin situated in the city of London, reported that as soon as he gave the dust he had collected, in water, to the sick boy, he came out of the illness completely. He added also that he filled the nostrils of the sick boy with the slight odor of the incense which he had found in the same wooden shrine and, as if the incense were driving it forth, banished every trace of the disease.

Miracle 15   *Concerning the man who was cured of his fever by the saint, who visited him in person*

Now I would like to recall briefly how two men, gravely ill with fever, were made well at the tomb of the same father, our Erkenwald, in order that people now and in the future might have hope and confidence in his goodness and mercy if they should make their request there out of the fullness of their hearts.

Quidam de transmarinis partibus aduena, baldewinus nomine, pluribus notus lundonie intolerabiliter igne febrium anxiatus est. Quesiuit
ubique refrigerium medele, sed inuenire non ualuit. Quadam igitur die,
dum inter manus suorum comitum debilis sursum et deorsum sustentatus uagaretur, ut pestilentia febrium saltem eundo excuteretur, preterit
10   casu ante monasterium[1] doctoris gentium, et audiens altisonis uocibus
canonicos psallere, sciscitatus est clerum quamobrem tam solenniter diem
illam celebrarent. Dictum est ei a circumstantibus quia ob festiuitatem
sancti erkenuualdi tam deuote concinerent. Continuo supplicauit ut ad
tumulum ipsius deduceretur, sperans sospitatem sibi per eius merita reddendam. Dum ergo allatus esset secus introitum chori,[2] admodum las-
sus et languidus resedit et obdormiuit.

Vidit igitur sopitus assistere sibi uirum elegantem cum baculo pastorali,
uestibus niue candidioribus ac sacerdotalibus indutum, quemadmodum
archiepiscopi[3] missam celebraturi uestiuntur. Qui perscrutatus est, quid
20   haberet uel cur aduenisset. Respondit eger, "Domine, febrium molesta
passio me fatigat et iugiter torquet, et ut remedium consequerer ad por-
tum salutis et sepulchrum sancti, cuius hodierna solennitas agitur,
confugi."

Dicit ei sanctus, "Ego sum. Fiat tibi sicut uis, et sicut credidisti." Deinde
uero in modum crucis, ante et retro dextrorsum et sinistrorsum caput
illius molliter et suauiter comprimens, dicessit, signo sancte crucis fron-
ti ipsius impresso.

Ipse autem febricitans, immo iam sanus, sopore adhuc fluctuans, exclamauit, "Domine, domine, miserere mei, et alleuia dolorem meum!"
30   Et expergefactus, leuita euuangelium incipiente,[4] propriis uiribus sospes
surrexit, oblationem obtulit, prostratus in terram gratias egit, et post
missam sospes domum rediit.

De ipsius socio ab eodem morbo eodem modo et loco et hora sanato

Avdiens uero consodalis ipsius, eodem morbo grauatus, eadem hora
baiulatus inter manus suorum ad sepulchrum beati uiri peruenit et,
opitulante ipso, eodem modo sanatus est.

A certain foreigner from across the sea, who was known to many in London by the name of Baldwin, was afflicted unbearably by the fires of fever. He sought everywhere for the consolation of a remedy but was unable to find one. One day, when the enfeebled man was being walked up and down, supported by the hands of friends, in the hope that simply walking might shake off the plaguing of the fever, by chance he passed by the minster of the doctor of the gentiles and hearing the canons chanting the psalms in their high voices he enquired what it was that the clergy were celebrating so solemnly that day. He was told by some bystanders that they were singing so fervently because it was St. Erkenwald's festival. Immediately he begged to be taken to the latter's tomb, hoping to have his health restored to him through the saint's merits. When he had been brought within the entrance to the chancel he sat down utterly worn out and weakened and fell asleep.

And while he slept he saw standing next to him a man with a pastoral staff clothed in white priestly vestments such as are worn by archbishops when celebrating mass, who questioned him as to what he wanted and why he had come. The sick man answered: "Lord, I am suffering from a grievous fever which exhausts me and tortures me continuously, and I have come seeking a refuge and a remedy, at the door of salvation and the tomb of the saint whose festival is being solemnized today."

The saint said to him, "I am he. It shall be as you wish and as you have believed it would be." Then he traced the form of the cross, pressing gently and softly on his head, at the front and back and on the right and left side, and then he went away, after making the sign of the cross on his forehead.

But the man with the fever, who was now whole and well but still moving restlessly in his sleep, cried out, "O Lord, have mercy upon me and take away my affliction!" And being awakened by the deacon beginning the gospel, he arose by his own strength happy and whole, and made his offering, and prostrating himself on the ground gave thanks, and after mass the fortunate man returned home.

Concerning a friend of his who was healed of the same illness in the same way and at the same place and time
When a friend and companion of this man, who was laboring under the same malady, heard about this, he arrived within the hour at the blessed man's sepulcher supported on the arms of his men and with his help was healed in the same way.

XVI *De puella ab eadem ualitudine, eodem ordine, ibidem alio tempore[1] repente curata*

Similis ferme curatio facta est in puella quadem lundoniensi. Multis enim diebus languebat febre fatigata, nec ullo genere medendi potuit re|f. 44v|staurari. Sed dominus noster clementissimus pater, qui filios suos interdum patrono uerbere corripit et ad se reuocat, modo blanditur et modo sanat,[2] huiusmodi remedium ei conferre dignatus est.

Nam dilectus suus erkenuualdus noctu illi uisus est astitisse, et in hunc modum sibi sermocinari. "Diu excocta es in fornace huius temptationis, non quod aliquo criminali peccato uitam tuam commaculaueris, sed ut in futuro iuuenilem petulantiam uirga correctionis studeas edomare,
10   moresque maturos imitari. Crastina die accelera sepulchrum meum uisitare, ibique oratura dominum ihesum christum ab hac debilitatis catena liberaberis."

Illa quidem, tremebunda cum uellet nomen eius percunctari, sed nimius pauor ipsam elinguem redderet, hoc seruus dei sentiens subiecit, "Erkenuualdus nuncupor, habens sepulchrum in dextro latere altaris sancte fidis uirginis et martyris.[3] Quo cum perueneris credens firmiter, salua eris."

Cum hoc somnium, immo rem gestam pater et mater mane ipsa narrante didicissent, nimis hylares effecti, deumque laudantes in eadem hora
20   filiam suam inter brachia fulcientes adduxerunt, et, ut sanctus presul docuerat, iuxta mausoleum ipsius eam collocauerunt. Cunque in puncto momenti esset in somnum soluta, statim totius doloris egritudo euacuata, et ipsa toto corpore incolumis est reddita.

XVII *Qualiter ipsius pictor festi eius temerator punitus est ipso sancto apparente causamque protestante*

Sepe legimus et audiuimus plerosque in hac uita castigatos esse nolentes celebrare festiuitates sanctorum, sicut quidam pictor, teoduuinus nomine,[1] flagellatus est, quod presumpsit operari in solenni die presulis erkenuualdi, quod hoc modo gestum est.

Eo tempore quo ipsius sancti presulis corpus adhuc in crypta in sarcofago seruabatur, testudo eiusdem cripte pingenda erat. Interea solen-

Miracle 16 *Concerning the girl who, in the same place, by the same power and in the same way, but at a different time, was suddenly healed*

A very similar cure was effected in the case of a London girl, who for many days languished in a state of collapse due to fever, nor could she be restored to health by any kind of medicine. But our most merciful lord and father, who sometimes chides his children with his paternal rod and thereby calls them back to him, and then sometimes soothes and heals them, deigned to provide a remedy for her in this wise.

For her beloved Erkenwald seemed one night to stand next to her and speak to her, as thus: "For a long time you have been scorched in the furnace of this trial, not because you have stained your life with any particular sin, but so that in future you will be zealous to overcome any of the wantonness of youth with the rod of self-discipline, and to emulate the habits of grown-ups. Tomorrow hasten to visit my sepulcher, there to pray to the Lord Jesus Christ to free you from the chain of this crippling infirmity."

She indeed, all atremble with the desire to ask him his name, was rendered speechless from fear. But the servant of God perceived this and added, "I am called Erkenwald—my sepulcher is on the right side of the altar of St. Faith, virgin and martyr. If you go there in firm belief you will be made whole."

When on the following morning she told her father and mother what had happened and they learned of her dream, they were boundlessly happy, and praising God they led her off the self-same hour, supporting her in their arms, and put her down next to the saint's tomb as he had instructed her. There she slipped into a slumber and in that same instant all the ill-effects of her malady disappeared and she was restored to health and well-being in her whole body.

Miracle 17 *How one of the saint's painters, who violated his festival, was punished, the saint himself appearing to him and declaring the reason for the punishment*

We have read and heard about the many people who have been chastised in their own lifetime for their unwillingness to celebrate the festivals of the saints; just such a one was a painter by the name of Teodwin, who was scourged because he dared to work on the holy day of bishop Erkenwald. It happened thus.

During the period when the body of the holy prelate was still being kept in its coffin in the crypt, the vault of the crypt had to be painted. Now

nitas illius illuxit. Nullus ibi missam illa die celebrauit. Altare dis-
coopertum fuit propter instrumenta erecta pictoris officio idonea.

Innumerabilis multitudo utriusque sexus conuenit ad oratorium, orare
10   uolentes et oblationem ac luminaria ferentes, sed introitus eis non patuit.
Pictor enim ianuam serauit, et ipsam arcuatam testudinem coloribus uer-
miculauit.

Dum autem diligentius colores protraheret, repente destitutus est uiribus, et repentino dolore arreptus ueluti exanimatus corruit. Cum diu
sic cruciaretur, somnus eum inuasit. Ecce, supradictus antistes, infula
pontificali exornatus, uenit et baculo pastorali grauiter eum flagellauit,[2]
recapitulans negligentiam ipsius, uidelicet quod illa die pertinaciter oper-
atus est et quod populum exclusit.

Hanc uisionem et castigationem pluribus innotuit, postquam de infirmi-
20   tate illa conualuit.

XVIII   *De sanctimoniali claudicante sancta ethelburga sanctoque erkenwaldo*
      uisitantibus reformata

Sermo diuinus, fratres karissimi, cibus et refectio est animarum nos-
trarum, et sicut in uaniloquio peccatum accumulatur, sic in uerbis celes-
tibus homo noster interior sa|f. 45r|ginatur. Semper igitur laus dei sit
in ore nostro, nec tedium sit nobis frequenter ad memoriam reuocare
sanctorum suorum miracula, quum ad laudem et honorem eius creati
sumus.[1]

Ciuis lundonie ualde locuples habebat filiam multum quidem facie
decoram et spectabilem, sed claudicabat. Talibus enim flagellis deus pres-
cius futurorum plerosque arguit, et in eternam paradisi mansionem ingredi
10   compellit, qui eternaliter perirent, si ad uoluntatem suam per omnia
momentanea mundi prosperitas illis arrideret.[2]

Plures proci uolebant illam consortem thalami petere, non inferiores
genere uel facultate, sed incessus debilis, ut dictum est, illis displicuit.
Vterque parens eius et cognati super hoc detrimento dolentes, tandem
iudicauerunt salubrius esse ut ad collegia sanctarum monialium
dedicaretur. Cum ergo credita esset, uenerabili abbatisse aeluiue[3] Ber-

Erkenwald's festival took place while this was going on, but on this particular day mass was not being celebrated there and the covering had been removed from the altar on account of the erection of the scaffolding the painter needed for his work.

However, a great crowd of people of both sexes, who wished to pray, assembled at the oratory bearing offerings and candles. But they were denied entrance. For the painter had barred the door and carried on painting the curve of the vault with his paints and dyes.

When he was painting away with great industry, however, he was all at once bereft of his strength and, gripped by a sudden pain, he fell to the ground as if his life had left him. When he had suffered thus for a long time, sleep enveloped him and lo, the aforesaid prelate, garbed in his episcopal regalia, came to him and beat him hard with his pastoral staff, reminding him how disrespectful he had been to persist in working on that day and to lock the people out.

After he had recovered from his illness, he made known to many people this vision and chastisement.

Miracle 18   *Concerning the crippled nun who was visited by SS. Ethelburga and Erkenwald and made whole and straight*

Godly speech, dearest brothers, is the food and refreshment of our souls. And while sin grows big on idle prattle, the interior man in each of us is nourished with heavenly words. Therefore, let the praise of God be in our mouths always, and let it not be wearisome for us to call often to mind the miracles of his saints, since we are created for his praise and glory.

A very wealthy citizen of London had a daughter whose face was remarkably lovely, but she walked with a limp. With such scourgings God in his foreknowledge of future events chastises many folk and drives them on to gain entrance to the eternal house of paradise, who might eternally perish if the fleeting happiness of the world were to smile on them in everything as they desired.

Many suitors sought her out as partner for the marriage bed, but her limping gait, which we mentioned, displeased them. Both her parents and her kin, in their sorrow over this disability, finally decided that it would be more beneficial to dedicate her to a community of holy nuns. And so they entrusted her to the care of the venerable Abbess Alviva, of the convent of

kingensis ecclesie, cotidianis orationibus frequentauit sepulchrum sancte adelburge uirginis, sororis sancti erkenuualdi, eiusdem loci fundatoris, et ut directo gressu potiretur obnixe orauit, spondens deo celibem omni
20   tempore uitam.

Dum fidelis uirgo sepius peteret et sepissime celi palatium pulsaret, efficatium sui desiderii consecuta est. Nam sponsa christi, aedelburga, nocturno tempore uisa est taliter eam alloqui. "Filia, nimium depone dolorem, quoniam tua sanitas iam iam approximat. Tantum memor esto ut fratrem meum erkenuualdum crebro ad intercessionem tuam inuoces, quia suis opitulantibus meritis sospes redderis."

Talem uisionem cum ipsa diluculo sororibus suis explanasset, exorta-cionibus omnium, ieiuniis et orationibus plus solito inuigilabat, uniuer-sa quoque congregatio specialiter pro ipsa domino supplicabat.

30   Non multo igitur post tempore lapso, dum sanctimoniales matutinales laudes concinerent circa tumbam beate uirginis aedelburge, tam dulcis sopor irrepsit oculis ipsius claudicantis ancille christi, ut nequaquam reniti posset. Sed dum in loco dormitasset opaco non longe a sepulchro, ecce sanctus pontifex erkenuualdus in uultu angelico illi apparuit et, paterne consolatus eam, manum eius apprehendit, dicens, "In nomine domini nostri ihesu christi, surge, et sicut petrus et iohannes claudum erexer-unt, sic et tu erigaris."[4]

Quo dicto, statim euigilans et exurgens, conclamauit dicens, "Sanc-tissime pater erkenuualde," nomen enim suum ipse prius innotuit, "Sanc-
40   tissime pater, miserere miserere."

Interim uero dum ad integritatem restauraretur, tantus fragor a cir-cumstantibus auditus est, ac si arida sepes confringeretur. Vbi autem sanctimoniales rei euentum didicerunt, unanimi uoce *te deum laudamus* inchoauerunt.

XIX   *De puella surda auditu sanata*

Vir erat in finibus episcopatus linconiensis ecclesie, in territorio luitonie,[1] agricola inter suos haud infimus, timens deum et recedens a malo, et conuersationis bone. Cuius filia, elegantis forme, debilitatis uer-

Barking. And here every day she prayed at the tomb of St. Ethelburga, sister of St. Erkenwald who was founder of the convent, and begged persistently that she might come to have a normal, upright way of walking, vowing to God that she would live as a celibate all her life.

When the faithful virgin had prayed many times, and many times had beat upon the door of heaven, she obtained the fulfillment of her desire. For Ethelburga, bride of Christ, appeared to her at night and spoke to her thus: "Daughter, lay aside your boundless grief, for now the time of your healing draws near. Only remember to call continually to my brother Erkenwald and ask him to intercede for you; for with his merits to help you, you will be restored to health."

When she had related this vision at daybreak to her sisters, urged and encouraged by them all, she devoted herself even more than usual to her fastings and prayers, and the whole community beseeched the Lord especially for her sake.

Not long afterwards, when the nuns were singing lauds in the morning, by the tomb of the blessed virgin St. Ethelburga, such a sweet sleep stole upon the eyes of that crippled handmaiden of Christ that she could in no wise resist it. But while she was sleeping in a shady corner not far from the sepulcher, lo, the holy bishop Erkenwald appeared to her in the guise of an angel and, comforting her like a father, he took her hand and said, "In the name of our Lord Jesus Christ, arise, and just as the lame man was raised up by Peter and John, be thou likewise made straight."

At these words, she awoke immediately and rose up crying out and saying, "O most holy father Erkenwald," for he himself had made his name known to her earlier, "O most holy father have mercy on me in my misery."

And while there and then she was being restored to full health, a great cracking sound was heard by all those present, as of a dry hedge being torn down. And when the nuns learned how the thing had come about, with one voice they burst into *Te Deum Laudamus*.

Miracle 19   *Concerning the deaf girl whose hearing was restored*

There was a man in the episcopal see of Lincoln, in the district of Luton, who was a farmer, and not the least among his fellows, a God-fearing man who avoided evil and lived a godly life. He had a daughter who was beautiful to see but who was stricken with the lash of disease. She finally became

bere flagellata est, et tandem collectis sordibus obsur|f. 45v|duit et au-
ditus officium omnino amisit.

Parentes igitur, ipsius graui meroris fulmine perculsi, medicos condux-
erunt, ut sospitati redderetur. Sed medicorum ars et subtilitas ibi efficatiam
inuenire non potuit. Statuerunt autem opem diuinam experiri, et eam
ad limina sanctorum circumducere, ut multiplicatis intercessoribus
10 curaretur. Quo facto, cum nusquam salutem corporis recuperare posset, ad ultimam deducta est ante tumbam patroni nostri uenerabilis erkenuualdi presulis. Ibi sopita, cum expergisceretur patefactis auribus et
sanie guttatim effluente redintegrata est.

Nos quoque, fratres karissimi, ad deum toto corde conuersi deprecemur,
ut interuentu preclari pontificis erkenuualdi nos inter prospera et aduersa
sic dirigat, quatinus, uiciis omnibus absolutos, ad libertatem glorie celestis
perducat ihesus christus dominus noster, qui uiuit et regnat deus per
infinita secula, amen.

EXPLICIUNT miracula sancti erkenwaldi episcopi.

deaf with the accumulation of putrid matter in her ears, and lost altogether the faculty of hearing.

Her parents, in their utter desolation, as if smitten by lightning, called in the doctors to see if she could be restored to health. But the doctors' art and ingenuity were powerless to find a remedy. So then they decided to try for help from heaven and to take her to the houses of the saints in the hope that by multiplying their intercessions, she might be cured. They did this, but nowhere was she able to recover the health of her body, until she was brought at the last before the tomb of our worthy patron, bishop Erkenwald. There she was healed, when her ears opened and were cleansed, and as the poisonous matter flowed forth she was made whole again.

Let us likewise turn to God with all our hearts, dearest brothers, and pray to him that, by the intervention of the preeminent bishop Erkenwald, he may so guide us amidst prosperity and adversity that, when we are finally absolved from all our imperfections, we may be led to the freedom of heavenly glory by our Lord Jesus Christ, who lives and reigns and is God for ever and ever, amen.

Here end the miracles of St. Erkenwald, bishop.

Textual Notes

Textual Notes

Vita Sancti Erkenwaldi

For descriptions of the manuscripts, see Introduction, Chapter One. Manuscript sigla:

A = B. L. Cotton Claudius A.v.
C = Cambridge, Corpus Christi College 161
L = B. L. Lansdowne 436
D = Dugdale, *History of St. Paul's Cathedral* (1658)
Dm = Dugdale, *Monasticon*, vol. 3 (1673).

The text of the present edition of *VSE* is that of manuscript **A**, except where indicated otherwise. Manuscript spelling has been retained, but punctuation, paragraph divisions, and line numbering are editorial. **D**'s alterations of *e* to *ae*, *u* to *v*, *i* to *j* have not been recorded in the variant notes. **Dm** variants are given only where different from **D**. Editorial intrusions are in italics. The INCIPIT and EXPLICIT are not included in the numbered lines but their variants are listed at the beginning and end of the following notes.

INCIPIT VITA, etc.] *Unique to* C *is a set of* capitula, *before the* INCIPIT *proper, as follows:* INCIPIUNT CAPITULA IN VITAM sancti erkenwaldi lundoniensis episcopi. Qualiter beitus *[sic]* erkenwaldus ad sanctitatis apicem profecerit et duo cenobia construxerit. **Post passionem** etc. *[VSE 1].* ii. Qualiter ad pontificium promotus sermone et opere populum edificaret. **Contigit,** etc. *[VSE 27].* iii. Qualiter cum pro infirmitate nec proficisci ualeret, tamen prouinciam peragraret, et de uehiculi eius salutifera uirtute. **Post multa,** etc. *[VSE 34]. [iv.]* Qualiter nouo prodigio uehiculum eius una rota cursum suum *[i]*erit. **Quadam uero die,** etc. *[VSE 43].* v. Vt uocationem suam precognitam suis edixerit. **Sed quoniam,** etc. *[VSE 51].* vi. De sacro eius transitu ac mira fragrantia. **Beatus uero,** etc. *[VSE 56].* vii. De corporis eius transuectione humanitus decertata et diuinitus multimode mirificata. **Audientes,** etc. *[VSE 63].* EXPLICIVNT CAPITVLA: INCIPIT VITA sancti erkenwaldi episcopi ii kalendas maii.

1 Post] pridie kalendas maii *(inside bowl of capital* P*)* Post A. ac] AC et D.
3 dauiticis . . . tympanis] AC Daviatici . . . hympnis D.
5 aduolarunt] AD aduolauit C. 6 papa] AD papa romano C. missum. Qui] ACD Beatus Augustinus anglorum apostolus qui L.

6–7 tramitem uite] A in ibi uite tramitem C tramitem tute D vite tramitem L.
7 docendo in] AD docendo CL. sede] AD sedem CL.
7–8 radius fulgere cepit] AD radium fulgere fecit CL.
8 Mellitum igitur sancti] ACD sanctum Mellitum commonachum suum et sancti L.
9 lundonia] ACD Londonia L (*same variation throughout*).
10 tamense] AD tamensim C Tamensi L. athelbertus] AL ethelbertus CD. honorem]
    AD honore CL.
11 pauli] ACD sancti pauli L.
11–12 pontificali fungeretur officio] ACD fungeretur officio pontificali L.
12 puerulus quidam] AD quidam puerulus CL.
13 nomine] ACD nomine, genere nobilis, nacione Anglicus L. paruus] ACD peruus L.
14 uita eius . . . fuisse tam] AD eius uita . . . tam fuisse CL.
17 adleburgam] AD ethelburgam C aethelburgam L.
18 uirgo uita et] AD uirgo et uita et CL.
22 quod] ACD et quod L.
23 instituerat] ADL in instituerat C. quidem in regione] ACD quidam regione L.
24 fluuium tamensem] ACD flumen tamese L. ceroteseya] AD certesya C ceroteseya ubi
    primo monachus et postea Abbas fuerat L.
25 berchingum] AD berkingum C Berthingum L.
27 Contigit] AD .ii. Contigit C Capitulum Secundum. Contigit L. ut] ACD post hec
    ut L. lundonice] ACD londoniensis L. migrauit] AD migraret CL.
28 Consensu . . . uocabulo] ACL *omit* D.
29 domini] ACL dei D. in cathedra] AD cathedra C cathera L.
34 Post] ADL .iii.(*in margin*) Post C. siquidem imminentis] ADL presentis C.
35 caballarium preparari] AD preparari caballarium CL.
38 grauati essent] AD essent grauati CL.
39 hastule] AD astule CL. abscise] AC abscisse DL.
40 citam] ACD cito L. parabant] AD prestabant CL.
41–42 Aduenit . . . reportarentur] ADL *omit* C.
42 horreum] ADL hurreum Dm.
43 Quadam] AD .iiii. Quadam C Capitulum Tertium. Quadam L.
45 semite difficultate] AC semite diffultate L semitis difficultate D.
47 currus] ACD currus qui L.
49 immo insolito] A imo insolito D immo solito CL. mirabiliter] CDL mirabiter A. O
    deus] ACD oculus L.
51 Sed] ADL .v. Sed C.
56 Beatus] AD .vi. Beatus C Capitulum Quartum (*in margin*) L. erchenwaldus] AD
    erkenwaldus CL.
57 infirmitate graui] ADL infirmitate C. finiuit. Qui] ADL finiret. Qui posteaque L.
59 admonitione] AD ammonitione CL.
60 transitu] ACD transsitu L.
62 perfunderetur] AD effunderetur CL.
63 Audientes] ADL .vii. Audientes C.
64 scilicet] ADL s̶c̶i̶l̶i̶c̶e̶t̶ C.
66 restiterunt] AD illis restiterunt CL.
67 illic] ACD illuc L.
67–68 loci ipsius] AD ipsius loci CL. de hac] AD hac de CL.
69–70 abbas, noster erit] ACD Abbas, erat L. huc] ACD huic L.
71 uestram] ACD nostram L. ecclesiam fundauisse] ADL fundauisse ecclesiam C.
72 fundator] AD constructor CL.
73 Tum] ADL Tunc C. ac] AD et CL.

74 certamine] ADL certaminie C.
79 dicerentur] AD dicuntur CL.
81 uerum etiam] ADL ꞇerum ꞇrꞇam C. beati uiri] AD beati CL.
82 prosecuntur] A prosequuntur CL persequuntur D. illis] ADL autem illis C.
83 tempestas] AD illis tempestas CL. uento] ADL de uento C.
84 declarandum] ACD declarudum L.
84–86 Nec . . . extincti] ADL *omit* C.
86 Sequentes] ACD Capitulum Quintum. Sequentes L. igitur] AD itaque CL.
87–89 fluuium . . . fluuium] AD flumen . . . flumen CL.
89 qui de] AD et de CL. riuulis] ACL fluviis D.
90 creuisse] AD succreuisse C sic creuisse L. superhabundasse] AD superundasse C superundauisse L.
91 transire] ADL *omit* C.
92 aliqua] ADL *omit* C. etiam] ACD autem L.
92–93 per . . . posset] ADL *erased* C.
97 disposuerit] ACL disposuerat D.
98 summopere] AD sumopere CL.
100 inportunitatem] ACL importunitatem D. uestram] ACDmL nostram D (*corrected to* uestram *in "corrigenda,"* 1658 *ed.*)
101 et incomparabile] AD in mirabile et incomparabile CL. iccirco ad nos] ACD idcirco ad nos Dm idcirco nos L.
104 eius corpus] AD corpus illius CL.
104–110 Sed . . . exspoliastis] ADL *omit* C.
107 laniando] AD lamando L. quascunque] AL quoscunque D. possent] AD possunt L.
108 et sic] A et hic D sic L. seuiendo] AD seuiende L. minitando] AD inuitando L.
109 exspoliastis] AD expoliastis L.
110 dominus deus omnipotens] AC deus omnipotens D dominus deus L.
111 hoc] AD hec CL.
111–114 e contra . . . differatis: quia] ADL *omit* C.
112 quod] AD est quod L.
113 nichil] AL nihil D. pro] AD quid pro L.
114–115 nec . . . habebitis;] AD *omit* CL.
115 nec nos unquam] AD Numquam nos C nec nos vnquam L.
117 et uos scire] AD scire et uos CL.
117–118 non . . . strenuos] ADL *omit* C.
118 et uerum] AD uerum CL.
123 rexit tempore] ADL tempore C. ipsoque] ADL rexit (*in margin, contemp. hand*) ipsoꝗue C.
125 et nos ipsi uolumus] ADL uolumus C.
126 ut] ACD *omit* L.
128 Interea] ACD Capitulum Sextum. Interea L.
129 obtinendo] ACD optinendo L.
132 est ac] ACD ac L.
134 opus] ACD corpus L. aggredimini] ADL agredimini C.
135–139 Scriptum . . . caritas est] ADL *omit* C.
136–137 estis discordes] AD discordes L. quomodo] AD qualiter L. holocaustomata] AL holocostomata D.
140 inplorate] A implorate CDL.
141 reliquias] ACD requies L. collocari] ACD collocare L.
142 exhortatorie] AD exortatorie C exhortacione L.

143 preciniuit] A precinuit CL praecinnivit D.
144 pusilli] ACD pusillii L. ac] ACL et D.
145 indicio] ACD iudicio L.
146 Ut] ADL Vere ut C.
147 inuocantibus] ADL inuocatibus C.
151 helias] AD helyas CL.
151-152 intronizandus] ACD inthronizandus L. uidissent] ACD omit L.
154 flumen quod] AD fluuium qui CL.
156 paulisper] ACD pausis per L. locus amenus] ACD amenus locus L.
158 nequaquam] AD ne unquam C nequequam Dm nemquam L.
159 sopita esset] ACD esset sopita L.
160 ac decrescerent] ACD omit L. rutilantes] ADL rutilantis C.
161 quisquamne] ACL quisnamne D.
162 uero] ACD ergo L.
167 inenarrabiliter] ACL enarrabiliter D. colletantes] ACD collocantes L.
168 sublimatus sit] AD sublimandus fuit CL.
168-169 tetigerunt] ACL tetegerunt D.
170 prestante] ACL et prostante D et prostrante Dm.
172 seculorum] ACLDm seculorium D.
Explicit uita sancti erkenwaldi episcopi] ACD Explicit uita de Sancto Erkenwaldo episcopo
L. et confessoris] AD omit CL.

Textual Notes
Miracula Sancti Erkenwaldi

For descriptions of the manuscripts of *MSE* see Introduction, Chapter One. Manuscript sigla:

C	= Cambridge, Corpus Christi College 161
Ch	= Bodley Latin Liturg. e.39 (the Chertsey Breviary)
J	= John Leland's *Collectanea* 1: 20–21
T	= B. L. Cotton Tib. E.i. (*Sanctilogium Anglie*)
E	= Bodley Tanner 15
Y	= York Minster XVI. G. 23 (**E** & **Y** are 15th-century recensions of the *Sanctilogium*).

The text of this edition of *MSE* is that of manuscript **C**, except where indicated otherwise. Some **C** readings are emended where obviously corrupt, and in Mir. I, IV, VI some readings are adopted from **Ch** and **J**. In the remaining miracle chapters, some **T** readings may well reflect the archetype but are not adopted here owing to lack of corroboration. Variant readings designated **T** in the notes are in most cases common to **ETY**, but where a **T** reading is unique, significant variants are supplied where appropriate. Horstmann's collation of **T** and **E** with the text of De Worde's *Nova Legenda Angliae* has been checked against the manuscripts where possible. **Y**, which is independent of **E** and **T**, but similar to **E**, is collated here for the first time.

In this edition the spelling and capitalization of the manuscripts have been retained, but punctuation, paragraphing, and line numbers of individual miracle chapters are editorial. Variations of c/t, v/u, ae/e, ch/h and i/j are not recorded for their own sakes, nor is **T**'s habitual preference for "London-" over **C**'s "Lundon-." Chapter headings (rubrics) are from **C** and are not included in the line count. Occasional page references to **T** are to Horstmann's *NLA*, vol. 1. Editorial intrusions are in italics.

PROEMIUM (C *only*)
29 de] de de C.

MIR. I (C, Ch, T; J, *lines 1–4 only, and a rubric, viz.*, Elwinus grammaticus, cujus discipulus, ferulam timens, ad Erkenualdi sepulchrum supplex confugit.)
1–11 Fuit . . . differenda] CCh *omit* T.
1 lundonie didasculus] C londonie didascalus ChJ. elwinus] CJ elwynus Ch.
9–10 ea . . . credens] Ch *omit* C. negotia] C se negocia Ch.
12 autem] CCh quidam T. lubrico et] ChT et C.
13 didascalice comminationis] CCh didasculi sui comminationis T.
14 pre oculis] CT oculis Ch.
15 occursaret puerili memorie] Ch occursaret C puerile memoria occuparet T.
16–17 qui . . . remedium] ChT (redderet valeat T) *omit* C.
17 ergo] CCh igitur T.
18 uel alicuius] CCh alicuius T. deuitaret ac euaderet] CCh evitaret T.
18–19 uel saltem . . . differet.] Ch *omit* CT.
20–21 Circumspiciens . . . uellet] CCh *omit* T.
21 cum . . . diffugium] Ch *omit* CT.
22 et] CT *omit* Ch. ibique] C et Ch.
22–23 ibique . . . iacebat] *omit* T.
25–29 Quibus . . . miraculo] *omit* ChT.
30 more solito] ChT *omit* C.
31–32 modo . . . deuenit] Ch ńé ueNit (*over an erasure*) C modo deuenit T.
32–41 Ira . . . fidutia] CCh *omit* T.
37 abduci posset] C abducli possit Ch.
42 animaduersione] CT animauersione Ch. offirmato] CT affirmato Ch.
43 quatinus . . . ratione] ChT *omit* C.
45 clementissimum] CT sanctissimum Ch.
46–52 At miro . . . audiuit] CT *omit* Ch.
47 hunc] ńé hunc C. hunc . . . studio] C preelegit modum qui pueri studio T.
51 magistrorum ante] C ante magistrorum T.
52 lectionem puer] C puer leccionem ChT.
53 atque adminiculo] C atque diminiculo T *omit* Ch.
56 didasculus] C didascalus Ch didascolus T.
59–81 Penitentis . . . concedat] *omit* ChT.

MIR. II (C, T)
1–6 Illud . . . innotuit] *omit* T.
3 iustitia] institia C.
7 Gloriosi enim] CEY glorio T. solennitate] solempnitate iam T.
9 quem] quam T.
13–30 Cum ergo . . . egressus] *omit* T.
30 ecce . . . graui] Et ecce quidam miser T.
31 et] cuidam ecclesie et T.
32 uacuus] vacans T.
32–35 de . . . neglexerat] *omit* T.
36–37 At minister . . . intermisit] Minister vero prefatus T.

37 uerbisque] uerbis T.
38 impium] ipsum T. inquit] *omit* T.
39 et sancti] sancti T. aliis indiges] aliis hominibus indigens T.
40 festinantibus] festiuitatibus T.
41 accedis] attendis T.
41–87 Quotiens . . . temptatis] *omit* T.
63 aduoca] aduoca*ré* C.
87 Uult] Qui proterue (respondit EY), Uult T.
88 ridiculus essem] ridiculum esset T.
90 habetote] habete T.
91–96 Qui . . . multare] *omit* T.
96 Sed] Sic T.
97 sic] *omit* T.
98 inquam] *omit* T.
99–101 Dumque . . . offendens] quod ad caput sepulchri cuiusdam mortui pedem offendens T.
101 caput] capud C.
103–107 Ut autem . . . perscrutatus] *omit* T.
109 incurrisse] meruisse atque incurrisse T.
109–110 dum . . . diuulgaret] dum se suaque amaret, vt correctionem irridens, in sanctos dei contumeliam grauem diuulgaret T.
111–129 His igitur . . . extat] *omit* T.

MIR. III (C, T)
1–3 Quodam . . . concitari] *omit* T.
3–4 quantum . . . illuc] iussu regio compeditus, ire T.
4 templumque dei] ad ecclesiam eo die T.
4–5 sancti colebatur] sancti Erkenwaldi celebratur; et T.
6 uanus] inuanus (*with* in- *erased*) C.
6–7 tua ueritate] *omit* T.
8 norim . . . tibi] mihi quid expediat, orare possim, tibique T.
9–34 Multa . . . populo tuo] *omit* T.
16 irasci] irascr C.
20 misericordia] mia (*excised*) misericordia (*superscript*) C.
35–36 Dum . . . populo] Cum in hunc modum custodes quererent illum, nunciatum est illis, hominem quem querebant ad solempne gaudium festiuitatis sancti Erkenwaldi peruenisse, nec latitare voluisse, sed in conspectu fidelium altari assistere, oculis ac manibus in altum leuatis ad dominum intentius orare. Tunc custodes, nunc reperto captiuo letati, nunc vero ipsius euasione commoti, ad templum dei cursum instituerunt, et suum commendatum non sine pena reducere proposuerunt T.
36 intuente] intnte C (*possibly* intrante; *the emendation* intuente *is supported by* T's *in conspectu fidelium*).
40 uiri] miraculi T.
42 cunctis . . . iniuriare] acius (arcius Y) ne predicto homini per custodes iniuriaretur T.
44 nullius] nullum T.
46–63 Rogitemus . . . misericordiam] *omit* T.

MIR. IV (C, T; *brief extracts in* J; T *is so heavily abbreviated and rewritten as to be worthless for collation: see NLA* 1: 395–96.)

22 Enim uero] J's *extracts begin here.*
25 inuolueret] inuoluere J.
31 matrici] matricae J.
33–39 Quasi . . . sarcinulis] *omit* J.
39 quippe . . . nocturno] J *omit* C.
42 eiulatibus] ejulantibus J.
43–48 Adhuc . . . dimittitur] *omit* J.
49 dampna pareant] damna pariant J. sedem] J s̷éd̷é C.
50 uidelicet . . . memoratam] J *omit* C. ausibus truculentis] J *omit* C.
51 miserabiliter] J mirabiliter C.
56 testudine] testitudine J.
57 diruitur; dissipata] diricitur dissipta J. et scissa et dilacerata] J *omit* C.
59 tradunt] *end of* J's *main extract.*
66 uirtutem] nirtutem C.
73 preciosissima] preciossima C.
88 execrabile] exiciabile C.
111 nature] ṷéṋéŕáḃi̷ĺé̷ nature C.
112 dicam] *The second scribe begins here, at quire VI.*
136 Erubesce] *Capital E is lined in red, with red paragraph marker.*

MIR. V (C; J: *a few lines re. the bishops of London;* T: *in* T *the two parts of* Mir. V, *continuous in* C, *are separated: NLA 1: 396, 400–401.*)
1 nouitate] igitur nouitate T. supradictus] sepedictus T.
2 uidetur] uidebatur T.
5 autem] itaque T. dominus Ricardus] Ricardus primus T.
7 quidem] siquidem T. incepte muros] CT muros inceptae J.
9 obsesse] obsessae J obcesse T.
10 aliisque quam plurimis] aliis plurimis T aliisque plurimis Y.
12 Post hunc cathedram] Demum, diuino procurante consilio, dura per quinquennium et eo amplius infirmitate concutitur, sicque homine mundano demum relicto pace quieuit. Vacuam quoque per vnum annum cathedram T.
15 uetus instrumentum ad] veteris instrumenti gibbum planauerat, explanationi quoque tecto superposito ad J veteris hominis imperfecti gibbum planaverat, explanatumque opus tecto superposito ad T. exposuerat] CJ composuerat T.
16 episcopii] episcopi T.
17–20 cum . . . anno] *omit* T.
20 quedam] Quedam T (T's *account of the Benedicta miracle f. 20v, NLA 1:400 is narrated separately from the preceding*).
21 ut] et T.
23–24 manus . . . contractio] vt preter manum aridam, quam gestabat ac si adhuc matris vtero foueretur, pugni concreta congeries et digitorum pollici suppositorum integralis conglutinatio, manus obseruationem penitus denegaret T.
25 Hec italicam] Preterea Ytalicam T. et] ortam apud Marcilliacum in prouincia lugunensi et T.
27–29 Certe . . . passa] *omit* T.
31 abdicarat] *omit* T. reseruat] CT (re- *superscript* C).
34 alumnam] alumpnam T.
35–46 Habundat . . . denegarat] *omit* T.
46 ut] dum supramemorata mulier ut T.
49 Enim] Cum T.

53 uiuificus] CEY viuicus T. manum . . . sanitati] et venarum pororumque repletio naturalis membrum restituunt T.
56 discretionem] discretio CT. nature] natura T.
57-58 humane] humanum T.
59-66 Sanata . . . ostendit] omit T.

MIR. VI (C, Ch, T)

1-3 Igitur . . . Ubi] CCh omit T.
1 Igitur cum dispensatori] Dum dispensatori igitur Ch.
4 cum quedam mulier, ut] CCh Cum quedam mulier ad feretrum argenteum parandum in quo sancto Erkenwaldi corpus poneretur, ut T. mente] CCh ibidem mente T.
6 Sequenti] CCh Sequente T.
8-9 Saluabitur] CCh sanabitur T.
10 noster] CCh Erkenwaldus T.
11 quatinus] quatenus ChT.
12 ipsius] CT eius Ch. se ferri] CT ferri se Ch. Itaque mane facto] CT Mane itaque facto Ch.
14-15 languoris sui sanitate] ChT sanitate C.
15-16 et . . . reuertitur] ChT omit C.
17-19 Nimirum . . . pietatis] C omit ChT.

MIR. VII (C, T)

1-22 Ea tempestate . . . fecit] omit T.
22 dominum] domnum C. Erat ibi] Tempore Stephani regis Anglorum erat quidem T.
23 gallia] galliis T.
24 nostros] Londoniarum T. Qui, completa processione] et in presentia sanctissimi corporis Erkenwaldi die solempnitatis sue inter populos assistebat. Completa itaque processione T.
24-25 ad . . . conuiuantes] inter ceteros supramemoratus homo repedauit ad sibi delegata hospitia; et dum inter conuiuantes T. socius discumberet] socios medius, et quasi nulli tunc secundus discumberet T. infirmitate] et pessima infirmitate T.
26 cathalepticum] cathalempticum C.
27 minitares] imitares T (Horstmann, NLA 1:401, prints intimares from De Worde; ASS Apr., 3:785 has putares).
28-36 In tam . . . sensualitate] omit T.
39 paratis] peractis T.
41-59 O genus . . . subintrauerat dies] omit T.
59-60 aliquis erkenwaldi] erat aliquis qui erkenwaldi T. implorarat] imploraret T. ubi] CYE omit T.
62-63 ad . . . elementia] omit T.
63 repente] pedes repente T.
64 a sacerdote] omit T.
65 uoueat] moueat T.
68 hastam . . . imminebat] astam . . . eminebat T.
70-71 sentire . . . hic] omit T.
72-74 Res . . . palpitabat] omit T.
74 et qui] et egrotus qui T.
81 hoc] omit T.
82 uobis] CY nobis ET.

84 lumine preuio] primo T.
85–101 O raphaelis ... christo] *omit* T.

MIR. VIII (C, T)

1 pretereundum] pretermittendum T.
2 asilum] sepulchrum T.
4 cunctis] cuncctis C.

MIR. IX (*Here supplied from ETY only: it was omitted by the C scribe, presumably in error, after he had written the rubric for Mir. IX. The text of Mir. X follows immediately in C. There is no way of knowing whether or not T preserves all or part of Mir. IX. The corresponding episode in the Middle English Gilte Legende, BL Add. 35298, f. 55v, occurs in the same position as in C.*)

2 diu] E *omit* TY.
5 voluero] EY *omit* T.

MIR. X (C, T)

1 Nec ... uir] *omit* T. quidam, eustachius nomine] Quidam argentarius, nomine Eustachius T.
2 domus] limina domus T. supramemorata theca] sancti Erkenwaldi feretrum T. limina sepius] sepius T.
3–8 erat ... Porro] *omit* T.
8 ibi] ubi T.
9 erkenwaldi] sancti Erkenwaldi T. condere] conderentur T.
9–12 fixeramus ... uero] *omit* T.
12 fatui] statim T. supramemorato] super memorato T.
16 sanctissimus] *omit* T.
17 ferculum] feretrum T.
18 his] hiis T.
19 ad lectum satis] *omit* T ad locum suum Y.
20 diuino ... iudicio] *omit* T.
21 erkenwaldi] beatus Erkenwaldus T beati Erkenwaldi Y. eiusdemque] eius denique T.
22 penitus animarat] animauerat T.
22–25 Nec ... tradat] *omit* T.

MIR. XI (C, T)

6 refertus] refertur T. prouectione] prouentione T.
8–22 Rerum ... debilior] *omit* T.
15 pretaxatus] pretaxtatus C.
22 misericordiam] quoque misericordiam T.
23 orationibus] et orationibus T.
25 mereatur] CEY mereantur T.
26–28 Properantibus ... habuimus] Die tertia post horam vespertinam apparuit subito T.
29 in huiusmodi] et huius T.
30 resolutum] resonantem T.
33 etiam omnium] omnium membrorum T.
34 uestri] nostri T (*Horstmann's reading, but MS illegible*) uiri Y.
35 uerum] seu ceteros naturales corporis sensus possim exercere, uerum T.
38–55 Si fuerit ... curaretur] *omit* T.
46–47 narrando] h̸o̸c̸ ̸a̸u̸t̸e̸m̸ narrando C.

MIR. XII (C, T)

1–5 Illud. . .preualuit] *omit* T.

6 etenim] *omit* T.

6–7 nomine . . . indumentum] *omit* T.

8 ipse] CY ipsi T.

9 pellemque] *Quidam enim pelliparius in eius solemnie* pellemque C festinus assendit pellemque T. radere cepit] radendi opera dedita cepit T.

11–12 festinantes. Vt] festinantes quo patronum suum in celo cum deo regnantem interpellarent ne in causa extremi examinis illis deesset qui eius memoriam eiusque gloriam dulciter recolerent. Vt T.

12 intendere] CY intendi T.

13 persenserunt] presumpserat T. eorum] illorum T.

14 defuerunt] fuerunt T.

15 temperarent] reuocare temptarent T.

15–24 Hi . . . prophanis] *omit* T.

25 His . . . admonitionibus] Horum autem monitionibus T.

26 uitalis] *omit* T. illi] sibi T. fuit] CY dignus T.

27 neglegeret, addidit] negligeret: Accidit T.

27–28 derisionem] subsannationem et derisionem T.

28 ingereret] gereret T. ergo] igitur T.

30 inprouidus] imperuidus T.

32–43 Et qui . . . gestum] *omit* T.

MIR. XIII (C *only; for a Middle English paraphrase, see* Gilte Legende, BL Add. 35298, *f. 56r.*)

MIR. XIV (C, T)

1 Imponebatur . . . quibusdam] Propter immensa sancti Erkenwaldi merita, circumquaque diuulgata per crebra miraculorum insignia que facere dignabatur dei prouidentia pro salute fidelium ad laudem sui sancti, imponebatur quibusdam T.

2 attonita] attoniti T. noctu] CT nocte EY.

7 clericulis] clericis T. in ecclesia] CT (*superscript in* C).

9 perculsi] percussi T. tanti] tantilli T.

11 ecclesie . . . editui] ad ecclesie . . . aditum T.

15–16 presbiteros . . . delegauimus] presbiteri tam uenerabilis thesauri custodes delegati fuerunt T.

16–17 parato sancti reliquias clauderemus] peracto sancti reliquie clauderentur T.

18 paratis] peractis T. etiam] CY et T.

20 tumbam uenimus] tumulum venientes T.

21 repperimus corpus] repertum fuit cuius T.

23 Certe . . . nuntiatum] *omit* T. et diuina tamen] Tandem diuina T.

24 renitentibus] reluctantibus T.

26 defraudari] defraudati T. una nobiscum] *omit* T.

26–27 perspicerent] prospexerunt T.

28–41 Quid . . . nequiui] (*paraphrased in* T: NLA 1:397, His itaque gestis . . . reliquiis locum daret.*)

34 dexteram] *dextendentis* dexteram C.

42 Affirmabant] quod affirmabant T. eadem] *omit* T. edelburge, olim] Athelburge solum T.

43–47 Nec . . . perfunderetur] *omit* T.

48 igitur] itaque T. anno] et cum tanta pietate repositum, anno T.
49-50 mense ... sextodecimo] mensis nouembris die quartodecimo T.
51 posuimus et alia] describitur, alia T.
52 omittimus] obmittuntur T. duo] *omit* T.
58-60 Referebat ... canonicus] *omit* T.
60 quod collectum] Quidam uero deo (de T) deuotus collectum TY.
61 Adiungebat] Adiungebatur T.
62 tenui fumigatione ... impleuerit] tenuis fumigatio ... impleuerat T.
63 depulerit] depellebat T.

MIR. XV (C, T)

1-4 Libet ... petierint] *omit* T.
5 Quidam] Erat quidam T. baldewinus] CY Baldwinus T.
6 intolerabiliter] q̶u̶i̶ intolerabiliter C qui intolerabiliter T.
8-12 inter ... quia] *omit* T.
12 ob festiuitatem] ministri ecclesie doctoris gentium festiuitatem T.
13 sancti] e̶t̶ h̶o̶n̶o̶r̶e̶m̶ d̶e̶i̶ e̶t̶ sancti C et honorem dei et sancti T.
14 sospitatem] sicut contigit, sospitatem T. per] esse per T.
15 Dum] CY Cum T.
18-19 quemadmodum archiepiscopi] et infula mitratum quemadmodum episcopi T.
22 sepulchrum] ad sepulchrum T.
24 Ego sum] *omit* T.
26 dicessit] discessit T.
27 ipsius] eius T.
28 immo] *omit* T.
30 sospes] *omit* T.
31 oblationem] et oblationem T.

MIR. XVI (C, T)

1 Similis ... Multis] Puella ex civibus londonie, multis T.
2 enim] *omit* T.
3 noster] *omit* T.
3-5 pater ... sanat] *omit* T.
5 huiusmodi] huius T.
8 ut] *omit* T.
10 die] enim die T.
11 ihesum] nostrum Ihesum T.
14 elinguem redderet] inlignem reddidit T iplignem reddidit EY.
15 altaris] CEY aliris T.
16-17 salua eris] sanaueris T sana eris EY.
23 et ipsa] est et T est et ipsa EY. toto ... reddita] reddita toto corpore incolumis T.

MIR. XVII (C, T)

1-4 Sepe ... est] *omit* T.
5 corpus] prefati corpus T.
6 erat] fuit T.
6-7 solennitas illius] reuoluti anni circulo, solempnitas ipsius sancti patris Erkenwaldi T.
10 oblationem] oblationes T. patuit] paruit T.
11 serauit et] serrauit ut T.
11-12 uermiculauit] uermicularet T.

15 somnus eum inuasit] *omit* T.
17 ipsius] illius T.

MIR. XVIII (C, T)

1-6 Sermo . . . sumus] *omit* T.
2-3 celestibus] celcstibus C.
7 Ciuis . . . locuples] Quidam ciuis nobilis Londonie T.
8-14 Talibus . . . tandem] *omit* T.
15 iudicauerunt] Parentes sui iudicauerunt T. sanctarum monialium] sanctimonialium T.
16 Cum] et ecclesiasticis disciplinis eruderetur. Cum T. aeluiue] Alwine T.
18 adelburge] Ethelburge T Athilburge EY. sancti] CY beati ET.
19 obnixe] gemitu, lachrymis, poplitibus flexis obnixe T. omni] et illibatam omni T.
21 Dum] Et dum T. pulsaret] humili prece pulsaret T.
23 taliter] se taliter T. eam] *omit* T. nimium] *omit* T.
24 iam iam] iam T.
27 ipsa] CEY *omit* T.
28-29 uniuersa . . . supplicabat] *omit* T.
30 post] *omit* T.
39 nomen . . . innotuit] *omit* T.
42 Vbi] Vt T.
43-44 *te* . . . inchoauerunt] dominum in sanctis suis gloriosum deuote laudauerunt T.

MIR. XIX (C, T)

1-3 Vir . . . bone] *omit* T.
3 Cuius filia] Filia cuiusdam deo deuoti de partibus lincolnie T.
4 collectis . . . et] *omit* T.
6 perculsi] percussi T.
7 redderetur] rederetur T.
8 experiri] experire T.
8-9 et eam ad] ad eam ET ac eam ad Y.
13 effluente] confluente T. est] est pristine sanitati, ad laudem domini nostri Ihesus Christi, cui est honor et gloria in secula seculorum amen T.
14-18 Nos . . . amen] *omit* T.

Abbreviations
Notes
Bibliography
Index

Abbreviations

AB   *Analecta Bollandiana*

ASS   *Acta Sanctorum quotquot orbe coluntur* . . . Januarius–Novembris. Ed. J. Bolland
          et al. Antwerp, Paris, Brussels, 1643–1925

BHL   *Bibliotheca hagiographica latina antiquae et mediae aetatis.* 2 vols. Brussels,
          1898–1901; *Supplément* (Brussels, 1911)

Camd. Soc. Camden Society

CCSL   *Corpus Christianorum Series Latinorum*

CSEL   *Corpus Scriptorum Ecclesiasticorum Latinorum*

Dugdale, Sir William Dugdale. *A History of St. Paul's Cathedral.* 3rd ed., Sir
ed. Ellis Henry Ellis. London, 1818

EETS   Early English Text Society

Gesta   *Guillielmi Malmesburiensis de gestis pontificum Anglorum.*
pontificum   Ed. N. E. S. A. Hamilton. Rolls Series 52. London, 1870

Gibbs   Marion Gibbs, ed. *Early Charters of the Cathedral Church of St. Paul's, Lon-
          don.* Camd. Soc., 3rd ser. 58. London, 1939

HBS   Henry Bradshaw Society

Hist. eccles. Bede. *Historia ecclesiastica gentis Anglorum.* Ed. Bertram Colgrave & R. A.
          B. Mynors, *Bede's Ecclesiastical History of the English People.* Oxford, 1969

MGH   *Monumenta Germaniae Historica:* SRM = *Scriptores Rerum Merovingicarum;*
          SS = *Scriptores*

Mir.   Arcoidus. *Miracula sancti Erkenwaldi* (as edited here; Roman numerals denote
          miracle chapters, Arabic numerals denote line refs. within chapters)

Mir. Pr. Ibid., *Proemium* (Arcoidus' prologue to the *Miracula sancti Erkenwaldi*)

MSE   Arcoidus. *Miracula sancti Erkenwaldi* (the whole work)

NLA   *Nova Legenda Angliae.* Ed. Carl Horstmann. 2 vols. Oxford, 1901

PL   *Patrologia Latina.* Ed. J. P. Migne. Paris, 1844–1880

RS   Rolls Series (Rerum Britannicarum Medii Aevi Scriptores)

SRM   (see above, MGH)

SS   (see above, MGH)

VSE   *Vita sancti Erkenwaldi* (the whole work; also, with line refs., the work as
          edited here)

NB. Biblical refs. are to the Vulgate, ed. P. Michael Hetzenauer, *Biblia sacra vulgatae
editionis Sixti V . . . et Clementis VIII . . . ,* Ratisbon & Rome, 1914.

NOTES TO CHAPTER ONE

1. The Tudor antiquary, John Leland, describes a *Vita Erkenwaldi* that is clearly *VSE: De rebus Britannicis collectanea*, 2nd ed. (London 1770), 1:19–20. His younger contemporary, John Bale, *Index Britanniae scriptorum*, ed. Reginald Lane Poole & Mary Bateson, Anecdota Oxon., Med. & Mod. Ser., 9 (Oxford, 1902), 98, 498, refers to a *Vita Erkenwaldi* in a manuscript which Bale found in Leland's library but which is apparently different from that mentioned by Leland himself.

2. Untraced MS copies of *MSE* include that from which Leland transcribed the extracts designated J below, another used by John of Tynemouth for the redaction found in his *Sanctilogium Anglie*, designated T below, and yet another used by the author of the Erkenwald chapter in the Middle English prose legendary known as the *Gilte Legende*.

3. See further Reginald P. Darlington, *The Vita Wulfstani of William of Malmesbury*, Camd. Soc., 3rd ser., 40 (London, 1928), vii, n. 4; Mary P. Richards, "The Medieval Hagiography of St. Neot," *AB* 99 (1981): 272–77; A. W. Wade-Evans, *Vitae Sanctorum britanniae et genealogiae*, Bd. of Celtic Studies, Univ. of Wales, History & Law Ser., 9 (Cardiff, 1944), xvi–xvii, where the MS description is by Robin Flower.

4. N. R. Ker, *The Medieval Libraries of Great Britain*, 2nd ed. (London, 1964), 102.

5. BL Cotton Faustina B iv (Holme Cultram, s.xiii in.) includes lives of Alban & Amphibalus, Ulric of Haselbury, Bee of Northumbria, Aldhelm, and John of Beverley; Harvard College Lat. 27 (Holme Cultram, s.xii ex.) contains lives of Anselm and the Cluniac saints Maiolus, Odilo, and Odo.

6. Before the Norman Conquest, to judge from the evidence of surviving calendars, Erkenwald was something of a national saint, but after the conquest veneration is confined to London and a few mainly southeastern monasteries. His feast is absent from all the manuscript copies of the Sarum Breviary I have been able to locate (except where added later, as in MS S below), and in the early printed ed. his feast is designated "non Sarum sed Sinodalis Londinensis." F. Proctor & C. Wordsworth, eds., *Breviarum ad usum insignis ecclesiae Sarum*, 3 vols. (Cambridge, 1879–86), 3:1038. On the history of Erkenwald's cult, see below, chap. 4.

7. On the life and work of Ralph Diceto, see Antonia Gransden, *Historical Writing in England c. 550 to c. 1307* (Ithaca, N.Y., 1974), 230–36; on the remains of Liber B see W. H. Hale, *The Domesday of St. Paul's of the year M.CC.XII*, Camd. Soc. 69 (Westminster, 1858), 109–17, and Gibbs, xi–xii, and xi, nn.1–4.

8. Dugdale (1658), 181–85, gives the impression that VSE and several charters, including those mentioned above, are all on the same folio, 20r. It must therefore have been huge and folded, since Bodl. Rawl. A.372 is only 356 mm. high.

9. For similar combinations of hagiographical and legal documents, see BL Cotton Vitellius A xiii, f. 20 et seq., a collection of Chertsey Abbey charters introduced by selections from VSE and Goscelin's life of Ethelburga; and the better known Liber Eliensis, ed. E. O. Blake, Camd. Soc., 3rd Ser., 92 (London, 1962).

10. Ker, 164.

11. The contents were listed by Horstmann, NLA 1:ix, n.2, and the manuscript is analyzed by Paul Grosjean, "Vita S. Roberti Nova Monasterii in Anglia abbatis," AB 56 (1938): 335–39.

12. E.g., VSE 12–13: Erkenwaldus nomine ACD, erkenwaldus nomine, genere nobilis, nacione Anglicus, L. Sir Thomas Duffus Hardy, Descriptive Catalogue of Materials Relating to the History of Great Britain and Ireland, RS 26, vol. 1 (London, 1862), 295, gives the impression that L is a distinct version of the life of Erkenwald, but this is misleading.

13. I am grateful to Andrew Watson of University College, London, for answering my queries regarding N. R. Ker's unpublished notes on S.

14. M. R. James, A Descriptive Catalogue of the Manuscripts in the Library of Corpus Christi College, Cambridge (Cambridge, 1912), 1:358–63; Ker, Medieval Libraries, 39; Denis Bethel, "The Miracles of St. Ithamar," AB 89 (1971): 427. Nigel Morgan, Early Gothic Manuscripts. Part 1: 1190–1285 (Oxford, 1982), 52, suggests that the manuscript originated with the Cluniacs of Faversham, Kent.

15. The summer saints, in C's order, are Martial (June 30, BHL 5552, prologue of 5551, 5561, first miracle of 5562, etc.: an eclectic compilation); Nicholas (Dec. 6 & May 9, BHL 6210, with unprinted prologue); Dunstan (May 19, the sermon printed in W. Stubbs, ed., Memorials of St. Dunstan, RS 63 (London, 1874), 454; Aldhelm (May 25, epitome of BHL 256); Erkenwald (April 30, BHL 2600 & 2601); Swithun (July 15, BHL 7943, 7944–46, abridged, & unprinted miracles added); Neot (July 31, BHL 1428); Ithamar (June 10, BHL 4501). Exceptions to the summer pattern are David (March 1, BHL 2107) and Edward the Confessor (Oct.13, BHL 2423, 2422 abridged). The four Cluniac saints are: Odo (Nov.18, BHL 6292–95), Maiolus (May 11, BHL 5182), Odilo (Jan.1, BHL 6282), Hugo (Apr.29, BHL 4012).

16. Mir. IX, textual note.

17. Only Lat. Liturg. e.6 is in the printed Bodley catalogue, the other portions having been acquired by the library relatively recently.

18. Attention was first drawn to the artistic value of the breviary by J. J. A. Alexander, "English Fourteenth Century Illumination: Recent Acquisitions," Bodley Library Record 9 (1974), 2:72–80.

19. Dean W. Sparrow Simpson, who wrote the only existing study of the liturgy of St. Erkenwald, in his Documents Illustrating the History of St. Paul's Cathedral, Camd. Soc., New Ser. 26 (London, 1880), xxi–xxix, 15–24, was unaware of the offices in the Chertsey Breviary, since Ch was in private hands. Helmut Gneuss first announced that it contained "Lesungen aus einer Textfassung" of VSE, in "Die Handschrift Cotton Otho A.XII," Anglia 94 (1976): 315–16.

20. Horstmann, NLA 1:xxxiii–lxv, associated John of Tynemouth with St. Albans, but see V. H. Galbraith, "The Historia Aurea of John, vicar of Tynemouth, and the sources of the St. Alban's chronicle (1327–77)," in H. W. C. Davis, ed., Essays in History presented to Reginald Lane Poole (Oxford, 1927), 379–98.

21. Horstmann's ed. is based on De Worde, collated with T and E (not Y).

22. A text almost identical to Horstmann's is in ASS Apr.3: 790–96, under the

name John Capgrave, long thought to be the original author or at least the fifteenth-century reviser. For refutation of these attributions, see Peter J. Lucas, "John Capgrave and the *Nova Legenda Anglie*: a survey," *The Library*, 5th Ser., 25 (1970): 1–10.

23. On the *Gilte Legende* sources and manuscripts, see Richard Hamer, ed., *Three Lives from the Gilte Legende*, Middle English Texts 9 (Heidelberg, 1978), who is collaborating with Vida Russell on a critical edition. On the GiL Erkenwald see Whatley, "A 'Symple Wrecche' at Work: the Life and Miracles of St.Erkenwald in the *Gilte Legende*, BL Add. 35298," in Brenda Dunn-Lardeau, ed., *Legenda aurea: sept siècles de diffusion*, Actes du colloque international sur la Legenda aurea: texte latin et branches vernaculaires, à l'Université du Québec à Montréal 11–12 Mai, 1983 (Montréal & Paris, 1986), 333–343.

24. Apparent corrections in grammar and usage include *VSE* 27: migrauit AD, migraret CL; 40: parabant AD, prestabant CL; 79: dicerentur AD, dicuntur CL; 168: sublimatus sit AD, sublimandus fuit CL. Stylistic changes, some of which seem quibbles, include *VSE* 6–7: tramitem uite A, uite tramitem CL; 14–15: uita eius . . . fuisse tam AD, eius uita . . . tam fuisse CL; 35: caballarium preparari AD, preparari caballarium CL; 38: grauati essent AD, essent grauati CL; 68: de hac AD, hac de CL.

25. Erkenwald's relics were translated twice, in 1140 and 1148. See Mir. XIV, 48–50, and Sir Frederic Madden, ed., *Matthei Parisiensis . . . historia Anglorum*, RS 44, vol. 1 (London, 1866), 285. Canon Arcoid, nephew of Bishop Gilbert the Universal, wrote MSE between 1140 and 1145 (see below, ch.3), and it would be logical to assume that fresh copies of *VSE* would be prepared to accompany the first edition of the book of miracles at this time. Another likely time for the *r* reviser to be at work would be in the 1180s, under Bishop Gilbert Foliot and Dean Ralph Diceto, when the literary aspirations of the St. Paul's chapter were more evident than earlier. See C. N. L. Brooke & Gilian Keir, *London 800–1216: the Shaping of a City* (Berkeley & Los Angeles, 1975), 350 ff.

26. The dates of feast days are supplied in the table of contents (f. 1v) and at the beginning of all but the first four lives in the manuscript, but the format of each work as copied does not suggest liturgical needs. For instance *VSE* has seven chapters, the *Vita S. Swithuni* has five, with over fifty miracle chapters. Such divisions are not liturgical. The book was evidently intended for private reading or public *lectio* in refectory or chapter house.

27. The wheel miracle that is introduced immediately after *VSE* 41–42 may well be an interpolation into an even older layer of *VSE*, and this in turn would explain why 41–42 seem awkwardly placed. See *VSE*, n. 14.

28. On page 180 of his first edition of D, Dugdale mentions only the *b* manuscript as the authority for his text of *VSE*: "Ex Cod. MS. penes Decanum et Capit. Eccl. Cath. S. Pauli Lond. [B] f. 20a . . . ." He cites the A manuscript, Cotton Claudius A.v, only in his list of "Faults in the Printing thus to be corrected," on the last page of the book. This may be an indication that he consulted the Cotton manuscript only as an afterthought. Certainly his preference for *b*'s readings would suggest it.

29. Cf. also *VSE* 45: semite ACL, semitis D; 89: riuulis ACL, fluviis D; 97: disposuerit ACL, disposuerat D; 107: quascunque AL, quoscunque D; 108: sic AL, hic D; 167: inenarrabiliter ACL, enarrabiliter D.

30. *VSE* 66: restiterunt AD, illis restiterunt CLCh; 69: certeseye AD, certeseie CLCh; 72: fundator AD, constructor CLCh; 73: ac AD, et CLCh; 79: dicerentur AD, dicuntur CLCh; 81: beati uiri ADCh, beati CL; 82: prosecuntur ACh, prosequuntur CL; 83: est AD, est illis CLCh; 86: igitur AD, itaque CLCh; 87: fluuium AD, flumen CLCh; 111: hoc AD, hec CLCh.

31. For example, it is clear from the text fragment on the reverse of Lat. Liturg. d. 42, f. 46, that Ch not only retained the enigmatic *VSE* 41–42 omitted by the C scribe, for example, but lacked altogether *VSE* 43–55, the wheel miracle episode. It would be

surprising if in eight lections space could not be found to recount, however briefly, the one interesting and specific miracle said to have taken place during the saint's lifetime, unless the contents of those eight lections were dictated by a tradition that pre-dated the first inclusion of the wheel miracle in the saint's *vita*. I argue in chap. 2, from external evidence, that a pre-*VSE* form of Erkenwald's *vita* was the only one available to Goscelin of Canterbury in the 1080s, and that the wheel miracle and other features of *VSE* are the *VSE* author's additions to this older, shorter life of the saint. The lections in S also, it seems to me, attest to the existence of this older tradition.

32. The relevant variants are as follows:- *VSE* 27: migrauit ADS, migraret CL; 29: dei DS, domini ACL; 34: presentis CS, siquidem imminentis ADL; 35: caballarium [S caballorum] preparari ADS, preparari caballarium CL; 39: hastule ADS, astule CL; abscise ACS, abscisse DL; 40: parabant AD, prestabant CLS.

33. See below, chap. 2.

34. Cf. also Mir. XV 5, where T's reading was "Erat quidem de transmarinis partibus aduena, Baldwinus nomine . . ., qui intolerabiliter igne febrium anxiatus est." C omits "Erat" and after first writing "qui" excises it, which indicates that his exemplar contained not only "qui" but also T's "Erat."

35. J's other readings are of varying quality. See Mir. IV 56, 57, 59.

36. Cf. Mir. XV 13 where the words "et honorem dei et" are in both C and T, but excised in C. See also *VSE* 64, "scilicet," and 81, "uerum etiam." Dr. Michael Lapidge, of Cambridge University, who will shortly publish an edition of various texts associated with the cult of St. Swithun, has informed me by letter that he has observed a similar pattern of deliberate abridgement by the scribes in the C copy of the miracles of St. Swithun, ff. 47v et seq.

37. For a further example of the abridging work of the C scribe or his exemplar (since there are no visible excisions in this case), see Mir. I 12, "puer . . . seductus" (and the textual notes) where I have adopted the reading of ChT against C.

38. The breviary sanctorale, Lat. Liturg. e.39, ends at Nov. 6, at least two gatherings having been lost after the last surviving leaf, f. 152.

NOTES TO CHAPTER TWO

1. On Arcoid, see chap. 3, pt. 2.

2. Hardy, 1, pt. 1:294.

3. Henry Wharton, *Historia de episcopis et decanis Londinensibus* (London, 1695), 18. It is possible that Hardy had seen, in addition to Wharton, the following passage in Leland, *Collectanea*, 1:21, "Autoris [sic] librorum de vita et miraculis D. Erkenwaldi floruit tempore huius Gilberti, utipsemet testatur. Ego colligo eum fuisse canonicum Paulinae ecclesiae."

4. C. N. L. Brooke, in W. R. Matthews & W. M. Atkins, eds. *A History of St. Paul's Cathedral* (London, 1957), 6; also Brooke & Keir, *London 800–1216*, 356; Gibbs, xxxiii & n. 2; Rose Graham, "An Appeal about 1175 for the Building Fund of St. Paul's Cathedral Church," *Journal of the British Archaeological Association*, 3rd Ser., 10 (1945–47):

43; B. Scholz, "The Canonization of Edward the Confessor," *Speculum* 36 (1961): 40–41 & nn. 14–16.

5. On the Corpus, Cotton, and Lansdowne MSS, and on John of Tynemouth's recensions, see chap. 1.

6. Arcoid's personal voice is particularly evident in Mir. V 27, 61, 64, where he records apparently personal impressions of a woman from Tuscany whose withered hand was healed at Erkenwald's shrine in 1138. See the other refs. in chap. 5, n. 34.

7. Mir. Pr. 11–14 seems to allude to *VSE* 30–35; in Mir. II 51–52 the anonymous canon is alluding to the storm, river miracle and candle miracle described in the later portion of *VSE*. In Mir. IV the narrator assumes the voice of someone ostensibly present during the great fire of 1087, alluding to a number of figures and episodes from the distant past while appealing to Erkenwald to demonstrate his miraculous powers lest his relics be destroyed. Cf. Mir. IV 69–71, 80–83, with *VSE* 12–13, 27–28, 35–36, 38–40.

8. Chap. 1, n. 24.

9. *Gesta pontificum*, 142–44.

10. Cf. William's picture of the river: "qui stans seorsum crispantibus undis se collegerat in cumulum" with Ios. 3.16: "steterunt aquae descendentes in loco uno, et ad instar montis intumescentes apparebant. . . ." Cf. also William's "alveo suo redditus est" with Ios. 4.18: "reversae sunt aquae in alveum suum."

11. E.g., *Gesta pontificum*, 155–56, where William conflates into one episode two separate stories out of Hermann of Bury's *Miracula sancti Edmundi*, viz. Abbot Leofstan's sacrilege and the arrival of Baldwin "medicus" at Bury. Thomas Arnold, *Memorials of St. Edmund's Abbey*, RS 96 (London, 1890–96), 1: 53–54, 56. A similar conflation of different passages, from Alcuin's letters, is described by Rodney M. Thomson, *Medievalia et Humanistica*, n.s. 8 (1977): 156. I am grateful to Dr. Thomson for this reference and for other suggestions concerning William's treatment of Erkenwald. In two articles on William's literary sources ("The Reading of William of Malmesbury," *Revue Bénédictine* 85 (1975): 362–402; 86 (1976): 327–35) he nowhere lists *VSE* as among William's literary sources, but he has indicated to me by letter that the account of the river miracle in *Gesta pontificum* could very well be a conflation of the two miracles in *VSE*.

12. According to Thomson, "William of Malmesbury as Historian and Man of Letters," *Journal of Ecclesiastical History* 29 (1978): 391, most of William's travelling to other libraries for research purposes was complete by ca. 1115, which pushes the *terminus ante* of *VSE* even closer to ca. 1100. Arcoid presumably came to London with or after his uncle the bishop, consecrated in 1128. Greenaway dates the first occurrence of Arcoid's name in contemporary documents ca. 1132. See John Le Neve, *Fasti Ecclesiae Anglicanae, vol. 1: St. Paul's Cathedral 1066–1300*, ed. Diana Greenaway (London 1975), 27.

13. "(Erkenwoldum) in miraculis perspicuum fuisse confirmat et recens fama et vetus memoria. . . . Habetur ergo Erkenuoldus Lundoniae maxime sanctus, et pro exauditionum celeritate favorem canonicorum nonnichil emeritus." *Gesta pontificum*, 142–44.

14. The most recent and fullest study of Goscelin's life and corpus of works is Thomas J. Hamilton, "Goscelin of Canterbury: A Critical Study of his Life, Works, and Accomplishments. Parts One and Two" (Ph.D. Diss., U. of Virginia, 1973). Important published studies are Marvin L. Colker, "Texts of Jocelyn of Canterbury which relate to the history of Barking Abbey," *Studia Monastica* 7 (1965): 383–417, and Frank Barlow, *The Life of King Edward* (London, 1962), Appendix C., 91–111.

15. Bale, *Index*, 98, 498. A work with the same incipit and entitled "De s.erkenwoldo" is known to have been in a collection of saints' lives at Dover Priory in the 14th century. M. R. James, *The Ancient Libraries of Canterbury and Dover* (Cambridge, 1903), 458.

16. Colker, "Texts of Jocelyn," 384 ff., who is uncertain as to the year of Goscelin's stay at Barking. But the translation of the three Barking saints' relics, at which Goscelin

was present and of which he wrote the account (ibid., 435–54), took place on Laetare Sunday, which was also March 7. The two coincided in 1087, according to A. Cappelli, *Cronologia, Cronografia e Calendario Perpetuo* (Milan, 1930), 48.

17. Gneuss, 317.

18. Our knowledge of the *lectiones de S. Erchenwaldo* in Cotton Otho A. xii derives from two sources: the manuscript itself and a handwritten note by Thomas Smith, who compiled the first printed catalogue of the Cotton manuscripts, *Catalogus librorum manuscriptorum bibliothecae Cottonianae* (Oxford, 1696), before the infamous fire. In a collection of Smith's personal papers (Bodley, MS Smith 94, p. 155) there is a note on Cotton Otho A. xii recording the incipit of the Erkenwald lections as "Cum ad laudem et gloriam constet nos creatos." Examination of the small, shrivelled fragment, which is all that remains of Otho A. xii, f. 155, reveals that Smith's incipit is actually an abbreviation of the first line of the first lection. This lection evidently consisted of seven lines, but only the last few syllables of each have survived the fire, and not all are legible. Following is my transcription of the Erkenwald lection, with reconstructions of missing letters where possible:

> [D e e r k e n] w a l d o
> [Cum ad laudem et gloriam creator]is nostri constet nos cr[ea-
> tos]   . . . .   glorificare d[..]
>   . . . .sumus(?) Miraba[..]
>   . . . .seruis suis glo-
>   . . . .ipso demonstra-
>   . . . .are est. mira-
>   . . .m diligent[is/ibus]

One sentence of Arcoid's proem, Mir. Pr. 14–17, shows faintly possible links with the Cotton fragment: "sed ne mors quidem defunctum retinere potuit, quin ad dei laudem fidelium salutem argumenta uiuentes animae certissima daret precelseque uirtutis acta fidelibus populis demonstraret." Cf. also the incipit recorded by Bale, "Veterum vestigium herentes," with Mir. Pr. 37, "Sanctorum igitur patrum exempla sequentes." A closer parallel is that between the wording of the Otho A. xii fragment, quoted above, and Mir. XVIII 5–6: "Quum ad laudem et honorem eius creati sumus." Mir. XVIII, significantly, recounts a Barking miracle. See also next note. I am grateful to Professor Gneuss for supplying me with his photograph of the Cotton fragment and for referring me to the Smith papers in Bodley.

19. On the lack of earlier accounts of the miracles, see Mir. Pr. 22 ff. Besides the Barking miracle recorded in Mir. XVIII (see previous note), a second is related by John of Tynemouth (*NLA*, 1:383), in which Erkenwald and his sister stretch a wooden beam between them to its required length during the building of Barking Abbey. Since Goscelin tells a similar story in his *Miracula S. Augustini* 6 (ASS Mai., 6:400 F), it is conceivable that he was responsible for the Barking beam-miracle also and that John of Tynemouth, who was evidently happy to increase Ethelburga's role in her brother's legend, borrowed it from the earlier hagiographer.

20. Cf. Barlow, *Life of King Edward*, 111, and C. H. Talbot, "The *Liber Confortatorius* of Goscelin of St. Bertin," *Analecta Monastica*, Ser. 3, *Studia Anselmiana*, fasc. 37 (1955): 5–22.

21. E.g., the opening of *VSE*, 1–4.

22. With *VSE* 1–4, cf. the following opening to Goscelin's life of St. Augustine of Canterbury: "Potentissimus Triumphator mundialis tyranni, omnia trahens ad seipsum in Crucis examine, habens per olim praescripti nominis insignia, Velociter spolia detrahe,

festina praedari; universa captivi praedonis spolia suis ducibus victoribus distribuit; Petrus arcem rerum Romam comprehendit, Paulus procinctu belli omnia subegit, Andreae Achaia, Joanni Asia, Matthaeo Aethiopia, Thomae & Bartholomaeo contigit vastissima a solis ortu India: & ne per singula prolonger, tandem summus Dominicarum nuptiarum praecentor Gregorius, orbem terrae Apostolicis alis amplexus est; Augustinus vero, cui haec corona gemmis aethereis texitur, alterum Britannici Oceani orbem suo Apostolatu praecinxit. Felix Romae, quae, post primos theoricae fidei Principes, tam principales Ecclesiae edidit Consules" (ASS Mai., 6:377).

23. VSE's account of Erkenwald's death for example (VSE 56–62) shows some traces of internal rhyme, as in "Commendauit . . . exalauit," but the entire passage is remarkably restrained when compared to Goscelin's account of the death of St. Ivo (PL 155:82–83): "Hic vero tanta flagrantia coelestem conversationem induit, quasi hinc demum coepisset, et quasi post longam sitem fontem petitum reperisset. Hic, inquam, tam suae quam omnium saluti jugiter invigilando, hic Dominum usque in finem expectando, ardentibus lucernis virtutum cum castitatis baltheo, tandem venienti et pulsanti aperuit cum gaudio; et Yvo Domini ivit ad Dominum, qui exivit a Patre et venit in mundum, ac de mundo triumphato revexit electorum triumphum," etc. Note here the characteristic parallelism in "Hic . . . induit quasi . . . coepisset, et quasi . . . reperisset. Hic . . . invigilando, hic . . . expectando. . . ," the stiffly figurative language of "ardentibus lucernis virtutum cum castitatis baltheo" (cf. Luc. 12.35–36 and Exod. 28.4, 39) and the laboriously playful pun "Yvo . . . ivit . . . exivit."

24. VSE 12–22. On the italicized passages, see VSE nn. 7– 9.

25. Horstmann, ed., The Life of St. Werburge of Chester by Henry Bradshaw, EETS o.s. 88 (1887; rpr. New York, 1973), xxi. The traditional ascription of the Vita Werburgae to Goscelin (BHL 8855) is affirmed, on convincing grounds, by D. H. Farmer, Oxford Dictionary of Saints (Oxford, 1978), 401.

26. Vita Ethelburgae 1–3, Colker, "Texts of Jocelyn," 400–4.

27. Colker, "Texts of Jocelyn," 388.

28. E.g., in his additions to Bede's account (Hist. eccles. 2. 4–7; Colgrave & Mynors, 114–56) of St. Laurence of Canterbury in Cotton Vespasian B. xx, ff. 200–4, consisting mainly of amusing stories of Laurence's supposed missionary travel in Scotland.

29. Goscelin does not describe Erkenwald's death or burial, merely mentioning the saint's "transitum . . . ad caelestia" while paraphrasing Bede's account of the horse-litter. All the verbs Goscelin uses here are in the present or perfect tense, whereas VSE uses the imperfect. With VSE 38–40 "grauati essent . . . liberabantur . . . parabant," cf. Goscelin: "Quod feretrum . . . multis febricitantibus . . . integre medetur. Sed et absentes infirmos astulis inde abscisis et ad eos delatis . . . salus sepius erexit. Adeo . . . vehiculum egrotos . . . sanat. Vbi etiam ipse pontifex offerebat Domino incensa orationum . . . inde affatim redundant beneficia sanitatum." Colker, "Texts of Jocelyn," 403–4. If the horse litter itself, or some suitable replica, did still exist when Goscelin wrote his Vita Ethelburgae, it was very likely destroyed in the great fire of 1087, described in Mir. IV. Hence the past-tense verbs in VSE and the shift of attention to the body of the saint, which had supposedly survived the fire by a miracle.

30. Colgrave & Mynors, 354–64.

31. Goscelin claims that anything he has added to Bede's account of Ethelburga derives from what he has read in other sources: "Sed et siquid his addimus, alibi legendo accepimus."

32. Colker, "Texts of Jocelyn," 400–1.

33. See VSE 27–30 and n. 10. For Goscelin's account, see Colker, "Texts of Jocelyn," 403.

34. Bede certainly gives the impression that Theodore appointed bishops at will and independently. But this was not the case. The situation described by Barlow as effective

in 11th century England (*VSE*, n. 10) also applied in the 7th c. Theodore's appointments could not have gone forward without the consent of kings such as Wulfhere of Mercia and his successor Ethelred.

35. Colker, "Texts of Jocelyn," 403, and *VSE* 13, 17, 20–21, 31, 32–34.

36. Colker, "Texts of Jocelyn," 401, and *VSE* 15–16, 30.

37. See also the parable of the sower in Luc. 8, especially v. 14.

38. Albert Blaise, *Lexicon Latinitatis Medii Aevi*, Corpus Christianorum Continuatio Mediaevalis 1 (Turnhout, 1975) 123.

39. A possible source for the phrase in *VSE* is a few lines from the hymn "Iesu redemptor omnium," which was sung regularly at the feast of a confessor bishop such as Erkenwald, in both monastic and secular uses:

> qui rite mundi gaudia
> huius caduca respuens
> cum angelis caelestibus
> laetus potitur praemiis.

See A. S. Walpole, *Early Latin Hymns* (Cambridge, 1922; rpt. Hildesheim, 1966), 387. Cf. also the following verses from Paulinus's life and passion of St. Felix of Nola, which may well have been in Goscelin's mind when he wrote his account of Erkenwald (Paulinus is contrasting Felix with his worldly brother Hermias):

> Hermiam mundus abegit,
> Felicem Christus sibi sustulit; ille caduca
> maluit, hic solida; praesentibus ille cohaesit,
> iste solum caelo uertit, patrimonia regnis;
> ille heres tantum proprii patris, iste coheres
> Christi.

G. Hartel, ed. *S. Paulini Nolani carmina*, CSEL 30 (Vienna, 1884), 54, vv. 79–84.

40. Gibbs, xxx–xxxi. The first known master of the school, Durand, was a noted grammarian. See R. E. Hunt, "Studies on Priscian in the eleventh and twelfth centuries," *Med. & Ren. Studies* 1 (1943): 206, 208, 224–25.

41. See below, chap. 4, nn. 18–19.

42. *Gesta pontificum*, 145–46.

N O T E S   T O   C H A P T E R   T H R E E

1. On hagiography as propoganda, see Graus, 39. On the protective relationship of saint and community, see, e.g., A. M. Orselli, "Il santo patrono cittadino: genesi e sviluppo del patrocinio del vescovo nei secoli VI e VII" in Gajano, 85–104; B. de Gaiffier, "Les revendications de biens dans quelques documents hagiographiques du XIe siècle," *AB* 50 (1932): 123–38; Patrick J. Geary, "The Humiliation of the Saints," in Stephen Wilson, ed. *The Saints and their Cults, Studies in Religious Sociology, Folklore and History* (Cambridge, 1983), first published in French in *Annales E.S.C.* 34 (1979): 27–42. I am grateful to Professor Geary for this reference.

2. Gibbs, xvi–xxxix; Brooke, "The Composition of the Cathedral Chapter of St. Paul's, 1086–1163," *Cambridge Historical Journal* 10 (1951): 111–32; Brooke, "The Earliest Times to 1485," in Matthews & Atkins, eds., *A History of St. Paul's*, especially 15–38; Brooke & Keir, *London 800–1216*, 338–59.

3. Gibbs, xxxii–xxxiii; Matthews & Atkins, 24–28; Brooke & Keir, 356–57.

4. Chap. 2.

5. Gibbs, xvii–xviii and n. 1, xxii–xxv; Brooke, "Composition," 115, 118–119, and, on the pre-Conquest "rule" and the Norman chapter, Matthews & Atkins, 12–22.

6. Gibbs, xxiv–xxvi.

7. Described in Mir. IV; on Maurice's role as rebuilder, see also Mir. V 1–4.

8. *Gesta pontificum*, 143. William toned down the passage in later editions.

9. *Historia ecclesiastica* 11.31, ed. M. M. Chibnall, *The Ecclesiastical History of Orderic Vitalis*, 8 vols. (Oxford, 1969–80), 6:144. Contemporaries of Orderic's at St. Evroul became abbots of Crowland and Thorney (Chibnall, 2:348–50, 6:148–54), and Orderic himself, a native of England, returned for at least one visit (Chibnall, 1:25).

10. "Richard of Belmeis and the Foundation of St. Osyth's," *Trans. Essex Archaeol. Soc.*, 3rd Ser., vol. 2 (1970): 301–2. Bethel adds that Maurice, according to William of Malmesbury, was a good preacher, but this seems to be a mistranslation of "efficatiae praedicabilem," i.e. "outstandingly efficient."

11. Bethel, "Richard of Belmeis," 302.

12. Colker, "Texts of Jocelyn," 398.

13. Bale, *Index*, 498.

14. H. W. C. Davis, ed., *Regesta regum Anglo-Normannorum 1066–1154*, vol. 1 (Oxford, 1913).

15. For the most recent study of Richard's career, emphasizing the later years, see Bethel, "Richard of Belmeis" (above, n. 10). The fullest account, still valuable, is that of Robert W. Eyton, *Antiquities of Shropshire*, 12 vols. (London, 1854–60), 2:192–201.

16. Gibbs, xxxii and 215–17. The standard account of the medieval St. Paul's school is that of A. F. Leach, "St. Paul's School before Colet," *Archaeologia* 62 (1910): 191–238.

17. Brooke, "Composition," 126–27; see also the several entries for "Belmeis" in Le Neve/Greenaway, "Index."

18. *Gesta pontificum*, 146.

19. Mir. V 7–11. Arcoid's assessment is corroborated by Ordericus Vitalis, *Historia ecclesiastica* 11.31, ed. Chibnall, 6:144: "summopere laborauit, et inceptum opus magna ex parte consummauit."

20. Bethel, "Richard of Belmeis," 302–3, 307, 321.

21. Ibid., 309–10.

22. Ibid., 327–28.

23. Mir. V 5–11.

24. W. Sparrow Simpson, "Two Inventories of the Cathedral Church of St. Paul, London," *Archaeologia* 50 pt. 2 (1887): 487.

25. Brooke, "Composition," 122–25.

26. Gibbs, xxvi–xxviii.

27. Simpson, *Registrum statutorum et consuetudinum ecclesiae cathedralis sancti Pauli Londinensis* (London, 1873), 50.

28. *Miracula sancti Dunstani auctore Osberno* 23, ed. Stubbs, *Memorials of St. Dunstan*, 155–56: ". . . amplexus foeminarum, amplas domus, amicorum societates." The story concerns one Edward, monk of Christ Church, Canterbury, and former archdeacon of London. See Le Neve/Greenaway, 8. The story is retold by Eadmer, in his life and miracles of St. Dunstan, at greater length but omitting the passage from which the quotation above is taken: Stubbs, *Memorials of St. Dunstan*, 241–44.

29. Brooke, "Composition," 120.

30. Archbishop Thurstan of York had been a non-resident canon of St. Paul's for a time, as well as chaplain to Henry I. His father, Canon Anger (*alias* Ansker), may have been chaplain to William Rufus. Brooke, "Composition," 124.

31. Ibid., 125–26.

32. The only thorough study of Gilbert the Universal is that of Beryl Smalley, "Gilbertus Universalis, bishop of London (1128–34), and the Problem of the 'Glossa Ordinaria,' " *Recherches de théologie ancienne et médiévale* 7 (1935): 235–62.

33. M. Brett, *The English Church under Henry I* (Oxford, 1975), 112.

34. Smalley, 238–39. Her source, previously unnoticed, is Hugh the Chanter.

35. *Epistolae* 24, PL 182:128–29; quoted in Smalley, 242.

36. Brooke, in Matthews & Atkins, 26.

37. Smalley, 245.

38. Mir. V 16–17.

39. Smalley, 245, and Frank Barlow, *The English Church 1066–1154* (London & New York, 1979), 118. Smalley quotes Henry of Huntingdon on Gilbert's parsimony: "multa perquirens, pauca largiens."

40. Smalley, 245–47 and n. 53.

41. Smalley, 242, n. 46, and 247; E. W. Williamson, *The Letters of Osbert of Clare, Prior of Westminster* (Oxford, 1929), 16–17.

42. Matthews & Atkins, 26, and Brooke & Keir, *London*, 356 and n. 2, citing Eleanor Rathbone, "Master Alberic of London, Mythographus tertius Vaticanus," *Journal of Medieval & Renaissance Studies* 1 (1941): 35 and 38. But Miss Rathbone nowhere connects Alberic with Gilbert.

43. Le Neve/Greenaway, 86.

44. Le Neve/Greenaway, 27.

45. L. DeLisle, *Rouleaux des Morts* (Paris, 1886), 342. Cited by Rathbone, "The Influence of Bishops and of Members of Cathedral Bodies on the Intellectual Life of England, 1066–1216" (Ph.D. diss., London U., 1935), 169. Ralph, son of Fulcred, does not appear, at least by that name, in Le Neve/Greenaway. Barlow, *English Church 1055–1154*, 234, thinks Ralph may have migrated, before 1129, to the court of William Warelwast, bishop of Exeter. It should be noted here also that Master Durand, who headed the St. Paul's school under Maurice and early in Richard's episcopacy, was a distinguished grammarian. See Barlow, 235, and n. 93.

46. Smalley, 240, and n. 29, corrects some errors in previous accounts of Gilbert's death, including the mistaken notion that he died on the way to Rome. This error continues to be made, however: cf. Brett, 54–55, 146, citing Smalley as his authority.

47. On the recruitment of bishops under Henry I, see Brett, 104–12. On the tight control of bishoprics under Norman kings in general, and the slight relaxation under Stephen, see Barlow, *English Church 1066–1154*, 115–18.

48. The council began March 22 at Westminster, was extended into April, and moved to Oxford where oaths were given and Stephen's charter of liberties to the church was issued. R. H. C. Davis, *King Stephen 1135–1154* (London, 1967), 22–23. For the Oxford charter and the list of ecclesiasts and lay barons present, see Stubbs, *Select Charters*, 10th ed. rev. W. H. C. Davis (Oxford, 1921), 142–44.

49. The following account is based on Ralph's *Abbreviationes chronicorum*, entries for the years 1136–1138, in Stubbs, ed., *The Historical Works of Master Ralph de Diceto*, RS 68, 2 vols. (London, 1876), 1:248–52.

50. The fullest account of Anselm is that of Williamson, *Letters of Osbert*, 192–200. See also David C. Douglas, ed., *Feudal Documents from the Abbey of Bury St. Edmunds*,

Records of the Social & Economic History of England and Wales, 8 (London, 1932), cxxxv–vii.

51. Ralph records also that in the following year Stephen profited further from the London canons, because of their failure to comply with a decree of the same council forbidding concubinage among the higher clergy. He imprisoned several of their "housekeepers" (focariae) in the Tower until they redeemed them for a hefty fine. Thus Hildebrandine ideals were bent to the service of the Exchequer. Diceto, 1:249.

52. ". . . si vitam et opinionem ejus sequamur, multo tutius est eum ab abbatia removere, quam in Lundoniensi ecclesia promovere." Diceto, 1:250. Cf. also Donald Nichol, *Thurstan, Archbishop of York (1114–1140)* (York, 1964), 232–33.

53. For Stubbs' brief account of Robert de Sigillo, see Diceto, 1:xxiv. The rumor of poison is recorded by John of Salisbury, *Historia pontificalis*, trans. Chibnall (London, 1956), 88.

54. See above, n. 3.

55. Eadmer wrote a tract defending the feast: *De conceptione sanctae Mariae*, PL 159:301–18; see Southern, *St. Anselm and his Biographer* (Cambridge, 1963), 290–96.

56. Williamson, *Letters of Osbert*, 67.

57. Edmund Bishop, *Liturgica Historica* (Oxford, 1918), 245–46. According to Smalley, 242, n. 35, Gilbert prevented young Richard of Belmeis (nephew of the former bishop) from assuming the archdeaconry of Middlesex, which had been conferred on him as a boy by his uncle. The latter's chaplain, Hugo, who had been given the office until young Richard's majority, apparently found favor with Gilbert and held on to the office until forced to relinquish it in 1138, when the matter was referred to the papal legate, Alberic. Diceto, 1:250–52.

58. Brooke & Keir, *London*, 356–57.

59. Williamson, *Letters of Osbert*, 13–14. Edward J. Kealey, *Roger of Salisbury, Viceroy of England* (Berkeley, 1972), 137–42, discusses the controversy over the feast and Osbert's role, but evidently does not consider the theory about the Belmeis faction's opposition worth mentioning.

60. Smalley, 241.

61. "Canonici . . . quia quod fecerunt tam regi quam toti concilio videbatur iniquum, regis indignationem plurimam meruerunt. . . ." Diceto, 248.

62. "Willelmo decano Lundoniae consanguinei sui maxime restiterunt, non quae Dei sed quae mundi sunt sapientes." Diceto, 249.

63. Anselm became a monk when a young boy in his native Lombardy. At age 18 or 19 he appears to have become his uncle Anselm's ward, his father Burgundus having died on pilgrimage. After completing his literary and monastic education at Christ Church school, he returned to Italy on Anselm's death in 1109, and not long afterwards obtained the abbacy of St. Saba in Rome, through personal ties with Pope Paschal. The same friendship, plus his English education and connections, secured his appointment as papal legate to England in 1115. Reappointed as legate the following year, he failed to gain entry to the country during his three year term, King Henry keeping him in Normandy the whole time, while treating him well. After his recall to Rome in 1119, Anselm apparently expected the offer of an English bishopric but settled for the abbacy of St. Edmund instead, in 1121. Such evidence as exists indicates that he did so reluctantly. Williamson, *Letters of Osbert*, 194–97, and Douglas, *Feudal Documents*, cxxxv. For an amusing interpretation of Anselm of Bury's career and character, see R. H. C. Davis, "The monks of St. Edmund's, 1021–1148," *History*, n.s. 40 (1955), 236–39. Davis asserts at the outset, 236, that Anselm was "not . . . intended either by his parents or by nature for a monastic life."

64. One of Anselm's early acts as abbot was to obtain a papal privilege (he was back in Rome in 1123) allowing for the possibility that Bury St. Edmunds might become a

bishopric and ensuring that the bishop must always be a monk. Williamson, *Letters of Osbert*, 194.

65. On Anselm's son, whom I have not seen mentioned by modern scholars, see charters 112 & 125 in Douglas, *Feudal Documents*, 113, 123. Dated 1121–35 and both of Abbot Anselm, the charters list a William "son of Anselm" among the witnesses in each case. On Thurstan as promoter of the Cistercian presence in Yorkshire, and as founder of the convent of St. Clement's, York, see Nicholl, 150–91, 199–200; for his protection of the recluses Roger of Caddington and Christina of Markyate, see Talbot, *The Life of Christina of Markyate*, 21, 27, 110–13, 126–27.

66. E. H. Webb, *Records of St. Bartholomew's Priory*, 2 vols. (Oxford, 1923), 1:40, 46, 48.

67. Gibbs, nos. 154, 156, pp. 119–22; see also Talbot, *Life of Christina*, 29–30.

68. Le Neve/Greenaway, 62.

69. Brooke & Keir, *London*, 356, echoed by Barlow, *English Church 1066–1154*, 96. There is no evidence for such a friendship.

70. See part two of this chapter.

71. Empress Matilda fled from London barely a month after Robert's consecration, and he with her, presumably. *Simeonis monachi opera omnia. Historia regum*, ed. Thomas Arnold, RS 75, 2 vols. (London, 1882–85), 2:310. After a short period of exile, during which time he got no help from the St. Paul's chapter, according to John of Salisbury (*Historia pontificalis*, trans. Chibnall, 48), Robert resumed control of the see by Easter, 1142 (Gibbs, 173, charter no. 219). It is possible that Arcoid would have omitted to mention or address Robert during this period of uncertainty, viz., July 1141 to March/April 1142. Cathedral chapters were habitually jealous of their corporate independence (Brett, 186–96), and after almost seven years without a bishop the canons of St. Paul's might have felt themselves more independent than most.

72. Arcoid explains, Mir. VII 96–97, that after this miracle occurred, he was given the task of recording it. It is possible therefore that he wrote a rough account soon after the event, which he later reworked. This may be true also of some of the other miracles. In a slightly different category is Mir. XVIII, concerning the novice of Barking in the time of Abbess Alviva (who held the office from the age of fifteen, ca. 1061, until her death in or after 1122). This episode may be based on a portion of the lost *Miracula Erkenwaldi* composed by Goscelin of Canterbury, although Arcoid denies the existence of previous written accounts of the miracles: Mir. Pr. 22–24. On Alviva, see Mir. XVIII, n. 3. For the lost set of *miracula* see above, Chap. 2, n. 18.

73. Le Neve/Greenaway, 1.

74. Smalley, 238. See above, n. 32.

75. Le Neve/Greenaway, 27; Gibbs, xxxii, n. 2; Brooke, in Matthews & Atkins, 26, 28. Arcoid's name appears quite frequently in the charters printed by Henry C. Maxwell-Lyte in *Historical MSS Commission Reports*, Vol. 9 *Appendix* (London, 1883), 63–68. Arcoid's name is variously spelt Arcoidus, Archoidus, Arcordus. I follow Brooke and Barlow in using the anglicized form, Arcoid.

76. Le Neve/Greenaway, 57.

77. Le Neve/Greenaway, 27.

78. "Composition," 120.

79. Smalley, 239.

80. On Robert de Auco, see Le Neve/Greenaway, 69. His son John is mentioned in a charter of ca. 1150; see Maxwell-Lyte, *Reports*, 62. For the schoolhouse of Master Hugo and his successor, see the charters of Bishop Richard of Belmeis, in Gibbs, 215–17.

81. Arcoid is named first of twenty-three canons after the archdeacons Richard and Geoffrey, in a charter (after 1138) concerning land leased to Agnes and Cecilia, *Reports*,

68, col.i; he heads the whole list, with the cognomen "presbiter," in a charter of uncertain date, granting a wharf to Walter, son of Bishop Richard I (ibid.).

82. Simpson, *Registrum*, 23; Gibbs, xxxi–xxxii, 216–217; Leach, "St. Paul's School," 192–95; Barlow, *English Church 1066–1154*, 225, n. 40, and 235.

83. Canons Geoffrey. and Robert, who appear in several of the same witness lists as Arcoid, were the sons of Wlfred [sic], who held the prebend of Weldland in the time of Bishops Maurice and Richard I. Le Neve/Greenaway, 83. Robert de Auco, prebendary of St. Pancras, witnessed his first charter, not yet as a canon, in 1104 (*Reports*, 61, col.ii); he inherited from his father, Osbern. Le Neve/Greenaway, 69. Master Henry, appointed schoolmaster 1127 by Bishop Richard, had been pupil and foster son of his predecessor, Master Hugo, who in turn had succeeded Master Durand, a noted grammarian (see above, n. 45), early in Bishop Richard's time. Le Neve/Greenaway, 25, 92–93.

84. Mir. VII, for example, makes some apparent allusions to the anarchy of Stephen's reign. The language with which Arcoid describes the increase in human wickedness and criminality at this time (Mir. VII 11–15), the doleful tone of the miracle itself, especially the homiletic digression on the misery of the human condition (Mir. VII 41–56) and the unique allusion to King Stephen at the end (Mir. VII 99), combine to evoke the grim atmosphere of the famous annal for 1137 in the Anglo-Saxon Chronicle. Cecily Clark, ed. *The Peterborough Chronicle 1070–1154*, 2nd ed. (Oxford, 1970), 55–56. Even here, however, the allusions to the chaos in the secular realm are carefully set within the context of the supernatural order. Immediately after mentioning that the miracle occurred "when the episcopal throne was vacant, under King Stephen," Arcoid adds (Mir. VII 98–101) that the year was "one thousand, one hundred and thirty-nine after the Virgin gave birth, this universal frame being governed by the King of Kings, our Lord Jesus Christ."

85. Henry of Huntingdon, a near-contemporary of Arcoid's and like him a secular clerk (archdeacon of Huntingdon) exhibits a similar theory of the genre of *miracula* (although his attitude towards miracles as such is clearly more cautious and critical than Arcoid's). Rather than interweave the miraculous and the mundane in a continuous narrative pattern, as Bede and many other historians had done, Henry in his *Historia Anglorum* sets aside a separate book, the ninth, *De miraculis*, for the miracles of English saints. Books I–VIII and the additional Book X contain no "hagiographical miracles." Gransden, *Historical Writing in England c. 550–c. 1307*, 197. Henry originally intended Book IX to be the last, "so that the merely temporal deeds of kings and nations might find their conclusion in the glorious works of eternal God" (ut temporales regum et gentium actiones in eterni dei gloriosis terminentur operibus). Cambridge University Library MS Ii. 2. 3, f. 385 (193). Henry's *De miraculis* is unprinted except for a few extracts. See Benedicta Ward, *Miracles and the Medieval Mind* (Philadelphia, 1982), 205, for other instances, among twelfth-century writers, of this tendency to separate the miracles of the saints from the non-miraculous history of human affairs (e.g., Eadmer's *Vita Anselmi*, which includes Anselm's miracles, and the *Historia novorum in Anglia*, which recounts Anselm's public career but relates no miracles).

86. The question of structure in collections of miracles is addressed by P.-A. Sigal, "Histoire et hagiographie. Les miracles aux XIe et XIIe siècles," *Annales de Bretagne et des Pays de l'Ouest* 87:2 (1980), 237–57. See also J. P. Valéry Patin & Jacques le Goff, "A propos de la typologie des miracles dans le Liber de Miraculis de Pierre le Vénérable," in *Pierre Abélard, Pierre le Vénérable, les courants philosophiques, littéraires, et artistiques en occident au milieu du XIIe siècle*, Colloques internationaux du Centre National de la Recherche Scientifique, 546 (Paris, 1975), 182. On the definition of *miraculum* as a distinct genre, see Peter Assion, "Die mittelalterliche Mirakelliteratur als Forschungsgegenstand," *Archiv für Kulturgeschichte* 50 (1968): 172–80. The studies by Dieter Harmening,

"Fränkische Mirakelbücher," *Würzburger Diöcezangeschichtsblätter* 28 (1966): 54 ff., and Hermann Bach, *Mirakelbücher bayerischer Wahlfahrtsorte* (diss., Munich, 1963), are mainly concerned with late medieval and early modern miracle collections in the German vernacular, but each begins with useful preliminary surveys of the origin, development, and purpose of miracle literature; see especially Bach, 21–27.

87. Recent general surveys of saints' cults and sanctity have focused either on late antiquity (Brown) or on the earlier Middle Ages (Geary, Graus, Poulin), or on the later Middle Ages after 1200: A. Vauchez, *La sainteté en occident aux dernières siècles du moyen âge*, Bibliothèque des écoles françaises d'Athènes et du Rome, 241 (Rome, 1981); Michael Goodich, *Vita Perfecta: The Ideal of Sainthood in the Thirteenth Century*, Monographien zur Geschichte des Mittelalters, 25 (Stuttgart, 1982); Donald Weinstein & Rudolph M. Bell, *Saints and Society* (Chicago, 1982); Richard Kieckhefer, *Unquiet Souls: Fourteenth Century Saints and their Religious Milieu* (Chicago, 1984). New comprehensive studies of 11th and 12th century saints, however, are lacking. (P.-A. Sigal, *L'homme et le miracle dans la France médiévale* (Paris, 1985) appeared too recently for me to use it here.)

88. Vauchez, 122, prints a table of figures compiled from earlier attempts to quantify the new saints created from the 10th to the 14th century. His table shows a steady rise in the number of new saints during the 12th and 13th centuries, the latter being the "bumper" century. A rather steep decline ensued in the 14th and 15th centuries.

89. This is not to say that local cults did not continue to appear and thrive. Witness that of the boy "martyr" St. William of Norwich (d. 1144), discussed by Ward, *Miracles*, 68–76. See also E. W. Kemp, *Canonization and Authority in the Western Church* (Oxford, 1948), 116–28, for other examples of uncanonized late medieval saints.

90. Still the best and most detailed treatment of the making of saints before the late twelfth century is that of Kemp, *Canonization*, 3–81.

91. D. W. Rollason, "The cults of murdered royal saints in Anglo-Saxon England," *Anglo-Saxon England* 11 (1983): 1–22.

92. Kemp, *Canonization*, 97–104, 106. Cf. Vauchez, 27: "Dès la fin du XIᵉ siècle, on croyait, dans certains milieux ecclésiastiques, à l'existence d'un décret interdisant *ne quis sine apostolica auctoritate canonizaretur.*" See also Kemp, *Canonization*, 74, for the source of Vauchez's quotation.

93. See next chapter.

94. For an account of the growth of "papal business" see Southern, *Western Society and the Church in the Middle Ages* (Harmondsworth, 1970), 107–25.

95. Vauchez, 26.

96. A valuable survey is Klaus Schreiner, "*Discrimen Veri et Falsi.* Ansätze und Formen der Kritik in der Heiligen- und Reliquienverehrung des Mittelalters," *Archiv für Kulturgeschichte* 48 (1966): 1–53. Although he cites some examples of the critical spirit from the early Middle Ages, particularly among the Carolingians, Schreiner's evidence is mainly drawn from after 1100.

97. For example, in 1131 Innocent II canonized Godehard of Hildesheim (d. 1038), and a contemporary chronicler wrote that the papal canonization was needed to ensure that "demonic illusions" were not responsible for the miracles that promoted the cult. Kemp, *Canonization*, 74.

98. Schreiner, 28–29, cites Lethaldus of Micy as an early example of the critical spirit, as evidenced in his preface to his life of St. Julian of Le Mans. PL 137:782. See also the prologue to his *Miracula S. Martini Vertavensis*, MGH SRM 3:567: "Maxime namque de his quae veritas gessit falsitas fugienda est."

99. The standard English discussion of this aspect of hagiography is Charles W. Jones, *Saints' Lives and Chronicles* (Ithaca, N. Y., 1947), especially 51–79. On the general subject of the saints' life as "pia fraus," see Schreiner, "Zum Wahrheitsverständnis im Heiligen-

und Reliquienwesen des Mittelalters," *Saeculum* 17 (1966): 131–69.

100. For Charlemagne's legislation on this subject, and several examples of its implementation, see Kemp, *Canonization*, 37, 45, 48–52.

101. Ibid., 52; Vauchez, 41.

102. E.g., the prologue to the *Vita S. Martini Vertavensis* by Lethaldus of Micy: "Ceterum quicumque dignatus pauperculae hujus schedae apices revolveris, ne verborum tibi displiceat rusticitas: verum sinceriter praelibatae historiae complaceat veritas. Regnum quippe Dei non in sermone constat, sed in virtute (1 Cor. 4.20)." ASS Oct., 10:805. See Gerhard Strunk, *Kunst und Glaube in der Lateinischen Heiligenlegende zu ihrem Selbstverständnis in den Prologen*, Medium Aevum, Philologische Studien 12 (Munich, 1970), 150–62, re. "sermo humilis" and "veritas" among hagiographers of the post-Merovingian period. The topos is already evident in the work of Sulpicius Severus. Strunk, 14–26.

103. Cf. Schreiner, "Zum Wahrheitsverständnis," 145, for a similar view. Schreiner also cites the interesting admission of Peter Damian that some of his miracle stories were not properly substantiated, but that the truths they expressed were of everlasting worth.

104. Strunk, 159–61.

105. For the topos "non ab oratoribus sed a piscatoribus" see Strunk, 15–16, 152–53.

106. The standard account of the Norman "purge" of the Anglo-Saxon saints' cults is that of E. Bishop & A. Gasquet, *The Bosworth Psalter* (Oxford 1908), 27–34, 63–64. See also Southern, *St. Anselm and his Biographer*, 249–50. David Knowles, *The Monastic Order in England* (Cambridge, 1940), 118–19, and D. J. A. Matthew, *The Norman Conquest* (London, 1966), 201–05, recount several anecdotes of Norman disrespect for the native English saints. Bishop & Gasquet's original argument is based on their assumption that the calendar in British Library MS Arundel 155, from which so many of the Anglo-Saxon saints are omitted, is a post-Conquest calendar from Christ Church. It now appears that the calendar is pre-Conquest and thus not the product of any reforms of Lanfranc's. Michael Korhammer, "The Origin of the Bosworth Psalter," *Anglo-Saxon England* 2 (1973): 179 (I am indebted to D. W. Rollason for this reference). The general picture painted by Bishop & Gasquet is confirmed, however, by comparison of the pre- and post-Conquest calendars printed by Francis Wormald, *English Kalendars before A.D. 1100*, HBS 72 (London, 1934), and *English Benedictine Kalendars after A.D. 1100*, HBS 77 (London, 1939). See also Barlow, *English Church 1066–1154*, 191.

107. The episode is described by Eadmer. See Southern, *Life of St. Anselm*, 50–54.

108. "pro confessione nominis Christi." Southern, *Life of St. Anselm*, 51.

109. Charles Plummer, ed., *Two Saxon Chronicles Parallel*, 2 vols. (Oxford, 1892; rpt. 1965), 1:142–43, translated Dorothy Whitelock, *The Anglo-Saxon Chronicle* (London, 1961), 91–92.

110. St. Elphege seems to have satisfied the same need in the 11th century as St. Edmund in the late 9th. King Canute, whose countrymen had murdered both saints, played a major role in establishing both their cults. For his part in the cult of St. Edmund, see Francis Hervey, *The History of Edmund the Martyr* (Oxford, 1929), 30–35; for his participation in St. Elphege's translation to Canterbury in 1023, see Plummer, 1:156 and Whitelock, 99–100.

111. Southern, *Life of St. Anselm* , 52–54.

112. Eadmer inserts a brief anecdote between Lanfranc's question and Anselm's response, in order, as he says, to provide a "historical perspective" before he repeats Anselm's theological argument. He tells how Elphege attempted to preach to and convert the heathen Danes as they were burning Canterbury and slaughtering its inhabitants, and how this provoked the Danes to kill him. Southern, *Life of St. Anselm*, 52. Eadmer's "historical" anecdote seems to be a conflation of several separate incidents culled from

Osbern's earlier *Vita S. Elphegi*. PL 149:380–84. I am working on a separate study of the hagiography of St. Elphege.

113. PL 157:313–404. To my knowledge, the only comparable work prior to Thierry's is the 4th c. *De laude sanctorum* of Victricius of Rouen. PL 20:443–59. Kemp, *Canonization*, 4–5, offers a brief assessment. See also Renée Herval, *Origines chrétiennes de la IIe Lyonaise gallo-romaine à la Normandie ducale (IV–XI siècles)* (Rouen, 1966), 108–53. Carolingian treatises on the iconoclastic controversy, by Agobard of Lyons, Claudius of Turin, and the Irishman Dungal, deal incidentally with relics. See K. Guth, *Guibert von Nogent und die Hochmittelalterliche Kritik an der Reliquienverehrung*. Studien und Mitteilungen zur Geschichte des Benediktiner-Ordens und seiner Zweige, Ergänzungsband 21 (Ottobeuren, 1970), 115, where he describes Thierry's work as the first theologically learned effort to come to terms with external features of saints' relics and cults.

114. *Flores* 2.1–6. PL 157:337–58.

115. A. Wilmart, "Edmeri Cantvariensis cantoris nova opuscula de sanctorum veneratione et obsecratione," *Revue des Sciences Religieuses* 15 (1935): 190–91. On the autograph manuscript, see Southern, *St. Anselm and his Biographer*, Appendix III, 367–74.

116. "Totis corporibus ante eorum reliquias prosternuntur, flexis genibus in humum usque deiciuntur, pronis uultibus incuruantur supplices eorum—et ipsi ante deum ad haec rigidi starent, auditum auerterent, horum aliquid non curarent?—Quis hoc dixerit? Itaque supplicum deuotio non erit inutilis, non erit uana, non erit a gratia uacua." Wilmart, 190.

117. PL 156:607–80. The most recent study is that of Guth (above, n. 113). A brief conventional account of book 1 of Guibert's *De pignoribus* is Colin Morris, "A Critique of Popular Religion: Guibert de Nogent on the *Relics of the Saints*," in G. J. Cuming & Derek Baker, eds., *Popular Belief and Practice. Studies in Church History* 8 (Cambridge, 1972), 55–60. Early studies, stressing Guibert's quasi modern "critical spirit" and historiographical enlightenment, are B. Monod, *Le moine Guibert et son temps* (Paris, 1905), 282 ff., and Abel le Franc, "Le traité des reliques de Guibert de Nogent et les commencements de la critique au moyen âge," *Études d'histoire du moyen âge dediées à Gabriel Monod* (Paris, 1896), 285–306. For a corrective view, see Jacques Chaurand, "La conception de l'histoire de Guibert de Nogent," *Cahiers de civilization médiévale* 8 (1965): 387–95. See also Roger D. Ray, "Medieval Historiography through the Twelfth Century: Problems and Progress of Research," *Viator* 5 (1974): 46–47.

118. "*Terra es, et in terram ibis.* . . . Et quae dignitas ut quis argentove claudatur, cum Dei Filius saxo vilissimo obstinatur?" PL 156:626.

119. The most useful essay in this direction is that of Schreiner, "*Discrimen Veri et Falsi*," cited above, n. 96. Guth (above, n. 113) provides a valuable survey of the relevant theological treatises that preceded Guibert's, but like Monod, Le Franc, and Morris, he emphasizes the uniqueness and splendid isolation of the *De pignoribus*. Nor does he deal with hagiographical evidence. Cf. also H. Delehaye, *Sanctus. Essai sur le culte des saints dans l'antiquité*, Subsidia hagiographica 17 (Brussels, 1927), 202–3, who regards Guibert "comme un véritable phénomène, en avance sur son temps de plusieurs siècles." On the other hand, Vauchez, 40, speaking of the rather restrained attitude, among hagiographers of 12th c. Latium, towards the miraculous element in saints' cults, goes so far as to claim that their restraint exemplifies the same spirit as Guibert's *De pignoribus*. Clearly there is room for re-evaluation of this entire topic.

120. For a recent discussion of the heresies of Henry of Lausanne and Peter of Bruys, see R. I. Moore, *The Origins of European Dissent* (New York, 1975), 82–114. A convenient collection of translated extracts from relevant contemporary sources is that of Walter L. Wakefield & Austin P. Evans, *Heresies of the High Middle Ages* (New York, 1969), 107–26, espec. 117, 120 re. the heretics' rejection of "churches built of stone or wood." On the traditional associations of holiness with specific locations, see Moore, 277–78.

121. On St. Bernard and Henry of Lausanne see Wakefield & Evans, 122–23, 125, translating St. Bernard's *Epistolae* 241 (PL 182:434–36) and *Sancti Bernardi vita . . . auctore Gaufrido* 6.16, 17 (PL 185:312–13). On the Cologne heretics, see Wakefield & Evans, 126 ff., especially 131, translating *Epistolae* 472 (PL 182:679).

122. *Venerabilis Hildeberti Cenomanensis episcopi epistolae* 2.23 (PL 171:237–42). There is unfortunately no modern edition of Hildebert's letters. Antoine Beaugendre, whose 1708 edition is reprinted in Migne (rev. ed. J. J. Bourasse), identifies the anonymous addressee of Letter 23 as Henry of Lausanne himself. But in a more recent analysis, F. Vernet rejects this as "invraisemblable," in view of the relatively mild tone of the letter and on grounds of chronology. *Dictionnaire de théologie catholique* 6:2180.

123. "Quod si nulla quae scribi debeant suis temporibus fieri contingant, non ideo nos statim falsitatis arguant, quasi quod alio tempore occulta Dei providentia non fit, pro corrigenda vel corripiendis hominibus fieri non possit. . . ." Stubbs, *Memorials of St. Dunstan*, 129.

124. Stubbs, *Memorials of St. Dunstan*, 130. The allusion is to the famous incident from the apocryphal Acts of St. John. See M. R. James, *The Apocryphal New Testament* (Oxford, 1924; rpt. 1953), 262–64.

125. ". . . illi praemium fidei habeant quandoque videre posse quod narrantibus nobis indubitata fide potuerunt credere." Stubbs, *Memorials of St. Dunstan*, 130.

126. "Maxime autem populus simplex et nonnulli nomine et habitu religionis perspicui delinquere uidentur, quod miraculis uel fictis uel certitudine nulla probabilibus statim credentes adquiescunt. Quod populus quidem causa stultissime nouitatis, religiosi uero, causa lucri uel causa loci sui sancti irrationabiliter ampliandi, mendaciter et mendose consuescere presumunt. Preterea si quid absque certo auctore scriptum repperiunt coram reuerenda dei presentia et sacrosancto altari legere et predicare domini timorem negligentes audent. Michi autem si narrentur huius miracula non aperte contradixero nisi aperte friuola sint, nec constanter affirmauero nisi notissimis indiciis et probatissimis personis ad plenum roborari perspexero." Cambridge U. Library MS Ii.2.3, f. 385 (193).

127. Printed by Thomas Arnold, ed., *Henrici archidiaconi Huntendunensis historia Anglorum*, RS 74 (London, 1879), xxvi ff.

128. PL 156:615.

129. *Miracles and the Medieval Mind*, 22.

130. Ward, *Miracles*, 14.

131. Ward, *Miracles*, 5–7; Cf. M. D. Chénu, *Man, Nature and Society in the Twelfth Century*. Selected, edited, and translated by Jerome Taylor & Lester K. Little (Chicago, 1968), 4–18; *La théologie au douzième siècle* (Paris, 1957), 21–30.

132. Chénu, 11, translated by Taylor and Little from William of Conches, *Philosophia mundi*. PL 172:56.

133. Chénu, 11.

134. Ward, *Miracles*, 30–31.

135. "Quotiens enim dei uicarius festum omnipotentis dei et sanctorum ipsius denuntiat et contempnitur, indignissima deo iniuria exoritur" (*Mir.* II 41–43).

136. The same topos of "negligentia," or failure to record the deeds of the saints, appears in Lantfred's miracles of St. Swithun, Herman's miracles of St. Edmund, and Peter the Venerable's *De miraculis*. E. P. Sauvage, "Sancti Swithuni wintoniensis episcopi translatio et miracula auctore Lantfredo monacho wintoniensi," *AB* 4 (1885): 373; Arnold, *Memorials of St. Edmund's Abbey*, 1:26–27; PL 189:851, 907.

137. Arcoid seems to combine two complementary interpretations of the passage from Matthew. On the one hand, there is the exegesis of St. Jerome, in which the swine are clearly identified as the unbelievers who refuse to hear the Gospel, "and who wallow in the vice and slime of their incredulity." *S. Hieronymi presbyteri opera*, I, 7, *Comm. in*

Mattheum libri IV, ed. D. Hurst & M. Adriaen, CCSL 77 (Turnhout, 1969), 42. The Ps.-Bede commentary and Rhabanus Maurus follow Jerome in calling the swine "contemptores veritatis" (PL 92:36; PL 112:1032). Cf. also Peter the Venerable, *Contra Petrobrusianos*, ed. James Fearns, CCCM 10 (Turnhout, 1968), 89: "Sed quia novi hec magis dicenda esse fidelibus venerantibus quam infidelibus irridentibus, recondantur interim margaritae, ne a porcis conculcentur." Ruper of Deutz and the *Glossa ordinaria*, on the other hand, view the verse as explaining why the scriptures are veiled in allegorical "figuris" and "aenigmatibus" and can only be understood by an elect few. So many are unworthy to know the mysteries of God's kingdom (PL 168:1454; PL 114:108). Arcoid is thus warning his audience not to treat his miracle stories with contempt and incredulity, as "contemptores veritatis," but rather to read them as the elite should, for their spiritual significance. Echoes of the complex of ideas and images surrounding the biblical verse occur here and there later in MSE, e.g., in Mir. IV 144 where Arcoid denounces Vigilantius as "vile heretic," and in XI 41–42 where he imagines the incredulous detractors "muttering and carping in the slimy dregs of their filth."

138. Some contemporary miracle collections contain large numbers of brief, monotonous healing episodes, e.g., the 102 miracles of St. Gibrien of Rheims, ca. 1145 (ASS Mai., 7:618–50), all but four of them healing episodes. The collection is analyzed by Sigal, "Maladie, pèlerinage et guérison au XIIᵉ siècle. Les miracles de saint Gibrien à Reims," *Annales. E.S.C.* 24 (1969):1522–39. Vauchez, 40–41, comments on the "flot tumultueux" of miracles submitted to the Pope by promoters of new saints' cults in hopes of canonization. One finds in the case of the miracles of St. Swithun an obsession with precise numbering of the crowds who were healed at the saint's shrine. Sauvage, 398, cc. XXI–XXIII.

139. S. *Hieronymi presbyteri contra Vigilantium*, PL 23:339–52. English trans. in *Post-Nicene Fathers* 6:417 ff. Vigilantius is discussed briefly in J. D. N. Kelly, *Jerome* (New York, 1975), and Brown, *The Cult of the Saints*, 27, 32. See also Guth, 11–12, and n. 57.

140. *Hildeberti episcopi epistolae* 23, PL 171:237–38, 240: "Tu quoque tanquam doleas oblivione suppressam Vigilantii perversitatem, suscitare eam perhiberis. . . . Porro . . . ad Vigilantium, cujus pedissequam fecisti animam tuam, Hieronymus scribens, his redarguit verbis . . ."

141. Arcoid refers at one point to Vigilantius's "confederates" (complices), Mir. IV 148.

142. *De pignoribus* 1.4, PL 156:626.

143. *De civitate Dei* 23.8–9, PL 41:760–72. See the account by Brown, *Augustine of Hippo* (Berkeley, Cal., 1969), 413–18; also *Cult of the Saints*, 27–28, 77–78.

144. Cf. Thierry of Echternach, *Flores* 1.3, PL 157:324–25 "excepta carne Christi . . . nulla carnis substantia carne sanctorum est nobilior . . . in morte nascitur ad requiem et gloriam. Ad gloriam, inquam, nascitur . . . aliud esse ex natura, aliud ex meritis et gratia. Ex natura est putribilis; ex meritis et gratia longissimo tempore etiam contra naturam durat imputribilis. . . . Caro sanctificata, per naturam *induta putridine, et sordibus pulveris, dormit in pulvere* (Iob 7.5, 20); per gratiam et meritum, vigilat in mirifico opere, et eum *cujus dulcedo est vermis* (Iob 24.20) resuscitat de pulvere, et reddit gratiae." Thierry's book II dwells repeatedly on the idea that the saints' shrines are symbolic of their heavenly glory (PL 157:337 ff.).

NOTES TO CHAPTER FOUR

1. Colgrave & Mynors, 354–57. The best modern accounts are those of Stubbs, in Stubbs & Henry Wace, *A Dictionary of Christian Biography* (London, 1880), 2:177–79; Whitelock, *Some Anglo-Saxon Bishops of London*, 5–10; and C. R. Hart, *The Early Charters of Eastern England*, Studies in Early English History 5 (Leicester, 1966), 117–19. See also Kenneth Harrison, *The Framework of Anglo-Saxon History to A.D. 900* (Cambridge, 1976), 68–72.

2. A. W. Haddan & W. Stubbs, *Councils and Ecclesiastical Documents Relating to Great Britain and Ireland*, vol. 3 (Oxford, 1871), 214; Colgrave, ed., *The Life of Bishop Wilfred by Eddius Stephanus* (Cambridge, 1927), c. xliii, p. 86; Alistair Campbell, ed., *Frithegodi monachi breuiloquium uitae beati Wilfredi et Wulfstani cantoris narratio metrica de sancto Swithuno* (Zurich, 1950), 45, vv. 1002 ff.

3. The other two are Oswald's cross of Hefenfeld, and Aidan's buttress, in *Hist. eccles.* 3.2, 17; Colgrave & Mynors, 214–19, 262–64. For further discussion, see chap. 5. Cf. also the wooden stake on which Oswald's head was impaled, *Hist. eccles.* 3.13; Colgrave & Mynors, 254.

4. Already by the mid-eighth century he was venerated as a saint at Chertsey, according to a letter of Sigebald, presumed Abbot of Chertsey, to Boniface: "et si supervixero tibi, cum nomine patris nostri Ercnwaldi (sic) Episcopi tuum adscribo nomen." Haddan & Stubbs, 3:350.

5. Arnold, *Memorials of St. Edmund's Abbey*, 1:42–43.

6. Felix Liebermann, *Die Heiligen Englands, angelsächsich und lateinisch* (Hannover, 1889), 13–14. The *Secgan* and its Latin affiliates are discussed by Rollason, "Lists of saints' resting-places in Anglo-Saxon England," *Anglo-Saxon England* 7 (1978): 61–93.

7. Wormald, *English Kalendars before A.D. 1100*, prints nineteen pre-Conquest English calendars. Erkenwald's April 30 feast day is in thirteen of these, many of which are from Wessex and the west midlands.

8. Colker, "Texts of Jocelyn," 403–4.

9. *VSE* 36–40. The fire is described in Mir. IV. On the shrine, see Mir. IV, n. 7.

10. On Maurice and the new church, see Mir. V 1–4, and n. 1.

11. *Gesta pontificum*, 142–44. According to Rodney Thomson, "William of Malmesbury as historian and man of letters," *Journal of Ecclesiastical History* 29 (1978): 391, William's research tour of English libraries was complete by ca. 1115. On his knowledge of *VSE* see above, chap. 2.

12. B. de Gaiffier has collected the eleventh-century evidence for the practice of reciting the saints' legends in the vernacular: "L'hagiographie et son public au XIe siècle," *Études critiques d'hagiographie et d'iconologie*, Subsidia hagiographica 43 (Brussels, 1967), 495–97.

13. Oxford, Bodleian Library Lat. Liturg. e. 39, ff. 42r–42v, 47r–48v. The manuscript is lacking at least two gatherings at the end and the sanctorale breaks off at November 6 (St. Leonard).

14. John of Tynemouth's version of this passage is a good example of the considerable differences between his *De Erkenwaldo* and Arcoid's *MSE*. John says that Erkenwald lay for many years "in terra," below ground, near the main altar under a wooden "theca" which was "shamefully covered with a piece of cheap cloth." He makes it seem that the great fire of London in 1087 was God's way of punishing the Londoners for allowing his servant to remain in such lowly circumstances. *NLA* 2:395.

15. I know of no modern study of the full-sized saints' shrines of medieval England. Daniel Rock, *Church of Our Fathers*, ed. G. W. Hart & W. H. Frere, 4 vols. (London,

1903), 3:306-43, collects a good deal of useful information relating to English shrines in the 12th and 13th centuries, much of which is incorporated in James Charles Wall, *The Shrines of British Saints* (London, 1905). Josef Braun, *Der Christliche Altar* (Munich, 1928), 546-55, an exhaustive study of the early medieval shrine in continental Europe, includes some English examples.

16. The fire is briefly described in the Anglo-Saxon Chronicle. Clark, *Peterborough Chronicle*, 10. For other historical refs., see Mir. IV, n. 43.

17. Neither Maurice nor Walkelin, who had been in frequent attendance on King William in the 1080s, appears to have accompanied the king to Normandy for the Vexin campaign. Thus, their being together on this occasion, while not confirmed by other sources, is not improbable.

18. W. D. Macray, ed. *Chronicon monasterii de Evesham*, RS 29 (London, 1863), 323-24, 335-36. See also Delehaye, *Sanctus*, 205, and Nicole Hermann-Mascard, *Les reliques des saints. Formation coutumière d'un droit* (Paris, 1975), 134-36, for earlier and later examples.

19. It is interesting that Arcoid not only emphasizes the absence of fire damage to the linen "pallium," to which he refers more than once as "pannus," but also rates the miracle as an act of power superior to that in Dan. 3.19-94, the survival of the three Hebrew youths in the fiery furnace. Cf. the following from the church's rite "ad probandas reliquias":

> Dominus Deus . . . qui sacerdotibus tuis sancta mysteria revelasti et *tribus pueris flammas ignium mitigasti*; concede nobis indignis famulis tuis . . . ut *pannus* iste, vel filum istud quibus involuta sunt corpora sanctorum, si vera non sint crementur ab hoc igne; et si vera sint, evadere valeant, ut iustitiae non dominetur iniquitas, subdatus falsitas veritati. [Italics mine]

Quoted by Delehaye, *Sanctus*, 205, n. 3.

20. Florence of Worcester mentions the fire of 1132: *Florenti Wigornensis monachi chronicon ex chronicis*, ed. Benjamin Thorpe, 2 vols. (London, 1848-49), 2:93. The same fire is described in some detail in the 15th century *Cartulary of Holy Trinity Aldgate*, ed. Gerald A. J. Hodgett, London Record Society 7 (London, 1971), 3:230-31. The fire of 1135/36 is mentioned briefly by Matthew Paris, *Chronica majora*, ed. Henry C. Luard, RS 57, 7 vols. (London, 1872-83), 2:163. Rose Graham says that "after the fire of 1136 the bishops gave up to the fabric fund half of the Pentecostals," i.e., Whitsuntide offerings, from all the lesser churches of the diocese. "An appeal about 1175 for the building fund of St. Paul's Cathedral Church," *British Architectural Association Journal*, 3rd Ser., 10 (1945-47):73. In 1136, however, there was no bishop, nor would there be one until 1141. This custom, referred to only vaguely in a later charter (Gibbs, 45-46), might have begun after the 1136 fire as Graham suggests, or later; but since the charter in question specifically refers back to Maurice and Richard I for other reasons, it is more likely that the custom originated with them and was necessitated by the fire of 1087.

21. See the plan of the crypt and the engraving in Dugdale, ed. Ellis, between 74 & 75.

22. See the notes to Mir. V for refs. to some analogues.

23. At least according to Ralph de Diceto, the abortive electon of Anselm of Bury in 1136-37 had cost the chapter a great deal of money (Stubbs, ed., *Historical Works of Master Ralph*, 1:248-52). Further, the king himself had sequestered some prebends in reprisal for the canons' conduct at the Easter council in 1136. It is not known whether he followed the custom of his predecessors in appropriating the income from the episcopal estates (as opposed to those of the chapter), but it is likely that he did. See Barlow, *English Church 1066-1154*, 116-17. Finally, the continuing burden of the building program must have been aggravated by the fire damage of 1132 and 1135/36.

24. For *MSE*'s evidence that the choir was ready for use by ca. 1140, see below and n. 28.

25. A similar shrine for the relics of St. Alban took "a few years" to build and decorate,

and this was thought to be fast work. Matthew Paris, *Gesta abbatum monasterii sancti Albani*, ed. H. T. Riley, RS 28 (London, 1867), 1:60. An early witness to the St. Alban shrine is Henry of Huntingdon, *Historia Anglorum* 9, in Cambridge U. Library MS Ii.2.3, f. 385 (193), where we learn that Abbot Geoffrey translated the relics to the new shrine, "feretrum mirabiliter auro et gemmis choruscum," in 1129, in the presence of Alexander, bishop of Lincoln, and a great crowd of people.

26. The charter is in St. Paul's MS W. D. 4 ("Liber L"), f. 40b, printed in Maxwell-Lyte, *Reports*, 65, cols. i–ii. It is undated, but two of the witnesses, Bretel and Ailwin Serehog the priest, appear elsewhere only in charters of the time of Dean William of Belmeis, viz. 1111–38; William of Wochend (Ockendon, Essex), another signator, was steward to the bishop and chapter from quite early in Richard I's episcopacy until about 1142. W. Hale, *Domesday of St. Paul's*, Camd. Soc. 69 (Westminster, 1858), 129. There being no St. Paul's canons among the witnesses to Galio's charter, it is probable that William was the chapter representative, though not necessarily as steward. On William of Ockendon, see further Brooke & Keir, *London*, 353, and Bethel, "Richard of Belmeis," 302–3 and n. 40.

27. Sandon is near Clacton in eastern Essex, near the sea. Galio's own manor was at Pentlow, somewhat closer to London.

28. By February, 1140, according to Mir. XIV 11, the upper church was sufficiently advanced to merit more than one night watchman, implying that at least part of it was furnished with movables that required protection. This tallies with the allusions, in Mir. XV, to the presence of the canons singing Erkenwald's festival mass in the choir. The story of Baldwin in Mir. XV seems to follow chronologically the translation episode in XIV, whereas XVI, as the rubricator of the Corpus manuscript points out, occurred earlier, when the shrine was still down in the crypt.

29. *Chronica majora*, ed. Luard, 2:183; Joseph Stevenson, ed., *Radulphus de Coggeshall chronicon Anglicanum*, RS 66 (London, 1875), 12.

30. Thomas S. R. Boase, *English Art 1100–1216* (Oxford, 1953), 95–96.

31. Simpson, "Two Inventories," 469–70.

32. The *Annales Paulini* record that in 1326 the saint's body was moved "from the place to which it had been translated before, *near the main altar*," presumably referring to the last translation proper, in 1148. Stubbs, *Chronicles of the Reigns of Edward I and Edward II*, RS 76 (London, 1882), 1:311.

33. Webb, 1:77, 489; Maxwell-Lyte, *Reports*, 67, col.ii. He also witnesses a charter only partially printed in *Reports*, 68, i. Le Neve/Greenaway, 95, lists him among the canons of St. Paul's, because he witnesses St. Paul's charters, but admits his prebend is unidentified. He is not in either of the prebendal lists. MSE provides an explanation: he was an intimate of the St. Paul's circle of resident canons, but his prebend was at St. Martin's. In one of the St. Bartholomew's charters he is listed next but one to Hugh, canon of St. Martin's. See also E. Ekwall, *Early London Place Names* (Lund, 1947), 66.

34. Stubbs, *Chronicles*, 1:cxxvii.

35. Cf. the story of the attempted theft of St. Edmund's relics by Bishop Aelfhun of London, when they were being kept in St. Gregory's church near St. Paul's, during Danish inroads ca. 1010. Arnold, ed., *Memorials of St. Edmund's Abbey*, 1:44–45. On relic thefts in general prior to the eleventh century, and for further bibliography, see Geary, *Furta sacra*.

36. Scholz, "The Canonization of Edward the Confessor," 40–41.

37. M. Bloch, "La vie de S. Édouard le Confesseur par Osbert le Clare," *AB* 41 (1923): 5–131. Bloch's view is repeated by Kemp, *Canonization*, 76–78.

38. Scholz, 43, n. 25; Williamson, *Letters of Osbert*, 17–19, 80–85, 87–88.

39. Bloch, 13.

40. Scholz, 48–49.

41. On Osbert's activities as a forger of charters on Westminster's behalf, see Brett, 59–60, 133–34; also Scholz, "Two Forged Charters from the Abbey of Westminster," *English Historical Review* 76 (1961): 477.

42. On the new choir see Matthews & Atkins, *History of St. Paul's*, 326; for the engraving see Dugdale, ed. Ellis, 108–9, especially the view next but one before 109, looking eastward down the long choir towards the main altar behind which is a partition: the shrine was on the far (east) side of the partition, as is made clear from the ground plan that immediately follows 108.

43. "in media nocte, propter tumultum populi evitandum. . . ." *Annales Paulini,* ed. Stubbs, *Chronicles,* 311. The shrine is depicted in Dugdale, ed. Ellis, 74. My impression is that the upper portion of the shrine, which appears to be a mere two-dimensional facade resting against the plain wall behind it, is all that remains of a much deeper three-dimensional structure, that would have been shaped like a miniature church occupying the flat top of the stone base. Presumably the shrine had been partially wrecked during the first wave of Puritan vandalism in the mid-sixteenth century (Dugdale, 31–32), but it may have been dismantled earlier, in Henry VIII's reign, by the commissioners of the crown for the sake of its treasure.

44. Dugdale, ed. Ellis, 15.

45. Braybroke's letters are printed by Simpson, *Documents,* xxiv–xxv, 15; and in *Registrum,* 393–95. Braybroke's action may have been part of a wider movement, spearheaded by Archbishop Courtenay, at reasserting the traditional sacramental modes of worship in the face of popular apathy and Lollard activism. On Courtenay and the Lollards, see Joseph Dahmus, *Metropolitan Visitations of William Courtenay, 1381–96* (Urbana, Ill., 1950), 45, 156–57, 170–73.

46. Dugdale, ed. Ellis, 15–16, 239.

47. Wormald, *English Benedictine Kalendars after 1100 A.D.,* 1:5, 37, 103, 120; 2:11, 66.

48. Bodley Lat. Liturg. e. 39, ff. 38v–48v, described in chap. 1; the historiated initial is in Lat. Liturg. d. 42, f. 46v.

49. J. B. L. Tolhurst, ed., *The Ordinale and Customary of the Benedictine Nuns of Barking Abbey,* HBS 65, 66 (London, 1927–28), 2:221–24, 336–37.

50. NLA 1:391–405; see above, chap. 1.

51. Tolhurst, *Ordinale,* 2:336. Cf. Simpson, *Documents,* 20; F. Proctor & C. Wordsworth, eds., *Breviarum ad usum insignis ecclesiae Sarum,* 3 vols. (Cambridge, 1879–86), 3:1038–48. Other previously unnoticed items testifying to Erkenwald's cult in the later Middle Ages include three lections for his deposition, based on a portion of *VSE,* in Stonyhurst College Library MS 52, f. 468v, as printed here in the appendix to *VSE,* and described in chap. 1; various collects, responds, and versicles in Bodley MSS Digby 38, f. 91v, Gough Liturg. 16, f. 2, and Bodley 790, f. 164; and a proper hymn, "Festiua dies annua," in Trinity College, Cambridge, MS O.3.54, a hymnary from Barking Abbey, f. 51v.

52. Dugdale, ed. Ellis, 15.

53. W. P. Baildon, *Records of the Honourable Society of Lincoln's Inn. The Black Books* (London, 1897–1902), 1:4.

54. Dugdale, *Origines Judicales,* 2nd ed. (London, 1671), 117, col.1.

55. Thomas M. C. Lawler, et al., eds., *Thomas More. A Dialogue Concerning Heresies,* 2 vols. (New Haven, 1981), 1:71, 81.

56. See Foreword, nn. 1 & 4.

57. BL Add. 35298, ff. 53–57. See Whatley, "A 'symple wrecche.' "

58. See above, n. 48.

59. Philip Nelson, *Ancient Painted Glass in England 1170–1500* (London, 1913), 186;

J. De Le Couteur, *English Medieval Stained Glass* (London, 1926), 118, fig. 28.

60. R. L. P. Milburn, *Saints and their Emblems in English Churches* (London, 1949), 89; Mrs. Arthur Bell, *The Saints in Christian Art*, vol. 3 (London, 1904), 49–50.

61. Christopher Woodforde, *The Norwich School of Glass Painting in the Fifteenth Century* (Oxford, 1950), 18–20. I am grateful to the Rev. David Sharp, M.A., Vicar of St. Peter Mancroft, and Mr. Dennis King, the Norwich glazier, for kindly providing me with information and photographs.

62. New York, Pierpont Morgan Library MS 105, f. 58. See Seymour de Ricci & W. J. Wilson, *Census of Medieval and Renaissance Manuscripts in the United States and Canada*, 3 vols. (New York, 1935–40). 2:1386; also *Supplement*, ed. W. H. Bond (New York, 1962), 337.

63. Morgan Library MS 46, ff. 44v–45. The verses, f. 45, were printed by Simpson, *Documents*, 16, when the manuscript was still in England. Cf. De Ricci & Wilson, 2:1374, and Bond, *Supplement*, 335–36. For a list of 15th c. *horae* in Bodley in which Erkenwald appears in calendar and/or litany, see Peterson, *Saint Erkenwald*, 65, n. 138. To these may be added Lambeth Palace MS 474, the so-called "Hours of Richard III and the Lady Margaret" and Huntington Library (San Marino) MS 1344, which appears to have belonged to a London Franciscan house. Finally Peterson, 64, n. 126, who does not mention the Morgan MSS, records a possible portrait of Erkenwald in a letter patent of Henry VII, dated 1486–87, along with a coat of arms. See also Peterson, n. 129.

NOTES TO CHAPTER FIVE

1. Barlow, *English Church 1066–1154*, 57–65, provides a crisp summary of the changes in personnel. For the impact of the Normans on the monasteries, and the initial friction between natives and newcomers, see David Knowles, *The Monastic Order in England* (Cambridge, 1941), 103–6, 114–17.

2. Barlow, 191, and nn. 62 & 63.

3. William of Malmesbury complains about the lack of written evidence and, in many cases, oral tradition: *Gesta pontificum*, 144. Similar complaints are voiced by other contemporary writers. While the Viking wars of the 9th and 10th centuries were doubtless responsible for actual loss of some early Anglo-Saxon works of hagiography (e.g. the *libellus* of St. Ethelburga's miracles, used by Bede in *Hist. eccles.* 4.7–10, ed. Colgrave & Mynors, 356–64), other factors were equally to blame for the shortage of proper *vitae* by the end of the 11th century. For example, the general lack of competent latinity in late Anglo-Saxon England: see Barlow, *The English Church 1000–1066*, 2nd ed. (London & New York, 1979), 280. The surviving Latin hagiography from the Anglo-Saxon period is surveyed by Gransden, *English Historical Writing*, 67–92; see also Wolpers, *Die englische Heiligenlegende*, 70–94. For a list of the vernacular prose lives besides Aelfric's, see Stanley Greenfield & Fred Robinson, *A Bibliography of Publications on Old English Literature to the end of 1972* (Toronto, 1980), 375–78. Of the dozen or so listed, only four are native saints (Chad, Guthlac, Mildred, Neot). Aelfric provided homilies or lives for only six native saints (Alban, Cuthbert, Edmund, Etheldreda, Oswald, and Swithun). See Ben-

jamin Thorpe, ed., *The Homilies of the Anglo-Saxon Church. The First Part, Containing the Sermones Catholici, or Homilies of Aelfric,* 2 vols. (London, 1843–46), 1:132–55, and W. W. Skeat, ed., *Aelfric's Lives of the Saints,* EETS 76, 82, 94, 114 (1881–1900); rpt., 2 vols. (Oxford, 1966), I:414–23, 432–69; II:124–43, 314–33. See also Malcom Godden, "Aelfric and the Vernacular Prose Tradition," in Paul Szarmach & Bernard Huppé, eds., *The Old English Homily and its Background* (Albany 1978), 108. In Old English Verse, only the two Guthlac poems have survived, ed. Jane Roberts, *The Guthlac Poems of the Exeter Book* (Oxford, 1979). R. M. Wilson, *The Lost Literature of Medieval England,* 2nd ed. (London, 1970), 85–91, posits the former existence of several vernacular lives, some in prose, some verse: Dunstan, Etheldreda, King Oswald, and Sexburga of Ely. He believes, however, that "little of importance in Old English religious or didactic prose has been lost." See also Wolpers, 151–56. D. W. Rollason is at work on a study of Anglo-Saxon saints' cults, and will no doubt throw more light on this topic.

4. Knowles, *Monastic Order,* 118–19; also Denis Bethel, "The Miracles of St. Ithamar," 422–23.

5. Barlow, *English Church 1066–1154,* 191, n. 63. See also Southern, *St. Anselm and his Biographer,* 248 ff., 291–92.

6. Barlow, *English Church 1066–1154,* 190. A Norman bishop, for example, presided when Abbot Gilbert Crispin translated Edward the Confessor's relics at Westminster, 1102. See J. A. Robinson, *Gilbert Crispin, Abbot of Westminster* (Cambridge, 1911), 24–25. Bishop Maurice of London (1087–1107) refurbished the shrine of St. Osyth and enhanced her cult around this time (see above, chap. 3, n. 10). The remains of Etheldreda and other Ely saints were translated in 1106 into a new abbey church completed by the Norman Abbot Richard, while Bishop Herbert of Norwich presided and preached a sermon on the virtues of St. Etheldreda. Blake, ed., *Liber Eliensis,* 228–30.

7. Southern, "The Place of England," 208.

8. On Goscelin see Barlow, *The Life of King Edward,* Appendix C, 91–111; Colker, "Texts of Jocelyn," 383–86; and Thomas J. Hamilton, "Goscelin of Canterbury: A Critical Study of his Life, Works, and Accomplishments. Parts One and Two" (Ph.D. diss., Univ. of Virginia, 1973). Gransden, 107–111, gives a selective survey of Goscelin's oeuvre. On Folcard, see Gransden, 107. On Osbern see, e.g., Southern, *St. Anselm and his Biographer,* 248–52, and Gransden, 127–29; on Eadmer see Gransden, 129–35, and Southern, *St. Anselm,* espec. 229–374. William of Malmesbury's lives of Dunstan and Wulfstan are discussed by D. Farmer in T. A. Dorey, ed., *Latin Biography* (London, 1967), 157–76; his life of Aldhelm is book 5 of the *Gesta pontificum,* 330–43; he also wrote an early and influential collection of miracles of the Virgin, on which see Southern, "The English Origins of the Miracles of the Virgin," *Medieval and Renaissance Studies,* 4 (1958): 176–216, and Peter Carter, "The Historical Content of William of Malmesbury's Miracles of the Virgin Mary," in R. H. C. Davis & J. M. Wallace-Hadrill, eds., *The Writing of History in the Middle Ages. Essays presented to Richard William Southern* (Oxford, 1981), 127–65. The miracles are printed in J. M. Canal, "El Libro De laudibus et miraculis sanctae Mariae de Guillermo de Malmesbury, O.S.B. (d. c. 1143)," *Claretianum* 8 (1968): 71–242. Dominic of Evesham's several saints' lives are briefly discussed by Gransden, 112–14, and his miracles of the Virgin are dealt with by Southern, "The English Origins." On the hagiography of Osbert of Clare, see Williamson, ed., *The Letters of Osbert,* 22–32.

9. Among authors of single works are Faricius, Abbot of Abingdon 1100–17, who wrote a life of St. Aldhelm ca. 1080, while a monk at Malmesbury: ASS Mai., 6:83–93; and Robert of Shrewsbury, whose life of St. Winifred, ASS Nov., 1:708–31, was composed ca. 1140. Some examples of anonymous vitae, besides VSE, are the *Vita S. Swithuni,* formerly attributed to Goscelin of Canterbury, printed by E. P. Sauvage in *AB* 7 (1888): 374–80 (a new edition by Michael Lapidge is forthcoming); the *Vita S. Birini* (BHL 1361),

unprinted; and the Ely lives of Ermenilda (BHL 2611), Sexburga (BHL 7693–94), and Wihtburga, with the latter's miracles (BHL 8979–80), all unprinted (cf. Blake, ed., *Liber Eliensis*, xxxiv, nn. 1 & 2, xxxvi–vii, n. 3). Other examples are the *passio* of St. Kenelm composed at Winchcombe ca. 1170, and based on a pre-Conquest source, ed. Rurik von Antropoff, *Die Entwicklung der Kenelm-Legende* (diss. Rheinischen Friedrichs-Wilhelms-Universität, Bonn, 1965), Appendix, and two lives of St. Neot, recently discussed by Richards, "The Medieval Hagiography of St. Neot."

10. Bethel, "Miracles of St. Ithamar," 424.

11. Southern, "The Place of England," 208. For a recent response to Southern and Bethel, see the valuable essay by James Campbell, "Some Twelfth-Century Views of the Anglo-Saxon Past," *Peritia*, 3 (1984), 131–50, which came to hand after the present study was complete.

12. Southern, ed., *The Life of St. Anselm*; Talbot, ed., *The Life of Christina of Markyate*.

13. In another paper, "Aspects of the European Tradition of Historical Writing. 4. The Sense of the Past," *Trans. Royal Hist. Soc.*, 5th Ser., 23 (1973): 249–50, Southern expresses the view that the most important historical work of the 12th century was the collection, classification, and copying of documents, for legal purposes involving property, exemptions, privileges, etc.

14. Cf. the typical exegetical commentaries on this section of Joshua by Isidore of Seville and Hrabanus Maurus, PL 83:371–72 and PL 108:1013. For a detailed introduction to the typological, as opposed to historical, mode of thought, see Jean Daniélou, *Bible et liturgie* (Paris 1951), Eng. trans., *The Bible and the Liturgy* (Notre Dame, Ind., 1956; rpt., 1966), espec. 99–113 on the river Jordan and baptism. On the general importance of typology in hagiography, see James W. Earl, "Typology and the Iconography of Style in Early Medieval Hagiography," *Studies in the Literary Imagination*, 8,i (1975): 15–46.

15. M. T. Clanchy, *From Memory to Written Record. England 1066–1307* (Cambridge, Mass., 1979), 249.

16. See Clanchy, 253, for remarks on Osbert's forging of documents and writing of saints' lives; also above, chap. 4, n. 4.

17. Stubbs, *Memorials of St. Dunstan*, 141–42.

18. ASS Mai., 6:375, translation mine.

19. *Hist. eccles.* 1.23–2.3, ed. Colgrave & Mynors, 68–145. The account of Augustine's life is much shorter than it seems, because Bede transcribes verbatim a good deal of the correspondence between Augustine and Pope Gregory.

20. ASS Mai., 6:377–78.

21. Ibid., 380–81.

22. See VSE, n. 17.

23. William Bright, *Chapters in Early English Church History*, 3rd ed. (Oxford, 1897), 294.

24. On the growing distance between clergy and laity in the performance of the sacraments, see Francis Oakley, *The Western Church in the Later Middle Ages* (Ithaca, N. Y., 1979), 82–85. The green sun-filled meadow where the canons and priests pause with the saint's funeral bier to let the people go on ahead is recognizably a "locus amoenus," the symbolic landscape that is a topos throughout medieval literature: E. R. Curtius, *Europäische Literatur und lateinisches Mittelalter* (Bern, 1948), English trans. by Willard Trask, *European Literature and the Latin Middle Ages* (New York, 1963; rpt. Princeton, 1973), 195–200, and Derek Pearsall & Elizabeth Salter, *Landscapes and Seasons of the Medieval World* (London, 1970), 46 ff., 56–75. The paradisal "pleasance" in *VSE* corresponds to the "terra coelestis repromissionis" awaiting those whose souls are saved through the priestly rite of baptism. See the commentaries cited above, n. 14.

25. Brooke, "The Earliest Times to 1485," in Matthews & Atkins, *History of St. Paul's Cathedral*, 12–15.

26. See de Gaiffier, "Les revendications de biens."

27. For the details see the account by Ralph Diceto, cited above, chap. 3, n. 51. On de Mandeville's seizure and surrender of the castle at Bishop Stortford, see Gibbs, *Early Charters*, 277.

28. Mir. Pr., n. 8.

29. A convenient sketch of the development of the theology of history is that of Robert Hanning, *The Vision of History in Early Britain* (New York, 1966), 1–43. For a more recent survey of relevant scholarship, see Roger Ray, "Medieval Historiography through the Twelfth Century: Problems and Progress of Research," *Viator*, 5 (1974): 33–59, espec. 38 ff.

30. For the hagiographical analogues, see Mir. I, n. 2.

31. See Mir. I, n. 5.

32. Southern, *Life of St. Anselm*, 37–39.

33. There is one example of apostrophe, *VSE* 49–51, and one piece of narrative exegesis, *VSE* 83–84.

34. Mir. VII 96–97: "Mihi qui aderam, scribendi miraculum onus iniungitur." Cf. also Mir. V 27, 61, 64; VII 4; X 9; XI 26–28; XIII 2; XIV passim.

35. Sigal, "Un aspect du culte des saints: le châtiment divin aux XIe et XIIe siècles d'après la litterature hagiographique du Midi de la France," *Cahiers de Fanjeaux* 11 (1976): 53–54.

36. See above, chap. 3, pt. 3.

37. See above, Foreword, nn. 1 & 4.

NOTES TO
VITA SANCTI ERKENWALDI

1. Cf. 2 Reg. 6.5. The phrase in the text is a circumlocution for "psalter."

2. Ps. 18.5. Cf. Rom. 10.18.

3. Cf. Ecclus. 50.7. The Epistle for the Mass on Erkenwald's feast day, along with the Little Chapter of the Office, was taken from the same chapter of Ecclesiasticus. See Tolhurst, *Ordinale*, 2:223.

4. Cf. Bede's *Hist. eccles.* 2.3, ed. Colgrave & Mynors, 142: "Augustinus . . . ordinauit . . . Mellitum . . . ad predicandum prouinciae Orientalium Saxonum qui Tamense fluuio dirimuntur a Cantia . . . quorum metropolis Lundonia ciuitas est super ripam praefati fluminis posita. . . ."

5. Cf. Bede: "Vbi uero et haec prouincia uerbum ueritatis praedicante Mellito accepit, fecit rex Aedilberct in ciuitate Lundonia ecclesiam sancti Pauli apostoli, in qua locum sedis episcopalis et ipse et successores eius haberent." (Ibid.)

6. Whitelock denies that Erkenwald could have been Mellitus's pupil, on the grounds of chronology (*Some Anglo Saxon Bishops of London*, 6, n. 6). But if Erkenwald were in his eighties when he died (693), he could as a boy have known Mellitus during the latter's final years as Archbishop of Canterbury (619–24). As Professor Whitelock points

out herself (ibid., 5, n. 5), Erkenwald with his Frankish name-element, *Eorcen*, was probably of Kentish royal stock, so contact with the Archbishop at Canterbury, the royal Kentish city, would be not unlikely. Legend, as represented here in *VSE*, implies that he was a Londoner. John of Tynemouth promoted the fiction that Erkenwald was the son of a certain Offa, King of the East Angles. *NLA* 1:391.

7. The *hystoria anglorum* is Bede's *Historia gentis Anglorum ecclesiastica*. The words quoted here are in *Hist. eccles.* 4.6, in Bede's account of Erkenwald, ed. Colgrave & Mynors, 354: "Cuius uidelicet uiri et in episcopatu et ante episcopatum uita et conuersatio fertur fuisse sanctissima, sicut etiam nunc caelestium signa uirtutum indicio sunt."

8. Cf. Eph. 3.16.

9. Cf. *Hist. eccles.* 4.6 (Colgrave & Mynors, 354).

10. Erkenwald did not actually succeed Cedd, who had died in 664 (*Hist. eccles.* 3.23; Colgrave & Mynors, 288). Wine, former bishop of Winchester, as Bede reports (*Hist. eccles.* 3.7; Colgrave & Mynors, 234), at some point in the interim bought the see of London simoniacally from Wulfhere, king of Mercia, and held the see till 675, presumably when he died. It was then Archbishop Theodore who, says Bede, "appointed" (constituit) Erkenwald to the London bishopric. *VSE* thus suppresses the saint's unsavory predecessor so as to render Erkenwald third in a line of three saintly bishops of London. At the same time *VSE* improves on Bede by describing the process of Erkenwald's elevation more in accordance with 11th and 12th century practice. Both before and after the Norman Conquest bishops were formally elected by clergy and people of the diocese, and the king gave his consent. But in practice the king nominated, after consulting with the leading seculars and ecclesiastics of the kingdom, and the cathedral chapter usually had no choice but to confirm the king's nominee. Barlow, *The English Church 1000–1066*, 99 ff. *VSE* implies this process by putting the consent of King Sebbe first, before that of the people, while the church's role is submerged in the passive verb, *sublimatus est*, a technical term for the elevation of a bishop. Such a formulation would not have offended either Bishop Maurice (1086–1106) or Bishop Richard (1106–27), both of whom were civil servants promoted to the episcopacy by William I and Henry I, respectively, as a reward for their loyal service to the Crown.

11. Cf. Eph. 3.17: "in caritate radicati."

12. The italicized words and phrases in this paragraph are taken directly from *Hist. eccles.* 4.6, Colgrave & Mynors 354. The rest is paraphrased from the same source. *VSE* differs from Bede, however, in referring to the healing properties of the horse-litter in the past tense, avoiding Bede's *usque hodie* or any such suggestion. On the importance of this difference, especially in relation to Goscelin of Canterbury's *Vita S. Ethelburgae*, see above, chap. 2. With *VSE* 37–39, "plurimi, . . . liberabantur," cf. the hymn for the Common of a Confessor bishop in Tolhurst, ed., *The Monastic Breviary of Hyde Abbey*, vol. 5, HBS 71 (London, 1934), 425: "membra languentum modo sanitati / quolibet morbo fuerint grauati restituuntur."

13. Matt. 25.14–30, the parable of the talents, was the usual Gospel text prescribed for Erkenwald's feast day. However, the "talentum preciosum" of this passage appears to be an echo of Venantius Fortunatus's famous hymn to the Holy Cross, "Pange Lingua," which was adapted for use as anthems and responds in the liturgy of Passion week and the feasts of the Holy Cross. Line 28 of the hymn, "sola digna tu fuisti ferre pretium saeculi," was rephrased to form a portion of the anthem of the Magnificat at First Vespers of the Invention of the Holy Cross (May 3) at both Chertsey Abbey and Hyde Abbey, Winchester: "sola fuisti digna portare talentum mundi." Bodley Lat. liturg. e. 39, f. 42v, and Tolhurst, *Monastic Breviary*, vol. 3, HBS 76 (London, 1938), 248v. The phrase "talentum pretiosum" in the text of *VSE* seems to be a conflation of "talentum" and "pretium."

14. Cf. Ps. 125.6: "veniunt cum exsultatione portantes manipulos suos." The whole

psalm echoes the image patterns of VSE up to this point. C omits VSE 41–42, however, recognizing most probably that the lines arouse expectations (that Erkenwald's death is to be described next) that are not fulfilled in the immediate sequel regarding the wheel miracle (VSE 43–51). See n. 15. Notice also how the substance of VSE 41–42 is merely repeated, less poetically, at VSE 51–54. On the other hand, in the Chertsey and Stonyhurst breviary lections it is the wheel episode and the redundant lines later that are omitted, not VSE 41–42, which are followed immediately and naturally by the account of the saints's death, leading one to suspect that the composer of the extant VSE interpolated the wheel episode rather awkwardly into a pre-existing narrative, the "old vita," to which the liturgical lections are the only witness. See also n. 23 on VSE 102–3, and above, chap. 2, regarding other evidence for the existence of the earlier shorter life.

15. For the cartwheel miracle, see the analogous episode in the Vita sancti Aedi episcopi in Charles Plummer, ed., Vitae sanctorum Hiberniae, 2 vols. (Oxford, 1910; rpt., 1968), 1:36–37. Other analogues are in the Vita S. Brigidae, by Chilien, in Latin verse, ASS Feb., 1:151; and Miracula sancti Edmundi, by Hermann, in Arnold, Memorials of St. Edmund, 1:43. The latter is probably later than VSE, and a response to it.

16. A sweet aroma at the saint's death is a common hagiographical motif. Cf. Felix's Life of St. Guthlac, ed. Bertram Colgrave (Cambridge, 1956), 158–61. Also Alcuin's life of St. Willibrord, ed. Krusch & Levison, MGH SRM 7:135.

17. From here to the end of VSE is essentially one continuous episode, consisting of Erkenwald's funeral procession from Barking to London, with the strife preceding it and the miracles accompanying it. Like the cart-wheel miracle, it seems to have been incorporated in the saint's legend late in the 11th c. It is an artful synthesis of various hagiographical topoi or commonplaces, chief of which is the "contentio" or "lis de corpore sancto." This topos, as far as I can discover, was initiated by Gregory of Tours in his accounts of the strife over the bodies of Martin of Tours (see next note) and Lipicinus the hermit (Vitae patrum, MGH SRM 1:716–17). See Michel Carrias, "Étude sur la formation de deux légendes hagiographiques à l'époque mérovingienne. Deux translations de Saint Martin d'après Grégoire de Tours," Rev. d'histoire de l'église de France 57 (1972): 7, n. 160. The topos was progressively elaborated in a succession of early medieval vitae, including those of Avitus of Orléans, Leodegar (Léger) of Autun, and Martin of Vertou. A fairly complex late example is in the mid-11th c. life of St. Modwenna of Burton-on-Trent. See below, nn. 25 & 33. VSE's handling of the topos, however, is particularly elaborate and successful, synthesizing and surpassing all previous versions (cf. the more or less contemporary but relatively weak example in the life of St. Kenelm, ed. Antropoff, appendix, xii–xiii). I have in hand a separate study of this aspect of VSE and its analogues.

18. Gregory of Tours, Historia Francorum, ed. Krush, MGH SRM, 1:55: "Dicebant enim Pectavi, 'Noster est monachus, nobis abba extetit, nos requiremus commendatum.' "

19. Ibid., 56: "Virum si mus antiquitus institutus servatur, in urbe qua ordenatus est habebit Deo iubente sepulchrum."

20. Dugdale, ed. Ellis, 290, identifies the hyla as the River Lea, which flows southwards into the Thames just east of London, dividing into several channels at Stratford (see below, VSE 154, and n. 36). But hyla is the name of a stretch of the River Roding some distance east of the Lea, and close to Barking itself. It was called the Hul or Hil in Anglo-Saxon times, a name which survives in that of Ilford, i.e., the ford over the Hile. See P. H. Reaney, Place Names of Essex (London, 1935), 97. The ford that became Ilford was on the Roman road, just north of the abbey. The procession is to be imagined as having followed the Hile northwards along its east bank until they came to the road, "ubi sine dubio transire putabant."

21. Ostensibly a piece of natural description, this explanation is actually part of the traditional biblical episode which lies behind this event. Cf. Ios. 3.15: "Jordanis autem

ripas aluei sui tempore messis impleuerat," harvest time being in April, when the mountain snows melted. See also the very early *Vita S. Marcellini* (in which a river, flooded by melting snows, "tumescens resolutione niuium," has to be forded by similarly miraculous measures), ASS Apr., 2:753; and the supposedly 9th-century *Vita S. Serenici confessoris*, ASS Mai., 2:164. The latter, in which the wonder-working saint is compared to both Joshua at the Jordan and Elisha the prophet, may have suggested the pairing Joshua/Elijah to *VSE*'s author.

22. Cf. *Vita S. Serenici*: "Interea fluvium transire experiens,. . . nam neque navis aliqua prae oculis aderat, neque alia facultas fluminis transeundi uspiam apparebat."

23. Cf. Stonyhurst College MS 52, f. 468v: "eosque multis exhortationibus spiritualiter et in dei famulatum fortiter ut facient exhortans." The borrowed phrase fits more smoothly into the Stonyhurst text than into *VSE*, strengthening my conviction that *VSE* built upon an older life of Erkenwald, which survives at least partially in the Stonyhurst lections. See above, n. 14; see also Appendix to *VSE*, where the lections are printed in full.

24. Bede, in *Hist. eccles.* 2.3 (*VSE* 8–10), calls the city of London itself *metropolis*, i.e., chief city of the *prouincia* of the East Saxons. The Londoners are here referring to the people of the city and of its diocesan province, i.e., mainly Essex, and the city's church, which is *metropolitana* not because the bishopric is highest in rank but because the city is a "metropolis." Gregory the Great had himself intended London, not Canterbury, to be the archiepiscopal see (*Hist. eccles.* 1.29; Colgrave & Mynors, 104–5, & n. 3). See also Whitelock, *Some Anglo-Saxon Bishops of London*, 25–26, for another use of the epithet "metropolitana" for London.

25. With the role played by the "uir religiosus" here, compare that of Eleusius, "uir insignis," in the 9th century *Vita S. Aviti Aurelianensis*, ed. Krusch, MGH SRM 3:384–85, and see also the *Vita S. Modwenna*, ASS Jul., 2:311, where the arbitrator is Bishop Columchille.

26. *Opus* here seems to mean the task of laying the saint's body to rest. One of the MSS., Lansdowne 438, reads *corpus*. But this MS usually agrees in its better readings with either Corpus or Cotton, or the Chertsey Breviary. Its unique reading here is therefore to be rejected as a late emendation.

27. Rom. 13.10. "Plenitudo ergo legis est dilectio."

28. Cf. Iac. 2.10. "Quicumque autem totam legem servaverit, offendat autem in uno, factus est omnium reus."

29. Cf. Ier. 6.20. "Holocaustomata vestra non sunt accepta."

30. 1 Ioh. 4.16.

31. Cf. Eph. 4.2–3. ". . . supportantes invicem in charitate, soliciti servare unitatem spiritus in vinculo pacis."

32. Ps. 144.18–19.

33. Cf. *Vita S. Martini Vertavensis*, ASS Oct., 10:809–10, and J. Mabillon, *ASS Ord. S. Ben.*, 1 (Venice, 1728), 357: "siccisque praebuisse itinere plantis."

34. Ios. 3.11–17; 4.1–18.

35. 4 Reg. 2.8, 14.

36. Having crossed the Hile (now Roding: see above, n. 20) at what was later to be Ilford, the procession follows the Roman road westward to the River Lea, several arms of which cross the road at Stratford. There may have been a small bridge over the Lea by the late 11th century, to judge from Hermann's *Miracula S. Edmundi*, ed. Arnold, *Memorials of St. Edmund's Abbey*, 1:42, but soon after 1110 Henry I's wife Matilda was swept from her horse crossing the Lea at Stratford. As a result of this mishap two bridges were built, with a connecting causeway, and Barking Abbey was endowed with the income from lands and a mill, with which to maintain the bridges. James Edwin Oxley, *A History of Barking* (Barking, 1935), 9.

37. The miracle of the candles, with the accompanying storm and sunshine, is not to be found in any of the analogues to the main episode. Miracles involving candles and supernaturally rekindled flames, however, are common enough in saints' lives. Cf. the examples from Aimon's miracles of St. Benedict (early llth c.) and from the life of St. Remaclus, cited by J. Bonifacius Bagatta, *Admiranda orbis Christiana* (Venïce, 1700), 1:76–77. *VSE*'s version is different in that the extinguishing and rekindling are not consecutive, as in all the analogues I have seen, but separated by other events.

NOTES TO
MIRACULA ERKENWALDI

PROEMIUM

1. The plural noun "apices," with or without "litterarum," commonly meant "writing," or "a piece of writing," in Medieval Latin. Arcoid is here contrasting the written word, as represented in this case by his *Miracula S. Erkenwaldi* (MSE), with the oral art of the lecturer or preacher, "eruditionibus doctorum." For "eruditiones" in the sense of "speeches" or "lectures," cf. Aulus Gellius, *Noctes Atticae*, Praef., ed. P. K. Marshall (Oxford, 1968), 1:1, note on line 16.

2. Arcoid here combines phrases from several of the Psalms. Cf. Ps. 71.18, "qui facit mirabilia solus"; 67.36, "mirabilis Deus in sanctis suis"; 27.7, "ut clara voce praedicem, laudem, et narrem mirabilia tua"; 150.11, "Laudate Dominum in sanctis suis."

3. An allusion to *VSE* 34, "Post multa siquidem imminentis uite certamina," but *VSE* makes no mention of struggles with demons or sexual lust. However, Erkenwald is said to be "corpore castus," *VSE* 32.

4. "Neglexit." A recurring rhetorical topos of medieval hagiography is that of the "negligentia" of the author's predecessors, who have failed to record the life and miracles of the saint properly, if at all. Examples close to Arcoid's London milieu are Hermann's *Miracula S. Edmundi* (written ca. 1100), ed. Arnold, *Memorials of St. Edmund's Abbey*, 1:27, and the anonymous *Miracula S. Ithamari* (ca. 1160 at Rochester), ed. Bethell, "The Miracles of St. Ithamar," 428–29.

5. "pauca de pluribus." Arcoid is employing the common rhetorical topos of "brevitas," but not with the usual justification, i.e. to avoid boring one's readers (cf. Bethel, "Miracles of St. Ithamar," 428); Arcoid's brevity is forced upon him by the literary negligence of his predecessors at St. Paul's.

6. "est sacerdos magnus." Cf. the "capitulum" or Little Chapter, "Ecce sacerdos magnus," prescribed for the Common of a Confessor Bishop in the monastic and secular uses of medieval England, and also in the offices for St. Erkenwald's feast at Chertsey and Barking. See Chertsey Breviary, Bodley Lat. liturg. e.39, ff. 38v, 39r, and Tolhurst, ed., *Ordinale* 2:222; see also Whatley, "The Middle English St. *Erkenwald* and its Liturgical Context," *Mediaevalia* 8 (1982): 279–81.

7. Ps. 144.19. Cf. *VSE* 147–48.

8. The word "sacramentum" had a wider range of meanings in the Middle Ages than its modern English derivative. As defined by St. Augustine, its basic meaning was "invisibilis gratiae visibilis forma." *Quaest. in Hept.* 3, qu. 84; PL 34:712. Besides the familiar meaning of an ecclesiastical rite, such as baptism or holy communion, the word in patristic usage could also have typological force. Tertullian refers to the miracle of Elijah's floating iron axe, 4 Reg. 6.1–7, as a "sacramentum" of the role of the holy cross in the baptismal rite and the salvation of mankind. Likewise Joshua was given his name because of its "futurum sacramentum." J. de Ghellinck, "Pour l'histoire du mot Sacramentum, 1, Les Antinicéens," *Spicilegium sacrum Lovaniense, études et documents*, fasc. 3 (Louvain & Paris, 1924), 115–17. This tendency to use "sacramentum" in a figural, symbolic, or allegorical sense was reinforced by early medieval exegetical traditions and was particularly noticeable by the 11th and 12th century, by which time it is virtually synonymous with "miraculum" and "mysterium." Peter the Venerable calls the miracle of the Transfiguration (Luc. 9.28–36) "magnum sacramentum" and "novum miraculum," and Peter Damian uses "sacramentum" to refer to nonbiblical miracles, replete with spiritual meaning. Miracles are "sacraments," in other words, because they are revelations of mysteries. Denise Bouthillier & Jean-Pierre Torrell, " 'Miraculum.' Une catégorie fondamentale chez Pierre le Vénérable," *Revue Thomiste* 80 (1980): 368–69; Ward, *Miracles and the Medieval Mind*, 26, and n. 24. Moreover, "sacramentum" by this time could denote not only the "visibilis forma" but also the "invisibilis gratia" itself. Cf. Alger, *De sacramentis*: "ut sit . . . sacramentum signans et signatum," PL 180.751C. This is how Arcoid seems to use the word here. The miracles of Erkenwald are earthly events, "gesta," wonderful in themselves and for their visible effects, but they "breathe the heavenly sacraments" of power and wisdom that lead men to salvation. Superficially acts of healing or other triumphs over physical nature, the miracles are in essence vehicles for imparting "divine grace to the deaf ears of men." They are sacramental events. Hence his exhortation to his fellow canons (Mir. Pr. 43–49) to receive and interpret the stories in a spiritual sense, as they would the "margaritae" of holy scripture, as an "exemplum spirituale salutis nostre."

9. Cf. Act. 2.11.

10. Matt. 7.6. In alluding to this verse, Arcoid is apparently advising his "fratres" to interpret the miracle stories spiritually, for their moral and allegorical significance, as "sacramenta" (see above n. 8), and not to scorn them as factually incredible or ludicrous. On the exegetical associations of the verse and their relevance to this context, see above, ch. 3, n. 137.

11. Rom. 15.4.

MIRACULUM I

1. "Doctor gentium" was a common medieval epithet for St. Paul. Cf. 1 Tim. 2.7.

2. On the early history of St. Paul's school, see A. F. Leach, "St. Paul's School before Colet," *Archaeologia* 62 (1910): 191–238; also Gibbs, xxxi–xxxii, 215–17. Although there were several priests called Elwin (or variants of the same) in Anglo-Norman London, there is no record of a schoolmaster of that name. See Eilert Ekwall, *Early London Personal Names* (Lund 1947), 11–12; see also the list of St. Paul's "magistri scholarum" from ca. 1090, in Le Neve/Greenaway, 25. If not wholly fictional, the story must represent an 11th-century tradition. English analogues include Osbern's *Miracula S. Dunstani* 15, ed. Stubbs, *Memorials*, 140–42; Eadmer's revision of the same episode, ibid., 227–28; Eadmer's *Vita S. Anselmi* 1.22, ed. Southern, *Life of St. Anselm*, 37–39; the life of St. Ermenilda (BHL 2611), in, e.g., Trinity College Cambridge, MS O.2.1, ff. 230r–230v. Celtic analogues include the story of SS. Finan and Columba and the angel in Plummer, ed.,

Vitae sanctorum Hiberniae, 2:97. See also C. Grant Loomis, *White Magic* (Cambridge, Mass., 1948), 24–25, for other examples of what Loomis calls the "wonder-child" topos. But see also the second preface to the Old Irish martyrology of St. Oengus, ed. Whitley Stokes, *Felire Oengusso Celi De. The Martyrology of Oengus the Culdee*, HBS 29 (London, 1905), 12–13, and Tom Peete Cross & Harris Clark Slover, *Ancient Irish Tales* (New York, 1936), no. V 223.4.1. For a brief discussion of Mir. I, see above, ch. 5.

3. It would certainly be known to Arcoid that the St. Paul's "magister scholarum" who retired or died in 1127, Master Hugh, realized the ambition that Arcoid here attributes to Elwin, since he was succeeded in his office by his pupil and "nutritus" (foster son), Henry. Le Neve/Greenaway, 25.

4. "Scolasticus" was a common designation at this time for the master of a cathedral school. The earliest known head of St. Paul's school, Durandus, is designated "scholasticus" in the chapter's entry in St. Bruno's mortuary role of 1102. Le Neve/Greenaway, 25.

5. Arcoid's description of Elwin's teaching method anticipates John of Salisbury's famous account of the pedagogy of Bernard of Chartres (d. 1112). C. J. Webb, ed., *Ioannis Sarisberiensis metalogicon* (Oxford, 1929), 55–56. Like Elwin, Bernard would "expound" a passage of Latin himself for his pupils, then have them memorize it, for recitation the following day. On occasion he would administer a flogging, a time-honored pedagogical aid. If Arcoid is to be trusted as to the general truth of this anecdote, it is the earliest English account of school life outside the monasteries.

6. The "magister scholarum" of St. Paul's was a busy man. In addition to actual teaching duties, he was librarian, secretary of the chapter, keeper of its seal, and supervised the cathedral lectors and table of lessons. At some point in the twelfth century, he began to leave all his teaching to assistant masters and concentrated wholly on his "alia negotia." Leach, "St. Paul's School," 196; also Nicholas Orme, *English Schools in the Middle Ages* (Oxford, 1973), 80–81, 173–74. As early as Arcoid's time, the schoolmaster was also supervisor and regulator of the other schools in London, with the exception of St. Martin's-le-Grand and St. Mary-le-Bow. Orme, 169; Gibbs, 217.

7. For a similar use of "lubricum" as a neuter singular noun, rather than the more usual adjectival or neut. plu. noun usages, cf. William of Malmesbury, *Gesta pontificum*, 358: "lubricum carnis." For a sympathetic approach to the sins of youth in a similar context, see Eadmer's *Vita S. Anselmi* 1.11, ed. Southern, *The Life of St. Anselm*, 21: "consideres puerum, aetate et scientia tenerum, nec bonum nec malum discernere valentem."

8. "uel saltem . . . differet." Cf. the Medieval Latin proverb: "Vindictam differ, donec pertranseat ira: Nec meminisse velis odii post verbera." Hans Walther, *Carmina Medii Aevi Posterioris Latina*, 2. *Proverbia Sententiaeque Latinitatis Medii Aevi*, 6 vols. (Göttingen, 1963–69), 5:738, no. 33453. Arcoid seems to be also aware of the ultimate source of the proverb, Cicero's *Tusculan Disputations* 4.36.78, ed. J. E. King (London & New York, 1927), 416: "si quam habent ulciscendi vim, differant in tempus aliud, dum defervescat ira."

9. The plural form "scolas" was commonly used to refer to a single school. Orme, 59, n. 1.

10. The "palla" or coffin drape is likewise a prominent item in the miracle of the great fire. See Mir. IV 19–20, 104, 108–13, 123–25.

11. The word "censura" with its strong judicial overtones is appropriate here, since the cathedral schoolmaster had jurisdiction at law over the scholars in his charge. Orme, 120. Cf. Leach, ed. *Educational Charters* (Cambridge, 1911), 232–33, 240–43, 252–61.

12. Sap. 10.21.

13. "a nullo magistrorum." According to Orme, 121, schools with more than one master were rare in medieval England, and even in the largest urban schools the staff would not exceed three, i.e. master, usher, and possibly parish clerk or another usher. He cites

the 1518 statutes of Colet's St. Paul's, where there was a master and usher for grammar, with a chaplain for catechism and articles of faith. Yet here Arcoid quite plainly implies more than one "magister."

14. "ad cor reuersus." Cf. Is. 46.8: "redite praevaricatores ad cor." See also Mir. IV 99–100.

15. This admission that he was an old man when composing *MSE*, in 1140–41, supports the evidence of the charters that Arcoid was dead probably by 1142 and certainly by 1145. Le Neve/Greenaway, 27.

16. "ipsisque . . . studio." Cf. Ecclus. 6.27–28.

17. An echo of Rom. 2.23, the immediate context of which it seems Arcoid's intention to recall at this point. Paul is speaking of the type of person who glories in the law ' and sets himself up as "eruditorem insipientium" and "magistrum infantium, habentem formam legis." Such a one dishonors God and breaks the law, "per praevaricationem legis Deum inhonoras."

18. "delicta . . . cumulamus." Cf. 2 Par. 28.13.

MIRACULUM II

1. This is the first of three episodes in which people are punished for "unrihtweorc," secular work on feast days when such "servile opus" has been prohibited. See also Mir. XII and XVII. The general study by Edith C. Rogers, *Discussion of Holidays in the later Middle Ages* (New York, 1940), largely ignores hagiographical data. Mir. II, XII, and XVII are in turn part of a larger group, II, VI, X, XII, XVII, in each of which the miracle is one of punishment rather than healing. Mir. I also belongs in this group, at least from the point of view of the schoolmaster. On the punitive type of miracle, see P.-A. Sigal, "Un aspect du culte des saints: le châtiment divin aux XIe et XIIe siècles d'après la litterature hagiographique du Midi de la France," *Cahiers de Fanjeaux* 11 (1976): 35–59. Like Mir. I, Mir. II combines two hagiographical topoi: first, dishonoring the saint's feast day by working, and second, desecrating the shrine by attempting to work near it and by verbally abusing the saint and his church. An early example of the former is Gregory of Tours, *Gloria confessorum* 97, ed. Krusch, MGH SRM 1:810–11. Cf. also the miracle of St. John of Beverley, in J. Raine, ed., *Historians of the Church of York*, RS 71, 3 vols. (London, 1879–94), 1:332–34. Arcoid's Mir. XII about Vitalis the skinner, and XVII about Teodwin the painter, are more typical of the basic topos than Mir. II. For other examples, see below, n. 12. A good example of the second topos, desecration, is Gregory of Tours, *Gloria martyrum* 60, MGH SRM 1:529–30, the story of Britto and the priest of St. Nazaire, in which, as here, there is a dialogue between profaner and priest, but the act of desecration is more physical than verbal. (See Whatley, "Opus dei, opus mundi: patterns of conflict in a twelfth century miracle collection," in published proceedings of *De cella in seculum*, 1986 Lincoln conference in honor of St. Hugh of Avalon; forthcoming, Cambridge, Boydell & Brewer, 1988.)

2. "prerogatiuam." Brett, *The English Church under Henry I*, 148–50, discusses illegal work on feast days in connection with a charter of Henry I granting Bishop Maurice jurisdiction in such cases. Gibbs, 20–21, no. 23. Here in Mir. II the dead saint acts as though he were the living bishop exercising his pontifical prerogative. Cf. also Mir. XII 17–19, to which reference is made by Brett, 150 and n. 1.

3. The phrase "denuntiatum est" and the general tenor of ll. 7–12 imply an official diocesan edict by bishop or dean. No such edicts or statutes survive from Arcoid's era or earlier, but for a 13th-century synodal statute concerning observance of feast days in London, see C. R. Cheney, "Rules for the Observance of Feast-Days in Medieval England," *Bulletin of the Institute for Historical Research* 34 (1961): 127–28, 138–39. Accord-

ing to these statutes, Erkenwald's feast was one of only two April feasts on which all work was forbidden. The other was that of St. Mark. Cheney, 138.

4. "seruili operi." The common, official term for work done by layfolk, especially manual work, and forbidden on Sundays and feast days.

5. "diuitias . . . bonam famam. . . ." Cf. Prov. 22.1: "Melius est nomen bonum, quam multae diuitiae."

6. "dei uicarius," i.e. the Pope. By invoking papal authority, the cleric implies that Erkenwald is a canonized saint, which of course he was not. On the shift from local to papal control of saints' cults during the 12th century, see above, chap. 3, n. 92.

7. Luc. 10.16.

8. "ministros dei sacerdotes." Cf. Ioel 2.17. Arcoid makes considerable use of Ioel 2 in Mir. IV 23 ff.

9. The canon implies that Erkenwald performed more than one miracle while still alive, whereas VSE records only the one miracle, of the cart-wheel, and even this happened apparently without the saint's conscious involvement. However, the canon does use the impersonal construction, "mirabilia . . . ipsius uitam commitata sunt." In the phrase "mox et post modum" he is referring presumably to the miracles of the river and the candles, which happened soon after the saint's death, and also the miscellaneous miracles of healing which later took place at the tomb in London and in connection with the wonder-working cart or litter. Cf. VSE 34-40, 43-49, 148-55, 161-64, 168-70.

10. On Arcoid's defensiveness with regard to the validity of Erkenwald's sanctity, see above, ch.3, part 3.

11. "canonicus" here is probably a double entendre: as a noun designating the ecclesiastical rank and station of the cleric; as an adjective denoting the "canonical" propriety of his warning to the "prophanum."

12. The layman's diatribe against the life of the beneficed clergy is interesting in that it avoids the usual topics of anti–clerical satire: viz., venality and greed; sexual immorality, ignorance and illiteracy, hypocrisy, worldliness. It is an attack on the basic idea of a privileged class of people who do no "useful" work, but whose sole occupation is, as the layman puts it, "to keep holidays," feriari. His argument, in other words, is that the "opus dei," the work of prayer and liturgy and performing the sacraments, is not work at all, but a mere game. The layman's complaint, that Erkenwald will not feed him if he stops work to celebrate the feast, is common enough in this type of miracle episode. Cf. two episodes from the miracles of St. Benedict composed by Ralph Tortaire, monk of Fleury, in the early 12th century (BHL 1129), in both of which the feastbreaker insists that he must work in order to eat. E. de Certain, ed., Les Miracles de Saint Benoît (Paris, 1858), 330, 331. The layman's emphasis on the usefulness and necessity of his kind of work, and his suggestion that the clergy envy such things, is echoed in the late twelfth-century miracles of St. Otto of Bamberg, by a disgruntled farmer on being chastized by a priest for working in the fields on the second day of the Feast of the Assumption: "quae est haec doctrina, quae hominibus a rebus necessariis et bonis jubet cessare . . . vos invidere utilitatibus nostris?" ASS Jul., 1:369, quoted by Bagatta, Admiranda orbis Christiana, 2:330.

13. "in patrocinium . . . producitis," literally, "you produce as witness for your defense." The legal language recalls, mockingly at this point, the priest's own legal language in lines 62-63.

14. Arcoid's "seculis," meaning "for generations," is unspecific, but it certainly implies that the story is to be thought of as taking place before the strictly historical period (1087-1140) to which Arcoid gives more specific attention in Mir. IV-XV.

MIRACULUM III

1. Arcoid emphasizes that this miracle takes place, like the previous one, on Erkenwald's feast day. The figure of the devout and penitent prisoner, struggling in his chains to the church to observe Erkenwald's feast, is an obvious foil for the irreverent, obdurate artisan of Mir. II.

2. On Erkenwald's devotion to his pastoral duty to preach the Gospel, see VSE 35–36.

3. The ahistorical character of this miracle, which it shares with Mir. I & II, is underlined by Arcoid's inability to name the bishop of London at the time in question. There is also a touch of fantasy in the idea that the bishop could forbid all further prosecution of the escaped convict (unless he had been the bishop's prisoner in the first place!). It is true that the bishop could protect a fugitive within the church precincts for a limited period of time, usually 40 days. But after that the accused must either surrender to the civil arm or go into exile abroad and never return (abjuratio regni). John Charles Cox, *Sanctuaries and sanctuary seekers of medieval England* (London, 1911), especially 155–56 re. the bishop's jurisdiction in the early twelfth century. See also Cox's article in *The Archaeological Journal* 68 (1911): 273–99, especially 280–81, and 284 for the remark that many sanctuary-seekers were escaped convicts, in part because escape from most jails was relatively easy. I have not encountered any study of the sanctuary laws, and related historical records, that considers the relevance or influence of this common miracle type. Early analogues to Mir. III include Gregory of Tours, *De virtutibus S. Martini* 1.23, 2.35, MGH SRM 1:600, 622. More contemporary examples include Osbern's *Miracula S. Dunstani* 22, ed. Stubbs, *Memorials*, 153–54, and two episodes from the miracles of St. John of Beverley, ed. Raine, 1:276–78, 302–7. The ultimate inspiration for this miracle topos may be the various miraculous escapes of the apostles, as in Act. 12.6–10, 16.25–27.

4. "flagellis." Arcoid's thoughts on divine providence are in accord with those of Gregory the Great, in whose works the word "flagellum," as an image of God's acts of correction, purgation, and trial, occurs hundreds of times. Pierre Boglioni, "Miracle et nature chez Grégoire le Grand," *Cahiers d'études médiévales* 1 (1974): 51–62, especially 56–58.

5. "Vtilis . . . utilis." For similar thoughts on the utility of miracles, see Peter the Venerable's prefaces to his two books of miracles. PL 189:851, 907–9.

MIRACULUM IV

(See below, nn. 37, 41–45, 47, for narrative analogues.)

1. Maurice, former clerk and chancellor of William the Conqueror, was bishop of London from 1086–1107. He had been archdeacon of Le Mans possibly before and certainly during his royal service. On his character and career, see Mir. V 1–5, and above, ch.3, part one.

2. Cf. 2 Cor. 5.7; 2 Tim. 3.5.

3. "honore doctoris gentium." The "honor" of St. Paul in London was the land in London legally held by the bishop and chapter as a feudal fief. On St. Paul as "doctor gentium," see Mir. I, n. 1.

4. Stone roofs were uncommon in pre-Norman churches. As Arcoid informs us later, IV 53–56, the Anglo-Saxon St. Paul's did not have stone vaulting, and it is unlikely therefore that it could support a heavy roof. The framework of the ceiling and roof was of timber. Perhaps Arcoid here means some form of slate or tile.

5. What was believed to be Sebba's tomb was still in St. Paul's in the 17th century. Dugdale, ed. Ellis, 64. For an account of him see Bede, *Hist. eccles.*, 4.11, ed. Colgrave

& Mynors, 364–68. Cf. also below, ll. 70–71, and Mir. XIV 43–45. The identities of the "aliorum sanctorum" are uncertain. One is probably Cedd (Mir. IV 69) who apparently had no cult; the others are presumably the former bishops of London from between Erkenwald's day and the time of the fire, who were buried in the minister. See below, ll. 72–74, and n. 24.

6. Tob. 13.21.

7. The details given here and later, ll. 107–8, suggest that Erkenwald's pre-Conquest shrine was very old. Not only does Arcoid specify that the cloth covering the top of the shrine was itself "ueteri," but the shrine itself conforms to the type commonly described in Merovingian and Carolingian sources: namely a stone tomb of sarcophagus type containing a lead coffin (cf. Mir. XIV 29) and sitting on the floor of the church a short distance behind the main altar, at right angles to it. On top of the stone tomb, and sometimes of later date, was a miniature building or "domunculus" of wood, with a gabled roof, towering above the altar in front of it and drawing all eyes towards it. Frequently such "structurae" were elaborately carved, decorated with precious metals and gems, or covered with rich fabric. See Braun, *Der Christliche Altar*, 546–55, the standard modern account. See above, chap. 4, n. 15, for works on British shrines. It is interesting that Arcoid reveals that the *pallium*, in addition to being old, was also made of interwoven silk and linen threads (108), with which cf. the early 9th-century *Historia translationis SS. Marcellini et Petri*, by Einhard (d. 840): "Et sicut in Francia mos est, supposito ligneo culmine linteis et sericis palliis ornandi gratia conteximus." Braun, 547, n. 4.

8. This defensive coda reflects a contemporary controversy. For arguments *in favor of* burying the saints' bodies below ground, see Guibert de Nogent's *De pignoribus* 1.4, PL 157:626–30. For further discussion, see above, ch. 3, part three. John of Tynemouth distorts this passage by insisting that Erkenwald's coffin was buried below ground and for this disrespect God destroyed London by fire. NLA 1:395.

9. St. John's day is June 24. At the end of the fire episode, IV 134–35, Arcoid gives the date of the fire as June 7. Since there was no major feast between June 7 and St. John's day, Arcoid's' "paulo ante natiuitatem beati iohannis" is appropriate. For the year, 1087, and for references to the fire in other sources, see below, n. 43.

10. In other words, the fire began at Ludgate, the old western entrance to the city, only a few hundred yards from St. Paul's, and burned everything in its path as far as Aldgate, the east gate.

11. "tonantis." A classical epithet for Jupiter, adopted by Christian writers such as Augustine and Prudentius with reference to God.

12. Adapted almost verbatim from Ioel 2.3–6.

13. "Unusquisque . . . sarcinulis." An interesting adaptation of Ioel 2.8.

14. Cf. Ioel 2.10.

15. Cf. 1 Tim. 1.20.

16. Arcoid's description of the timber superstructure of the building suggests a basilican form of church. The vaulting in stone or brick that Arcoid refers to here was not common in England until after the early twelfth century. On the absence of groined vaults in Anglo-Saxon and late eleventh-century Anglo-Norman churches, except over side aisles, see A. W. Clapham, *English Romanesque Architecture After the Conquest* (Oxford, 1934), 55–59. Clapham also says, 4–8, that early groined vaulting was developed specifically as a fire preventive measure.

17. Nahum 2.7, 10, which confirms the C MS reading, "diruitur," as against that of Leland's transcript (J), "diricitur," but also endorses J's inclusion of "et scissa et dilacerata," omitted by C. See textual notes.

18. "Stat erkenwaldus in medio" is probably an echo of Dan. 3. 24–25: "Et ambulant in medio flammae . . . stans autem Azarias orauit. . . ." Arcoid later alludes directly to

the story of the three youths in the fiery furnace, ll. 131–32.

19. Ioel 2.21.

20. This implies that Erkenwald resuscitated the dead during his own lifetime, but there is nothing in VSE or any other early source to suggest that he did so. It was a common enough saintly feat, however, and Arcoid may be simply invoking the hagiographer's license to attribute to his patron the virtues of other saints. It is interesting that in the Middle English St. Erkenwald, composed ca. 1400, Erkenwald does raise a corpse, temporarily, to life. See the edition of Clifford Peterson (Philadelphia, 1977), ll. 177 ff. This passage in the Miracula may have suggested to the poet the possibility, or at least the suitability, of reshaping the Gregory/Trajan legend around St. Erkenwald.

21. Arcoid is following VSE 12–13 in regarding Mellitus as Erkenwald's teacher. See also Goscelin's Vita Ethelburgae 1, ed. Colker, "Texts of Jocelyn," 400. After being driven out from London when the citizens relapsed into paganism, Mellitus became archbishop of Canterbury, 619–24, and was entombed there. Bede, Hist. eccles. 2.7, ed. Colgrave & Mynors, 158–59. Goscelin's life of Mellitus, which includes several miracles not in Bede, is unprinted (BHL 5896). By the early 13th century St. Paul's was in possession of some of Mellitus's relics, as listed in the inventory of 1245, and a reliquary containing them shared the main altar with that of Erkenwald. W. Sparrow Simpson, "Two Inventories of the Cathedral Church of St. Paul, London," Archaeologia, 50, pt.ii (1887), 441, 470.

22. Arcoid again follows VSE in giving the impression that Erkenwald was preceded by Cedd, rather than the simoniac Wine. See VSE 27 ff. and n. 10.

23. Bede informs us that Sebba was joint king of the East Saxons when Erkenwald became bishop of London, and that he later adopted the monastic life under the influence of Erkenwald's successor, Waldhere. Hist. eccles. 4.6, 11, ed. Colgrave & Mynors, 354, 364–68. Arcoid goes further than VSE or Bede here, by implying that Erkenwald had a close friendship with Sebba. Erkenwald does seem to have been associated with Ine, king of the West-Saxons. See Whitelock, Some Anglo-Saxon Bishops of London, 4 ff. In the later Middle Ages at St. Paul's, it was believed that Erkenwald actually converted Sebba to Christianity in 677. Dugdale, ed. Ellis, 64.

24. This is a polite way of saying that the bishops of London between Erkenwald and the time of the fire were buried in oblivion and worked no miracles. Cf. William of Malmesbury, Gesta pontificum, 144, who says not even their tombs were known. See Whitelock, 10–24. William of Malmesbury made an exception for Bishop Theodred, whose tomb, he tells us, was in the crypt of the new cathedral. According to a list of saints' resting-places, preserved in Hugh Candidus' mid-12th century Peterborough Chronicle but probably of an earlier vintage, there must have been a cult of Theodred before the Conquest. On Theodred and his extant will, see Whitelock, 17–21, and for further speculation on his contributions to St. Paul's, see Brooke in Matthews and Atkins, History of St. Paul's Cathedral, 12–13.

25. The allusion here is to those of Erkenwald's miracles that involved not healing of bodily ailments but the cleansing, and in some cases punishment, of the soul. Cf. Mir. I, II, III, VI, X, XII, XVII. The healing miracles are alluded to below, ll. 85–86.

26. Arcoid echoes VSE 36–40 in saying that the wooden horse-litter, which was Erkenwald's mode of transportation when he went out to preach to the people of the diocese, was a powerful healing relic after his death. But VSE says nothing of other funerary relics. It is pretty certain that even the wooden horse-litter itself had disappeared long before Arcoid's time, either in the 1087 fire or earlier. St. Paul's possessed what was believed to be a wooden goblet of the saint's, according to the 13th century inventories. Dugdale, ed. Ellis, 315. There was also a bell of Erkenwald's at Barking, which figured prominently in his feast day rites. See Tolhurst, Ordinale, 2:222.

27. "Lapis superpositus." This is obscure. The phrase suggests the saint's tombstone

described in Mir. XIV (cf. also Ioh. 11.38). But no healing miracles are linked with it, as is indicated by the context here, particularly ll. 83–85. Arcoid may be referring instead to the medieval practice of healing bodily ills with gemstones, which was one reason why the shrines of the saints were usually studded with precious stones, many of them donated by pilgrims and devotees after the completion of the shrine or reliquary proper. Erkenwald's silver "feretrum" was encrusted with about a hundred and thirty such stones by 1245, and Dean Geoffrey de Lucy (d. 1241) gave a sapphire ring to the shrine, as did a wealthy London grocer, Richard de Preston, in the late 14th century, stating explicitly that his sapphire was good for curing diseases of the eyes. Simpson, "Two Inventories," 444, 469.

28. "ligni vermiculus." Cf. Lev. 14.4, 49; also Exod. 38.18.

29. Alluding presumably to Mir. VII, VIII, XIII (caecus); XVIII (claudus); V (aridus).

30. "nouitas" is one of Arcoid's favorite words for a miracle. See below, VII, n. 1, for a possible explanation.

31. Mich. 1.2.

32. Ioel 1.2.

33. Cf. Mir. I 56.

34. Ioel 1.2–3. Since Arcoid is not speaking in propria persona here, but in the voice of the prophet Joel, it would be unwise to attach too much importance to the phrase, "filiis vestris . . . et filii vestri filiis suis" (ll. 101–02). He is speaking as if present at the time of the fire, addressing the people of London in general rather than the St. Paul's canons in particular. For an account of inherited prebends in the chapter and their gradual disappearance during the 12th century, see Brooke, "Composition," 124–26.

35. "ethneas," i.e. "aetneas," the adjective from "Aetna," the volcano in Sicily.

36. "artare," i.e. "arctare."

37. Cf. Dan. 3.4. See also below, nn. 41 & 42. Mir. IV incorporates this biblical motif, in which the bodies and garments of saints are unharmed by fire, into a related hagiographical topos, in which a saint's relics survive when all else is destroyed owing to God's anger with the sinful people. For example, Gregory of Tours tells how the Huns burned Metz to the ground, slaughtering the people and the priests, but the oratory containing the relics of St. Stephen was spared because the saint appealed to SS. Peter and Paul to save it. The apostles agreed but insisted that the town was due for destruction on account of the wickedness of its inhabitants. Hist. Franc. 2.6, 2nd ed., Krusch & Levison, MGH SRM 1, pt. 1 (Hannover, 1951), 47–48.

38. For a brief appraisal of Walkelin, Bishop of Winchester (1070–98), and for further refs., see Barlow, The English Church 1066–1154, 62. Although both Walkelin and Maurice were used to being in constant attendance on the king, there is no evidence that they were with William on his campaign in the Vexin in the summer of 1087. Neither is mentioned as present at his deathbed later that year. See David C. Douglas, William the Conqueror (London, 1964), 358–59; Douglas & George W. Greenaway, English Historical Documents 1042–1189 (London, 1968), 279–89.

39. Mir. IV is the first miracle of the "historical" period (1087–1140), the first three being of indeterminate date. Arcoid is careful to stress that he has two named and highly respectable witnesses for this miracle, "non dubitamus," and the phrase "fides certior" may be taken to mean not only a surer faith in God, which was a major purpose of any miracle, but also more certain trust in the sanctity of St. Erkenwald's relics. The handling of Mir. IV shows some parallels with the ecclesiastical rite for testing relics by fire. For discussion and further refs., see above, chap. 4, nn. 18 & 19.

40. A Latin proverb. See Walther, Proverbia Sententiaeque Latinitatis Medii Aevi, 5:431, no. 32036.

41. Cf. Gregory of Tours' account, much briefer, of a similar occurrence at the shrine

of St. Melaine of Rennes: *Liber in gloria confessorum* 54, MGH SRM 1:779–80: "Haec vero palla non solum non usta, verum etiam nec summo tenus ab igne decolorata est." See also next note.

42. An allusion to Dan. 3.19–94, of which v. 94 is especially relevant to Arcoid's account of the discovery of the miracle by the bishops and other notables.

43. Other historical sources are less specific about the date of the fire. The Anglo-Saxon Chronicle says it was before harvest time in 1087: Cecily Clark, *The Peterborough Chronicle*, 2nd ed. (Oxford, 1970), 10. The fire is also mentioned in Ordericus Vitalis, *Historia ecclesiastica* 11.31, ed. Chibnall, 6:144, but not by William of Malmesbury. An inscription in old St. Paul's, on a column next to John of Gaunt's tomb, dated the fire July 7, 1087. Dugdale, ed. Ellis, 62.

44. Vigilantius, a former protégé of Sulpicius Severus, was a priest and pamphleteer in Aquitaine in the time of St. Jerome, who knew him personally. In about 406 Vigilantius wrote a treatise criticizing, among other things, the cults of relics that were proliferating at this time. Jerome wrote a vituperative response, *Contra Vigilantium*, PL 23:353–68, which unfortunately is the sole source of our knowledge of what Vigilantius actually wrote.

45. Cf. Jerome, *Contra Vigilantium* 1; PL 23:355.

46. Arcoid has made up these supposed quotations himself, to convey the general tenor of Vigilantius' criticisms, as far as these can be inferred from Jerome's counter-arguments.

47. Vigilantius, of course, was long dead. Arcoid may be using his name to typify critics of relics' cults in his own day. Hildebert of Lavardin, an older contemporary of Arcoid's, in a letter to an unknown proponent of similar ideas, compared his correspondent to Vigilantius. PL 171:237–38, 240. See above, chap. 3, part 3, for further discussion of the contemporary context of Arcoid's outburst. Cf. also William of Malmesbury, *Gesta pontificum*, 288–89, re. the fire at the tomb of Wulfstan of Worcester. William concludes his account, which has certain features in common with Arcoid's Mir. IV, with a disquisition on incredulity.

48. Cf. Mir. Pr. 5–6.

MIRACULUM V

1. William of Malmesbury commented on the slow pace of construction, which he attributed to the immoderate size of Maurice's ambitious design. *Gesta pontificum*, 145–46. Despite a disastrous fire in 1135/36, not mentioned by Arcoid, it is pretty certain that the Romanesque choir was complete by the 1140s, but the whole building, which was the largest in England and among the largest in all Europe, was not finally complete until 1240. The most recent account is that of G. H. Cook, *Old St. Paul's Cathedral* (London, 1955), which should be used with caution, at least where St. Erkenwald and his shrine are concerned.

2. Maurice died in September, 1107. Le Neve/Greenaway, 1.

3. Richard of Belmeis, consecrated by St. Anselm in July, 1108, died in January, 1127, and was buried in St. Osyth's Priory, Essex, which he had founded. For the dates, see Le Neve/Greenaway, 1. Arcoid's estimate of his character and achievements as a builder is more favorable than that of William of Malmesbury, *Gesta pontificum*, 146, but it is echoed by other authorities. Cf. Ordericus Vitalis, *Historia ecclesiastica* 11. 31, ed. Chibnall, 6:144, and Richard's epitaph and memorial verses at St. Osyth's. The fullest account of him is still that of Eyton, *Antiquities of Shropshire*, 2:192–201, but see also the recent article by Bethel, "Richard of Belmeis." On the clerical dynasty of the Belmeis at St. Paul's, see Brooke, "Composition," 126–27, and also in Matthews & Atkins, 22–23. Arcoid's statement that Richard acquired the streets and laymen's houses round the

churchyard at his own expense is certainly feasible. As Henry I's sheriff and virtual viceroy of Shropshire, he was a great provincial landholder and his non-ecclesiastical income was presumably sufficient to allow him to devote his episcopal rents to the building fund at St. Paul's. For some external evidence as to Richard's work on the wall around the cathedral, see Gibbs' charter no. 28, pp. 23-24. For further discussion of Richard's character, see above, chap. 3, part 1.

4. Gilbert the Universal, former head of the cathedral school of Auxerre, was consecrated bishop of London in January, 1128, and died in August, 1134 (Le Neve/Greenaway, 1). The most thorough account of his career as teacher, theologian, lawyer, and finally bishop, is that of Smalley, "Gilbert the Universal."

5. On Gilbert's role in the compilation of the *Glossa Ordinaria*, see Smalley (1935) 247-62, (1936) 24-60. The scribe of the C MS has here abbreviated a passage from MSE that was evidently corrupt quite early in the history of the text, to judge from the variants in J and T. Smalley discusses this passage in a lengthy footnote, 240-41, n. 30, referring to a statement of John Leland, in his *Itinerarium*, that Gilbert built the roof of St. Paul's cathedral. Smalley points out that this mistake of Leland's was due to his reliance on a MS of Tynemouth's *Sanctilogium* or later recension thereof. Smalley does not appear to have known Leland's transcriptions from MSE, our J, which are in the *Collectanea*. On Gilbert's "frugality," which was seen as avarice by Henry of Huntingdon and Hugh the Chanter, see above, chap 3, part 1.

6. The author here identifies himself as nephew of Gilbert the Universal. Smalley, 238, identifies the nephew as Arcoidus, who witnessed St. Paul's charters ca. 1132-45. For further discussion of Arcoid's authorship, see above, chap. 3, part 1.

7. From what is said below, Mir. VII 20-21, it can be deduced that Mir. V, concerning Benedicta, occurred in late April or early May, 1138, during the time of Erkenwald's feast. This was "in the fourth year after the death" of Gilbert.

8. For a fuller description of Benedicta's affliction, see the variant reading from T in the textual notes. The C scribe has again summarized what was apparently the more prolix rendering of the original, preserved in this case in T, where we learn that the fingers of the withered hand were clenched rigidly over the thumb as if glued together, so that the fist was a solid, inflexible mass, "concreta congeries." Arcoid does not explain the cause of the paralysis in so many words, but he links it with the dryness of the hand. Desiccation of the nerves was a common hagiographical explanation for paralysis, whereas in fact the learned tradition of medieval medicine recognized that paralysis was often caused by a lesion in a nerve, due to excess of fluids, incision, external pressure, or frost, each of which prevented the "animal spirits" from passing along the nerve to the organ affected. See P.-A. Sigal, "Comment on concevait et on traitait la paralysie en Occident dans le Haut Moyen Age (Ve–XIIe siècles)," *Revue d'Histoire des Sciences* 24 (1971): 193-211, especially 195-99, where Sigal distinguishes between a "medical" view of paralysis, derived from Galen, and a "hagiographical" interpretation, derived from popular belief and observation of plant biology. See also below, ll. 50-55 and n. 12.

9. Cf. VII 21, where Benedicta is said to be from Tuscany.

10. The relation between, on the one hand, human suffering and affliction and, on the other, divine providence, is one of Arcoid's favorite themes. In Mir. IV London and St. Paul's are destroyed by fire, partly as punishment for men's sins, partly so that they could witness the power of Erkenwald's relics and grow in faith as a result. Here Benedicta has been subjected to the rigors of her long pilgrimage to glorify the saint of London. See also, for example, Mir. III, XI, and XVI. Among analogous stories, about pilgrims who endure long journeys to widely scattered shrines before finding the one saint's relics that can cure them, are Goscelin of Canterbury's *Miracula S. Augustini* 2 (Leodegar the Saxon cripple), ASS Mai., 6:397-98, and the wanderings of the parricide in the *Miracula S. Swithuni*, ASS Jul., 1:335.

11. "absconditorum cognitor deus." Cf. Dan. 13.42.

12. The description of the healing is an apparent mixture of what Sigal (see above, n. 8) regards as the "hagiographical" and "medical" explanations of paralysis. The references to "nimia . . . strictione" and "animalis . . . uiuacitatis" seem to reflect the learned tradition, whereas what follows reverts to the cruder medicine of the hagiographers: viz., the explanation that it is the blood, "succus uiuificus," that restores the hand to health. It is possible that Arcoid had some slight acquaintance with a work such as the *Practica breuis* of Johannes Platearius. In Mir. XI we learn that he was friendly with a chancery clerk who was also a "medicus."

13. "manum ceream." Wax images of limbs or human and animal figures were offered at saints' shrines either in hope of healing or, as here, in gratitude for healing received. Cf. Mir. VII, below, where wax eyes are offered to Erkenwald on behalf of a blind man, who is given his sight soon afterwards. For some interesting illustrations of such votive offerings from the later Middle Ages, see U. M. Radford, "The Wax Images Found in Exeter Cathedral," *The Antiquaries Journal* 29 (1949): 164–68.

14. Efforts to locate a convent of nuns in a Marcillac or Marcilly on the Loire in the province of Lyons have failed. Marcilly-le-Chastel (Marcilliacus castri) had a priory, founded ca. 1128, which was a daughter-house of the abbey of Savigny. But there is no evidence of nuns there. Auguste Bernard, ed., *Cartulaire de l'Abbaye de Savigny* (Paris, 1853), 1:489–90. Either Arcoid or an early copyist has apparently made the mistake of substituting Marcilliacum for Marciniacum, i.e., Marcigny, a famous Cluniac convent, founded in the eleventh century, situated on the Loire in the province of Lyons. Henry I's sister, Adela of Blois, retired here, and Archbishop Thurstan of York suggested to Christina of Markyate that she do the same. Barlow, *The English Church 1066–1154*, 194. I am grateful to Mme. Mulon, conservateur, Centre d'Onomastique, at the French Ministry of Culture in Paris, for help and advice on this problem. Benedicta's name does not appear at the appropriate point in the list of nuns of Marcigny printed by M. F. Cucherat, *Cluny au onzième siècle*, 2nd ed. (Autun, 1873), 233 ff., but since she does not seem to have entered the priory for life, but merely for a period of retirement, her absence from the list is not surprising.

MIRACULUM VI

1. This episode, divided into three parts, formed the lections for the second nocturn at Mattins on May 2 at Chertsey Abbey in the early 14th century. Bodley MS Lat. Liturg. e.39, f. 42r–42v.

2. "ferculum." A rather unusual word, which Arcoid uses again below, Mir. X 17. It seems to be interchangeable with the more normal word for a portable shrine, "feretrum." Both words were current in classical Latin and meant a bier or litter on which images of the gods or the spoils of war were carried in public procession.

3. For evidence from a contemporary charter that the public was contributing to the fund for Erkenwald's silver shrine, see above, chap. 4, n. 26. With Arcoid's use of the word "collectas" cf. 1 Cor. 16.1–2, where it means the money collected from donors. Arcoid seems to use it of the places where such collections were made, possibly temporary booths.

4. "collectione." A medical term, for which the earliest citation in Latham's *Dictionary of Medieval Latin from British Sources* is from the 13th-century *Compendium medicinae* of Gilbertus Anglicus. The word also meant, in Medieval Latin, the same as "collecta," i.e., a collection of money for alms or other pious purposes, so there is a sardonic play on words here. The punishment fits the crime.

5. Cf. 1 Cor. 7.14.

MIRACULUM VII

1. Cf. Peter the Venerable's letter to Louis VII (1146): "Renouantur iam nostro tempore antiqua secula et in diebus nouae gratiae, uetusti populi miracula reparantur." Giles Constable, ed., *The Letters of Peter the Venerable*, 2 vols. (Cambridge, Mass., 1967), 1:327. For the importance of this theme in early medieval hagiography, see Marc Van Uytfanghe, "La controverse biblique et patristique autour du miracle et ses repercussions sur l'hagiographie dans l'Antiquité tardive et le haut Moyen Age Latin," in *Hagiographie, cultures et sociétés (IVe–XIIe siècles). Actes du Colloque organisé à Nanterre et à Paris (2–5 mai 1979)* (Paris, 1981), 214. For the typological character of many saints' lives, see Earl, and for the relevance of the Pauline theology of the "corpus mysticum" of Christ, see Whatley, "The Figure of Constantine the Great in Cynewulf's 'Elene,' " *Traditio* 37 (1981), 192–98. Arcoid refers here to the renewal of the early Christian miracles; Mir. VII, however, goes on to show how Erkenwald's miracles surpass those of the Old Testament. Cf. Mir. VII 85–92 and Mir. IV 130–32. New Testament parallels are made explicit in Mir. XVIII 36, and are implicit in Mir.III, of which the ultimate "type" is Act. 5.17–21 and 12.6–10.

2. 1 Cor. 14.22. This verse was once invoked by those who denied that miracles occurred, or were necessary, in a society of converted Christians. They argued that Christ and the apostles performed miracles as a part of their missionary work, to inculcate faith in their teachings. For those who supposedly were Christians, miracles were superfluous. Augustine himself subscribed to this view until towards the end of his life. Uytfanghe, 210–212.

3. The "opus" is the new silver shrine referred to in Mir. VI for the first time. Arcoid uses the future infinitive here, "fore," because the shrine is to take some time to complete. Mir. VII takes place April 30–May 2, 1139. I argue above, chap. 4, that it was finished in time for Nov. 14, 1148.

4. The passage seems to be about the "anarchy" of Stephen's reign. See above, chap. 3, n. 84.

5. Cf. Ier. 19.3. Also 1 Reg. 3.11; 4 Reg. 21.12. The collective "stupor" of the Londoners, in their state of sin and infidelity to Christian principles, is typified in the cataleptic stupor of the young man in the miracle that follows.

6. Cf. Lam. 3.21–22.

7. Cf. above, Mir. V 20, 25, and notes 7 & 8. The date of Mir. VII is pretty certainly April 30–May 2, 1139. A "statio" of the sort mentioned in l. 32 would normally happen on Erkenwald's feast day (see next note), April 30; the T recension specifies that the occasion was "die solempnitatis sue," a statement that may derive from the original *MSE* or it may be John of Tynemouth's own interpolation (either way it supports our explanation of the "statio"); Arcoid (line 21) adds that the day was a Sunday, and later (99–100) that the year was 1139. In 1139, April 30 fell on a Sunday. A. Capelli, *Cronologia* (Milan, 1969), 100.

8. In a stational mass such as this, priests and congregation processed (see l. 24) from one church to another, or in their own church to a side altar, chapel or crypt, as here. At their destination they would stand during mass, rather than occupy pews or choir stalls, for reasons of space. The occasion might be to honor a particular saint or to commemorate an important event associated with the station. While Erkenwald's shrine was in the Romanesque crypt, either next to St. Faith's altar (Mir. XV 15–16) or in its own enclosed oratory (XIV 4, XVII 5 ff.), a stational mass would be the normal procedure on the saint's feast day, though exactly where the main altar of the church was located during the period before the choir was habitable is unknown. On "stationes" see *Iohannes Beleth summa de ecclesiasticis officiis*, ed. Heribert Daniel, CCCM 41A (Turnhout 1976),

18. For the origins and early semantic development of the word "statio," see Christine Mohrmann, *Études sur le Latin des Chrétiens*, vol. 3. Storia et Letteratura raccolta di Studi e Testi, 103 (Rome, 1965), 307–330.

9. According to Latham's *Dictionary* the earliest English occurrence of "cathalepticus" is in the 13th-century *De proprietatibus rerum* 7.10 of Bartholomeus Anglicus.

10. There seems to be no reason to doubt the existence of Hamelin and Albereda, but I have found no external evidence for it.

11. "toruis luminibus." Cf. Virgil, *Aen.* 3.677, for the glaring eyes of the Cyclopes, "Aeteneos fratres." Also Ovid, *Met.* 9.27.

12. "malphationibus." i.e., "malefac(t)ionibus," an old classical medical term for swooning. Cf. Du Cange, *Glossarium Mediae et Infimae Latinitatis* (Paris, 1845), 4:204, "Malefactio = Lipothymia . . . fit ex nimitate aut evacuatione sanguinis."

13. Iob 14.2.

14. Iob 13.25.

15. Cf. Iob 23.2–3, 7.

16. Eccles. 4.10.

17. Iob 23.8–10.

18. Ioh. 19.5.

19. 1 Cor. 15.52.

20. Arcoid implies with the word "nostram" that he was present in the dying man's room, and later, l. 96, he states plainly that he was "present" at the miracle of his recovery. But in ll. 78–79 he reports William's speech on his recovery as if he had merely heard it from a bystander: "tale dicitur dedisse responsum."

21. The early 15th-c. stained glass of York Minster shows wax images hanging from a rack by the side of the shrine of St. William; a crude 15th-c. woodcut depicts a similar rack from which hangs, among other wax objects, a pair of eyes, at the shrine of St. Simon of Trent. The eyes hung from the railing by St. Erkenwald's shrine would presumably be strung together with candle wick. See Radford, 66, plate XXI c & d (cited above, Mir. V, n. 13). What William's friend does with the wax eyes in the first place, l. 67, seems similar to the medieval practice of "measuring," which involved donating to a shrine the amount of candle wick and wax roughly equivalent to the length of the limb or, in some cases, the person healed by a saint. For a brief account and further refs., see Ronald C. Finucane, *Miracles and Pilgrims: Popular Beliefs in Medieval England* (London, 1977), 95–96.

22. Luc. 2.12.

23. Cf. Tob. 6.15, 19; 7.2; 11.13.

24. The episcopacy was vacant during the first seven years of Stephen's reign. Gilbert the Universal died in August, 1134, Robert de Sigillo was consecrated in June, 1141. Abbot Anselm of Bury, elected in 1136 by a majority of the canons but without the consent of Dean William, was temporarily bishop from 1137–38, but his election was quashed by Rome, having been opposed by the king, nobility, and other bishops all along. On the vacancy and the election conflict, see above, chap. 3, part 1.

MIRACULUM VIII

1. This brief unremarkable episode may be compared with Mir. IX and Mir. XIII for lack of narrative detail and homiletic color. One is tempted to regard the three as interpolations by someone other than Arcoid. Mir. VIII is omitted entirely by the redactor of the Erkenwald chapter in the *Gilte Legende*, in BL Add. 35298. Verbal parallels between VIII and XIII are particularly close. See the note on Mir. XIII.

MIRACULUM IX

1. Like Mir. VIII, this anonymous, unspecific episode lacks any of the features (including any indication of the illness!) that lend conviction and purpose to Arcoid's work in the main. Mir. IX seems to be located here in the sequence of episodes because the "languidus" is young, like William in VII and Adam in XI, and also because like each of them he makes a short speech proclaiming his newly recovered health.

MIRACULUM X

1. On the silver shrine, see Mir. VI 1-2, VII 4-5, and above, chap. 4. That several silversmiths are at work on the shrine implies the considerable size of the object (cf. below, ll. 14-15 & n. 4) and the elaborate and costly decoration. I have found no contemporary references to a silversmith named Eustace.

2. "similem . . . querit." Cf. Walther, *Proverbia Sententiaeque Latinitatis Medii Aevi*, 1:934, no. 7418: "Est et semper erit: similis similem sibi querit." Cf. Eccles. 13.19.

3. The completed shrine, as described in the inventory of 1245, was of wood inside (cf. l. 14) while the outer surfaces were of silver embossed with images in relief, and studded with 130 precious gems (the latter probably added in subsequent years, through donations). Two silver angels perched on the top of the shrine. There is no mention of gold, however, despite Arcoid's "et auro" (l. 8). See Simpson, "Two Inventories," 444, 469.

4. Although it appears to have been a portable reliquary suitable for processions (it is said to rest *on* the main altar in the 1245 inventory), it was evidently long enough to imagine an adult male lying in it.

5. Cf. 4 Reg. 1.9-15, re. Elijah, and 4 Reg. 2.24, re. Elisha. With these allusions compare *VSE* 151-52, re. Elijah's crossing of the Jordan.

MIRACULUM XI

1. Arcoid is very respectful of this person, calling him "uenerabilis" and a clerk in the service of someone of high rank. Later we learn (ll. 21-22) that he was a young man named Adam, who was enamoured of the pleasures of the world. He may have been the chancery clerk of the same name whom King Stephen, in a charter of 1135-40, confirmed in possession of some land in Norfolk and Suffolk originally granted by Henry I. This Adam may also have been a clerk at St. Martin's-le-Grand, which had close links with the royal chancery through its absentee Dean, Roger of Salisbury. Henry A. Cronne & R. H. C. Davis, *Regesta Regum Anglo-Normannorum 1066-1154*, vol. 3 (Oxford, 1967), xi, 5. There is no evidence that Stephen's Adam was also skilled in medicine.

2. Luc. 15.11-32, the parable of the prodigal son.

3. Osee 2.7, which is linked with the parable of the prodigal son (see previous note) in Jerome's commentary *In Osee*, ed. M. Adriaen, *S. Hieronymi presbyteri opera.* I, 6, *Commentarii in prophetas minores*, CCSL 76 (Turnhout, 1969), 20-21. Arcoid may well have had Jerome's commentary in mind. Cf. Mir. XI 8-10, with Jerome, ibid., 21: "Ex quo intelligimus quod prouidentia Dei saepe nobis accidant mala, ne habeamus ea quae cupimus, et uariis oppressi calamitatibus huius saeculi ac miseris, ad Dei seruitutem redire cogamur."

4. Paraphrased from Amos 3.6, "Si erit malum in ciuitate, quod Dominus non fecerit," and from Is. 45.7, "Ego Dominus . . . , faciens pacem, et creans malum." The two passages

are linked by Jerome in his commentary *In Amos*, ed. Adriaen, CCSL 76, 245-47 (see previous note).

5. Cf., e.g., William Langland, *Piers Plowman*, B 15.268, ed. George Kane & E. Talbot Donaldson (London, 1975), 550.

6. Arcoid is somewhat obscure here. He says he was hurrying to the church after vespers so as to "complete" the twelfth hour. But the twelfth "hora" was traditionally vespers itself. Cf. Amalarius of Metz, *Liber de Ord. Ant.*, ed. J. M. Hanssens, *Amalarii episcopi opera liturgica omnia*, 3 vols. (Rome, 1948-50), 3:33, "vespertinam synaxin agimus circa duodecimam horam." Arcoid's "post vespertinam" and his use of the verb "compleremus" suggest he has compline in mind.

7. On this and similar outbursts, see above, chap. 3, part 3.

8. Early in the 13th c., a Londoner named Ralph of Cornhill granted a rent or annual subsidy of 12 pence for the maintenance of lights before the altar of St. Erkenwald, which was also the main altar. Gibbs, 187, no. 237. Early in the 15th c. Dean Thomas bequeathed money to have some houses built and rented out so as to furnish regular income for the upkeep of the shrine, including the burning of lights on the two annual feast-days. Dugdale, ed. Ellis, 15.

MIRACULUM XII

1. "aures . . . habentibus." Cf. Matt. 13.9: "Qui habet aures audiendi, audiat."

2. On episcopal jurisdiction over cases of illegal work on feast days, see Mir. II, nn. 2 & 3. Strictly speaking there was no bishop of London at the time this episode is supposed to take place, assuming the time is similar to the preceding and subsequent miracles. "Episcopo ciuitatis" (17-18), therefore, may refer to Erkenwald himself, as is the case in Mir. II, or possibly to the bishop in charge, Henry of Blois, Bishop of Winchester, who ruled the London diocese from 1138 to 1141, after the fiasco over the election of Anselm of Bury. I have been unable to trace Vitalis the skinner in any other sources.

MIRACULUM XIII

1. This miracle is very similar to Mir. VIII. However, its language is more interesting. Notice especially the word-games with the vocabulary of sight, including not only "in omnium oculis" (1 & 3), but also "euidentia," "claruit" (4), "spectaculum" (4), "uisa" (5), and "euidens" (6-7).

MIRACULUM XIV

1. See above, chap. 4, for the argument that the attempted theft story is fictitious, but that the translation to the upper church described later in this episode was carried out to allow visitors and pilgrims better access to the shrine, and therefore better publicity and more support for the cult, than was likely in the crypt. On the "translatio" as a distinct hagiographical genre, see Martin Heinzelmann, *Translationsberichte und andere Quellen des Reliquienkultes*, Typologie des sources du moyen âge occidental, vol. 33 (Turnhout, 1979).

2. One can only speculate as to which monasteries Arcoid means to implicate here. Bernard Scholz has suggested a rivalry between St. Paul's and Westminster Abbey (see above chap. 4, n. 36), *VSE* describes a conflict with the monks and nuns of Chertsey

and Barking, and the *Miracula S. Edmundi* suggests a similar spirit of rivalry between London and Bury (see above, chap. 4, nn. 5 & 35).

3. Cf. also below, l. 25, and Mir. XVII 11, where the area that included the altar and shrine is called an "oratorium."

4. "clericulis," l. 7, could also mean "lesser clerks of low rank," but alongside the "quidam . . . pueritiam exuens" the word more likely means boys from the choir school, which helps to make the consternation of the thieves more the result of "diuino . . . iudicio" (8–9), than of fear of three burly night-watchmen. It is surprising, however, that the vast and probably eerie crypt was left in charge of a youth and two small boys.

5. The sealed coffin, as we learn later (ll. 29, 37), is made of lead. Lead coffins, as well as those of stone and wood, were in use in early Christian Gaul. Braun, *Christliche Altar*, 549–50, cites an account from 9th-century Fulda, where the bodies of SS. Alexander and Fabianus, obtained from Rome, were encased in lead coffins and entombed, by Hrabanus Maurus, in a single stone tomb surmounted by an elaborately adorned "Aufbau" of wood. Braun also cites, 552 & n. 34, the opening in 1623 of an 11th-century stone sarcophagus in the crypt of St. Servatus, Maastricht, in which was found a lead casket divided into four compartments but containing the relics of five saints, including those of St. Servatus himself. On the clasp of the lead casket were five seals, inscribed with the name of the bishop, Hermann, who officiated at the translation in 1039.

6. The translation of Nov. 14, 1148, which became the official feast day, was presumably more public than this hasty affair. But in 1326 (Feb. 1), when the saint's relics were translated again, to a new shrine in the new Gothic choir, the ceremony was again done in private, "in media nocte, propter tumultum populi evitandum," with no higher ecclesiast than the Dean officiating, as was probably the case in 1140. Stubbs, ed., *Chronicles of the Reigns of Edward I and Edward II*, 1:311.

7. Cf. Ps. 103.2.

8. On St. Ethelburga, see *VSE* 17–26, and Bede *Hist. eccles.* 4.6–9, ed. Colgrave & Mynors, 354–63. None of the extant legends of St. Ethelburga contains a story like this one, although Goscelin's account of her translation mentions problems in finding and then moving her sarcophagus. See Colker, "Texts of Jocelyn," 441 ff. It is possible that the onlookers at St. Paul's had in mind the miracle performed jointly by Ethelburga and Erkenwald, when they miraculously stretched a wooden beam which had been cut too short by the carpenters building Barking Abbey. This story, included in Erkenwald's life by John of Tynemouth, but unknown to the author of *VSE* or at least ignored by him, may have been one of the miracles in the collection believed to have been written by Goscelin of Canterbury, but no longer extant.

9. The allusion is to *Hist. eccles.* 4.11, ed. Colgrave & Mynors, 364–68. Bede's story of Sebba presumably inspired the similar episodes in Alcuin's life of Willibrord, ed. Levison, MGH SRM 7:135, and Widric's life of St. Gerard of Toul (11th c.), ed. G. Waitz, MGH SS 4:498–99.

10. That this is the only complete piece of chronology in the whole work underlines the basically liturgical motive of MSE.

11. Le Neve/Greenaway, 95, lists one Teoldus among the St. Paul's canons "whose prebend cannot be identified," but who witnesses several St. Paul's charters between 1138 and 1142. Arcoid's description of the Theoldus in Mir. XIV as "consotius noster" and a canon of St. Martin's would explain why the Teoldus of the charters is not in the prebendal lists. He was not a canon of St. Paul's at all, but a respected neighbor whose signature and presence were valued on important business occasions. He was probably the same "Tioldus canonicus" who witnesses a charter at St. Bartholomew's Priory in 1137. E. A. Webb, ed., *Records of St. Bartholomew's Priory*, 2 vols., (Oxford, 1921), 1:77, 489. He was still a canon of St. Martin's in 1158, according to a charter printed by A. J. Kemp,

Historical Notices of the Collegiate Church . . . of St. Martin's-le-Grand, London (London, 1825), 65. On the name, see Ekwall, *Early London Personal Names*, 66.

MIRACULUM XV

1. "monasterium." During the Middle Ages this word was applied not only to monasteries proper but also to collegiate and cathedral churches with secular canons, like St. Paul's, London, and, for example, York "Minster."

2. The implication is that the saint's tomb is at or near the entrance to the choir where the canons are chanting the office. This miracle therefore takes place after the translation from the crypt, and confirms what was inferred from Mir. XIV: that by 1140 the choir of the new cathedral was ready for use, even if not complete to the last detail. That the time of Mir. XV is in fact *after* the 1140 translation, and not some earlier epoch before the fire of 1087, is confirmed by the rubric of Mir. XVI, which signals a shift in chronology back to the period when Erkenwald's relics were still in the crypt.

3. Pope Gregory the Great originally expected London to be the archdiocese for southern England, not Canterbury. Bede, *Eccles. hist.* 1.29, ed. Colgrave & Mynors, 104–05, n. 3. Bishop Richard of Belmeis had revived the idea during the time of Archbishop Anselm. Barlow, *English Church 1066–1154*, 35–36. Arcoid seems to be endorsing Bishop Richard's position. Cf. also the ME poem, *St. Erkenwald*, v. 107 (ed. Peterson), where Erkenwald is called "primate."

4. "leuita euuangelium incipiente." The gospel for St. Erkenwald's day, according to the late medieval liturgical sources, was that of the Common of a Confessor Bishop, as one would expect. In all likelihood, therefore, Baldwin awakens to the opening words of Matt. 25.13: "Vigilate. . . ."

MIRACULUM XVI

1. "alio tempore." This and the remaining miracles take place chronologically before the previous group, IV–XV.

2. Cf. Mir. XI 8–14, for similar reflections on the workings of divine providence. Mir. XVI, however, represents a more subtle example of this theme, since the girl's fever is in no way a punishment but rather a preventative trial (see below, ll. 7–10). Suffering this early in life and experiencing miraculous recovery will help the girl resist temptation in the future.

3. I.e., in the crypt. See Dugdale, ed. Ellis, 75, and the plan and plate between 74 & 75.

MIRACULUM XVII

1. There is no "Teodwinus pictor" in the surviving records of Anglo-Norman London, but a "Tedwinus pistor," i.e. a baker, witnesses charters in the time of Bishop Richard of Belmeis. Maxwell Lyte, *Historical MSS Commission Reports*, vol. 9, *Appendix*, 61b. See also Gibbs, 157, "Tidewinus."

2. An early analogue to this motif is in Bede, *Hist. eccles.* 2.6, ed. Colgrave & Mynors, 154, where St. Peter appears in a dream to an early archbishop of Canterbury, Laurence, and beats him for contemplating flight from England, which was relapsing into paganism.

MIRACULUM XVIII

1. "quum ad laudem et honorem eius creati sumus." These words are reminiscent of the incipit of the fragment from the lections, De Erkenwaldo, thought to be the work of Goscelin of Canterbury (see above, chap. 2, n. 18). This coincidence, plus the fact that Mir. XVIII concerns Barking and Ethelburga in the time of Abbess Alviva, strongly suggests that the episode is based on one of Goscelin's lections. Goscelin wrote lives of Ethelburga and other Barking abbesses, and an account of the translation of their relics in 1087, during the time of Alviva. It is interesting that in the Middle English version of Mir. XVIII, in the Gilte Legende, the father of the young crippled girl is given a name, whereas in the C manuscript, and in John of Tynemouth's redaction, he is not named. In the Gilte Legende his name is "Goslamis" (BL Add. 35298, f. 56v, col.b). It seems to me possible that this rather unusual name may have resulted from a mistaken reading of the name "Goscelinus," written perhaps as a marginal annotation in the GL redactor's exemplar or some earlier manuscript in the same family, identifying not the father of the girl but the author of the original version of her story.

2. Arcoid again treats the miracle as a "signum," or divine revelation of God's providence. Cf. Mir. III, IV, V, XI, XVI.

3. Aeluiua (OE Aelfgyfa) was abbess of Barking for an astounding period of time: ca. 1060–ca. 1122. According to Goscelin the hagiographer, she became abbess at age 15, which helps explain the length of her term. See Colker, "Texts of Jocelyn," 388, 437; Tolhurst, Ordinale, 1:5, 2:362; also David Knowles, C. N. L. Brooke, & Vera M. London, The Heads of Religious Houses. England and Wales 940–1216 (Cambridge, 1972), 208.

4. Cf. Act. 3.1–10.

MIRACULUM XIX

1. Luton in Bedfordshire was formerly included in the Anglo-Saxon see of Dorchester, but it became part of the great see of Lincoln as a result of Norman reorganization.

Bibliography

I. MANUSCRIPTS

Cambridge, Corpus Christi College 161; 393; Trinity College 0.2.1; 0.3.54; University Library Ii.2.3
Cambridge, Mass., Harvard College Lat.27
London, British Library, Additional 35298; Claudius A.v; Cleo A.ii; Faustina B.iv; Otto A.xii; Tiberius E.i; Vespasian B.xx; Vitellius A.xiii; Harley 2250; Lansdowne 436
London, Lambeth Palace Library 474
New York, Morgan Library 46; 105
Oxford, Bodleian Library, Bodley 790; Digby 38; Gough Liturg. 16; Lat. Liturg. d.42; Lat. Liturg. e.39; Smith 94; Tanner 15
San Marino, Huntington Library 1344
Stonyhurst College 52
York Minster XVI.G.23

2. PRIMARY SOURCES

(Lives of saints are listed alphabetically by saint's name and also, when known, by author's name.)

AEDUS, Saint. *Vita sancti Aedi*. Ed. Charles Plummer, *Acta sanctorum Hiberniae*. 2 vols. Oxford, 1910; rpt. 1968. 1:34–45.
AELFRIC. *The Homilies of the Anglo-Saxon Church. The First Part Containing the Sermones Catholici, or Homilies of Aelfric*. Ed. Benjamin Thorpe. 2 vols. London, 1846.
————. *Aelfric's Lives of the Saints*. Ed. W. W. Skeat, EETS 76, 82, 94, 114. London, 1881–1900; rpt., 2 vols., 1966.

————. *Lives of Three English Saints*. Ed. G. I. Needham. London, 1966.

ALCUIN. (See below, Saint WILLIBRORD.)

AMALARIUS of Metz. *Liber de ordine antiphonarii*. Ed. J. M. Hanssens, *Amalarii episcopi opera liturgica omnia*. 3 vols. Rome, 1948–50.

ANSELM, Saint. *Vita sancti Anselmi*. Ed. Richard W. Southern, *The Life of St. Anselm of Canterbury by Eadmer*. London, 1962; rpt. Oxford, 1972.

Antropoff, Rurik von, ed. (See below, Saint KENELM.)

ATTRACTA, Saint. *Vita sanctae Attractae*. ASS. Feb., 2:297–300.

AUGUSTINE of Canterbury, Saint. *Vita sancti Augustini ep. Cantuariensis auctore Goscelino*. ASS Mai., 6:375–95; *Miracula, historia translationis*, ibid., 397–430, 432–43.

AUGUSTINE of Hippo. *De civitate Dei*. Ed. B. Dombart & A. Kalb, CCSL 48. Turnhout, 1955. PL 41.

AVITUS, Saint. *Vita sancti Aviti confessoris Aureliensis*. Ed. B. Krusch, MGH SRM 3 (Hannover, 1896): 383–85.

Baildon, W. P., ed. *Records of the Honourable Society of Lincoln's Inn. The Black Books*. 4 vols. London, 1897–1902.

BEDE. *Historia ecclesiastica gentis Anglorum*. Ed. Bertram Colgrave & R. A. B. Mynors, *Bede's Ecclesiastical History of the English People*. Oxford, 1969.

BELETH, Johannes. *Iohannes Beleth summa de ecclesiasticis officiis*. Ed. Heribert Daniel, CCCM 41A. Turnhout, 1976.

BENEDICT, Saint. *Miracula sancti Benedicti*. Ed. E. de Certain, *Les miracles de Saint Benoît*, Soc. de l'hist. de France, publications in octavo, 96. Paris, 1858.

BERNARD, Saint. *Epistolae*. PL 182:67–662.

————. *Sancti Bernardi vita . . . auctore Gaufrido*. PL 185:225–366.

Bernard, Auguste, ed. *Cartulaire de l'Abbaye de Savigny*. Paris, 1853.

Biblia latina cum glossa ordinaria. 4 vols. Strassburg, 1480.

Bishop, E. & A. Gasquet, eds. *The Bosworth Psalter*. London, 1908.

Blake, E. O., ed. *Liber Eliensis*. Camden Soc., 3rd Ser. 92. London, 1962.

BRIGID, Saint. *Vita sanctae Brigidae adscripta Chilieno*. ASS Feb., 1:141–55.

CHILIEN. (See above, Saint BRIGID.)

CHRISTINA of Markyate. (See below, Talbot.)

CICERO, Marcus Tullius. *Cicero's Tusculan Disputations*. Ed. J. E. King. London & New York, 1927.

Clark, Cecily, ed. *The Peterborough Chronicle 1070–1154*. 2nd ed. Oxford, 1970.

Colker, M., ed. (See below, GOSCELIN.)

CONCHUBRAN. (See below, Saint MODWENNA.)

CONSTANTIUS. (See below, Saint GERMANUS.)

DICETO, Ralph de. *Radulphi de Diceto decani Lundoniensis opera historica.* Ed. William Stubbs. 2 vols, RS 68. London, 1876.

Douglas, David C., ed. *Feudal Documents from the Abbey of Bury St. Edmunds.* Records of the Social & Economic History of England and Wales, 8. London, 1932.

————, & George W. Greenaway, eds. *English Historical Documents 1042–1189.* London, 1968.

Davis, H. W. C., et al., eds. *Regesta regum Anglo-Normannorum 1066–1154.* 4 vols. Oxford, 1913–69.

Delisle, L., ed. *Rouleaux des morts.* Paris, 1866.

DUNSTAN, Saint. *Vita sancti Dunstani Cantuariensis archiepiscopi et confessoris, auctore Osberno. Liber miraculorum beatissimi patris nostri Dunstani . . . , auctore Osberno.* Ed. William Stubbs. *Memorials of St. Dunstan,* RS 63. London, 1874.

EADMER. *De conceptione sanctae Mariae.* PL 159:301–18.

————. A. Wilmart, ed., "Edmeri Cantuariensis cantoris nova opuscula de sanctorum veneratione et obsecratione," *Rev. des sciences religieuses* 15 (1935): 184–219, 354–379.

————. B. Scholz, ed., "Eadmer's Life of Bregwine, Archbishop of Canterbury," *Traditio* 22 (1966): 127–48.

————. *Vita sancti Anselmi* (see above, Saint ANSELM).

————. *Vita et miracula sancti Dunstani.* Ed. Stubbs. *Memorials of St. Dunstan* (see above, Saint DUNSTAN).

EDDIUS Stephanus. (See below, Saint WILFRED.)

EDMUND, Saint, king & martyr. *Passio sancti Eadmundi auctore Abbone Floriacensi.* Ed. Thomas Arnold. *Memorials of St. Edmund's Abbey,* RS 96, vol.1. London, 1890.

————. *Hermanni Archidiaconi liber de miraculis Sancti Eadmundi.* Ibid.

EDITH, Saint. (See below, GOSCELIN of Canterbury.)

EDWARD, Saint, king & confessor. *Vita Edwardi regis* [attrib. to Goscelin of Canterbury]. Frank Barlow, ed. *The Life of King Edward Who Rests at Westminster.* London, 1962.

————. M. Bloch, ed., "La vie de S. Éduoard le Confesseur par Osbert de Clare, " *AB* 41 (1923): 5–131, espec. 64–123.

EORMENHILD, Saint. *Vita sanctae Ermenhildae.* ASS Febr., 2:691 (epitome); Horstmann, *NLA* 1: 368–69 (epitome).

ERKENWALD, Saint. *Vita sancti Erkenwaldi episcopi Londoniensis.* Ed. Sir William Dugdale. *A History of St. Paul's Cathedral* (London, 1658); 2nd ed., E. Maynard (London, 1716); 3rd ed., Sir Henry Ellis (London, 1818); Dugdale, *Monasticon Anglicanum,* vol. 3 (London, 1673).

————. *De sancto Erkenwaldo episcopo et confessore* [epitome of *vita* and *miracula*]. Ed. Wynkin de Worde, *Nova Legenda Angliae* (London, 1516); ASS Apr., 3:781–87; Horstmann, *NLA* 1:391–405.

————. *St. Erkenwald.* Ed. Ruth Morse. Cambridge, 1975.

————. *St. Erkenwald.* Ed. Clifford Peterson. Philadelphia, 1977.

ETHELBURGA, Saint. (See below, GOSCELIN of Canterbury.)

FELIX. (See below, Saint GUTHLAC.)

FINAN, Saint. *Vita sancti Fintani.* Ed. Plummer. *Vitae sanctorum Hiberniae,* 1:96–106.

FLETE, John. *The History of Westminster Abbey by John Flete.* Ed. J. Armitage Robinson. Cambridge, 1909.

FLORENCE of Worcester. *Florentii Wigornesis monachi chronicon ex chronicis.* Ed. Benjamin Thorpe. 2 vols. London, 1848–49.

FOLCARD, Abbot of Thorney. (See below, JOHN of Beverley.)

FRITHEGODUS. (See below, Saint WILFRED.)

GELLIUS, AULUS. *Noctes Atticae.* Ed. P. K. Marshall. Oxford, 1968.

GEOFFREY of Auxerre. (See above, Saint BERNARD.)

GERARD, Saint. *Vita sancti Gerardi episcopi Tullensis auctore Widrico.* Ed. G. Waitz. MGH SS 4 (Hannover, 1841): 490–505.

GERMANUS, Saint. *Vita Germani episcopi Autissiodorensis auctore Constantio.* Ed. Wilhelm Levison. MGH SRM 7 (Hannover, 1919): 247–83.

Gibbs, Marion, ed. *Early Charters of the Cathedral Church of St. Paul's, London.* Camd. Soc., 3rd Ser., 58. London, 1939.

GIBRIAN, Saint. *Miracula facta Remis anno 1145.* ASS Mai., 7:619–51.

GOSCELIN of Canterbury. *Vita, miracula, historia translationis sancti Augustini archiep. Cant.* (See above, Saint AUGUSTINE of Canterbury.)

————. *Vita sanctae Edithae.* Ed. A. Wilmart, "La Légende de St. Édith en prose et vers par le moine Goscelin," *AB* 56 (1938): 5–101, 265–307.

————. *Vita sanctae Ethelburgae* [with the *vitae* of Hildelith & Wulfhild, and two accounts of the translation of the three saints]. Ed. Marvin Colker, "Texts of Jocelyn of Canterbury Which Relate to the History of Barking Abbey," *Studia Monastica* 7 (1965): 383–460.

————. *Vita sanctae Ivonis ep. Persa et soc.* PL 155:81–89.

————. *Vita sanctae Werburgae.* Ed. Horstmann. *Henry Bradshaw's Life of St. Werburghe,* EETS o.s. 88. London, 1887.

GREGORY of Tours. *Historia Francorum.* Ed. W. Arndt. *Gregorii Turonensis opera.* MGH SRM 1, pt. 1 (Hannover, 1885); 2nd ed., Krusch & Levison (Hannover, 1937–51).

————. *Liber in gloria confessorum, Liber in gloria martyrum, Liber vitae patrum,*

Libri quattuor de virtutibus beati Martini episcopi. Ed. Krusch, MGH SRM 1, pt. 2. Hannover, 1885.

GUIBERT of Nogent. *De pignoribus sanctorum.* PL 157:607–80.

———. *De vita sua.* Trans. John F. Benton. *Self and Society in Medieval France. The Memoirs of Abbot Guibert of Nogent.* New York, 1970.

GUTHLAC, Saint. *Vita sancti Guthlaci auctore Felice.* Ed. Bertram Colgrave. *Felix's Life of St. Guthlac.* Cambridge, 1956.

———. Jane Roberts, ed. *The Guthlac Poems of the Exeter Book.* Oxford, 1979.

Haddan, A. W. & William Stubbs, eds. *Councils and Ecclesiastical Documents Relating to Great Britain and Ireland.* 3 vols. Oxford, 1869–78.

Hale, W. H., ed. *The Domesday of St. Paul's.* Camd. Soc. 69. Westminster, 1858.

Hamer, Richard, ed. *Three Lives from the Gilte Legende.* Middle English Texts 9. Heidelberg, 1978.

Hart, Cyril. *Early Charters of Barking Abbey.* Colchester, 1953.

———. *The Early Charters of Eastern England.* Studies in Early English History 5. Leicester, 1966.

HENRY of Huntingdon. *Historia Anglorum.* Ed. Thomas Arnold, *Henrici archidiaconi Huntendunensis historia Anglorum,* RS 74. London, 1879.

HERMANN, Archdeacon. (See above. Saint EDMUND.)

Herzfeld, George, ed. *An Old English Martyrology.* EETS o.s. 116. London, 1900.

HILDEBERT of Lavardin. *Venerabilis Hildeberti Cenomanensis episcopi epistolae.* PL 171:135–312.

Hodgett, Gerald A. J., ed. *Cartulary of Holy Trinity Aldgate.* London Record Soc. 7. London, 1971.

Horstmann, Carl, ed. *Nova Legenda Angliae.* 2 vols. Oxford, 1901.

ISIDORE of Seville. *Mysticorum expositiones sacramentorum seu quaestiones in vetus Testamentum.* PL 83:207–424.

ITHAMAR, Saint. Denis Bethel, ed. "The Miracles of St. Ithamar," *AB* 89 (1971): 421–37.

JACOBUS de Voragine. Th. Graesse, ed. *Jacobi a Voragine legenda aurea.* 3rd ed. Bratislava, 1890; rpt. Osnabrück, 1965.

James, M. R., trans. *The Apocryphal New Testament.* Oxford, 1924; rpt. 1953.

JEROME, Saint. *Commentarii in Evangelium Matthaei.* Ed. D. Hurst & M. Adriaen. *S. Hieronymi opera,* 1,7. CCSL 77. Turnhout, 1969.

———. *Commentarii in prophetas minores.* Ed. Adriaen. Ibid., 1,6.

———. *Contra Vigilantium.* PL 23:353–68.

JOHN, Saint, of Beverley. *Vita S. Joannis Eboracensis auctore Folcardo.* Ed. James Raine. *Historians of the Church of York.* RS 71, vol. 1 (London 1879–94): 239–60.

———. *Miracula S. Joannis,* auctore Guillielmo de Kettel, ibid., 261–91.

JOHN of Salisbury. Marjorie Chibnall, trans. *Historia pontificalis. Memoirs of the Papal Court.* London, 1956.

———. *Metalogicon.* Ed. C. J. Webb. *Ioannis Sarisberiensis metalogicon.* Oxford, 1929.

JOHN of Tynemouth. *Sanctilogium Anglie.* Ed. Horstmann. *Nova Legenda Angliae.*

JULIAN of Le Mans, Saint. (See below, LETHALDUS.)

KENELM, Saint. *Passio S. Kenelmi.* Ed. Rurik von Antropoff, *Die Entwicklung der Kenelm-Legende.* Diss. Rheinischen Friedrichs-Wilhelms-Universität. Bonn, 1965.

LANDFERTH (Lantfredus) of Winchester. (See below, Saint SWITHUN.)

Leach, Arthur F., ed. *Educational Charters.* Cambridge, 1911.

LETHALDUS of Micy. *Vita et miracula sancti Juliani ep. Cenomannensis.* PL 137:781–96.

———. *Vita et miracula S. Martini Vertavensis* (see below, Saint MARTIN of Vertou).

LÉGER, Saint. *Passio Leudegarii episcopi Augustodunensis.* Ed. Krusch. MGH SRM 5 (Hannover 1910): 282–322.

———. *Passio Leudegarii ep. Aug.* auctore Ursino ["passio B"]. Ibid., 323–56.

Liebermann, Felix, ed. *Die Heiligen Englands, angelsächsisch und lateinisch.* Hannover, 1889.

Mabillon, Jean, & Lucas d'Achery, eds. *Acta sanctorum ordinis Sancti Benedicti.* 9 vols. Paris, 1668–1702; 2nd ed., Venice, 1733–40.

Macray, W. D., ed. *Chronicon monasterii de Evesham.* RS 29. London, 1863.

MALCHUS, Saint. Reginald of Canterbury, *Vita sancti Malchi.* Ed. R. L. Lind. Urbana, Ill., 1942.

MARCELLINUS, Saint. *Vita sancti Marcellini episcopi Ebredunensis.* ASS Apr., 2:750–53.

MARTIN of Tours, Saint. Sulpice Sevère. *Vie de Saint Martin.* Ed. Jacques Fontaine. 3 vols. Sources Chrétiennes 133–35. Paris, 1967-69.

———. *Miracula* (see above, GREGORY of Tours, *De virtutibus S. Martini*).

———. Paulinus of Périgueux (Petricordia). *De vita S. Martini libri vi.* Ed. M. Petshenig. *Poetae Christiani minores.* CSEL 16,1. Vienna, 1888.

MARTIN of Vertou, Saint. *Vita et miracula sancti Martini ab. Vertavensis* [attrib. Lethaldus]. Ed. Mabillon. Acta SS. ord. S. Ben. 2nd ed. (Venice 1733),1:357-70; ASS Oct., 10:805-17; ed. Krusch, MGH SRM 3:567-75 (excerpts).

MODWENNA, Saint (also known as Monenna or Darerca). M. Esposito, "Conchubrani vita sanctae Monennae, edited with an introduction," Proceedings of the Royal Irish Academy 28 (1910): Sect.C: 202-51; also ASS Jul., 2:290-96.

————. A. T. Baker & Alexander Bell, eds. St. Modwenna. Anglo-Norman Texts 7. Oxford, 1947.

MORE, Saint Thomas. A dialogue concerning heresies. Ed. Thomas M. C. Lawler, et al. 2 vols. New Haven, 1981.

ORDERIC Vitalis. Historia ecclesiastica. Ed. Marjorie Chibnall. The Ecclesiastical History of Orderic Vitalis. 6 vols. Oxford, 1969-80.

OSBERN of Canterbury. Vita et miracula sancti Dunstani (see above, Saint DUNSTAN).

————. Vita sancti Elphegi archiep. Cantuariensis. ASS Apr., 2:631-41; PL 149:375-86 (epitome).

OSBERT of Clare. The Letters of Osbert of Clare, Prior of Westminster. Ed. E.W. Williamson. London, 1929.

————. Vita sancti Edwardi regis et confessoris (see above, Saint EDWARD).

OTTO, Saint, b. of Bamberg. Vita sancti Ottonis ep. Bambergensis. ASS Jul., 1:425-49.

PARIS, Matthew. Matthaei Parisiensis chronica majora. Ed. Henry R. Luard. RS 57, 7 vols. London, 1872-83.

————. Gesta abbatum monasterii Sancti Albani. Ed. H. T. Riley. RS 28, 3 vols. London, 1867-69.

————. Matthei Parisiensis historia Anglorum sive . . . historia minor. Ed. Sir Frederic Madden. RS 44, 3 vols. London, 1866-69.

PAULINUS of Nola. S. Paulini Nolani carmina [on the life and passion of Saint Felix of Nola]. Ed. G. Hartel. CSEL 30. Vienna, 1884.

PAULINUS of Périgueux. (See above, Saint MARTIN of Tours.)

PETER the Venerable. Petris Venerabilis contra Petrobrusianos hereticos. Ed. James Fearns. CCCM 10. Turnhout, 1968.

————. De miraculis libri II. PL 189:851-954.

————. The Letters of Peter the Venerable. Ed. Giles Constable. 2 vols. Cambridge, 1967.

Peterson, Clifford, ed. (See above, Saint ERKENWALD.)

Plummer, Charles, ed. Two of the Saxon Chronicles Parallel. 2 vols. Oxford, 1892; rpt. 1965.

————. ed. *Vitae sanctorum Hiberniae*. 2 vols. Oxford, 1910; rpt. 1968.

Proctor, Francis & C. Wordsworth, eds. *Breviarum ad usum insignis ecclesiae Sarum*. 3 vols. Cambridge, 1879–86.

RALPH of Coggeshall. *Radulphus de Coggeshall chronicon Anglicanum*. Ed. Joseph Stevenson. RS 66. London, 1875.

Raine, James, ed. *The Historians of the Church of York and its Archbishops*. RS 71, 3 vols. London, 1879–94.

Rees, W. J., ed. *Lives of the Cambro-British Saints*. Llandovery, 1853.

Rickert, Margaret, ed. *The Reconstructed Carmelite Missal*. London, 1952.

SERENICUS, Saint. Vita S. Serenici confessoris. ASS Mai., 2:162–65.

SIMEON of Durham. *Historia regum*. Ed. Arnold. *Symeonis monachi opera omnia*. RS 75. London, 1885.

Smith, David M., ed. *English Episcopal Acta, I: Lincoln 1067–1185*. London, 1980.

Simpson, W. Sparrow, ed. *Documents Illustrating the History of St. Paul's Cathedral*. Camd. Soc., n.s. 26. London, 1880.

————. ed. *Registrum statutorum et consuetudinum ecclesiae cathedralis Sancti Pauli Londiniensis*. London, 1873.

————. "Two inventories of the cathedral church of St. Paul, London," *Archaeologia* 50 pt.ii (1887): 439–524.

Stokes, Whitley, ed. *Felire Oengusso Celi De. The martyrology of Oengus the Culdee*. HBS 29. London, 1905.

Stubbs, William, ed. *Chronicles of the Reigns of Edward I and Edward II*, RS 76. 2 vols. London, 1882–83.

————. ed. *Select Charters and Other Illustrations of English Constitutional History, from the Earliest Times to the Reign of Edward I*, 9th ed., rev. by H. W. C. Davis. Oxford, 1921.

SWITHUN, Saint. *Vita sancti Swithuni episcopi Wintoniensis*. Ed. E. P. Sauvage, AB 7 (1888): 374–80.)

————. "Sancti Swithuni Wint. ep. translatio et miracula auctore Lantfredo monacho wintoniensi." Ed. Sauvage, AB 4 (1885): 372–95. (See also ASS Jul., 1:331–37; PL 155:65–80.)

————. *Wulfstani cantoris narratio metrica de sancto Swithuno*. Ed. Campbell (see below, Saint WILFRED).

————. (For the Old English version of Swithun's miracles, see above, AELFRIC, ed. Needham.)

Talbot, Charles H., ed. *The Life of Christina of Markyate*. Oxford, 1959.

THIERRY of Echternach. *Flores epitaphium sanctorum*. PL 157:313–404.

Tolhurst, J. B. L., ed. *The Monastic Breviary of Hyde Abbey.* 6 vols. HBS 69–71, 76, 78, 80. London, 1932–42.

―――. ed. *The Ordinale and Customary of the Benedictine Nuns of Barking Abbey.* 2 vols. HBS 65–66. London, 1927–28.

URSINUS. (See above, Saint LEGER.)

VICTRICIUS of Rouen. *Liber de laude sanctorum.* PL 20:443–58.

Wade-Evans, W. A., ed. *Vitae sanctorum Britanniae et genealogiae.* U. of Wales, History and Law Ser., 9. Cardiff, 1944.

Walpole, A. S., ed. *Early Latin Hymns.* Cambridge, 1922; rpt. Hildesheim 1966.

Webb, E. A., ed. *Records of St. Bartholomew's Priory.* 2 vols. Oxford, 1921.

Whitelock, Dorothy, trans. *The Anglo-Saxon Chronicle.* London, 1961.

WILFRED, Saint. *The Life of Bishop Wilfred by Eddius Stephanus.* Ed. Bertram Colgrave. Cambridge, 1927.

―――. *Frithigodi monachi breviloquium vitae beati Wilfredi et Wulfstani cantoris narratio metrica de Sancto Swithuni.* Ed. Alistair Campbell. Zurich, 1950.

WILLIAM of Conches. *Philosophia mundi* [formerly attrib. Honorius of Autun]. PL 172:39–102.

WILLIAM of Kettel. (See above, Saint JOHN of Beverley.)

WILLIAM of Malmesbury. *De gestis pontificum Anglorum.* Ed. N. E. S. A. Hamilton. RS 52. London, 1870.

―――. *The vita Wulfstani of William of Malmesbury.* Ed. Reginald P. Darlington. Camd. Soc., 3rd Ser., 40. London, 1928.

WILLIBRORD, Saint. *Vita Willibrordi episcopi Traiectensis.* Ed. Krusch & Levison. MGH SRM 7. Hannover, 1920.

Wormald, Francis, ed. *English Benedictine Kalendars after 1100.* 2 vols. HBS 77, 81. London, 1939, 1946.

―――. ed. *English Kalendars before A.D. 1100.* HBS 72. London, 1934.

Wynkyn de Worde. *Nova Legenda Angliae.* London, 1516. STC no. 4601. See also above, Horstmann; and JOHN of Tynemouth.

3. SECONDARY SOURCES

Aigrain, René. *L'hagiographie: ses sources, ses méthodes, son histoire.* Poitiers, 1953.

Alexander, J. J. A., "English early-fourteenth century illumination: recent acquisitions," *Bodley Library Record* 9, 2 (1974): 72–80.

Bagatta, J. Bonifacius. *Admiranda orbis christiana.* 2 vols. in 1. Venice, 1700.

Bale, John. *Illustrium maioris Britanniae scriptorum . . . summarium*. Ipswich, 1548; 2nd ed., *Scriptorum illustrium m. Brytanniae . . . catalogus*, 2 vols. in 1. Basel, 1557–59; rpr., Farnborough, Hants., 1971.

———. *Index Britanniae scriptorum*. Ed. Reginald L. Poole & Mary Bateson. Anecdota Oxoniensa, Mediaeval & Modern Ser., 9. Oxford, 1902.

Barlow, Frank. "The effects of the Norman Conquest," in Dorothy Whitelock et al., *The Norman Conquest: Its Setting and Impact*. New York, 1966.

———. *The English Church 1000–1066*. 2nd ed. London, 1979.

———. *The English Church 1066–1154*. London, 1979.

Bell, Mrs. Arthur. *The Saints in Christian Art*. 3 vols. London, 1901–04.

Benson, Larry D. "The authorship of *St. Erkenwald*," *Journal of English & Germanic Philology* 64 (1965): 393–405.

Bethel, Denis. "Richard of Belmeis and the foundation of St. Osyth's," *Transactions of the Essex Archaeological Society*. 3rd Ser., 2 (1970): 299–327.

Bollandists. Socii Bollandiani, eds. *Bibliotheca hagiographica latina antiquae et mediae aetatis*. 2 vols. Brussels, 1898–1901. *Supplementum*. Brussels, 1911.

Bond, W.H. (see De Ricci).

Bishop, Edmund. *Liturgica historica*. Oxford, 1918.

Blaise, Albert. *Lexicon latinitatis medii aevi*. CCCM 1. Turnhout, 1975.

Boase, T. S. R. *English Art 1100–1216*. Oxford, 1953.

Boglioni, Pierre. "Miracle et nature chez Grégoire le Grand," *Cahiers d'études médiévales* 1 (1974): 11–102.

Bouthillier, Denise & Jean-Pierre Torrell, " 'Miraculum.' Une catégorie fondamentale chez Pierre le Vénérable," *Revue Thomiste* 80 (1980): 357–86.

Braun, Joseph. *Der christliche Altar in seiner geschichtlichen Entwicklung*. Munich, 1928.

Brett, Martin. *The English Church under Henry I*. Oxford, 1975.

Brewer, Cobham. *A Dictionary of Miracles*. London, 1884.

Bright, William. *Chapters in Early English Church History*. 3rd ed. Oxford, 1897.

Brooke, Christopher N. L. "The composition of the chapter of St. Paul's, 1086–1163," *Cambridge Historical Journal* 10 (1951): 111–32.

———. "The earliest times to 1485," in Matthews & Atkins, eds. *A History of St. Paul's Cathedral*. London, 1957.

———. & Gilian Keir. *London 800–1216: the Shaping of a City*. Berkeley & Los Angeles, 1975.

Brown, Peter. *Augustine of Hippo*. Berkeley, Cal., 1969.

———. *The Cult of the Saints*. Haskell lectures on the history of religions, new ser., 2. Chicago, 1981.

Butler, Alban. (See Thurston, Herbert.)

Campbell, James. "Some twelfth-century views of the Anglo-Saxon past," *Peritia* 3 (1984): 131–50.

Capelli, Adriano. *Cronologia, cronografia e calendario perpetuo.* Milan, 1930; rpt., 1969.

Carrias, Michel. "Étude sur la formation de deux légendes hagiographiques à l'époque mérovingienne. Deux translations de saint Martin d'àpres Grégoire de Tours," *Revue d'histoire de l'église de France* 57 (1972): 5–18.

Carter, Peter. "The historical content of William of Malmesbury's miracles of the Virgin Mary," in W. H. C. Davis & J. M. Wallace-Hadrill, eds. *The Writing of History in the Middle Ages. Essays presented to Richard William Southern* (Oxford, 1981), 127–65.

Chaurand, Jacques. "La conception de l'histoire de Guibert de Nogent," *Cahiers de civilization médiévale* 8 (1965): 387–95.

Cheney, C. R. "Rules for the observance of feast days in medieval England," *Bulletin of the Institute for Historical Research* 34 (1961): 117–47.

Chénu, M. D. *La théologie au douzième siècle.* Paris, 1957.

———. *Man, Nature and Society in the Twelfth Century.* Selected, ed. & trans. Jerome Taylor & Lester K. Little. Chicago, 1968.

Clanchy, M. T. *From Memory to Written Record. England 1066–1307.* Cambridge, Mass., 1979.

Clapham, A. W. *English Romanesque Architecture after the Conquest.* Oxford, 1934.

Clark, Cecily. "Aelfric and Abbo," *English Studies* 49 (1968): 30–36.

Colker, Marvin. "A Gotha codex dealing with the saints of Barking Abbey," *Studia Monastica* 10 (1968): 321–24.

Cook, G. H. *Old St. Paul's Cathedral.* London, 1955.

Cox, John Charles. *Sanctuaries and Sanctuary Seekers of Medieval England.* London, 1911.

———. "The sanctuaries and sanctuary seekers of Yorkshire," *The Archaeological Journal* 68 (1911): 273–99.

Crawford, V. M. (trans.) (See below, Delehaye.)

Craster, H. H. E. (See Madan).

Cross, Tom Peete & Clark Harris Slover. *Ancient Irish tales.* New York, 1936.

Cucherat, M. F. *Cluny au onzième siècle.* 2nd ed. Autun, 1873.

Curtius, Ernst Robert. *Europäische Literatur und lateinisches Mittelalter.* Bern, 1948.

———. *European Literature and the Latin Middle Ages.* Trans. Willard R. Trask. Bollingen Series 36. Princeton, 1973.

Daniélou, Jean. *Bible et liturgie.* Paris, 1951.

————. *The Bible and the Liturgy*. Notre Dame, Ind., 1956; rpt. 1968.

Davis, H. W. C. "London lands and liberties of St. Paul's, 1066–1135," *Essays in Medieval History presented to T. F. Tout*, ed. A. G. Little & F. M. Powicke. Manchester, 1925.

Davis, R. H. C. *King Stephen 1135–1154*. London, 1967.

————. "The monks of St. Edmund's, 1021–1148," *History*, New Ser. 40 (1955): 227–39.

De Gaiffier, B. "L'hagiographie et son public au XIe siècle," *Études critiques d'hagiographie et iconologie*. Subsidia hagiographica 43 (Brussels, 1967), 475–507.

————. "Les revendications de biens dans quelques documents hagiographiques du XIe et XIIe siècles," *AB* 50 (1932): 128–38.

De Ghellinck, J., et al. *Pour l'histoire du mot sacramentum. I, Les antinicéens*. Spicilegium sacrum Lovaniense, études et documents, fasc. 3. Louvain & Paris, 1924.

De Le Couteur, J. *English Medieval Stained Glass*. London, 1926.

Delehaye, H. *Les légendes hagiographiques*. Subsidia hagiographica 18a. 4th ed. Brussels, 1955.

————. *The Legends of the Saints*. Trans. V. M. Crawford. London, 1907; rpt. Norwood, Pa. 1974.

————. *Sanctus, essai sur le culte des saints dans l'antiquité*. Subsidia hagiographica 17. Brussels, 1927.

De Ricci, Seymour & W. J. Wilson, *Census of Medieval and Renaissance Manuscripts in the United States and Canada*. 3 vols. New York, 1935–40. *Supplement*. Ed. W. H. Bond. New York, 1962.

Dorey, T. A., ed. *Latin Biography*. London, 1967.

————. "William of Poitiers: Gesta Guillelmi," in *Latin Biography*.

Douglas, David C. *William the Conqueror*. Berkeley & L.A., 1964.

Du Cange, Charles du Fresne. *Glossarium mediae et infimae latinitatis*. 7 vols. Paris, 1840–50.

Dugdale, Sir William. *A History of St. Paul's Cathedral*. London, 1658; 2nd ed., E. Maynard (London, 1716); 3rd ed., Sir Henry Ellis (London, 1818).

————. *Monasticon anglicanum*. 3 vols. London, 1655–73.

————. *Origines judicales*. 2nd ed. London, 1671.

Dunn-Lardeau, Brenda, ed. *Legenda Aurea: sept siècles de diffusion*. Actes du colloque international sur la Legenda Aurea: texte latin et branches vernaculaires à l'Université du Québec à Montréal, 11–12 Mai 1983. Montreal & Paris, 1986.

Earl, James W. "Typology and iconographic style in early medieval hagiography," *Studies in the Literary Imagination* 8,i (1975): 15–46.

Ekwall, Eilert. *Early London Personal Names.* Lund, 1947.

Eyton, Robert W. *Antiquities of Shropshire.* 12 vols. London, 1854–60.

Farmer, D. H. *Oxford Dictionary of Saints.* Oxford, 1978.

———. "Two biographies by William of Malmesbury," in Dorey, ed., *Latin Biography,* 157–74.

Finucane, Ronald C. *Miracles and Pilgrims. Popular Beliefs in Medieval England.* London, 1977.

———. "The use and abuse of medieval miracles," *History* 60 (1975): 1–10.

Fros, Henry. "A mortuis suscitati, ut testimonium perhibeant veritati," *AB* 99 (1981): 355–60.

Gajano, Sofia Boesch, ed. *Agiografia altomedioevale.* Bologna, 1976.

Geary, Patrick J. *Furta sacra: Thefts of Relics in the Central Middle Ages.* Princeton, 1978.

———. "The humiliation of the saints," ed. Wilson, *Saints and their Cults,* 123–40.

Gneuss, Helmut. "Die Handschrift Cotton Otho A. xii," *Anglia* 94 (1976): 289–318.

Godden, Malcolm. "Aelfric and the vernacular prose tradition," ed. Szarmach & Huppé, *The Old English Homily and its Background,* 99–117.

Goodich, Michael. *Vita perfecta: the Ideal of Sainthood in the Thirteenth Century.* Monographien zur Geschichte des Mittelalters 25. Stuttgart, 1982.

Graham, Rose. "An appeal about 1175 for the building fund of St. Paul's cathedral church," *Journal of the British Archaeological Association,* 3rd Ser. 10 (1945–47): 73–76.

Gransden, Antonia. *Historical Writing in England c. 550 to c. 1307.* Ithaca, 1974.

Graus, Frantisek. *Volk, Herrscher und Heiliger im Reich der Merowinger. Studien zur Hagiographie der Merowingerzeit.* Prague, 1965.

Greenaway, Diana E. (See Le Neve.)

Greenfield, Stanley B. & Fred C. Robinson. *Bibliography of Publications on Old English Literature to the End of 1972.* Toronto, 1980.

Grosjean, Paul. "Vita s. Roberti Novi Monasterii in Anglia abbatis," *AB* 56 (1938): 334–60.

Guth, K. *Guibert von Nogent und die Hochmittelalterliche Kritik an der Reliquienverehrung.* Studien und Mitteilungen zur Geschichte des Benediktinerordens und seiner Zweige, Ergänzungsband 21. Ottobeuren, 1970.

Hamilton, Mary. *Incubation or the Cure of Disease in Pagan Temples and Christian Churches.* St. Andrews, 1906.

Hanning, Robert. *The Vision of History in Early Britain.* New York, 1966.

Hardy, Sir Thomas Duffus. *Descriptive Catalogue of Materials Relating to the History of Great Britain and Ireland to the End of the Reign of Henry VII*. RS 26. 3 vols in 4. London, 1862–71.

Harrison, Kenneth. *The Framework of Anglo-Saxon History to A.D. 900*. Cambridge, 1976.

Heist, William W. "Hagiography, chiefly Celtic, and recent developments in folklore," in Patlagean & Riché, eds., *Hagiographie, cultures, et sociétés*, 121–41.

Henken, Elissa R. "The saint as folk hero: biographical patterning in Welsh hagiography," in Patrick Ford, ed., *Celtic Folklore and Christianity. Studies in memory of William W. Heist* (Los Angeles, 1983), 58–74.

Hermann-Mascard, Nicole. *Les reliques des saints. Formation coutumière d'un droit*. Société d'Histoire du Droit. Collection d'histoire institutionelle et sociale 6. Paris, 1975.

Hervey, Francis. *The History of King Edmund the Martyr*. Oxford, 1929.

Herval, Renée. *Origines chrétiennes de la IIe Lyonaise gallo-romaine à la Normandie ducale (IVe–XIe siècles)*. Rouen, 1966.

Hunt, R. W. "Studies on Priscian in the eleventh and twelfth centuries, I: Petrus Helias and his predecessors," *Medieval & Renaissance Studies* 1 (1941–43): 194–231.

Hutton, W. *Lives and Legends of English Saints*. The Bampton lectures. New York & London, 1903.

James, M. R. *The Ancient Libraries of Canterbury and Dover*. Cambridge, 1903.
———. *A Descriptive Catalogue of the Manuscripts in the Library of Corpus Christi College, Cambridge*. 2 vols. Cambridge, 1912.

Jones, Charles W. *Saints' Lives and Chronicles*. Ithaca, 1947.

Kealey, Edward J. *Roger of Salisbury, Viceroy of England*. Berkeley, Cal., 1972.

Kelly, J. N. D. *Jerome*. New York, 1975.

Kemp, A. J. *Historical Notices of the Collegiate Church . . . of St. Martin's-le-Grand*. London, 1825.

Kemp, E. W. *Canonization and Authority in the Western Church*. London, 1948.

Ker, N. R. *The Medieval Libraries of Great Britain*. 2nd ed. London, 1964.

Knowles, David. *The Monastic Order in England*. Cambridge, 1941.
———, with C. N. L. Brooke, & Vera C. M. London. *Heads of Religious Houses. England and Wales 940–1216*. Cambridge, 1972.

Korhammer, Michael. "The origin of the Bosworth Psalter," *Anglo-Saxon England* 2 (1973): 173–87.

Latham, R. E. *Dictionary of Medieval Latin from British Sources*. London, 1975.

Leach, A. F. "St. Paul's School before Colet," *Archaeologia* 62 (1910): 191–238.

———. *The Schools of Medieval England*. London, 1916.

Le Franc, Abel. "Le traité des reliques de Guibert de Nogent et les commencements de la critique au moyen âge," *Études d'histoire du moyen âge dédiées à Gabriel Monod* (Paris, 1896), 285–306.

Le Goff, Jacques. (See Patin.)

Leland, John. *Joannis Lelandi antiquarii de rebus Britannicis collectanea*. 2nd ed., T. Hearne. 6 vols. London, 1770.

Le Neve, John. *Fasti ecclesiae anglicanae 1066–1300, I, St. Paul's, London*. Ed. Diana E. Greenaway. London, 1968.

Loftus, E. A. & H. F. Chettle. *A History of Barking Abbey*. London, 1954.

Loomis, C. Grant. *White Magic*. Cambridge, Mass., 1948.

Lucas, Peter J. "John Capgrave and the *Nova Legenda Anglie*: a survey," *The Library*, 5th Ser., 25 (1970): 1–10.

Madan, Falconer & H. H. E. Craster. *A Summary Catalogue of Western Manuscripts in the Bodleian Library at Oxford*. 7 vols. Oxford, 1895–1953.

Matthew, Donald J. A. *The Norman Conquest*. London, 1966.

Matthews, W. R. & W. M. Atkins, eds. *A History of St. Paul's Cathedral*. London, 1957.

Maxwell-Lyte, Henry C. *Historical Manuscripts Commission Reports*. Vol.9, *Appendix*. London, 1883.

Mayr-Harting, Henry. *The Coming of Christianity to England*. New York, 1972.

Milburn. R. L. P. *Saints and their Emblems in English Churches*. London, 1949.

Mohrmann, Christine. *Études sur le latin des Chrétiens, III*. Storia et letteratura raccolta di studi e testi 103. Rome, 1965.

Monod, B. *Le moine Guibert et son temps*. Paris, 1905.

Moore, R. I. *The Origins of European Dissent*. New York, 1975.

Morris, Colin. "A critique of popular religion: Guibert of Nogent on the Relics of the Saints," ed. G. J. Cuming & Derek Baker, *Popular Belief and Practice*. Studies in Church History 8. Cambridge, 1972.

Nelson, Philip. *Ancient Painted Glass in England 1170–1500*. London, 1913.

Nicholl, Donald. *Thurstan, Archbishop of York 1114–1140*. York, 1964.

Oakley, Francis. *The Western Church in the Middle Ages*. Ithaca, 1979.

Orme, Nicholas. *English Schools in the Middle Ages*. Oxford, 1973.

Orselli, A. M. *L'idea e il culto del santo patrono cittadino nella letteratura latina christiana*. Bologna, 1965.

———. "Il santo patrono cittadino: genesi e sviluppo del patrocinio del vescovo nei secoli VI e VII," ed. Gajano, *Agiographia altomedioevale*, 85–104.

Oxley, James Edwin. *A History of Barking*. Barking, 1935.

Patin, J. P. Valery & Jacques le Goff, "A propos de la typologie des miracles dans le *Liber de miraculis* de Pierre le Vénérable." *Pierre Abelard, Pierre le Vénérable, les courants philosophiques, littéraires, et artistiques en occident au milieu du XIIe siècle*. Colloques internationaux du Centre National de la Recherche Scientifique 546 (Paris, 1975), 181–89.

Patlagean, Evelyne & Pierre Riché, eds. *Hagiographie, cultures, et sociétés (IVe–XIIe siècles)*. Actes du colloque organisé à Nanterre et à Paris, 2–5 Mai 1979. Paris, 1981.

Pearsall, Derek & Elizabeth Salter. *Landscapes and Seasons of the Medieval World*. London, 1970.

Poulin, J.-C. *L'idéal de sainteté dans l'Aquitaine carolingienne d'àpres les sources hagiographiques (750–950)*. Travaux du Laboratoire d'Histoire Religieuse de l'Université Laval 1. Quebec, 1975.

Radford, V. M. "The wax images found in Exeter Cathedral," *The Antiquaries Journal* 29 (1949): 164–68.

Rathbone, Eleanor. "The Influence of Bishops and the Members of Cathedral Bodies on the Intellectual Life of England, 1066–1216." Ph.D. diss., London University, 1935.

———. "Master Alberic of London, Mythographus tertius Vaticanus," *Medieval & Renaissance Studies* 1 (1941–43): 35–38.

Ray, Roger "Medieval historiography through the twelfth century: problems and progress of research," *Viator* 5 (1974): 33–59.

Reaney, P. H. *Place Names of Essex*. London, 1935.

Richards, Mary P. "The medieval hagiography of St. Neot," *AB* 99 (1981): 259–78.

Robinson, J. Armitage. *Gilbert Crispin, Abbot of Westminster*. Cambridge, 1911.

Rock, D. *Church of our Fathers*. Ed. G. Hart & W. Frere. 3 vols. in 4. London, 1903.

Rogers, Edith C. *Discussion of Holidays in the Later Middle Ages*. New York, 1940.

Rollason, D. W. "The cults of murdered royal saints in Anglo-Saxon England," *Anglo-Saxon England* 11 (1983): 1–22.

———. "Lists of saints' resting-places in Anglo-Saxon England," *Anglo-Saxon England* 7 (1978): 61–93.

———. *The Mildrith legend. A Study in Early Medieval Hagiography*. Leicester, 1982.

Round, J. H. *The Commune of London*. Westminster, 1899.

Scholz, B. W. "The canonization of Edward the Confessor," *Speculum* 26 (1961): 38–60.

Schreiner, Klaus. "Discrimen veri et falsi. Ansätze und Formen der Kritik in der Heiligen- und Reliquienverehrung des Mittelalters," *Archiv für Kulturgeschichte* 48 (1966): 1–53.

——. "Zum Wahrheitsverständnis im Heiligen- und Reliquienwesen des Mittelalters," *Saeculum* 17 (1966): 131–69.

Scragg, D. G. "The corpus of vernacular homilies and prose saints' lives before Aelfric," *Anglo-Saxon England* 8 (1979): 223–77.

Sigal, P.-A. "Comment en concevait et on traitait la paralysie en occident dans le haut moyen âge (Ve–XIIe siècles)," *Revue d'histoire des sciences* 24 (1971): 193–211.

——. "Histoire et hagiographie: les *Miracula* aux XIe et XIIe siècles," *Annales de Bretagne et des pays de l'Ouest* 87,2 (1980): 237–57.

——. "Maladie, pèlerinage et guérison au XIIe siècle. Les miracles de Saint Gibrien à Reims," *Annales E. S. C.* 24 (1969): 1522–39.

——. "Un aspect du culte des saints: le châtiment divin aux XIe et XIIe siècles d'àpres la littérature hagiographique du Midi de la France," *Cahiers de Fanjeaux* 11 (1976): 35–59.

Smalley, Beryl. "Gilbertus Universalis, Bishop of London, 1128–34, and the problem of the 'Glossa Ordinaria,' " *Recherches de théologie ancienne et médiévale* 7 (1935): 235–62; 8 (1936): 24–60.

Smith, Thomas. *Catalogus librorum manuscriptorum bibliothecae Cottonianae.* Oxford, 1696.

Smith, William & Henry Wace. *A Dictionary of Christian Biography.* 4 vols. London, 1877–87.

Southern, Sir Richard W. "Aspects of the European tradition of historical writing, 4. The sense of the past," *Transactions of the Royal Historical Society,* 5th Ser., 23 (1973): 243–63.

——. "The English origins of the miracles of the Virgin," *Medieval and Renaissance Studies* 4 (1958): 176–216.

——. Ed. *The Life of St. Anselm of Canterbury by Eadmer.* London, 1962.

——. *Medieval Humanism and Other Studies.* New York, 1970.

——. "The place of England in the Twelfth-Century Renaissance," *History* 45 (1960): 201–16.

——. *St. Anselm and his Biographer.* Cambridge, 1963.

——. *Western Society and the Church in the Middle Ages.* Harmondsworth, Middlesex, 1970.

Stenton, Sir Frank. *Anglo-Saxon England.* Oxford, 1947.

Strunk, Gerhard. *Kunst und Glaube in der lateinischen Heiligenlegende zu ihrem*

Selbstverständnis in den Prologen. Medium Aevum. Philologische Studien 12. Munich, 1970.

Szarmach, Paul E. & Bernard Huppé, eds. *The Old English Homily and Its Background*. Albany, N.Y., 1978.

Thomson, Rodney. "The reading of William of Malmesbury," *Revue Bénédictine* 85 (1975): 362–402; 86 (1976): 327–35.

———. "William of Malmesbury and the letters of Alcuin," *Medievalia et Humanistica*, New Ser. 8 (1977): 147–61.

———. "William of Malmesbury as historian and man of letters," *Journal of Ecclesiastical History* 29 (1978): 387–413.

Van Uytfanghe, Mark. "La controverse biblique et patristique autour du miracle et ses repercussions sur l'hagiographie dans l'antiquité tardive et le haut moyen âge latin," ed. Patlagean & Riché, *Hagiographie, cultures, et sociétés*, 205–33.

Vauchez, A. *La sainteté en occident aux derniers siècles du moyen âge*. Bibliothèque des écoles françaises d'Athènes et de Rome 241. Rome, 1981.

Wall, Charles J. *Shrines of British Saints*. London, 1905.

Walther, Hans. *Lateinische Sprichwörter und Sentenzen des Mittelalters. Carmina medii aevi posterioris Latina*, II: *Proverbia sententiaeque latinitatis medii aevi*. 6 vols. Göttingen, 1963–69.

Ward, Benedicta. *Miracles and the Medieval Mind*. Philadelphia, 1982.

Weinstein, Donald & Rudolf Bell. *Saints and Society*. Chicago, 1982.

Wharton, Henry. *Historia de episcopis et decanis Londinensibus*. London, 1695.

Whatley, Gordon. "The figure of Constantine the Great in Cynewulf's *Elene*," *Traditio* 37 (1981): 161–202.

———. "Heathens and saints: St. *Erkenwald* in its legendary context," *Speculum* 61 (1986): 330–63.

———. "The Middle English St. *Erkenwald* and its liturgical context," *Mediaevalia* 8 (1982): 277–306.

———. "A 'symple wrecche' at work: the life and miracles of Saint Erkenwald in the *Gilte Legende*," in Dunn-Lardeau, 333–343.

Whitelock, Dorothy et al. *The Norman Conquest, its Setting and Impact*. New York, 1966.

———. *Some Anglo-Saxon Bishops of London*. Chambers Memorial Lecture, University College, London, 1974. London, 1975.

Wilson, R. M. *The Lost Literature of Medieval England*. 2nd ed. London, 1970.

Wilson, Stephen, ed. *Saints and their Cults. Studies in Religious Sociology, Folklore, and History.* Cambridge, 1983.

Wolpers, Theodor. *Die englische Heiligenlegende des Mittelalters.* Tübingen, 1964.

Woodforde, Christopher. *The Norwich School of Glass Painting in the Fifteenth Century.* Oxford, 1950.

Index

The Index is a guide to the persons, places, etc., named in the Introduction and Latin texts; for the most part, material in the notes has not been indexed. Arabic numerals, when alone, denote page numbers; when following VSE and Mir., they denote lines or note numbers. Where an indexed item occurs in both Introduction and Texts, page numbers in the Introduction appear first, followed by VSE and Mir. line numbers.

The Saint of London is the first edition and translation of Arcoid's *Miracula sancti Erkenwaldi* and the first translation of the anonymous *Vita* . . . . the two principal Latin memorials to the seventh-century monk Erkenwald who became the patron saint of medieval London. Erkenwald, founder of the great Benedictine abbeys at Barking and Chertsey, was also the bishop of London and the East Saxons from 675–693, and was made famous as the protagonist of a popular Middle English poem bearing his name.

Whatley's lively facing-page translations are accompanied by a substantial introduction which deals with the manuscripts, date and authorship, and historical background of each text. Included is a chapter on the cult of St. Erkenwald, and a brief overview of the English revival of haigiography after the Norman conquest. Critical apparatus and notes to the text, along with a full bibliography and an index, round off this volume.

Gordon E. Whatley has held an NEH fellowship and several research awards, and has published widely on St. Erkenwald and on hagiography in *Speculum*, *Mediaevalia*, *Modern Philology*, *Manuscripta*, *Viator*, *Traditio*, and other journals. He is currently an Associate Professor of English at Queens College of the City University of New York.

mRts

medieval & Renaissance texts & studies
is the publishing program of the
Center for Medieval and Early Renaissance Studies
at the State University of New York at Binghamton.

mRts emphasizes books that are needed —
texts, translations, and major research tools.

mRts aims to publish the highest quality scholarship
in attractive and durable format at modest cost.